THE RISE AND FALL OF KHOQAND, 1709–1876

CENTRAL EURASIA IN CONTEXT SERIES
Douglas Northrop, Editor

THE RISE AND FALL OF Khoqand
1709–1876

Central Asia in the Global Age

SCOTT C. LEVI

University of Pittsburgh Press

Published by the University of Pittsburgh Press, Pittsburgh, Pa., 15260
Copyright © 2017, University of Pittsburgh Press
All rights reserved
Manufactured in the United States of America
Printed on acid-free paper
10 9 8 7 6 5 4 3 2 1

Cataloging-in-Publication data is available from the Library of Congress

ISBN 13: 978-0-8229-6506-0
ISBN 10: 0-8229-6506-2

Cover art: Photomontage of the Palace of Khudáyár.

Cover design by Joel W. Coggins

*This book is dedicated to the memory of Ghulom Karimov,
a great scholar, and a great friend*

CONTENTS

Preface: Connecting Histories ... ix
Acknowledgments ... xiii
Transliteration and Abbreviations ... xvii
The Shahrukhid Rulers ... xix
Note on Geographic Terminology ... xxi
Note on Sources ... xxiii

INTRODUCTION ... 1
1. A NEW UZBEK DYNASTY, 1709–1769 ... 14
2. CRAFTING A STATE, 1769–1799 ... 50
3. THE KHANATE OF KHOQAND, 1799–1811 ... 74
4. A NEW "TIMURID RENAISSANCE," 1811–1822 ... 95
5. A NEW CRISIS, 1822–1844 ... 127
6. CIVIL WAR, 1844–1853 ... 159
7. KHOQAND DEFEATED, 1853–1876 ... 188
CONCLUSION ... 210

General Glossary ... 225
Bibliography ... 229
Index ... 247

PREFACE
On Connecting Histories

IN THE PROCESS of completing work on my first book, *The Indian Diaspora in Central Asia and Its Trade, 1550–1900*, an observation struck me. I had spent years studying chronicles and government records, travel accounts, legal records, previous scholarship in multiple languages and anything else I could get my hands on that would help me to locate Indian merchants in locations across Central Asia (and more broadly, Central Eurasia). In the seventeenth century, I was able to place Indian merchant communities across Afghanistan, Central Asia, Iran, and in the city of Astrakhan in Russia. I could even trace their movement up the Volga as far as Moscow and St. Petersburg. Focusing in on Central Asia, in one collection of official letters I found a seventeenth-century Bukharan mandate (*farmān*) that boldly declares the Bukharan khan's intention to protect the Hindu communities he hosted "in the territories of Bukhara, Balkh, Badakhshan, Qunduz, Taliqan, Aibek, Ghuri, Baghlan, Shabarghan, Termiz, Samarqand, Nasaf (Qarshi), Kish and Shahrisabz."[1] At any given time in the seventeenth century, I argued, there was a circulating population of tens of thousands of Indians orchestrating this far-flung merchant diaspora. The Indians pursued profit-oriented opportunities everywhere they could, and they served their hosts as commercial agents and professional moneylenders. In many

---

1. Mirakshah Munshi, Mullah Zahid Munshi, and Muhammad Tahir Wahid, comps., Maktubat munsha'at manshurat, IVANU, Ms. No. 289, fols. 185b–186a. The inclusion of both Kish and Shahrisabz in this list is puzzling as they are two names for the same city.

places their networks moved beyond urban centers into villages, where they operated rural credit systems that helped finance agricultural production. Their network in Central Asia was widespread, but I found no source that could place them in the Ferghana Valley in the seventeenth century.

I realized this only when I began to direct attention to the Russian colonial records of the late nineteenth century, by which time Indian communities had become at least as ubiquitous in the Ferghana Valley as they were everywhere else in the region. Contrasting Babur's memories of his youth in the Ferghana Valley—the Timurid prince and founder of the Mughal Empire was born in 1483 in the city of Andijan, at the eastern end of the valley—with the American diplomat Eugene Schuyler's description from four centuries later, I was struck by the remarkable differences in the Ferghana Valley's built environment, its ecology, its economy, the size of its population, its ethnographic composition, and more.[2] This prompted me to ask what had happened in the interim. Specifically, it drew my attention to the Khanate of Khoqand as a force for change and dynamism in the region.

The comparatively little work that had been directed to Khoqand added to my enthusiasm for this project. Focusing on Khoqand provides an opportunity to offer a historical counterpoint, both to the established narrative of Central Asian history as seen from the perspective of Bukhara, as well as the even more well-rehearsed narratives of Qing and Russian imperial expansion into the region. Beijing appears early and often in the discussions below, but it is distant, and readers will find that the smoke-filled imperial offices of St. Petersburg, London, and Calcutta remain beyond the horizon. The imperial perspective is an important one, but it is well represented elsewhere. There is no space for the poorly informed posturings of the Great Game literature that misrepresents Central Asians as two-dimensional figures scrambling in response to English or Russian imperial incentives. Attention here is on the ways that Central Asians exercised their own agency in shaping their future.

As I began to pursue my objectives in researching and writing this book, I settled on a connected histories methodology. This approach is well suited to my own interests, which tend to favor the investigation of transregional connections and the influences of global historical processes on local ways of life. I am fascinated by transregional connections and integrative structures, identifying the broad patterns that shape local histories but that may not be readily apparent to the historical actors living at the time. The factors that precipitated the expansion of the Indian merchant

---

2. See the description of the valley as experienced in 1873 by Eugene Schuyler, *Turkistan: Notes of a Journey in Russian Turkistan, Khokand, Bukhara, and Kuldja*, 2 vols. (New York: Scribner, Armstrong & Co., 1877), 2:1–60.

network into Central Asia during the mid-sixteenth century, at the very historical moment when long-held historiographical traditions tell us that the two regions would be growing farther apart, is one example.

There are some who are resistant to the notion that transregional connections are an important feature of early modern Central Asian history.[3] I argue that they are, and that the connected histories approach can illustrate their importance. This work argues that it was the convergence of integrative processes, and not regional isolation, that shaped the rise, efflorescence, and collapse of the Khanate of Khoqand. Readers will find a sustained effort to construct a more complete and meaningful understanding of the multiplicity of ways that Khoqand and its people were influenced by larger Eurasian, and global, historical processes. The chapters below examine a number of the ways that Central Asians responded to these influences as they endeavored to control their own circumstances and futures, achieving resounding successes and suffering cataclysmic failures in the process.

That is not to say that integrative processes fully determined the history of Khoqand. Glancing at the chapter titles one may get the impression that the history of Khoqand followed a familiar trajectory of birth, rise, crisis, and collapse. A critical reader may wonder, if Khoqand's history was so predictable, then what new insights does this book really have to offer? The discussions within these chapters demonstrate that the rise and fall of Khoqand was far from smooth and predictable: it was thoroughly uneven and heavily shaped by both macro-level world historical processes and micro-level contingencies and fortune, both good and bad.

I also do not claim that my application of a connected histories approach is entirely innovative—Sanjay Subrahmanyam has been championing connected histories for two decades now.[4] But I do argue that it is both relevant and valuable for Central Asian history, and I apply it here deliberately, and cautiously. I take seriously

---

3. For a recent example, see Paolo Sartori, "Introduction: On Kh^vārazmian Connectivity: Two or Three Things That I Know about It," *Journal of Persianate Studies* 9 (2016): 133–57.

4. Sanjay Subrahmanyam, "Connected Histories: Notes towards a Reconfiguration of Early Modern Eurasia," *Modern Asian Studies* 31, no. 3 (1997): 735–62. For two examples of connected histories in practice, see Sanjay Subrahmanyam's *From the Tagus to the Ganges: Explorations in Connected History* (Delhi: Oxford University Press, 2012) and *Mughals and Franks: Explorations in Connected History* (Delhi: Oxford University Press, 2012). In a number of important ways, Subrahmanyam follows what more than a decade earlier the Central Asian historian Joseph Fletcher had referred to as "integrative history." See Joseph Fletcher, "Integrative History: Parallels and Interconnections in the Early Modern Period, 1500–1800," *Journal of Turkish Studies* 9 (1985): 37–57. Fletcher was writing in the early 1980s, at a time when the field of world history was just beginning to take shape. Subrahmanyam's vision for connected history presents a considerably more refined articulation of the methods for, and merits of, conducting transregional historical studies.

Francesca Trivellato's insightful critique of the "global turn" and her assessment of the opportunities and problems that it presents. Trivellato articulates a determined defense of the merits of microhistory. She convincingly argues that "the potential of a microhistorical approach for global history remains underexploited" but that to realize that potential the historian must not lose sight of the often fraught and tense relationship between the micro-level narrative and the macro-level context.[5] Striking the right balance between the local and the global, she suggests, "can instill a healthy dose of critical self-reflexivity into the practice of global history," a field that too often suffers from overgeneralizations.[6]

It is in that spirit that I combine close attention to the Khoqand chronicles with a globally integrative perspective to advance a series of conclusions that I hope to be of value to scholars and students working both within and far beyond the field of Central Asian history. In assembling a history of the Khanate of Khoqand, this study explores the ways that historical processes unfolding in other parts of the world influenced Central Asian society, military strategies, and statecraft; it examines the ways in which local crises were catalysts for social change; and it draws attention to a number of ways that the more compact states of eighteenth- and nineteenth-century Central Asia resemble other states emerging on the frontier of expanding empires. I do not suggest that a connected histories methodology is the only approach for conducting historical research. But I do argue that it is a valuable one that stands to offer important new insights into Central Asian history.

---

5. Francesca Trivellato, "Is There a Future for Italian Microhistory in the Age of Global History?," *California Italian Studies* 2, no. 1 (2011), https://escholarship.org/uc/item/0z94n9hq.
6. Trivellato, "Is There a Future for Italian Microhistory in the Age of Global History?"

ACKNOWLEDGMENTS

I BEGAN THE spadework for this volume in 2002. As is often the case, I encountered many unanticipated obstacles along the way and what I had initially intended to be a project that would take four or five years to complete transformed into a much greater undertaking. But some delays are not all bad. Over the years, this project has developed in ways that would have been impossible for me to forecast when I initially set out to write a history of the Khanate of Khoqand. I hope that the end result is a more interesting and more valuable scholarly contribution. The road has been a long one, and I have amassed many debts along the way.

To recognize the institutions, I thank my first employer out of graduate school, Eastern Illinois University, for providing me a supportive environment in which to begin my career and an EIU Council on Faculty Research Summer Research Grant that enabled me to travel to Uzbekistan to begin work on this project. This was followed by a generous Social Science Research Council Eurasia Program Postdoctoral Research Grant, which I used to fund additional research trips to Central Asia over three successive summers. I then stepped away from Khoqand for some time to shepherd several smaller projects to completion, and twice shifted academic positions in the meantime. In 2008, I made my way to the Department of History at The Ohio State University and the support that I have received at OSU, both from my department and from the College of Arts and Sciences, has been critical to my ability to move this project forward. I was able to return to it fully in 2013–14 with the generous support of a National Endowment for the Humanities Fellowship from the Division of Research Programs. I would also like to thank Director Samuel Jubé of the Institut d'Études Avancées de Nantes, the extraordinary staff, and my great cohort of colleagues in the 2016–17 fellowship year for providing the exceptionally stimulating environment in which I was finally able to bring this project to completion. I am grateful to all of these institutions for their support.

In Tashkent, I worked primarily in the manuscript collection of the Abu Rayhan al-Biruni Institute of Oriental Studies. The librarian at the Biruni Institute, Rano Magrufova, known to all as Rano Opa, was a remarkable resource and I thank her for locating rare books in private collections and facilitating my work in other important ways. I am also grateful to my friends and colleagues Gulchekhra Sultonova and Sherzodhon Mahmudov for facilitating my visits to the Institute of History in recent years. Sherzodhon, a native of Qo'qan (as the historical city of Khoqand is known today), also arranged for me to visit the Ferghana Valley as a guest of his wonderfully hospitable family whose own history is bound together with that of the Khanate, and he graciously shuttled me across the valley from one historical site to the next. Bakhtiyar Babadjanov generously provided copies of a large number of rare resources pertaining to Khoqand. Aftandil Erkinov introduced me to the literary history of Khoqand and also to Benedek Péri, whom I thank for providing the English-language translations of the poems that 'Umar Khan and his wife, Mahlar Oyim, authored and which I have included in chapter 4.

I am profoundly grateful to my friend Ghulom Karimov, who on every visit to Tashkent welcomed me back with bear hugs and boundless hospitality, and who generously shared his Persian literary skills as I worked my way through the manuscripts. Sadly, in April 2014, Ghulom passed away. He was a devoted husband and father, a dedicated scholar, a kind and generous man, and a dear friend. I will never be able to thank him in person for all he has done over the years to help me find my way through the Central Asian manuscripts that fill the footnotes below. I dedicate this book to his memory.

My work on this project has benefitted from conversations with many colleagues over the years, and I am grateful to those who arranged opportunities for me to deliver my ongoing research as presentations at multiple venues. These include Robert McChesney at New York University's Hagop Kevorkian Center Research Workshop, Robert Crews at Stanford University, Douglas Northrop at the University of Michigan's Russian History Workshop, Christian Raffensperger at the Russian History Colloquium at Wittenberg University, and both Alexandre Papas and Isabelle Ohayon at the CNRS and EHESS in Paris. The feedback and criticisms that I received at these venues have proven immensely helpful in adding new insights and generally improving the value and accessibility of my work.

Timur Beisembiev, the world's leading scholar on the history of Khoqand, was in the process of working his way through the entire manuscript when he passed away on December 30, 2016. He generously offered me numerous valuable suggestions and has left behind an extraordinary scholarly legacy for future researchers in the field of Central Asian history. Mike Thurman has by now surely earned all the necessary credentials to serve as a *mirab*, in Ferghana or elsewhere, and his past work and more recent guidance have proven extraordinarily helpful in shaping my engagement with the history of water. I am equally grateful to Heather Sonntag for her help in locating many of the historical photographs that illustrate this volume.

I am also particularly indebted to the following friends and colleagues who generously read drafts of this manuscript in whole or in part, offered suggestions for its improvement, and directed me to helpful books and articles. Their feedback has helped me avoid embarrassing errors and present my work with greater nuance than I otherwise could have. This includes Adeeb Khalid, James Millward, Alexander Morrison, Douglas Northrop, Lakshmi Subramanian, and Ying Zhang. I thank Bill Nelson for his care and attention to detail in drafting the nine maps that illustrate this volume. I also thank Peter Kracht at the University of Pittsburgh Press for his guidance and good humor in supervising the production process of this book. Other colleagues not already listed whose valuable insights and suggestions have shaped the discussions in this volume include Nick Breyfogle, John Brooke, Phil Brown, Jane Hathaway, Nurten Kılıç-Schubel, Ousman Kobo, Morgan Liu, Beatrice Manz, Timothy May, Geoffrey Parker, Beatrice Penati, and Ron Sela. Needless to say, any remaining errors, oversights, and omissions are fully my responsibility.

Most of all, I thank my wife, Dr. Karen Spierling, and our two daughters, Madeleine and Abigail, for their love and support. I dedicate this volume to our departed friend Ghulom Karimov. Everything else, I dedicate to them.

TRANSLITERATION AND ABBREVIATIONS

THROUGHOUT THIS VOLUME, the transliteration of terms from the Persian, Turkic, and Arabic languages follows a slightly simplified version of the system employed by the *Encyclopaedia of Islam*. In the interest of accessibility, I have elected to present proper names, geographical locations, and other geographical features without diacritics.

AIKC: Beisembiev, Timur K. *Annotated Indices to the Kokand Chronicles.* Tokyo: Research Institute for Languages and Cultures of Asia and Africa, 2008.
EIR: *Encyclopaedia Iranica.* Ed. by Ehsan Yarshater. London: Routledge & Kegan Paul, 1982–.
IAN: *Izvestiia akademii nauk UzSSR.*
IVANU: Abu Rayhan al-Beruni Oriental Studies Institute of the Academy of Sciences of the Republic of Uzbekistan (Institut Vostokovedeniia Akademii Nauk, Uzbekistan).
KI: Beisembiev, Timur. K. *Kokandskaiia istoriografiia: issledovaniie po istochnikovedeniiu Srednei Azii XVIII–XIX vekov.* Almaty, 2009.
LA: Beisembiev, Timur K., ed. and tr. *The Life of 'Alimqul: A Native Chronicle of Nineteenth Century Central Asia*, by Mulla Muhammad Yunus Djan Shighavul Dadkhah Tashkandi. London: RoutledgeCurzon, 2003.

MK: Muhammad ʿUmar Marghīnānī ("Ummīdī"). *Maktūbcha-i khānī*. IVANU, Ms. No. 1902/V, ff. 130b–156b.

MT: Muhammad Hakimkhon. *Muntakhab at-tavarikh*. Ed. by A. Mukhtorov. 2 vols. Dushanbe: Donish, 1983–85. Facsimile edition of Hajji Muhammad hakīm Khān b. Saʿid Maʾsum Khān, *Muntakhab al-tavārīkh*. Institute of Oriental Studies and Written Legacy, Academy of Sciences, Republic of Tajikistan, Ms. No. 63.

MTF: Muhammad Fazil Bek b. Qadi Muhammad Atabek. *Mukammal-i tā'rīkh-i Farghāna*. IVANU, Ms. No. 5971.

ÖIF: *Özbekistonda ijtimoii fanlar.*

ONU: *Obshchestvennye nauki v Uzbekistane.*

ORE-AH: *Oxford Research Encyclopedia of Asian History*. Ed. by David Ludden. http://asianhistory.oxfordre.com.

TJN: Mulla ʿAvaz Muhammad b. Mulla Ruzi Muhammad Sufi (ʿAttar-i Khoqandi). *Tā'rīkh-i jahān-nūma-ī*. IVANU, Ms. No. 9455/I.

TJT: Muhammad Sālih Khwāja Tāshkandī. *Tā'rīkh-i jadīdah-i Tāshkand*. IVANU, Ms. No. 5732.

TS: Niyaz Muhammad b. ʿAshur Muhammad Khoqandī. *Tā'rīkh-i Shahrukhī*. IVANU, Ms. No. 1787.

THE SHAHRUKHID RULERS OF KHOQAND, 1709–1876

Shah Rukh Biy	1709–22
'Abd al-Rahim Biy	1722–34
'Abd al-Karim Biy	1734–51
Irdana Biy (first reign)	1751–52
Baba Biy	1752–53
Irdana Biy (second reign)	1753–69
Sulayman Biy	1769–70
Narbuta Biy	1770–99
'Alim Khan	1799–1811
'Umar Khan	1811–22
Muhammad 'Ali (Madali) Khan	1822–42
Sher 'Ali Khan	1842–44
Murad Khan	1844
Muhammad Khudayar Khan (first reign)	1844–58
Malla Khan	1858–62
Shah Murad Khan	1862
Muhammad Khudayar Khan (second reign)	1862–63
Sultan Sayyid Khan (as puppet of 'Alimqul)	1863–65
Muhammad Khudayar Khan (third reign)	1865–75
Nasr al-Din Khan	1875–76

NOTE ON GEOGRAPHIC TERMINOLOGY

HISTORIANS AND HISTORICAL geographers have developed an impressive toolbox of geographic terms that can be applied to Central Asia and its surrounding regions, and these require some explanation. *Central Asia* itself can take on various meanings depending on who is employing the term and in what context. As used in this book, it refers to the zone that includes the modern nation states of Uzbekistan, (southern) Kazakhstan, Tajikistan, Kirghizstan, and Turkmenistan, as well as northern Afghanistan, northeastern Iran, and historical *Altishahr*, the "Six Cities" region of some 350,000 square miles that Qing armies conquered in the mid-eighteenth century and incorporated into a very large, new territory that the Qing designated *Xinjiang* (also Sinkiang), the Qing "New Dominion" or "New Frontier." The list of the "six cities" that constitute Altishahr varies somewhat, and the lack of clarity provides insight into why Khoqandi sources often refer to the region as *Yetishahr*, or the "Seven Cities" region. The list most commonly includes the oasis cities of Kashgar, Yarkand, Aksu, Yangi Hisar (also Yangishahr), and Khotan, and occasionally includes Turfan or Uch Turfan (also Uch, or Osh), with Kucha occasionally taking the place of Aksu. The territory of Xinjiang became an official province only in 1884, seven years after the Qing recovered Altishahr from the Khoqandi adventurer Yaʻqub Beg. As it applies in the eighteenth- and nineteenth-century context, Central Asia is often referred to as *Turkestan* and is divided into Western and Eastern portions. Thus, Eastern Turkestan refers to Altishahr whereas Western

Turkestan includes the territories of the Bukharan Khanate in historical Transoxania (Gr.) or Mawarannahr (Ar. Mā warā' al-nahr, "that which lies beyond the river"), the Khivan Khanate of Khwarezm, and the Khanate of Khoqand in the Ferghana Valley, a small but exceptionally fertile zone of approximately 8,500 square miles.

This stands in contrast to *Inner Asia*, the vast and largely pastoral nomadic steppe to the north of Central Asia. This region is commonly referred to in historical sources as the Dasht-i Qipchaq, or the Qipchaq Steppe, the southern stretches of which include much of contemporary Kazakhstan. As used here, *Inner Asia* refers to the uninterrupted steppe zone that stretches from the plains north of the Caspian Sea eastward across Siberia to Mongolia. This region includes *Jungaria*, the portion of Xinjiang situated to the north of Altishahr and historically populated by pastoral nomadic peoples, as well as the northeastern parts of what is today Kazakhstan. The broadest of the geographic terms applied here is *Central Eurasia*, which references nearly the entire Eurasian interior including both Central Asia and Inner Asia, the Tibetan Plateau to the east, and the Caucasus of southern Russia to the west. Those interested in further investigations into the historical geography of the region will find much of interest in the essays and maps in Yuri Bregel, *An Historical Atlas of Central Asia* (Leiden: E. J. Brill, 2003). I have used that resource extensively in the preparation of the maps for this volume.

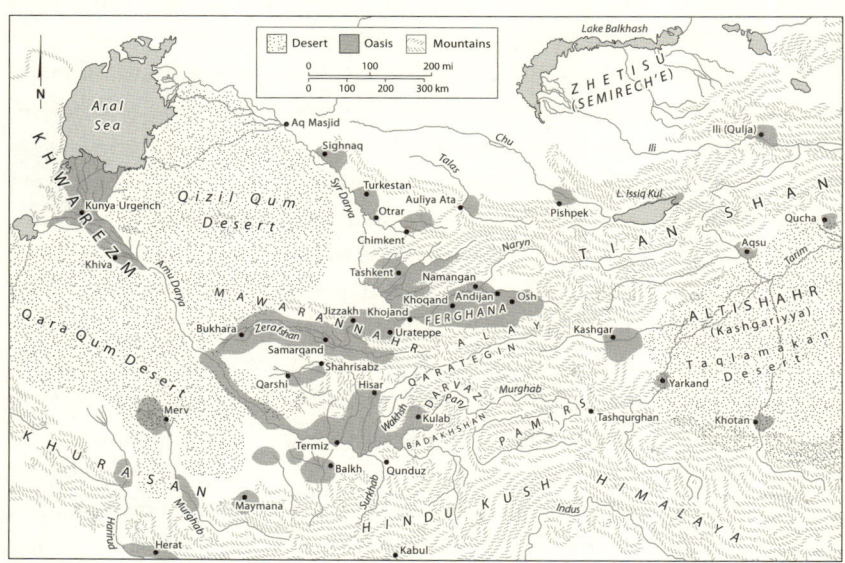

MAP 1 Central Asian Geography.
Map by Bill Nelson.

NOTE ON SOURCES

THE RESEARCH FOR this volume includes a close reading of a number of Khoqand chronicles and other primary sources, as well as engaging a rich scholarly tradition that dates back more than 130 years and has benefitted from a number of recent contributions. Research in the Khoqand chronicles equips the present study with an important perspective, one that is absent in Chinese and Russian sources and the scholarship based on those sources. But accessing the history of Khoqand is not without its challenges. I have found the Russian imperial-era scholarship that engages Central Asian sources to be quite valuable when used carefully. But a close analysis exposes gross errors and a bias that makes the genre as a whole problematic. A much greater complication is that nearly all of the official records of the government of Khoqand were destroyed by fire in the wake of the Russian conquest of the valley.[1]

The loss of such valuable documentary evidence presents no small obstacle to investigating the history of Khoqand, but that loss is mitigated by the abundance of narrative sources. Timur Beisembiev, the scholar most knowledgeable on Khoqand's

---

1. There still exists a small selection of archival records from the later years of the Khanate. See A. L. Troitskaia, comp., *Katalog arkhiva Khokandskikh Khanov XIX veka* (Moscow: Nauka, 1968); A. L. Troitskaia, *Materialy po istorii Kokandskogo Khanstva XIX v. po dokumentam arkhiva Kokandskikh Khanov* (Moscow: Nauka, 1969). A few of these have also been published in R. N. Nabiev, *Iz istorii Kokandskogo Khanstva (feodal'noe khoziaistvo Khudoiar-Khana)* (Tashkent: Fan, 1973).

historiography, notes that there are more than forty historical works in Persian and Chaghatai Turkic that are either largely or entirely dedicated to presenting the history of Khoqand.[2] These sources include roughly 12,000 pages of information on the history of Khoqand, a body of literature that is, in its size, "more than all known Bukharan and Khivan chronicles taken together."[3] In addition to providing an extraordinarily useful map to this information in his *Annotated Indices to the Kokand Chronicles*, Beisembiev has conducted an exhaustive historiographical analysis of these sources and their contents. In 2009, he published his results in the meticulously organized 1,263-page *Kokandskaiia istoriografiia: issledovanie po istochnikovedeniiu Srednei Azii XVIII–XIX vekov*.[4]

This book is nowhere near so comprehensive. The material employed here is drawn primarily from seven histories of the Khanate of Khoqand, carefully selected because of their value and the diverse viewpoints and coverage that they present. More than any other historical source, the *Muntakhab al-tawārīkh* has proven to be especially valuable. This "universal history" was completed in 1843 by Muhammad Hakim Khan Tore, a nephew of both 'Alim Khan (r. 1799–1811) and 'Umar Khan (r. 1811–22) and cousin to Madali Khan (r. 1822–42).[5] Hakim Khan's mother was an important and influential figure at court, and his father served as Khoqand's Sheikh al-Islam, the highest position in the Khanate's judicial administration, roughly akin to the supervisor of religious and legal affairs. In his lengthy section on Khoqand, Hakim Khan provides what is at times a deeply personal insight into the inner workings of the ruling family during a critical period in the history of the Khanate. The edition that I used is a published facsimile that the Tajik scholar Ahror Mukhtarov produced using the Dushanbe manuscript 63, which was produced by two copyists who were working from the original autographed manuscript in the city of Kitab in January or February 1844, just one year after the original was completed.[6] In cases where the orthography is questionable, I have relied on the critical text edition that Yayoi Kawahara and Koichi Haneda published in 2006.[7]

---

2. Timur K. Beisembiev, *Annotated Indices to the Kokand Chronicles* (Tokyo: Research Institute for Languages and Cultures of Asia and Africa, 2008 (henceforth AIKC), 19.
3. Beisembiev, *Annotated Indices*, 20.
4. Timur. K. Beisembiev, *Kokandskaiia istoriografiia: issledovaniie po istochnikovedeniiu Srednei Azii XVIII–XIX vekov* (Almaty: TOO Print-S, 2009) (henceforth KI).
5. Hajji Muhammad Hakim Khan b. Said Ma'sum Khan, *Muntakhab at-tavarikh*, ed. A. Mukhtarov (Dushanbe: Donish, 1985) (henceforth MT). The designation of Töre indicates that the person is a descendant of Chinggis Khan, much as a Sayyid is a descendant of the Prophet Muhammad.
6. See Mukhtarov's preface in MT, 9. See also the discussion in KI, 372–84.
7. Muhammad Hakīm Khān, *Muntakhab al-tawārīkh: Selected History*, vol. 2, ed. Yayoi Kawahara and

Later chroniclers appear to have held Hakim Khan's account in high esteem as they relied heavily on it. One such case is Mulla 'Avaz Muhammad "'Attar-i Khoqandi," who was witness to events in the Khanate from the early 1840s, just as Hakim Khan's narrative comes to an end, and whose accounts of earlier events are quite often copied verbatim from Hakim Khan's work.[8] Mulla 'Avaz Muhammad finished his *Tā'rīkh-i jahān-nūma-ī* in 1869, roughly two years before Niyaz Muhammad ("Niyazi") completed the first edition of his better known *Tā'rīkh-i Shahrukhī*.[9] Niyazi's history is also exceptionally important to the present study as it provides a history of the Khanate that differs substantially from the *Muntakhab al-tawārīkh* insofar as it draws from the author's significantly different personal experiences, textual sources, and oral traditions.

For his treatment of the early history of Khoqand, Niyazi relied heavily on the two earliest Khoqand chronicles, the *'Umar-nāma* written by 'Abd al-Karim Namangani and the *Shāh-nāma-i 'Umar-khānī* written by Mirza Qalandar Mushrif Isfaragi, both of which were completed circa 1821–22 under the patronage of 'Umar Khan himself.[10] A member of a military family, Niyazi's account is especially strong in terms of his own observations in that area. The *Tā'rīkh-i Shahrukhī* is the last of the official Khoqand chronicles, and it had a strong influence on later histories, including Muhammad Fazil Bek's *Mukammal-i tā'rīkh-i Farghāna*, a survey history written at the beginning of the twentieth century.[11]

Another source of special importance is the *Tā'rīkh-i jadīdah-i Tāshkand*, a substantial manuscript that presents an extraordinarily detailed history of Tashkent, Khoqand's most valuable territorial possession from 'Alim Khan's annexation of the city in 1807 until it was lost to Russian forces in 1865.[12] Muhammad Salih Khoja Tashkandi began writing this manuscript in 1862 and finished in 1886–87. His insight

---

Koichi Haneda (Tokyo: Research Institute for Languages and Cultures of Asia and Africa, 2006). For further discussion of Khoqand historiography, see xxix–xxxvii. Kawahara and Haneda address this edition of the manuscript on xxxiii.

8. Mulla 'Avaz Muhammad b. Mulla Ruzi Muhammad Sufi ('Attar-i Khoqandi), *Tā'rīkh-i jahān-nūma-ī*, Abu Rayhan al-Beruni Oriental Studies Institute of the Academy of Sciences of the Republic of Uzbekistan (henceforth IVANU), MS. No. 9455/I (henceforth TJN).

9. Niyaz Muhammad b. 'Ashur Muhammad Khoqandī, *Tā'rīkh-i Shahrukhī*, IVANU, MS. No. 1787 (henceforth TS).

10. Timur K. Beisembiev, *Ta'rikh-i Shakhrukhi: kak istoricheskii istochnik* (Alma-Ata: Nauka, 1987), 32–35.

11. Originally authored under the title, *Mufassal-i tā'rīkh-i Farghāna*, the manuscript referenced here was a copy of the original produced in 1941. Muhammad Fazil Bek b. Qadi Muhammad Atabek, *Mukammal-i tā'rīkh-i Farghāna*, IVANU, MS. No. 5971 (henceforth MTF). AIKC, 21; KI, 114, 385–86.

12. Muhammad Sālih Khwāja Tāshkandī, *Tā'rīkh-i jadīdah-i Tāshkand*, IVANU, MS. No. 5732 (henceforth TJT).

into the history of Tashkent was aided by the fact that 'Alim Khan appointed Muhammad Salih's uncle, Sarimsaq Tura (in some sources, Salimsaq Tura), to serve as his first hakim, or governor, of Tashkent and the steppe areas to the north. Over the intervening decades the history of Tashkent remained closely intertwined with Muhammad Salih's own family history.

The final chapter of this volume draws from two additional sources. Khudayar Khan, the last khan of Khoqand, fled Central Asia in the wake of the Russian conquest of the Ferghana Valley. After being robbed in Afghanistan of nearly everything he had, the former khan had the good fortune to encounter an Ottoman Turkish merchant named 'Abd al-Rahim Effendi, and the two became friends ("like brothers") as they traveled to India where they boarded a ship for Jiddah and together made the Hajj to Mecca. The Turkish merchant later commissioned Muhammad 'Umar Marghinani ("Umidi"), an accomplished chronicler and poet from Marghilan (known at the time as Marghinan), to compose a history of Khudayar Khan and his family in the *dastan* literary tradition. Umidi completed his Uzbek-language poem, the *Maktūbcha-i khān*, in 1884/85.[13] The poem presents valuable information on Khudayar Khan's life and travails when he was living in exile in Orenburg, Baghdad, and elsewhere.

The source used most heavily in the final chapter is the *Ta'rikh-i 'Alimquli Amir-i lashkar*, a Chaghatai-language chronicle long thought to have been anonymous. In his annotated critical translation of this manuscript, published with facsimile images under the title *The Life of 'Alimqul: A Native Chronicle of Nineteenth Century Central Asia*, Beisembiev identifies the author as Mulla Mirza Yunus Jan Tashkandi.[14] Mulla Yunus, as he was known, was a soldier of high rank who served under 'Alimqul, a Qipchaq (an Uzbek tribe separate from the Ming) and the de facto ruler of Khoqand for several years near the end of the khanate's history. Mulla Yunus's career in the Khanate's service began at least as early as 1852, and he authored his work in Russian-colonial Andijan in 1902/3. His generous treatment of 'Alimqul's role in late Khoqandi history is tilted decidedly in favor of the Qipchaqs. It therefore provides a useful counterpoint to Niyazi's *Tā'rīkh-i Shahrukhī*, which, while also an exceptionally valuable resource, exhibits disdain

---

13. Muhammad 'Umar Marghīnānī ("Umīdī"), *Maktūbcha-i khān*, IVANU, Ms. No. 1902/V, ff. 130b–156b (henceforth MK). See also the published modern Uzbek edition, Muhammad Umar qori Umidii Marghilonii, *Maktubchai khon*, ed. S. R. Hasanov (Toshkent: Fan, 2007).

14. Timur K. Beisembiev, ed. and tr., *The Life of 'Alimqul: A Native Chronicle of Nineteenth Century Central Asia*, by Mulla Muhammad Yunus Djan Shighavul Dadkhah Tashkandi (London: RoutledgeCurzon, 2003) (henceforth LA).

for 'Alimqul and his Qipchaq supporters and a clear bias in favor of Khudayar Khan and his loyal Sarts.

In studying the Khoqand chronicles, this is but a small selection of the textual sources available.[15] I have focused my efforts on these sources as they present an abundance of original information, and the authors exhibit contrasting perspectives and biases. That said, these are all official histories that were created for specific purposes, many were written well after the events that they describe unfolded, and they all draw on certain oral traditions that cannot be corroborated and are occasionally in conflict. Additionally, the information that the chronicles provide tends to focus on matters that pertain to political history and the inner workings of the Khoqandi elite and the Shahrukhid royal family: the biys and khans of Khoqand. A comparative textual analysis reveals varying degrees of harmony in many areas but also equally important lacunae, biases, rifts and contradictions, which call for a comparative analysis and a deeply critical perspective. The destruction of the official Khoqandi records that could have shed light on these points of friction is a terrible loss. Still, these sources offer a wealth of valuable information about the history of Khoqand, a topic that has too long remained in the dark in English-language scholarship in the field, and they add a great richness to this book.

Beisembiev calculates that the totality of Khoqand's historiography contains "chronological information on approx. 600 events, it holds genealogical data on 1,600 persons (including 230 members of the Kokand ruling clan of Ming); its prosopographical evidence covers 900 rulers, governors and commandants in 180 geographical locations, as well as 1,700 officials and notable persons who held 150 different ranks, posts, titles and degrees."[16] There is indeed an overabundance of information, and so I have worked to employ the information carefully and judiciously in order to achieve the goals and objectives of the present study, which is to analyze the ways in which Central Asia's integration with the outside world contributed to the rise, efflorescence, and collapse of the Khanate of Khoqand.

No work stands alone. For a study that was first conceived in 2002, readers will find that the following chapters reference an abundance of books, book chapters, journal articles and unpublished (or not-yet-published) PhD dissertations in Central Asian history and tangentially related fields that were completed well after I began work on this project. If this book has any new ideas, methodological innovations

---

15. Beisembiev provides a summary analysis of the historiography and the interconnections among the chronicles in AIKC, 19–24.
16. AIKC, 23.

and scholarly contributions to offer, it is because I have been able to incorporate into my own work the research achievements advanced in these studies. To my mind, this bodes well for the future of the field of Central Asian history.

What follows is the first English-language history of the Khanate of Khoqand. It neither claims nor aspires to be the last word on the matter.

THE RISE AND FALL OF KHOQAND, 1709–1876

INTRODUCTION

THE KHANATE OF Khoqand was an exceptionally dynamic Central Asian state that gradually emerged over the course of the eighteenth century in eastern Uzbekistan's Ferghana (Farghāna) Valley. The Shahrukhid dynastic family that ruled Khoqand belonged to the Ming, an Uzbek political group, or for want of a better word, tribe.[1] Although the term Uzbek is used more inclusively today, in Central Asian historical literature it refers to the descendants of the several hundred thousand Turkic people who migrated into the region from the Qipchaq Steppe under the leadership of Muhammad Shibani Khan (d. 1510) at the turn of the sixteenth century.[2] It therefore distinguishes the Uzbek tribes that were part of that migration from the many other Turkic peoples that had entered the region previously and others who would arrive later.

The Uzbeks were the dominant political force in eighteenth- and nineteenth-century Central Asia, and perhaps for that reason the Khanate of Khoqand is sometimes identified as an "Uzbek state." That designation falls short, however, as Khoqand's population was much more diverse than it suggests. In addition to the Uzbek

---

1. Despite their similar names, the Uzbek Ming had no relation to the Ming dynasty of China (1368–1644). In Uzbek, *ming* means 1,000, whereas the Chinese Ming dynasty chose that name to suggest the dynasty's "brilliance."
2. Yuri Bregel, "Turko-Mongol Influences in Central Asia," in *Turko-Persia in Historical Perspective*, ed. Robert L. Canfield (Cambridge: Cambridge University Press, 1991), 74 and note.

Ming, the Khanate of Khoqand was home to substantial populations of Kyrgyz, other Uzbek tribes (including especially the Qipchaq), "Uyghur" Turks (as they would be identified today) from Altishahr, and large numbers of Persian language–speaking Tajiks, all of whom played a role in the state's hierarchies of power, as well as its religious, cultural, and economic landscape.[3] The history of Khoqand is also closely intertwined with the histories of both Qing and Russian imperial expansion in the region, processes that unfolded over the eighteenth and nineteenth centuries and the legacies of which remain potent across the region today.

Khoqand's own legacy also merits close consideration as it continues to shape the lives and experiences of the contemporary peoples of the Ferghana Valley, the most densely populated region in modern Central Asia. This is apparent in the Ferghana Valley's religious heritage, ethnic demographics, and conflicts over water rights, all of which represent factors in the social tensions and recurrent unrest that have plagued the region in recent years, and all of which have roots that stretch back into the history of the khanate. Despite its relevance to both historical and contemporary concerns, comparatively little is known about the history of Khoqand, including the factors that contributed to its emergence, its remarkable territorial expansion and cultural efflorescence at the turn of the nineteenth century, and its ultimate demise under the weight of Russian colonial expansion into the region.[4]

---

3. The same critique could, of course, be applied to the Bukharan Amirate and the Khivan Khanate.
4. The Khanate of Khoqand has attracted some scholarly attention. The collective works that Timur Beisembiev has produced over the past several decades, many of which are cited throughout this volume and listed in the bibliography, mark the single greatest contribution to the field. Also notable is the recent Russian-language study by Bakhtiyar Babadjanov, *Kokandskoe khanstvo: vlast', politika, religiia* (Tokyo and Tashkent: Yangi Nashr, 2010). Babadjanov adds a critical voice to the earlier treatment by Haidarbek Nazirbekovich Bababekov, *Qŏqon tarikhi* (Toshkent: Fan, 1996). Some of Bababekov's conclusions are available in a sketchy and unreliable English translation, Victor Dubovitski and Khaydarbek Bababekov, "The Rise and Fall of the Kokand Khanate," in *Ferghana Valley: The Heart of Central Asia*, ed. S. Frederick Starr (Armonk, NY: M.E. Sharpe, 2011), 29–68. See also the Uzbek-language treatment by Shadman Vohidov, *Qo'qon khonligida tarikhnavislik (genezisi, funktsiyasi, namoyandalari, asarlari)* (Tashkent: Akademnashr, 2010). For a thorough study of the ways in which the government administration changed over the years, see Sherzodhon Mahmudov, "Sistema administrativnogo upravleniia v Kokandskom Khanstve (1709–1876 gg)" (PhD diss., Akademiia Nauk Respubliki Uzbekistan, Institut Istorii, 2007). The classic history of the khanate by the Russian Orientalist Vladimir Nalivkin, *Kratkaia istoriia Kokandskago khanstva* (Kazan, 1886), is based on his work with a number of chronicles, but his interpretations are problematic and often misleading, and so I have relied on it sparingly. In the English-language scholarship, the one work that merits attention here is Laura Newby, *The Empire and the Khanate: A Political History of Qing Relations with Khoqand c. 1760–1860* (Leiden: E. J. Brill, 2005). Newby's careful and reliable study combines deep original research in Qing archival records and other Chinese documentary sources with some Central Asian literature and thoughtful analysis. The discussions below reference her conclusions often, but New-

Khoqand emerged in the context of the eighteenth-century Bukharan crisis, the general contours of which are now well established in the scholarly literature.[5] From the late seventeenth century, the final Chinggisid (descendants of Chinggis Khan) rulers in the region, the Toqay-Timurid (1599–1747) Bukharan khans, suffered a diminished capacity to control their subordinate Uzbek amirs whose allegiance and loyalty was the cornerstone of their own military strength and legitimacy.[6] The chronicles detail a growing fiscal crisis over the seventeenth and eighteenth centuries, and numismatic evidence supports claims that silver became increasingly scarce. Ultimately, Bukharan coinage was debased to the point of losing nearly all its value. Fiscal problems made it increasingly difficult for an inherently decentralized regime such as the Bukharan Khanate to maintain patronage systems. It then became impossible.

Rebellions took root in the seventeenth century with increasing frequency in the early eighteenth century. The southern agricultural region of Central Asia meanwhile suffered debilitating invasions from nomadic peoples, most notably during the Kazakh "Barefooted Flight," a horrific event in Kazakh history propelled by a 1723 Jungar (also Zungar, Zhungar, Dzungar) Mongol invasion that pushed the Kazakhs southward, where they occupied Bukharan agricultural territories.[7] Efforts to achieve greater centralization by imposing military reforms met with failure, exacerbating rebellions and further undermining Chinggisid legitimacy. The traditional Bukharan forces crumbled under the weight of more technologically advanced Persian artillery in 1737, and they simply submitted when Nadir Shah returned in 1740. With the assassination of Nadir Shah in 1747, the Uzbek Manghit tribal leadership executed the final Chinggisid ruler, Abu'l Fayz Khan (r. 1711–47), and took over leadership for themselves.[8] None of these points are contested. In

---

by's primary concern is focused on Qing history as seen through Qing relations with Khoqand. It is not a history of Khoqand, nor does it set out to be one.

5. Wolfgang Holzwarth, "Relations Between Uzbek Central Asia, the Great Steppe and Iran, 1700–1750," in *Shifts and Drifts in Nomad-Sedentary Relations*, ed. Stefan Leder and Bernhard Streck (Wiesbaden: Dr. Ludwig Reichert, 2015), 179–216. For the most detailed, comprehensive history of the Bukharan state in this period, see Andreas Wilde, *What is Beyond the River? Power, Authority and Social Order in Eighteenth- and Nineteenth-Century Transoxania* (Vienna: Verlag der Österreichischen Akademie der Wissenschaften, 2016). See also the same author's essay in ORE-AH, s.v. "The Bukharan Amirate."

6. Thomas Welsford, *Four Types of Loyalty in Early Modern Central Asia: The Tūqāy-Tīmūrid Takeover of Greater Mā warā al-Nahr, 1598–1605* (Leiden: E. J. Brill, 2013).

7. I have opted to refer to this early modern nomadic power using the more straightforward (in English) spelling of Jungar, rather than Dzungar, Zhungar, Zungar, Züüngar, Jüün Ghar, or other more precise transliterations from the Mongolian, Manchu, Chinese, Kazakh, Russian, or Persian languages.

8. The Bukharan amirs maintained puppet khans until 1785, but from 1747 regal authority rested with the Manghit leadership.

retrospect, perhaps what is most remarkable is that the Toqay-Timurids were able to hold on for as long as they did.

To date, the sole explanation scholars have presented for this crisis is that a general shift in international trade to the maritime arena had usurped the early modern overland caravan trade passing through Central Asia, allegedly isolating the region and causing it to plunge into economic crisis. Starved of resources, Central Asian societies suffered a decline in commercial life, cultural production, and military strength. I have elsewhere argued that this explanation for the Bukharan crisis is flawed, and there is no need to repeat myself here.[9] It is worth noting, though, that even if this explanation were correct, it completely fails to explain why the Bukharan crisis became critical only in the first half of the eighteenth century. Why not a century earlier, or later? In fact, there is abundant evidence demonstrating Central Asia's continued economic integration with China, Russia, and India throughout the early modern era, including during the first half of the eighteenth century. Economic isolation cannot explain the Bukharan crisis.[10]

A central argument of this book is that integration, not isolation, shaped the trajectory of early modern Central Asian history. I do not mean to say that early modern Central Asia was uniformly on a trajectory of increased integration. One can identify many political, social, economic, and intellectual institutions and processes that had earlier linked Central Asia to distant regions and that deteriorated or even collapsed during this period. But the discussions below demonstrate that, even as some important aspects of Central Asian integrative structures unraveled, other processes emerged to weave new patterns. Building on that premise, this book examines how globalizing processes during the eighteenth and nineteenth centuries contributed to the rise, and subsequent fall, of the Khanate of Khoqand.

In pursuit of this goal, I have made a deliberate, sustained effort to connect Central Asian history and historiography to multiple other historical fields. While the geographical focus for this study remains centered squarely within Central Asia, and even more precisely within the Ferghana Valley, the discussions below take readers

---

9. My earliest engagement with this debate is found in Scott C. Levi, "India, Russia and the Eighteenth-Century Transformation of the Central Asian Caravan Trade," *Journal of the Economic and Social History of the Orient* 42, no. 4 (1999): 519–48. Additional references can be found in the bibliography.
10. I am currently preparing a separate study that aims to identify the causal factors behind the Bukharan crisis. This analysis suggests that there were multiple factors at play, some independent and some linked, some of which emerged slowly while others erupted more abruptly, and all of which converged in the early eighteenth century to the great detriment of the Bukharan Khanate and those dependent on it.

far afield, engaging the historiographies of Qing China, the Russian Empire, and the fields of Indian Ocean and world history. Integrating Central Asian history into these scholarly literatures highlights the transregional connections that linked those who lived in the heart of Asia with larger Eurasian and global historical process, and illuminates how those processes shaped Central Asian lives and the trajectory of Central Asian history.

This is a book about the rise and fall of the Khanate of Khoqand, so I dedicate a substantial amount of attention to the political history of that state, including the Shahrukhids's methods of establishing dynastic legitimacy and the power structures that they used to sustain their state. At the same time, the chapters below engage discussions of economic history, including commercial history but also monetary flows; diplomatic history; innovations in military technologies and their role in changing Central Asian statecraft and the ideas underpinning legitimacy; work in environmental history, including the history of water and the "hydraulic state"; as well as new perspectives on Khoqand made available through scholarly analyses of poetry and other historical literature. This book brings all of this literature together to provide new insights into early modern Central Asian history. These discussions give shape to the canvas on which the rise and fall of Khoqand took place.

THE HISTORICAL ARC OF KHOQAND

The chapters in this book trace the formation of the Khanate of Khoqand to the reign of Shah Rukh Biy (r. 1709–22), the leader of the Uzbek Ming tribe and progenitor of the ruling dynasty (the "Shahrukhids") of Khoqand, and they situate his achievements and those of his heirs in their larger Eurasian context. Bukhara lost its ability to assert authority in the Ferghana Valley in the late seventeenth century. Already in the early decades of the eighteenth century, the inhabitants of the valley benefited from their position along caravan routes leading to Kashgar, Yarkand, and other markets to the east. This position became substantially more important after 1756–59, when the Qing conquest of the territory that would later be designated Xinjiang (including both the pastoral-nomadic Buddhist Jungar state in the north and the settled Islamic region of Altishahr in the south) brought the Qing imperial frontier to the borders of Khoqand.[11]

---

11. For a summary of the literature on, and meaning of, the Qing frontier, see Mark Elliott, "Frontier Stories: Periphery as Center in Qing History," *Frontiers of History in China* 9, no. 3 (2014): 336–60.

The Ferghana Valley was fully brought under Shahrukhid authority during the long, prosperous reign of Narbuta Biy (r. 1770–99). By the time Narbuta Biy ascended the throne, the Shahrukhid ruling family had effectively neutralized threats posed by a politically ambitious network of Naqshbandi sufi khojas, established a new capital at Khoqand, defended the valley from multiple invasions, formed a political relationship with the Qing, and used that relationship to negotiate lucrative privileges for Khoqandi merchants in Qing territory.[12] During the second half of the eighteenth century, the Khoqandi khans began using these resources to expand irrigation agriculture in the valley and leverage their ability to provide access to water as a means to settle tens of thousands of migrants, increase their productivity, mediate their conflicts, and control their political ambitions. At the same time, Khoqand developed a formidable military arsenal equipped with cannons, muskets, and other artillery capable of subjugating rivals throughout the valley and beyond.

The state of Khoqand was formally restyled as a "khanate" during the reign of Narbuta Biy's son and successor 'Alim Khan (r. 1799–1811), the first in the Shahrukhid line to assume the lofty title of "khan." Doing so was a breach of tradition, as in Central Asia the use of that title had for nearly six centuries been restricted to rulers who could trace their male ancestry directly to Chinggis Khan (d. 1227). Undeterred, the Shahrukhids devised new mechanisms to support their claims to legitimacy. They leveraged the gravity associated with the title of khan for diplomatic influence abroad, and they consolidated their authority at home through the deliberate imitation of the fifteenth-century Timurids, whose legacy in the region had risen to mythical proportions in the eighteenth century as the Chinggisids teetered and fell. This most famously included crafting a new origin myth for the Shahrukhid khans of Khoqand, the Altun Beshik ("Golden Cradle") legend, that traced the ancestry of the dynasty's Uzbek founder, Shah Rukh Biy, to Zahir al-Din Muhammad Babur himself (1483–1530). Linking the Shahrukhid ancestry to Babur's legacy was ideal because he was the last Timurid prince to rule in the ancestral capital of Samarqand, the founder of early modern India's great Mughal Empire (1526–1857), and a native of the Ferghana Valley.

Some Shahrukhids also sought to imitate the Timurids in their method of governance by patronizing a broad base of constituencies that included tribal interests and the military, as well as the highly influential mystical orders (sufis), more orthodox-minded Muslim scholars ('ulama), poets, scholars, artists, and more. Through

---

12. For a discussion of political sufism in Central Asia, see Alexandre Papas, *Soufisme et politique entre Chine, Tibet et Turkestan: Étude sur les Khwajas Naqshbandis du Turkestan orientale* (Paris: Jean Maisonneuve, 2005).

much of its history Khoqand was on a centralizing trajectory, but at no point would one be justified in classifying Khoqand as a modern "centralized state." Rather, the Shahrukhid leadership flourished by balancing the interests of multiple constituencies and serving as the chief negotiator among them. This technique brought rewards, and, in the early decades of the nineteenth century, the khanate flourished as the epicenter of a brief Islamic cultural efflorescence in the region. In this way, too, the Shahrukhids reflected their Timurid models.

The comparison stops there. While the medieval Timurid state was built on nomadic military power, technological advancements in the early modern world offered Central Asian rulers new opportunities, and new challenges. The Shahrukhids exploited their access to a growing population, greater economic resources, and improved gunpowder-weapons technologies. Khoqand was able to develop a formidable standing army that the Shahrukhids used to extend their authority deep into the Pamirs and far into the Kazakh steppe. To the north, in 1820 Khoqand established the fortress of Aq Masjid (also Ak Mechet, the "White Mosque," and modern Kyzylorda) near the shores of the Aral Sea as a Khoqandi outpost on the lower course of the Syr Darya, and its territory stretched eastward across the steppe to the borders of the Qing Empire.[13] During the first four decades of the nineteenth century, Khoqand's territorial holdings increased by a factor of thirty. By 1840, with some 3,000,000 subjects and a territory that stretched over some 250,000 square miles, Khoqand rivalled Bukhara in population and greatly exceeded it in size.

Destabilization took root when Khoqand lost the ability to manage its constituencies. In an effort to explain that process, this book examines the dialectic between Russian colonial expansion in Central Asia and the escalating ethnic tensions that terminally undermined indigenous political authority in the valley. Russian imperial literature and a long scholarly tradition emanating from that literature have tended to portray the later rulers in Khoqand as shortsighted feudal warlords and tyrants, stereotypical "Oriental despots" most interested in extracting wealth from their own people to support their own debaucherous pursuits. To be sure, one can find evidence to support those notions, and that evidence is discussed in the chapters that follow. But that evidence represents only one part of the whole. The discussion here challenges that interpretation by examining Khoqandi motivations and agendas and approaching Russian imperial expansion into the region from a Khoqandi perspective.

The final chapters outline multiple ways that the Russian imperial presence itself

---

13. Timur Beisembiev, *Tarikh-i Shahrukhi kak istoricheskii istochnik* (Alma-Ata: Nauka, 1987), 17.

served as a destabilizing factor in the region. Russian generals repeatedly expressed their desire to reach a firm, stable frontier. But approaching their actions from the Khoqandi perspective, one finds that, more than anything else, it was Russian expansion itself that led to the deterioration of Khoqand's political climate, not least by undermining the support of political factions that had previously been loyal to Khoqand. The resulting instability, chaos, and conflict created both the opportunity for Russian colonial expansion into Khoqand's territory and a perceived need among some in the Russian administration to act on that opportunity in an effort to impose stability on their frontier. Russian forces took the Khoqandi steppe outpost of Aq Masjid in 1853, and, in the immediate wake of the Crimean War (1853–56), Russian troops redirected their attention to the other Khoqandi steppe fortresses. They continued southward, annexed Tashkent in 1865, defeated the army of Khoqand in 1868, and in 1876 Tsar Alexander II (r. 1855–81) formally extinguished the khanate altogether and incorporated the Ferghana Valley into the Russian Empire. Again, rather than casting Central Asians as ahistorical victims of Russian imperialism, this book emphasizes Central Asians' agency in the process.

As noted above, this study demonstrates the methodological merits of conducting "connected histories" and applying a world historical perspective to local and regional histories. In doing so, the book advances a number of conclusions relevant to Central Asian specialists as well as scholars working in other areas of Eurasian and world history. Perhaps most important, the broader community of historians may find value in directing attention to ways that the more compact states of Central Asia resemble—or differ from—other states emerging on the frontier of, and in contact with, expanding imperial powers during the eighteenth and nineteenth centuries. Globalization, with roots stretching back at least to the sixteenth century, is a driving force in this process.[14] I recognize that what constitutes "globalization" itself is a contested notion, but a rehearsal of the many volumes written on the subject would be more cumbersome than helpful.[15] I apply it here in reference to a dramatic increase in global mobility; the general intensification of early modern global commercial bonds; the development of transregional networks, technologies, and institutions that facilitated that intensification; the growing commodification

---

14. See Dennis O. Flynn and A. Giraldez, "Born Again: Globalization's Sixteenth-Century Origins (Asian/Global versus European Dynamics," *Pacific Economic Review* 13, no. 3 (2008): 359–87.
15. I will refrain from digressing into a discussion of the many dozens of articles and books authored by Immanuel Wallerstein, Andre Gunder Frank, and other historical sociologists and economic historians that debate when globalization began and whether a "world system" took shape in the nineteenth century, the fifteenth century, or already in the third millennium BCE.

of certain agricultural products and other merchandise; and the variegated impacts that this process had on localities across the globe in terms of politics, economics, culture, and more.[16]

I argue that globalizing forces contributed to the rise, efflorescence, and collapse of the Khanate of Khoqand, and that this Central Asian case merits comparative analysis with, for example, the Burmese kingdom in mainland Southeast Asia, both Bali and the Siak Sultanate in Indonesia, and the Sultanate of Aceh in Sumatra; Ranjit Singh's Sikh state in the Punjab, Hyderabad, and many of the other "princely states" and "agencies" of post-Mughal India; the Sokoto Caliphate and the Tijaniyya Caliphate of Umar Tal in western Africa, the non-Muslim Asante (Ashanti) Kingdom in contemporary Ghana, and the Zulu Kingdom of South Africa. These are just a few of many states and other regional powers that exploited opportunities brought about by globalizing forces to establish a trajectory of growth and centralization, only to suffer eventual crisis and collapse as a result of those same forces. But before one may compare Khoqand with any of these other case studies, it is first necessary to introduce the Ferghana Valley, the heart of Central Asia.

THE EARLY HISTORY OF THE FERGHANA VALLEY

Surrounded by the Tian Shan (Heavenly Mountains) and Pamir-Alay mountain ranges, the Ferghana Valley is today home to roughly 14,000,000 people, making it the most densely populated region in Central Asia.[17] In the arid climate of the region, the Ferghana Valley offers fertile soil and an abundance of water, drawn primarily from the annual snowmelt that feeds the Naryn and Qara Darya rivers, which—even before they join to form the Syr Darya—channel water into hundreds of miles of

16. See Jan de Vries, "The Limits of Globalization in the Early Modern World," *Economic History Review* 63, no. 3 (2010): 710–33. Where de Vries directs his attention to the limits of the maritime networks orchestrated by the European Companies, I am more interested in how the general early modern pattern of globalization shaped historical developments deep in the hinterland. For an exceptionally useful treatment, see C. A. Bayly, "'Archaic' and 'Modern' Globalization in the Eurasian-African Arena," in *Globalization in World History*, ed. A. G. Hopkins (London: Plimco Press, 2009), 47–93. For a recent study of the cultural implications of globalization in the field of literature, see Ning Ma, *The Age of Silver: The Rise of the Novel East and West* (New York: Oxford University Press, 2017.)
17. This section is an abbreviated and edited excerpt from Scott C. Levi, "Farghana Valley," *Encyclopaedia of Islam, Three*, ed. Kate Fleet, Gudrun Krämer, Denis Matringe, John Nawas, Everett Rowson, Brill Online, http://referenceworks.brillonline.com/entries/encyclopaedia-of-islam-3/farghana-valley-COM _27096. I am grateful to the editors for granting permission to reproduce that material here in a slightly altered format.

canals that today irrigate nearly every part of the valley. This fact, combined with the valley's long, hot summers, has for millennia enabled its farmers to produce a regular surplus of crops including the peaches, melons, and other fruits for which the area is famous. An extra measure of historical importance is afforded to the valley as it rests along caravan routes that connected Bukhara, Samarqand, and other urban centers of Mawarannahr to the west, with Kashgar and the other oasis cities of Altishahr to the east.

The recorded history of the valley stretches into antiquity. In the year 329 BCE, Alexander the Great (356–323 BCE) is said to have established a settlement known as Alexandria Eschatae ("The Farthest") near the western entrance to the Ferghana Valley, at or very near the location of Khojand, an important Khoqandi possession in the nineteenth century now located in Tajikistan. Population growth and urbanization were well underway by the second century BCE, when (c. 126 BCE) the Han Chinese ambassador to Bactria, Zhang Qian (Chang Chi'en) traveled through the Ferghana Valley (Dayuan, or Ta-yüan, in his account) and left one of the earliest written accounts of the region. Zhang Qian reported that, at that time, Ferghana was home to a sedentary civilization of several hundred thousand people, mostly farmers. He found that the people of the valley had developed a sharp commercial acumen, and his account was perhaps the first to identify the Ferghana Valley as a source of the legendary blood-sweating "heavenly horses" that would for centuries spark the Chinese imagination.

In the early centuries of the Common Era, the inhabitants of the Ferghana Valley continued to thrive. This is partly attributable to their relationship with the neighboring Sogdians, who orchestrated a merchant diaspora that spanned much of Asia and connected local Central Asian economies with the much larger economies of China, India, and the Middle East.[18] The valley's medieval importance peaked in the middle of the eighth century, when the Chinese Tang Empire (618–907) successfully extended its authority across the Tian Shan and the rulers of both Tashkent (known at the time as Chach, or Shash) and the Ferghana Valley accepted Chinese suzerainty. This was at least partially in the expectation of achieving a closer commercial relationship with the Tang.

In the 740s, the Tang took advantage of the political fragmentation of the Second Türk Qaghanate (682–742), a superpower in steppe politics, to expand their interests westward. But that was quickly brought to a halt. In the year 750, the Tang were

---

18. Étienne de la Vaissière, *Histoire des marchands Sogdiens* (Paris: Collège France, Institute des Hautes Études Chinois, 2004). See also the English translation, Étienne de la Vaissière, *Sogdian Traders: A History*, trans. James Ward (Leiden: E. J. Brill, 2005).

drawn into a minor conflict between their two Central Asian vassals, the kingdoms of Tashkent and Ferghana. Following orders from the emperor, the Tang governor of the western province interfered on the side of Ferghana, forced the ruler of Tashkent into submission, and brought him to China to be executed.[19] The Tashkent ruler's son fled the Chinese and made his way to nearby Samarqand, where he requested aid from the city's new Arab Muslim ruler. The following summer, in 751, an Arab army from Samarqand, bolstered with reinforcements from Khurasan and Qarluq deserters from the Chinese confederation, defeated the Tang near the city of Talas (Taraz, previously Jambyl), in contemporary southern Kazakhstan. Both Tashkent and Ferghana were left firmly in the hands of the Arabs, and Chinese forces were confined to the east side of the Tian Shan. Just a few years later, following the 755 An Lushan Rebellion, Chinese armies retreated all the way to China proper. It would be a thousand years before the Manchurian Qing dynasty would again conquer that far to the west.

In subsequent centuries, the people of the Ferghana Valley, along with others in the region, gradually set aside their Zoroastrian faith and other ancestral religious traditions in favor of Islam. The maturation of this process is evidenced by the anonymous author of the tenth-century *Ḥudūd al-ʿĀlam* (The limits of the world), a cultural and geographical survey of the Islamic world at that time.[20] Some five centuries later, Ferghana's established position in Central Asian Islamic civilization was recorded in Babur's personal memoir, the *Baburnama*.

In Babur's time, Ferghana was elevated in status as a political unit, a Timurid *soyūrghāl* (a land grant intended to provide revenue for a Timurid prince), but it remained subordinate to Samarqand and was in actuality little more than a collection of seven modestly sized cities surrounded by villages and abundant wilderness designated to a lesser Timurid heir.[21] Babur's capital city was Andijan, the largest city in Ferghana but smaller than Samarqand or Shahrisabz. Other urban centers in Babur's realm included Akhsi and Kasan in the northern part of the valley, Osh to the east, and Marghilan, Isfara, and Khojand to the south and west. Cities such as Namangan, Tura Qurghan, Chust, and of course Khoqand itself were later developments, either not yet established or little more than villages that grew into important urban centers only from the eighteenth century.

---

19. Bregel, *Atlas*, 18.
20. Vladimir Minorsky, *Ḥudūd al-ʿĀlam: "The Regions of the World," A Persian Geography, 272 A.H.–982 A.D.*, ed. C. E. Bosworth, 2nd ed. (London: Gibb Memorial Trust, 1970), 112–19.
21. See Babur's description in Wheeler M. Thackston, trans., *The Baburnama: Memoirs of Babur, Prince and Emperor* (New York: Oxford University Press, 2002): 3–8.

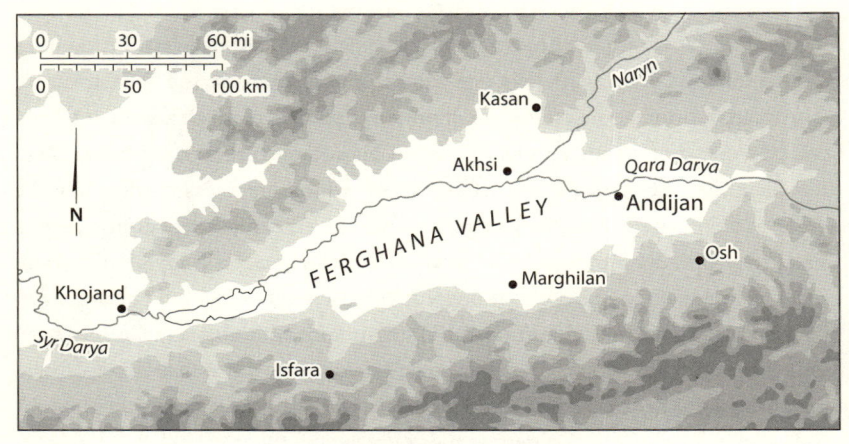

MAP 2 Babur's Ferghana Valley.
Map by Bill Nelson.

In his memoir, Babur describes his youth in Ferghana. He longingly recalls that the melons, grapes, and pears of Andijan were among the best anywhere; that peaches, pomegranates, and other fruit grew in abundance elsewhere in the valley; and that the valley offered a wealth of untouched wilderness for hunting deer, pheasant, hare, and other game. His account references a few locations where irrigation canals channeled water from rivers to agricultural lands, and he proudly asserts: "the income of Ferghana Province, if justly managed, will maintain three to four thousand men."[22] Exploring demographic and environmental change over time, the image of the Ferghana Valley Babur presents contrasts sharply with descriptions of the mid-nineteenth century, which depict a substantially more densely populated and heavily irrigated Ferghana Valley at the heart of a state that could produce an army as large as 100,000 troops.

What happened in the interim? With Babur's expulsion from Central Asia at the turn of the sixteenth century, the valley fell into Uzbek hands, and it remained a peripheral province of the Bukharan Khanate for nearly two centuries.[23] Bukharan

---

22. Thackston, *The Baburnama*, 7.
23. There is little historical work on the Ferghana Valley during this period. R. N. Nabiev has done some work on this theme. See R. N. Nabiev, "Iz istorii feodal'nogo zemlevladeniia v Fergane v XVI–XVII vekakh," IAN 3 (1960), 25–34; and his "Novye dokumental'nye materialy k izucheniiu feodal'nogo instituta 'suiurgal' v Fergane XVI–XVII vv.," IAN 3 (1959), 23–32. For another short treatment, see A. Juvonmardiev, "XVI va XVII asr boshlarida Farghonada dehqonlarning erga biriktirilishi masalasiga doir," ONU 2 (1963), 61–64.

control over its eastern territories, including the Ferghana Valley, slipped away during the latter half of the seventeenth century. At the turn of the eighteenth century, the valley was independent of Bukhara and home to multiple ethnic and religious groups with competing political visions. The valley's transformation from Babur's idyllic wilderness paradise into a much more densely populated and agriculturally rich commercial hub was a product of integrative structures that began to take shape only during the early eighteenth century, even as the neighboring Bukharan Khanate plunged into a deepening state of crisis and political decentralization. It is the story of Khoqand.

One
A NEW UZBEK DYNASTY, 1709–1769

IN THE NORTHWESTERN part of the Ferghana Valley, a small stream flows southward, bringing snowmelt from the distant peaks into the open plains. Observed from a distance, the brown, dusty landscape is interrupted by a shock of green as agriculture becomes possible along a long, narrow strip of land stretching little more than a hundred yards to either side of the frigid water. Moving closer, one spies neatly whitewashed houses tucked beneath ancient trees, a small stone mosque with goats grazing in its courtyard, a dirt road that follows the twisting and turning path of the stream, and farmers tending to their melon patches, vineyards, apple orchards, peach trees, and more. As in other places in the valley, the long and intensely hot summers combine with rich soil and a reliable supply of water from melting snow to provide an ideal environment for growing the intensely sweet fruit for which the region is famous. The trees also provide shade for the inhabitants of this small settlement of Chadak and the khojas, descendants of a lineage of Naqshbandi sufis, who lived among them.

Near the turn of the eighteenth century, the Uzbek amirs and other tribal powers in the region were not the only groups to take advantage of the diminished strength of the Bukharan Khanate. As Bukharan authority withdrew from the Ferghana Valley in the late seventeenth century, political power became localized in the hands of several Turkic tribes and a network of theocratic khojas centered in Chadak. While a number of these tribes, including the Ming, were relatively recent arrivals, the tension between

FIG. 1.1 Chadak.
Author photo.

the pastoral-nomadic tribes and the Islamic religious establishment was nothing new. Across western Central Asia, Naqshbandi sufi networks had been heavily engaged in the political arena since the fifteenth-century Timurid era.[1] And in nearby Kashgar, to the east, political authority had for decades been in the hands of two rival lineages of Naqshbandi khojas, established by Ishaq Khoja (d. 1599) and Afaq Khoja (d. 1694). Both were descendants of the famous Naqshbandi sufi Ahmad Kasani (1461–1542), renowned as Makhdūm-i A'zam, the "Greatest Master," who lived in Samarqand and was reputedly a sayyid, or descendant from the Prophet Muhammad.[2]

1. See Jo-Ann Gross and Asom Urunbaev, *The Letters of Khwajah 'Ubayd Allah Ahrar and His Associates* (Leiden: E. J. Brill, 2002); Jo-Ann Gross, "Multiple Roles and Perceptions of a Sufi Shaykh: Symbolic Statements of Political and Religious Authority," in *Naqshbandis: cheminements et situation actuelle d'un ordre mystique musulman*, ed. Marc Gaborieau, Alexandre Popovic, and Thierry Zarcone (Istanbul and Paris: IFEA et Editiones ISIS, 1990), 109–21; Bakhtiyar Babajanov, "La naqshbandiyya sous les premiers Sheybanides," *Cahiers d'Asie centrale* 3–4 (1997): 69–90; Robert D. McChesney, *Central Asia: Foundations of Change* (Princeton, NJ: Darwin Press, 1996), 69–115.

2. In addition to Papas, *Soufisme et politique entre Chine, Tibet et Turkestan*, see the same author's excellent summary analysis in ORE-AH, s.v. "Khojas of Kashgar." Cf. the following studies, Devin DeWeese, "The 'Competitors' of Isḥāq Khwāja in Eastern Turkistan: Hagiographies, Shrines, and Sufi Affiliations in the Late Sixteenth Century," in *Horizons of the World*, ed. İlker Evrim Binbaş and Nurten Kılıç-Schubel (Istanbul: İthaki Publishing, 2011), 133–215; David Brophy, "The Oirat in Eastern Turkistan and the Rise of Āfāq Khwāja," *Archivum Eurasiae Medii Aevi* 16 (2008–9): 5–28; Jeff Eden, "A Sufi Saint in Sixteenth-Century East Turkistan: New Evidence Concerning the Life of Khwāja Isḥāq," *Journal of the Royal Asiatic Society* 25, no. 2 (2015): 229–45. See also Isenbike Togan, "The Khojas of Eastern Turkestan," in *Muslims in Central Asia: Expressions of Identity and Change*, ed. Jo-Ann Gross (Durham: Duke University Press, 1992), 134–48; Henry Schwarz, "The Khwājas of Eastern

In the late sixteenth century, these sayyid khojas of Kashgar began to usurp authority from the nomadic Chaghataids, descendants of Chinggis Khan. Their influence grew and, by the late seventeenth century, the khojas had effectively replaced longstanding concepts of legitimacy based on steppe traditions with more theocratic concepts based on adherence to Naqshbandi interpretations of Islamic law and practice. In 1678, Galdan Khan (r. 1676–97), the Buddhist ruler who united the Jungar Mongols, defeated the Chaghataids and conquered Altishahr. While the region was made Jungar territory, Galdan Khan installed the leaders of the Afaqiyya (followers of Afaq Khoja, and also known as the Aqtaghlik or "White Mountain" Khojas) to serve as his subordinate governor of Altishahr, the "Six Cities" region of eastern Turkestan.[3] For eight decades prior to the Qing conquest of the region, political and religious authority in Altishahr were bound together in the hands of the khojas of Kashgar. The evidence presented in the Khoqand chronicles—albeit scanty, based on oral traditions, and codified well after the fact—suggests that the khojas of Chadak intended to follow in the footsteps of their eastern counterparts by replacing the Bukharan Khanate's Chinggisid authority with a similar theocracy in the Ferghana Valley. The khojas enjoyed some early successes in the wake of the Bukharan withdrawal in the late seventeenth century, but in the first decade of the eighteenth century the Ming thwarted their efforts.

There are no contemporary accounts of Shah Rukh (r. 1709–22), the Ming tribal leader who is identified as the progenitor of the ruling dynasty that later produced the khans of Khoqand. Chroniclers have, however, preserved several divergent versions of the rich oral history of the events surrounding his rise to power. According to this tradition, the elders of several of the Turkic tribes in the valley assembled early in the eighteenth century to assess their position vis-à-vis the Chadak Khojas. Citing the *Tārīkh-i Turkestān*, a source authored in 1915, the historian of Khoqand Haidarbek Bababekov identifies the coalition as constituting representatives from "Targhovaga, Jankat, Pilakhan, Tufantip, Partak, Tepe-Kurgan, Kainar and other

---

Turkestan," *Central Asiatic Journal* 20, no. 4 (1976): 266–96; Joseph Fletcher, "The Naqshbandiyya in northwest China," in *Joseph Fletcher: Studies on Chinese and Islamic Central Asia*, ed. Jonathan Lipman and Beatrice Forbes Manz (Aldershot: Variorum, 1995), 1–46.

3. As discussed in the Note on Geographic Terminology, after the Qing defeat of the Jungars and conquest of Altishahr in 1759, the Qing renamed Altishahr as Xinjiang, "New Frontier." On the persistent legacy of historical understanding among Turkic Muslims in the Altishahr region (our contemporary Uyghurs), see the methodologically innovative study by Rian Thum, *The Sacred Routes of Uyghur History* (Cambridge, MA: Harvard University Press, 2014). On the shaping of an Uyghur ethnic-national identity in the early twentieth century, see David Brophy, *Uyghur Nation: Reform and Revolution on the Russia-China Frontier* (Cambridge, MA: Harvard University Press, 2016).

towns."[4] Specific details regarding the alliance are lacking, but the Uzbek council reportedly decided to unite under Shah Rukh's leadership to rebel against Chadak and claim political authority from the khojas. The following is a distilled and combined summary of several different accounts as they have come down to us through oral tradition, relying most heavily on Niyazi's *Tārīkh-i Shahrukhī*.

> The Sultanate began with Shah Rukh, son of 'Ashur Biy.[5] Up to that time, there was no city of Khoqand. Chadak had become a center of power in the Ferghana Valley, and many khojas in that area supported its political position. At the same time, Uzbek tribes had begun to make their way into the valley and gather in various places. The Uzbeks decided that they would come together to make a council. One man announced, "Among us there is a man who is a descendant of Chamash Biy, he is Shah Rukh son of 'Ashur Bek. We shall make him khan and rebel against Chadak." The assembled Uzbeks agreed, and they devised a plan to achieve that goal.
>
> The plan began with an effort to convince the Chadak Khojas that they were prepared to establish an alliance and accept a subordinate role to the khojas. Toward this goal, the Uzbeks offered one of their girls to the hakim (governor) of Chadak to take as his wife. The hakim was pleased, and he agreed. On the wedding day, a group of forty Uzbeks came to Chadak to participate in the toi (wedding celebration). After the festivities, the Uzbeks were divided up and placed in various homes as guests. According to the plans that the Uzbeks had laid out, shortly after the groom should arrive that night, but before he would have a chance to consummate the marriage, one of the Uzbeks would rub a willow branch in the crook of a tree to issue a secret signal. At that moment, all of the Uzbeks would rise up and kill their hosts. This was done, and the rise to power of the Chadak khojas was brought to an end.
>
> From Chadak, the Uzbeks rapidly extended their reign (eastward) over Chust and Namangan, and then on to Shaidon and Panghaz ("Pansad Ghazi"). The Uzbeks distributed gifts to the populations of those conquered cities that submitted without resistance, and Shah Rukh appointed hakims to govern them.
>
> Shah Rukh then issued an order that, before searching out and defeating other enemies in the region, his followers should find a place to build a fortress that might

---

4. The author refrains from describing the nature of the Uzbeks' conflict with Chadak. Bababekov, *Qöqon Tarikhi*, 21–22. See Mullah Alim Makhdum Khoja, *Tārīkh-i Turkestān* (Tashkent, 1915), 8–11. For Beisembiev's analysis of the *Tā'rīkh-i Turkistān* as a historical source, see KI, 115. See also the slightly altered English translation of Bababekov's Uzbek-language work, Dubovitski and Bababekov, "The Rise and Fall," 30.

5. In Khoqand the Turkic honorific is transliterated as "biy" or "bī," where in references to other Turkic groups it may be transliterated as bey, beğ, beg, or bek.

FIG. 1.2   Chadak, Mausoleum of the Khojas.
Author photo.

serve as their new capital. He sent scouts around the valley and they found an old ruined fortress known as Koktonliq Ata at the juncture of two small rivers, a distance of some sixteen *farsakh* (about eighty-eight miles) west of Andijan. Shah Rukh ordered the construction of a new ark at that spot.

*The Sultanate Is a Garden
Without a Wall, It Is Difficult to Protect*

Shah Rukh had a wall built around the city with gates on all four sides: the Andijan Gate in the east, the Namangan Gate in the north, the Tashkent Gate in the west (also called the Khojand Gate, or the Samarqand Gate), and the Ispara Gate in the south (also known as the Chahar Kuh Gate). He ordered residences to be built within the ark for all of the high officials of his new state. The throne was established there, and the Uzbeks commemorated the event with a great celebration. Shah Rukh was installed as khan by the *āq kigīz* ceremony (the traditional Mongolian "White Felt" ceremony for elevating a Chinggisid khan). The year was 1121 (1709/10). People migrated to this fortress from all around, and the bazaar and surrounding areas grew large and became a city.[6]

6. TS, fols. 12a–16b; MTF, fols. 15a–18a; TJT, fols. 18b–19b. The account relayed by Muhammad Fazl Bek has the khojas divided up and staying as the Uzbeks' guests, though meeting the same end. On the continuation of the *āq kigīz* ritual, in altered format, among the non-Chinggisid Manghit rulers in eighteenth-century Bukhara, see Ron Sela, "Ritual and Authority in Central Asia: The Khan's Inauguration Ceremony" (papers on Inner Asia, no. 37, Indiana University Research Institute for Inner Asian Studies, Bloomington, 2003).

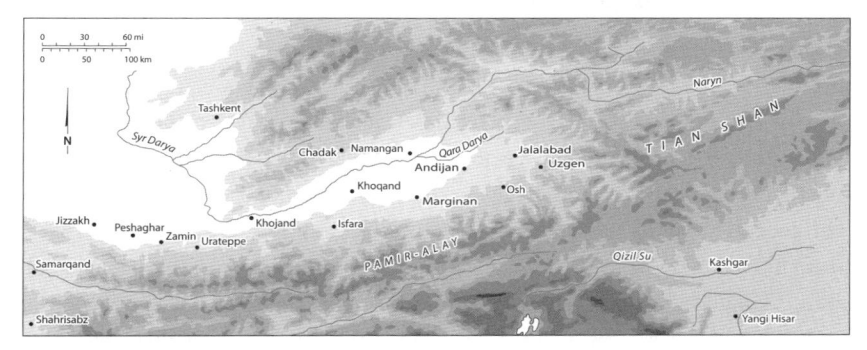

MAP 3 The Ferghana Valley and Its Environs.
Map by Bill Nelson.

In chapter 5 we will return to the relevance of tracing Shah Rukh's lineage through Chamash Biy (also referenced in historical sources as Chamash Sufi, Jamash Biy and Shah Mast Biy). For now, it is sufficient to note that doing so served two purposes. The historical Chamash Biy was believed to have been a *murid* (disciple) of the revered sixteenth-century Naqshbandi sufi Lutfallah Chusti.[7] Beisembiev repeats a tradition that Chusti "allegedly had given Chamash the good news that his posterity would be rulers."[8] At the same time, this legend goes on to trace the Shahrukhid lineage through the historical Chamash Biy to the mythical Altun Beshik and, through him, to Babur.

Shah Rukh's victory over Chadak and the elimination, or more accurately suppression, of the khojas is presented as if it were a momentous event. The resulting image is one of an Uzbek dynasty on an upward trajectory. In the greater context of the region, if the event did in fact unfold as reported through this oral tradition, it reflects nothing more than the good fortune of one Turkic political group—or for want of a better word, tribe—the Ming, in their efforts to take advantage of Bukhara's weakened stature even prior to the beginning of Abu'l Fayz Khan's long and ultimately failed reign.

A critical perspective exposes a number of problems with this narrative. For example, although it is possible that Shah Rukh led the coalition of Uzbek tribes that defeated the Chadak Khojas, the historical evidence shows that sufis remained exceptionally powerful in the valley through the duration of the history of the khanate that he launched. Over a century later, a different line of Naqshbandi khojas held sufficient influence to issue multiple campaigns against the Qing in

---

7. MT, 375.
8. AIKC, 14.

Kashghar, even taking the city in the 1826 and asserting their own rule for some months.[9]

Two more problematic aspects of the chroniclers' treatment of this account demand attention. First, the assertion that the Ming elevated Shah Rukh as khan is most certainly an invention of a later period. The Shahrukhids were not Chinggisids and, contrary to what some scholars have argued, they never sought to claim legitimacy by concocting a fictive Chinggisid lineage.[10] Rather, during the early eighteenth century, Shah Rukh emerged as one of a number of Uzbek tribal biys (nobles), who enjoyed positions of authority in the Ferghana Valley.[11] It does seem that Shah Rukh established an initial capital at what had been a ruined fortress in Deqan Tudah, some three farsakh (about seventeen miles) south of Khoqand.[12] But there is no presently reason to challenge the accepted position that Laura Newby has recently examined and reaffirmed, that Shah Rukh's great-great-grandson 'Alim was the first of his lineage to claim the title of khan, and that he did so at the very beginning of the nineteenth century for specific reasons pertaining to foreign diplomacy initiatives and his conquest of Tashkent.[13]

Equally implausible is the suggestion that Shah Rukh governed over a vast stretch of the Ferghana Valley. Based on the available information, it is reasonable to conclude that Shah Rukh successfully extended his control over some of the central and western portions of the Ferghana Valley. However, the extent of his territory is questionable, the sources do not address the degree of autonomy that his hakims enjoyed, and the centralization of whatever administration he did establish was quite limited and would remain that way for decades to come. Again, one must resist the temptation to read backward later achievements and assign any form of centralized statehood to Khoqand at this stage in its development. The chronicles attest to the Shahrukhids' impressive number of early military victories, but they neglect to place an equal emphasis on the fact that many of these were temporary and throughout the history of Khoqand power and authority were matters of constant negotiation.

---

9. For a thorough treatment of one of these sufi-led campaigns, see chapter 4 in Newby, *The Empire and the Khanate*, 95–123.
10. Others have argued that their efforts to link their ancestry to Babur stemmed from his Chinggisid parentage on his mother's side. This is despite the fact that Chinggisid legitimacy could only pass through the male, or agnatic, line. This argument is refuted in chapter 4.
11. It has long been established that the process of state consolidation began in the late eighteenth century. See Ol'ga Chekhovich, "O nekotorykh voprosakh istorii Srednei Azii 18–19 vekov," *Voprosy istorii* 3 (1956): 87.
12. AIKC, 608, 795.
13. Newby, *The Empire and the Khanate*, 62 and note.

In general, it is necessary to approach concepts of statehood in Central Asia during this period with great caution and sensitivity to the teleological nature of the sources. One thing we can assert with a reasonable degree of certainty is that the Shahrukhids did not bring the entire Ferghana Valley under their control in any meaningful way until much later in the eighteenth century.

Also problematic is that the above is not the only account of Shah Rukh's rise to power. Niyazi and Muhammad Fazl Bek both present versions of an alternate tradition that, when Shah Rukh was eighteen years old, one of the "Khans of Mawarannahr" traveled to the Ferghana Valley to go lion hunting (at that time the Toqay-Timurid ruler of Bukhara would have been either Subhan Quli Khan, r. 1681–1702, or his son and successor 'Ubaydullah Khan, r. 1702–11). Shah Rukh accompanied the khan into a forested area of the valley where the hunting party encountered a lion. The young Shah Rukh leaped forward and, engaging the beast, mortally wounded it with a dagger (or a spear). Shah Rukh's bravery is said to have impressed the khan to such an extent that he awarded Shah Rukh with the surrounding areas to rule as his own.[14]

Such an account seems highly unlikely, though Bukharan policies during the reign of Shah Rukh did indeed have a direct impact on developments in the valley. In 1716–17, the Khitay-Qipchaqs (modern Kazakhs) invaded southward and devastated agricultural areas around Samarqand and Qarshi by permitting their herds to feast on crops, which caused a famine. Abu'l Fayz Khan (r. 1711–47) intended to take control of the matter by "appointing" (perhaps "officially recognizing" would be more accurate) a nobleman named Ibrahim Biy Keneges to the position of *ataliq* (a senior advisor at court) in an effort to strengthen ties with the Keneges, a major independent tribal power in and around Timur's home city of Shahrisabz.[15] Although the Keneges have until recently tended to be written out of eighteenth- and nineteenth-century Central Asian history, their leaders had governed in Shahrisabz since the Toqay-Timurid ruler Subhan Quli Khan placed Rustam Bey Keneges as hakim in 1694, and they would remain the dominant political power there until the Russian conquests.[16]

Despite Abu'l Fayz Khan's best efforts at subjugating the Keneges, matters in the

---

14. TS, f. 12b; MTF, f. 14a–b. See also TJN, f. 23a. It is possible that this tradition is a case of attributing to the wrong person stories of an actual historical event that occurred nearly a century later. According to Hakim Khan, one of 'Alim Khan's sons, also named Shah Rukh, bravely killed a lion, although by gunshot and in the presence of his father, not the ruler of Bukhara. MT, 432–33.

15. Holzwarth, "Relations between Uzbek," 192.

16. For a unique and valuable look at Keneges Shahrisabz as an independent and sovereign city-state, rather than a diminutive Bukharan "province in rebellion," see James Robert Pickett, "The Persianate Sphere during the Age of Empires: Islamic Scholars and Networks of Exchange in Central Asia, 1747–1917" (PhD diss., Princeton University, 2015), 88–105.

region unfolded in a way that would work against the Bukharan advantage. Rather than joining forces with Bukhara, the Keneges struck an alliance with the Kazakhs that enhanced their position as a separate power in the region.[17] The Keneges leadership retained their independence, but at great cost. Already in 1717, some 12,000 Samarqandis fled their famine-ravaged home for India, and thousands more found refuge in the Ferghana Valley.[18] Over the next century and a half, Bukhara would unleash successive campaigns in an effort to reassert its authority over Shahrisabz. With only a few temporary exceptions, these efforts failed. The Keneges would effectively retain their independence until the Russian colonial period.

Little more is known about the specific details of Shah Rukh's reign, though he reportedly had ruled for twelve years and left three sons ('Abd al-Rahim, 'Abd al-Karim, and Shadi Biy) and at least one daughter when he died in 1722. The mantle passed to his eldest son, the quite capable 'Abd al-Rahim (r. 1722–34). Mulla Avaz Muhammad reports that, in his youth, Shah Rukh had sent 'Abd al-Rahim to take up a position at the court of Aq Buta Biy, hakim of Khojand and the leader of the Yuz (the word *yüz* is Uzbek for one hundred but here refers to the Uzbek Yuz tribe). At that time, the Yuz were the dominant tribal power in the region to the west of the valley, and their territory included the cities of Khojand as well as Jizzakh, Urateppe, Hisar-i Shadman and, early on, Qurama, a region that stretched between the valley and Tashkent.[19]

Shah Rukh had struck an alliance with Aq Buta Biy, which involved not only handing over 'Abd al-Rahim Biy to the Yuz, but also giving him his own daughter in marriage.[20] 'Abd al-Rahim is said to have quickly matured into a capable military commander, rising through the ranks and earning popularity and influence in the Yuz army. Over time, Aq Buta Biy's opinion of his young Ming guest shifted from a paternal pride to a deep fear. Suspecting that 'Abd al-Rahim was plotting to take Khojand for his father, Aq Buta Biy conspired to have him killed. According to Hakim Khan, Aq Buta Biy dispatched some 500 Kyrgyz soldiers to capture 'Abd al-Rahim, who narrowly escaped. Aided by the work of a talented sniper who is said to have single-handedly brought down forty of the Kyrgyz, 'Abd al-Rahim and his entourage fled Khojand and safely made their way back into the valley.[21]

Upon ascending the throne after Shah Rukh's death, 'Abd al-Rahim first had to

---

17. Pickett, "The Persianate Sphere," 193.
18. Timur Beisembiev, "Migration in the Qöqand Khanate in Eighteenth and Nineteenth Centuries," in *Migration in Central Asia: Its History and Current Problems*, ed. Komatsu Hisao, Obiya Chika, and John S. Schoeberlein (Osaka: The Japan Center for Asian Studies, 2000), 36.
19. AIKC, 13.
20. TJN, fols. 23a–24b.
21. MT, 375.

FIG. 1.3 Citadel of Khojand.

Turkestanskii Al'bom, 1865–72, Library of Congress, Prints & Photographs Division, LC-DIG-ppmsca-12262.

assert his authority over all of the hakims who had been loyal to his father but who viewed the transition following his death as an opportunity to jockey for increased autonomy or fully assert their own independence. 'Abd al-Rahim assembled an army of Uzbeks and Sarts (the latter term refers to settled farmers, either Turkic or Tajik, as a social category opposed to nomadic Turkic tribesmen), which he quickly put to work quashing rebellions across the valley.[22] He unleashed his forces against Khojand and personally killed Aq Buta Biy Yuz and his two sons. He then occupied both Khojand and Urateppe, thereby subjugating the Yuz and establishing his control over the only entrance into the valley not naturally protected by mountains.[23] After six (or seven) years, 'Abd al-Rahim assembled another army and continued his struggle against Bukhara. During this campaign, he occupied Samarqand without a fight

22. TJN, f. 23b.
23. The only significant variation in the accounts of this campaign is in the size of the army. Niyazi reports that it included 20,000 troops, Muhammad Fazl Bek places the figure higher, at 29,000, and Muhammad Salih estimates that the army was comprised of 40,000 troops. TS, f. 18a; MTF, fols. 19b–21a; TJT, f. 19b; TJN, f. 24a–b.

FIG. 1.4 Khojand, Market Square.
Turkestanskii Al'bom, 1865–72, Library of Congress, Prints & Photographs Division, LC-DIG-ppmsca-12224

and then went on to establish an immensely important alliance with the independent Keneges leadership in Shahrisabz.

For his part of the alliance, 'Abd al-Rahim received in marriage Oychuchuk Oyim, the young daughter of Ibrahim Biy Keneges, niece of the hakim and future grandmother of the Shahrukhid ruler Narbuta Biy (r. 1770–99).[24] It is a dramatic understatement to say that the chroniclers minimize the multiplicity of roles that women played in political matters pertaining to the history of Khoqand and the larger history of the region. But Oychuchuk Oyim, later known as Keneges Oyim, was so powerful and influential that she appears in virtually all accounts, and the chroniclers present her achievements in greater detail than those of many of her contemporary men.[25] Considering her historical importance, ambition, and acumen, Oychuchuk Oyim could be said to represent an eighteenth-century Uzbek analogy to the thirteenth-century Mongol princess Sorghaghtani Beki (d. 1252), wife of Chinggis Khan's

---

24. TS, fols. 18a–20b; MTF, fols. 19b–22b; TJN, f. 24b. According to Muhammad Salih, Khoqand received tribute from Samarqand, and the army left without conquering the city. TJT, f. 19b. See also AIKC, 80.
25. Muhammad Hakim Khan Tore, author of the *Muntakhab al-tawarikh* (MT), is her great-grandchild through her son, also named Hakim Khan, born to her during her third marriage.

youngest son Tolui and mother to both Mönke Khan (r. 1251–59) and Qublai Khan (r. 1259–94), albeit on a much smaller scale.

ANOTHER MONGOL INVASION

The eighteenth-century chronicler, Mir Muhammad Amin Bukhari, reports that in the year 1705, the Toqay-Timurid ruler 'Ubaydullah Khan (r. 1702–11) traveled from his capital of Bukhara to Samarqand. Upon his arrival, Uzbek amirs from throughout the eastern stretches of his realm "waited upon the khan with presents (*pīsh-kash*) and declarations of loyalty."[26] The chronicler presents an image of a strong Bukharan presence but, as is often the case, the political context of the region at that time was more complicated than the official record suggests. In the early decades of the eighteenth century, Central Asia was populated by a variety of ethnic and tribal groups, and a number of these, including those in the Ferghana Valley, were already effectively independent of Bukharan authority. In addition to a number of independent Uzbek tribes, the Kazakh khans were also a major political force within the region, having ruled the cities of Turkestan from 1628 and Tashkent from 1642.[27]

At the turn of the eighteenth century, the Bukharans and Kazakhs had worked in harmony, and there had long been a considerable movement of peoples between the two regions: Kazakhs came to occupy parts of Mawarannahr, and many thousands of Bukharan merchants moved with relative ease among the various commercial outposts in the steppe.[28] Settlements built alongside the Syr Darya as it stretched northward toward the Aral Sea served as important commercial outposts for the Bukharan caravan traders and others who moved between these two realms. Bukharans and Kazakhs also shared a common enemy in the pastoral-nomadic Jungars (again, Buddhist Mongols, the Jungars are generally referred to as Qalmaqs in Khoqandi and other "Islamic" sources), another major power in the steppe with expansionist aspirations.

---

26. Mir Muhammad Amin Bukharai, *'Ubaidullānāma*, IVANU, Ms. No. 1532, f. 39b and Russian tr. by A. A. Semenov, *Ubaidulla-name* (Tashkent: Nauka, 1957), 55. The reference and quotation are found in Holzwarth, "Relations between Uzbek Central Asia," 183.
27. Holzwarth, "Relations between Uzbek," 184.
28. See Audrey Burton, *The Bukharans: A Dynastic, Diplomatic and Commercial History, 1550–1702* (New York: St. Martin's Press, 1997), and Erika Monahan, *The Merchants of Siberia: Trade in Early Modern Eurasia* (Ithaca: Cornell University Press, 2016).

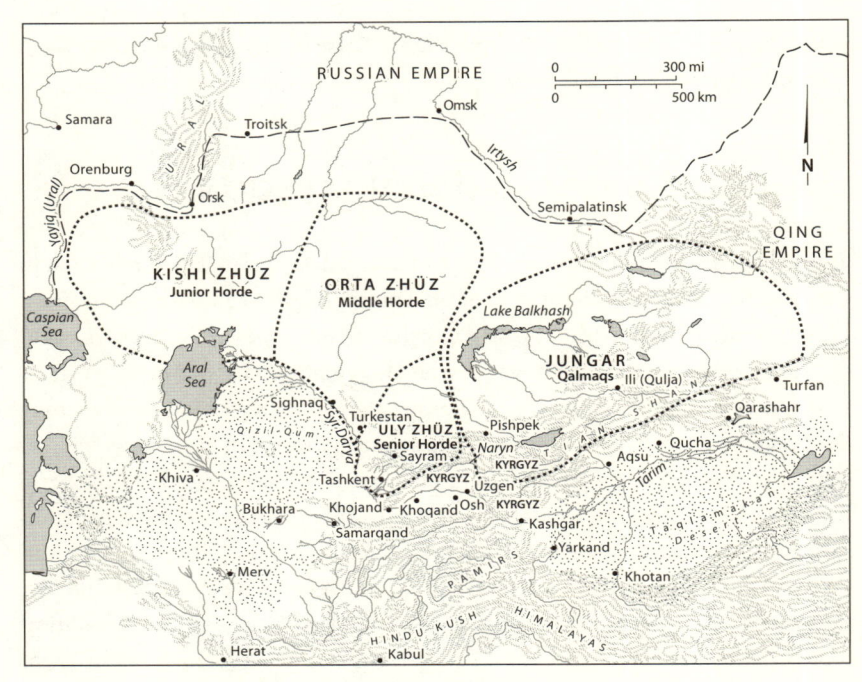

MAP 4 Steppe Powers in the Eighteenth Century.
Map by Bill Nelson.

The Jungar-Kazakh wars of the early eighteenth century were extraordinarily destructive and they severely destabilized key parts of the region. Resisting the temptation to recount the full extent of Jungar military exploits in this period, I have restricted the discussion here to those events that provide insight into later developments in Central Asia.[29] During the second half of the seventeenth century, the Jungar ruler Galdan Khan (1644–97) had effectively modernized the Jungar military by emphasizing gunpowder weapons over traditional nomadic techniques. Rather than relying on foreign supplies, his military program included developing a mining infrastructure to obtain iron ore for making canons, muskets, and mortars, and refining saltpeter to produce gunpowder.[30] Galdan's innovative approach was

---

29. This subject has received considerable attention in the secondary literature. For an insightful treatment, see the chapter "Imperial Overreach and Zunghar Survival, 1700–1731," in Peter Perdue, *China Marches West: The Qing Conquest of Central Eurasia* (Cambridge, MA: Harvard University Press, 2005), 209–55.
30. Perdue, *China Marches West*, 304–6.

exceptional, but it was during the reign of his nephew, Tsewang Rabdan (r. 1697–1727), that the Jungar would reach the height of their power in the region.

Near the beginning of his reign, in 1698–99, Tsewang Rabdan launched an attack against Kazakh settlements along the Irtysh and Xier rivers. This was at least partly motivated by his concerns that the Kazakh alliances with the Russians represented a threat to the Jungar interests in the west. In 1709, the Jungar attacked northern Kazakh settlements, killing many and bringing others back as prisoners.[31] In this instance, the Jungar appear to have withdrawn quickly, before the Bukharans could materially support their Kazakh allies. The following year, the Jungar attacked the Russian fortress at Bakan, in Siberia. Recognizing that their forward troops at that time were insufficiently supported and exposed, the Russians expressed an interest in peace, but the Jungar refused and instead demanded the full Russian withdrawal from their Siberian fortresses at Krasnoyarsk, Kuznetsk, and Tomsk.[32] In 1716, the Jungar then forced the Russians to retreat from their trading outpost at Lake Yamysh. The Russians quickly regrouped and built a stronger and more sustainable fortress at Omsk, which they bolstered with supplies before they returned to Yamysh two years later.

The speed of the Jungar nomadic military forces combined with their use of modern artillery had made them a formidable force in the region, and in 1716–17, Jungar forces inflicted a crushing defeat on the Qing army in Tibet. The ferocious nature of the Jungar victory and the importance the Kangxi emperor (r. 1661–1722) attached to Tibet seems to have steeled Qing resolve. The Qing dispatched reinforcements to Tibet, the Jungar were overpowered, and they withdrew.[33] The Qing had achieved the upper hand in open conflict, but both the Russian and Qing forces had acquired an acute appreciation for what the Jungar forces were capable of on the battlefield, and the Qing in particular appear to have become determined to identify a means to end the Jungar threat for good. But for the next three decades the Jungar remained an exceptionally powerful force in the region.

Shortly before the Kangxi emperor's death in 1722, the Qing managed to gain the upper hand and force the Jungar to agree to a truce that stripped the Jungar of much of their former grazing lands. Faced with insufficient lands, the Jungar were left with little option but to look westward for new pasture. In 1723, the Jungar again attacked the Kazakhs and occupied their eastern pastures, forcing the Kazakhs from land they had long considered their own and setting in motion a wave of devastation that

---

31. Holzwarth, "Relations between Uzbek," 187.
32. Perdue, *China Marches West*, 211.
33. Perdue, *China Marches West*, 235–37.

unfolded across much of Central Eurasia. This monumental loss for the Kazakhs has been memorialized as the "Barefooted Flight" (Aktaban Shubryndy).[34] Some of the displaced Kazakhs moved farther to the west, where they entered territories occupied by the Bashkirs and Qalmaqs in the Urals, and the Karakalpaks and others near the Aral Sea. Other Kazakhs moved southward, into the settled regions of Mawarannahr. Here again Holzwarth provides a detailed depiction of the Kazakh invasion of 1723 and its traumatic aftermath.[35]

Pushed by Jungar forces to the Syr Darya, the Kazakhs entered Mawarannahr and made their way into the Zerafshan Valley, initially settling not far from Khojand. There are no precise figures for the number of Kazakhs involved in this mass migration. One contemporary author ventures the rough estimate that it involved some 150,000 families, or several times that number in terms of individuals. This would be exceptional if accurate, but the figure is likely to be highly exaggerated.[36] Nevertheless, the number of Kazakhs was certainly very large and it set in motion a highly disruptive series of events. In advance of the invasion, the Keneges broke off from their conflict with Bukhara to defend themselves from the coming onslaught. Echoing events of just seven years earlier, the Keneges leadership sought out opportunity in the coming devastation. Soon after the Kazakhs arrived, the Keneges and Kazakhs established an alliance and they moved jointly against Bukhara, occupying Bukharan territory in 1724.[37] Threatened, weakened, and overpowered, the Bukharans countered the Kazakh-Keneges alliance by forming their own alliance with the Jungars.[38] The Kazakhs remained in Mawarannahr for three years. In 1727, they put Bukhara under siege for two months, after which they returned northward into the steppe. Holzwarth rightly observes that "the Kazakhs had come as refugees, and left as conquerors."[39]

These three years had lasting implications on political developments across the

---

34. See the treatment of the causal factors underpinning these events as laid out in chapter 2, "The Barefooted Flight in Historical Sources," in Michael Hancock-Parmer, "Running Until Our Feet Turn White: The Barefooted Flight and Kazakh National Identity" (PhD diss., Indiana University, Bloomington, 2017). For an analysis of how this momentous event in Kazakh history has been memorialized, interpreted, and politicized, see Michael Hancock-Parmer, "The Soviet Study of the Barefooted Flight of the Kazakhs," *Central Asian Survey* 34, no. 3 (2015): 281–95.
35. Holzwarth, "Relations between Uzbek," 193–98.
36. Holzwarth observes that the author is generally unreliable, perhaps stemming from the fact that he was in Lahore and not Central Asia, and his information came from exaggerated oral reports.
37. Holzwarth, "Relations between Uzbek," 194.
38. Holzwarth identifies this event as "unparalleled in the history of Uzbek Central Asia," Holzwarth, "Relations between Uzbek," 196–97.
39. Holzwarth, "Relations between Uzbek," 197.

region. With the Toqay-Timurids under siege, Ibrahim Ataliq and other Keneges had in the meanwhile attempted to elevate another Chinggisid, Rajab Khan from Urgench, as a rival khan in Samarqand.[40] Their attempt failed, but in the fallout Abu'l Fayz Khan was pressured to elevate Ibrahim Keneges as hakim of Samarqand. From the Bukharan perspective, he was now officially appointed by Bukhara, but in reality the appointment simply recognized and reinforced his already entrenched position. The Keneges thus consolidated their position as an independent power in the Zerafshan Valley, a powerful ally for Khoqand, and a persistent thorn in Abu'l Fayz Khan's eastern side.

Beyond their own migration, the Kazakhs's Barefooted Flight also had widespread implications for the large-scale movement of other peoples within the region. As 'Abd al-Rahim Biy was extending his authority within the Ferghana Valley and securing control over Khojand and Urateppe, his fledgling state began to draw refugees from the more troubled areas. The Jungar advances in the northern stretches of the Tian Shan had pushed Kyrgyz groups southward into the valley, and they were soon thereafter joined by large numbers of Kazakhs, referred to in the local sources as Qipchaqs, as most of the nomads who made their way into the valley appear to have belonged to the Qipchaq tribe. These migrants joined the many thousands who had fled Samarqand for Ferghana during the earlier nomadic invasion and occupation of the Zerafshan Valley. At the same time, the valley also absorbed a steady stream of Tajik "Kuhistanis," mountain dwellers who made their way northward from Qarategin, Badakhshan, and Chitral.[41]

Even as their own population was growing, from the vantage point of the Shahrukhids it was quite clear that the Eurasian arena was becoming more dangerous by the year. The Jungar wars with the Kazakhs and the devastation caused by the subsequent Barefooted Flight were followed by a Jungar victory over the Qing army in 1731.[42] For the Qing, this loss underlined that their current logistical system was insufficient to run campaigns that far to the west, and they began devising a solution for that problem. Meanwhile, Russian advances in Siberia and the establishment of new fortresses along the Irtysh represented another threat to the north and west. These advances sent shock waves through the region, as nomadic peoples were subsumed or, in some case, pushed from the steppe in search of refuge, or plunder, in the settled zones to the south. Additional wars between these powers seemed inevitable and, much like Bukhara, at that time the Shahrukhid military

---

40. Abdurrakhman-i Tali', *Istoriia Abulfaiz-khana*, trans. A. A. Semenov (Tashkent, 1959), 68–69.
41. AIKC, 13.
42. Perdue, *China Marches West*, 254–55.

forces were equipped with little more than bows and arrows, swords, and spears supplemented by a small supply of rudimentary muskets and field cannons in the face of much larger, more modern armies. Little more than good fortune had enabled residents in the valley to escape the Kazakh occupation following the Barefooted Flight. 'Abd al-Rahim Biy was determined to ensure that when the next invasion happened his forces would be ready. To achieve that end, he needed new, modern weaponry and instruction in how to use it. He would need help, and for that he looked to Istanbul, the greatest center of power—military and otherwise—in the Islamic world at the time.

Far to the west, overlooking the shores of the Bosphorus, one can only imagine the surprise, and perhaps even skepticism, with which the newly elevated Ottoman Sultan Mahmud I (r. 1730–54) welcomed a traveler who introduced himself as an ambassador sent to the Sublime Porte by an Uzbek noble by the name of 'Abd al-Rahim Biy. This embassy represents the earliest evidence of a diplomatic relationship between the Ottoman Empire and the state that would soon become known as the Khanate of Khoqand. This was the first of many such envoys, and it set in place a pattern that would become more familiar in later years. Ottoman archival records report that 'Abd al-Rahim Biy's ambassador delivered a letter to the Sultan requesting that Istanbul supply the Shahrukhids ruler with firearms, as well as military uniforms, to aid in his people's struggles against the infidel forces from Russia and China that were encroaching on the region. The archival records show that Sultan Mahmud approved the request and ordered the Finance Ministry to provide those materials.[43]

To be sure, there was no Turkish caravan headed to the Ferghana Valley loaded with cannons, barrels of gunpowder, and large numbers of state-of-the-art flintlock muskets, a technology that made muskets much faster and more effective than the earlier matchlocks and which by this time had been produced in Ottoman weapons foundries for several decades.[44] Rather, it seems clear that Sultan Mahmud presented this ambassador with a few examples of current military technology, materials that 'Abd al-Rahim Biy could have his own *miltīqsāz* (gunsmiths) replicate in Ferghana and which did indeed equip his troops with a strategic advantage over their enemies, both near and far.[45] The diplomatic relationship between Khoqand and the Sublime

---

43. Başbakanlık Osmanlı Arşiv, MMD, no. 2683. Cited in Abdulkadir Macit, "Başbakanlık Osmanlı Arşiv Belgerleri Işığında XIX. Yüzıl Osmanlı-Hokand Hanlığı Munasebetleri" (MA thesis, Marmara Üniversitesi, İstanbul, 2008), 105.

44. Gábor Ágoston, *Guns for the Sultan: Military Power and the Weapons Industry in the Ottoman Empire* (Cambridge: Cambridge University Press, 2005), 89.

45. I must therefore disagree with Holzwarth's position that the flintlock reached Bukhara only a century later, in the 1840s. Wolfgang Holzwarth, "Bukharan Armies and Uzbek Military Power, 1670–1870:

Porte continued through the eighteenth century and became closer in the first half of the nineteenth century, during Khoqand's greatest period of territorial expansion.[46]

Despite some early military successes, the Shahrukhid proto-state at this time remained underdeveloped and was periodically destabilized by localized political powers in the valley. Thus, their early advances out of the Ferghana Valley proved premature. While the Shahrukhids were generally able to hold on to Khojand, Samarqand was lost after just six months and nearby Urateppe was destined to remain a locus of nearly perpetual conflict between Bukhara and Khoqand for the next 140 years.[47]

Suffering from a debilitating mental illness and unwilling to relinquish his throne, in the year 1734 'Abd al-Rahim was assassinated in the ark of Khojand—the very location where he himself had killed Aq Buta Biy.[48] Leadership over the "Sultanate" then passed laterally to his brother, 'Abd al-Karim (1734–51/52), where it remained for the next eighteen years. Illustrating the critical importance that the Ming attributed to their alliance with the Keneges in Shahrisabz, 'Abd al-Karim married his brother's Keneges widow, Oychuchuk Oyim, even as she was pregnant with 'Abd al-Rahim's own daughter.[49]

A NEW CAPITAL

It was during 'Abd al-Karim's reign that the Shahrukhids established the city of Khoqand as their new capital. For the first six years of his reign, 'Abd al-Karim ruled from his father's capital at Koktonliq Ata. But as the valley attracted migrants

---

Coping with the Legacy of a Nomadic Conquest," in *Nomad Military Power in Iran and Adjacent Areas in the Islamic Period*, ed. Kurt Franz and Wolfgang Holzwarth (Wiesbaden: Dr. Ludwig Reichert, 2015), 291. Although Holzwarth is no doubt correct that it was not used widely until much later, perhaps when flintlocks would have become more affordable on the secondary weapons market, the technology would have been known by the 1730s, and perhaps even earlier.

46. See especially Sherzodhon Mahmudov's discussion of international relations in the chapter on Khoqand in D. A. Alimova, ed., *Istoriia Uzbekistana (XVI–pervaia polovina XIX v.)* (Tashkent: Fan, 2012), 374–473. The new research into commercial and diplomatic exchanges is especially interesting. See also Sherzodhor. Mahmudov, "The Interrelation of the Kokand Khanate with the Ottoman Empire in the First Half of the Nineteenth Century," in *Proceedings of the XVIth Turkish History Congress* (Ankara: Korzayayincilik, 2015), 287–90.
47. In the 1750s, even Khojand was temporarily lost to the Bukharan Muhammad Rahim Khan.
48. 'Abd al-Rahim is buried in Khojand. He is one of the few Shahrukhids not laid to rest in the Dakhm-i Shahan in Khoqand.
49. TJN, f. 24b; MT, p. 378.

seeking refuge from turmoil elsewhere, the population around the fortress had increased considerably. Even after the addition of new neighborhoods and a new citadel to the old capital, 'Abd al-Karim found it necessary to construct an entirely new capital. In the year 1740, a new fortress was completed a short distance to the northwest, at the ruins of an old fortress (Eski Orda). The new capital was named Khoqand (Khawaqand), and it quickly grew to become a substantial city.[50]

Urbanization was exceptional in this period, spurred by a general increase in the population of the entire Valley. Mulla Avaz Muhammad reports that the people who migrated to Khoqand during this period belonged to four distinct groups: "Samarqandi, Kashgari, Chankati and Kuhistani."[51] The reason that Samarqandis made their way into Ferghana has been addressed above, and the movement of Turkic Muslim populations fleeing Kashgar and its environs ahead of Qing expansion into Altishahr is a topic that will be addressed directly. The factors propelling the migrations from the other regions remain more obscure. Mulla Avaz Muhammad does note, however, that 'Abd al-Karim Khan directed considerable support to strengthening Islamic institutions in this period, and the religious landscape of the Ferghana Valley began to change as mosques, madrasas, and sufi hostels were constructed to adorn his new capital of Khoqand, and elsewhere.[52]

Within that same period, Khoqand narrowly escaped yet another series of potentially devastating events: namely, the two Persian invasions that Nadir Shah's armies launched across the Amu Darya in 1737 and 1740. Even as Nadir Shah spared the Ferghana Valley and moved to Khiva instead, Khoqand's future did not go unaffected as the Persian armies occupied neighboring regions.[53] But the Persian army was not the only threat facing Khoqand at the time. In 1745, just five years after Nadir Shah's forces encamped around Bukhara and then moved eastward to Samarqand, the Jungar Mongols launched an invasion from the other direction.

In explaining this event, Mulla Avaz Muhammad blames the Qing, asserting that "the Chinese pushed the Qalmaqs onto the head of Ferghana." Alternatively, Niyazi and Muhammad Salih limit their coverage of the event to confirming that, while the city of Khoqand was still young, the Qalmaq army invaded the Ferghana Valley from the direction of Qaynar, to the east of Osh, and put it under siege.[54] In fact, Chinese

---

50. Cf. TS, f. 21a–b; TJT, f. 21a; MTF, fols. 22b–23b.
51. TJN, f. 25a. See also MT, 391, 700. Other sources refer to the Chankati as Jankati. See Beisembiev, "Migration," 36.
52. TJN, f. 25a.
53. Pickett, "Persianate Sphere," 47.
54. Cf. TS, f. 22a; TJT, f. 21b; TJN, f. 25a.

sources suggest that Mulla Avaz Muhammad had it wrong: the Qalmaq invasion of the valley in 1745 had nothing to do with having been "pushed" by the Qing. During the early years of the Qianlong emperor's long reign (r. 1736–95), the Qing and Jungar had enjoyed a truce. In the early 1740s, the Qing pursued a policy of peaceful trade with their Jungar neighbors that continued into the 1750s.[55]

Whatever their motivations may have been, the Jungar did indeed invade Ferghana. Thousands of Qalmaq soldiers entered the valley from the east and put the new capital of Khoqand under siege. The army of Khoqand was able to break the siege only after Yuz reinforcements from Urateppe arrived and aided the Ming, presumably because they were eager to keep the Mongols from continuing onward and inflicting the same type of suffering they had caused in 1727. Together, the Ming, Yuz, Kyrgyz, and Qipchaqs were able to force the Qalmaq forces from Khoqand.[56] But they withdrew only as far as Qarateppe (later known as Muimubarak), a short distance to the east of Khoqand between Marghilan and Shahrikhan, and what was left of Khoqand's limited control over the hakims in the central and western cities began to slip away.[57]

Recognizing that his future was in jeopardy, 'Abd al-Karim sent an embassy to the Qalmaq nobles and invited them to Khoqand under the pretense that he would submit, accept a subordinate position, and pay tribute. The Mongols arrived expecting a ceremony and lavish gifts, but instead they walked into a slaughter. Those who managed to escape were chased down, hunted, and massacred.[58]

The remaining Jungar forces regrouped soon after and eventually agreed to depart the valley, but only after receiving a substantial amount of wealth ("gifts") and a Shahrukhid prince, Baba Bek, son of 'Abd al-Rahim Biy, as a hostage.[59] Those

---

55. Perdue, *China Marches West*, 256–70. The Qing permitted this trade to grow by a factor of ten within just three years, from 10,000 taels in 1738 to more than 100,000 in 1741. One tael is equal to approximately 1.3 ounces. Tael is synonymous with *liang*, and it is the more common term in English, having been borrowed from the Malay *tahil* through Portuguese.
56. Babadjanov, *Kokandskoe Khanstvo*, 108; V. N. Ploskikh, *Kirgizy i Kokandskoe Khansvto* (Frunze: Ilim, 1977), 72.
57. AIKC, 646. Hakim Khan tells that someone in India located a vegetable that would vibrate when the Qur'an was read in front of it and could identify when people were truthful, and when they were not. This vegetable was widely believed to have been enchanted by a holy relic, a hair of the Prophet. In the nineteenth century, an Indian man brought one of these to Khoqand, and Madali Khan built a shrine (*ziyoratgah*) for it at Qarateppe. It became heavily trafficked by pastoralists, who began to refer to Qarateppe as Muimubarak, Hair of the Prophet. Recognizing an opportunity, later entrepreneurs appear to have added another two Muimubarak shrines. MT, 709–10.
58. TJN, fols. 25a–26a.
59. Sources generally identify Baba Bek as 'Abd al-Rahim's eldest son, but he is occasionally identified as 'Abd al-Rahim's nephew through his sister. AIKC, 103.

Qalmaqs who remained in the southwest part of the valley did so having accepted a subordinate position to Khoqand, and they represented yet another ethnic group in the valley, alongside the Kyrgyz, Uzbeks, Qipchaqs, Tajiks, and others.[60] Khoqand next turned its army against the sizable population of Qipchaqs, who had sought refuge in the valley from the earlier Jungar invasions. These Qipchaqs had come to occupy the territory between Khoqand and Namangan, and they claimed loyalty to the Chinggisid (Tore) ruler Shighai Khan in Tashkent.[61] The Qipchaqs were overrun.

Baba Bek lived among the Qalmaqs until 'Abd al-Karim died in 1164/1751.[62] When news of the royal vacancy reached the Qalmaqs, they promptly dispatched Baba Bek back to Khoqand so that he might take the throne from his younger brother, Irdana Biy (also a son of 'Abd al-Rahim Biy), who had been elevated in his absence. The Qalmaqs used their military strength to force Baba Bek on Khoqand, and they met with temporary success. As one might expect, however, from the moment he was taken into Jungar custody Baba Bek's ascension to the throne would be challenged as illegitimate. Indeed, the *aqsaqals* (community elders, lit. "white beards") of Khoqand considered him a Qalmaq puppet. Within a year the Khoqandis had had enough: Baba Bek was taken to Besh Ariq, a small town a short distance to the west of Khoqand, he was executed, and Irdana was returned to the throne. Jungar forces made several additional forays into the Ferghana Valley during the 1740s, but Khoqand was able to repel them. During the 1750s, factors both internal and external to Jungar politics would ensure that those disruptions would soon be over.

IN THE WAKE OF THE QING CONQUEST

The Jungar Mongols were the last great Inner Asian nomadic state. Wedged between the Russian and Qing empires, Galdan Khan had overseen military reforms that gave his people a tactical advantage over their Kazakh neighbors and a fighting chance against the larger, wealthier, and considerably more populous sedentary imperial powers. But following the death in 1745 of Galdan Khan's nephew, Galdan Tseren, the Mongols could no longer hold back the Qing forces. The Qianlong emperor watched as the Jungar nobility fragmented into multiple factions and scrambled for power, and then he resolved to bring those conflicts—and the threat the Jungar had long represented to his own empire—to an end. With war on the horizon, some

---

60. Beisembiev, "Migration," 36.
61. TJN, f. 26a. For Shighai Khan, see also Nalivkin, *Kratkaia*, 63.
62. TS, f. 22a; TJN, f. 21b.

Jungar looked westward for support, but the Russians feared provoking the Qing and refused aid. Ablay Khan (1711–81), leader of the Kazakh Orta (Middle) Zhüz, took advantage of the situation and began advancing his people eastward into Jungar pastures.[63] Then in the spring of 1755, the Qianlong emperor dispatched two forces of some 25,000 troops each. Their victory was swift and the Qing claimed to have permanently settled the Jungar problem.[64] That claim was far from accurate.

In the wake of what had appeared to be a decisive victory, the Qianlong emperor was disappointed by the evasiveness of his Jungar opponents and the ineffective leadership that he perceived among his own military commanders. He had invested enormous resources in developing a supply chain that extended over thousands of miles to keep many tens of thousands of his soldiers fed for months at a time. He could marshal vast resources, but he was already stretched to the breaking point and suffering rebellion in two key regions of the empire as a result. Breaking completely with earlier methods of managing relations with China's nomadic neighbors, the Qianlong emperor resolved to do more than simply defeat the Jungars on the battlefield; he aimed to extinguish them completely. Perdue summarizes:

> Qianlong rejected all leniency. He now ordered the massacre of all Zungharian captives: "Show no mercy at all to these rebels. Only the old and weak should be saved. Our previous military campaigns were too lenient. If we act as before, our troops will withdraw and further trouble will occur." In another edict he declared: "If a rebel is captured and his followers wish to surrender, he must personally come to the garrison, prostrate himself before the commander, and request surrender. If he only sends someone to request submission, it is undoubtedly a trick. Tell Tsengünjav to massacre these crafty Zunghars. Do not believe what they say."[65]

Following those orders, the Qing military employed a hybrid force of fast-moving cavalry and musket-wielding infantry equipped with field cannon to massacre Jungar men, women, and children.[66] Hundreds of thousands were killed or died of disease. Some fled westward, while small numbers survived in China where they

---

63. The Kazakh term for a political unit (*zhüz*) is often mistranslated into English as horde. Horde carries with it a military connotation that is lacking in *zhüz*, which references a political unit. For further discussion of this period in Kazakh history, see Jin Noda, *The Kazakh Khanates between the Russian and Qing Empires* (Leiden: E. J. Brill, 2016).
64. Perdue, *China Marches West*, 272–75.
65. Perdue, *China Marches West*, 283 and note.
66. Wayne E. Lee, *Waging War: Conflict, Culture, and Innovation in World History* (Oxford: Oxford University Press, 2016), 301.

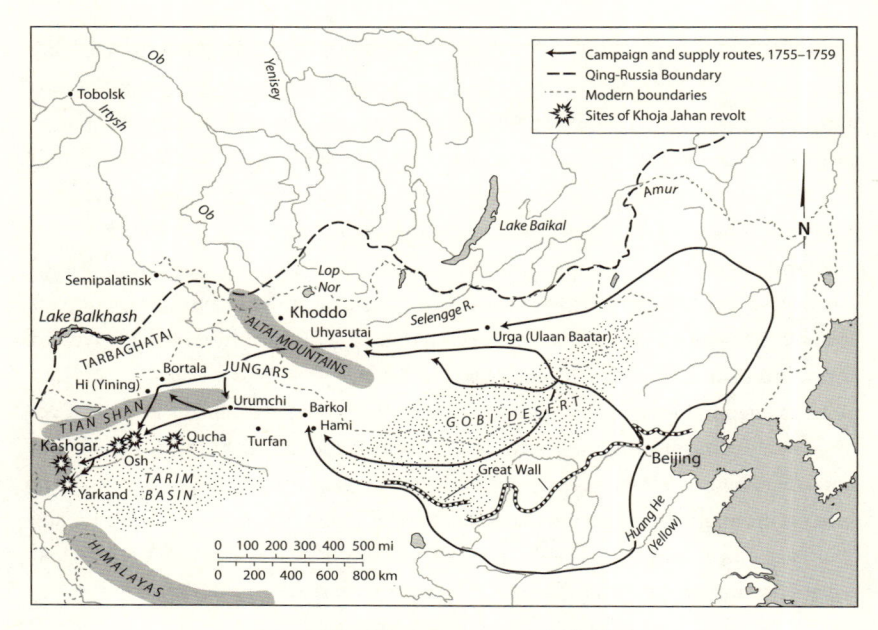

MAP 5 The Qing Conquest of Altishahr.

Map by Bill Nelson. Based on "The Qianlong emperor's western campaigns, 1755–1760," in Peter Perdue, *China Marches West* (Cambridge, MA: Belknap Press, 2005), map 7, 273.

were reduced to lives of servitude. Though assertions in some historiography that the Qing had completely extinguished the Jungars are overstated, their identity as a political body had effectively been erased.[67]

The Qing conquests did not end with the victory of the Jungars. The Qianlong emperor sought to make his victory so decisive that any Jungars who may have escaped extermination would not even be able to find a foothold in their former territory from which they could mount a recovery. With this in mind, the Qing next turned attention southward to Altishahr, a Jungar possession that, at 350,000 square miles, is more than twice the size of modern Uzbekistan and consisted of the six oases towns of modern Xinjiang—usually Kashgar, Yarkand, Aqsu, Yangi Hisar, Turfan, and Khotan, though other towns are sometimes included in the list of "six," and in Turkic sources the region is often referred to as Yetishahr, or the "Seven

---

67. Benjamin Samuel Levey, "Jungar Refugees and the Making of Empire on Qing China's Kazakh Frontier, 1759–1773" (PhD diss., Harvard University, 2014).

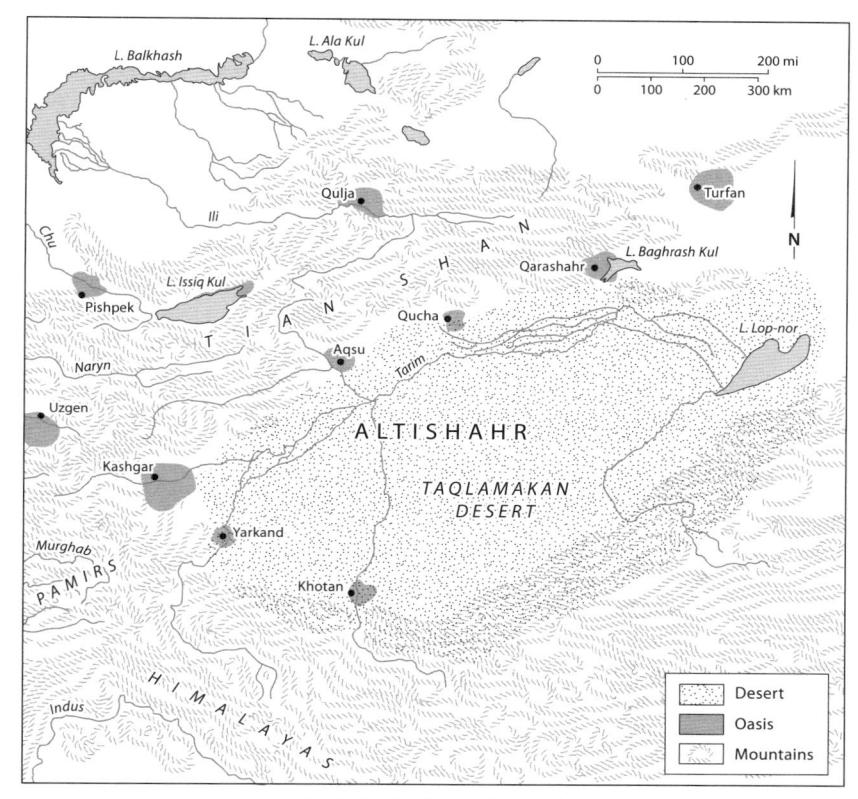

MAP 6 Altishahr in the Eighteenth Century.
Map by Bill Nelson.

Cities" region.⁶⁸ As part of their victory over the Jungar, the Qing ordered the release of two Afaqi Khojas, Burhan al-Din and his younger brother Khoja Jahan, who had been held captive. Now freed from the Jungar and permitted to return to Altishahr, the brothers quickly rose in rebellion against the Qing. When their supporters took up arms against the Qing and massacred one hundred Chinese soldiers in Qucha, they provoked an overpowering Qing response.⁶⁹

---

68. The estimate of Altishahr's size comes from Kwangmin Kim, *Borderland Capitalism: Turkestan Produce, Qing Silver, and the Birth of an Eastern Market* (Stanford: Stanford University Press, 2016), 3. On the shared Turkic-Muslim identity among the inhabitants of these oases settlements in this period, see Laura J. Newby, "'Us and Them' in Eighteenth and Nineteenth Century Xinjiang," in *Situating the Uyghurs Between China and Central Asia*, ed. Ildikó Bellér-Hann et al. (Aldershot: Ashgate, 2007), 15–31.
69. Newby, *The Empire and the Khanate*, 21.

Qianlong dispatched to Altishahr the same general who had overseen the Qing victory over the Jungar. The khojas's supporters were quickly defeated, and the khojas themselves fled southward to Badakhshan. Both died in exile, but their Afaqi descendants lived on and would remain a persistent and occasionally expensive source of anxiety for the Qing for the next century. In the meanwhile, the Qing incorporated the Jungar territories, including Altishahr, into their empire; the combined territory eventually came to be known in Chinese as Xinjiang, the "New Frontier."[70] Recalling earlier discussions of population movements in the region, at this point, some 9,000 families are reported to have fled Qing rule and abandoned Altishahr to take up residence in the Ferghana Valley.[71]

One of the defining features of Qing governance in their newly conquered territory was that the Qing aimed to maintain control over the region, but they aimed to do so using a limited number of troops and resources. Initially, the Qing placed some 40,000 Manchu and Mongol troops in the formerly Jungar steppe zone to the north and much smaller numbers in the sedentary districts of Altishahr.[72] That number was gradually raised to 50,000, but it quickly became clear that permanently garrisoning the tens of thousands more Qing troops that would be required to force submission would be prohibitively expensive.

The Qing instead early on established a system of indirect governance that involved relying on a smaller number of Manchu and Mongol administrators and troops to rule through the mediation of influential Turkic Muslim nobles, or biys (known as *bo-ke* in Chinese, and "begs" in most English-language materials on the region).[73] Uprisings did occur and they will be addressed below, but in general, over the century that followed the Qing conquest of the region, rebellions were rare. In fact, the Turkic Muslim begs of Altishahr proved quite willing to work with the "heathen" Qing so long as it was in their best interest to do so. Indeed, for a number of reasons, including efforts to mobilize against the (also heathen) Buddhist Jungars, some of these same Turkic Muslim begs had collaborated with the Qing even prior to their annexation of Altishahr.

---

70. Muslim inhabitants of Altishahr continued to refer to their region by that name. The Qing differentiated the northern and southern regions of Xinjiang, referring to the north as Zhunbu, named after the Jungars (or Zhungars), and the south as Huibu, or the "Muslim Region" of southern Xinjiang. James A. Millward, *Eurasian Crossroads: A History of Xinjiang* (New York: Columbia University Press, 2007), 97–98 and note 29.
71. Beisembiev, "Migration," 36.
72. Millward, *Eurasian Crossroads*, 99.
73. Nicola Di Cosmo, "Qing Colonial Administration in Inner Asia," *International History Review* 20, no. 2 (1998): 292–94.

In his study of this subject, Kwangmin Kim focuses attention on one member of the religious elite in particular, Emin Khoja, who fought alongside the Qing against the Jungar forces, and then later proved to be a staunch Qing ally as the Qing consolidated their control in Altishahr.[74] While thousands of Turkic Muslims left Altishahr, making their way to the Ferghana Valley, for example, the vast majority elected to stay put. The Qing spent an estimated 23,000,000 taels of silver on the 1753–59 campaigns that resulted in the annexation of Xinjiang, and they nearly doubled the size of the empire as a result.[75] Efforts to retain this vast territory solely through the use of force would represent a financial burden impossible to bear. Instead, the Qing devised an alternate means to retain authority over the region, one that emphasized collaboration over conflict. The Qing broadcast their intention to remain respectful of local traditions, both legal and religious, while providing an array of incentives to their loyal subjects.[76] Emin Khoja and other Turkic Muslim elite found themselves in an ideal position to exploit the commercial opportunities that Qing expansion had created—using commercial policies and financial incentives to link the regional economy of Altishahr with the thoroughly globalized economy of the eastern seaboard. Until the mid-nineteenth century, Qing rule in Xinjiang essentially functioned as a partnership with Qing administrators using Qing resources and policies to develop the regional commercial and agricultural economies and build wealth for their Turkic Muslim partners. Except, of course, when that partnership failed.

As the Qing were eliminating the Jungars and annexing Altishahr, Shah Rukh's grandson Irdana Biy (r. 1751–52, 1753–69) was concerned with more immediate, local problems. A few years earlier, the Manghit amir Muhammad Rahim had the last Astrakhanid ruler of Bukhara, Abu al-Fayz Khan (r. 1711–47), executed and from 1753 assumed regal authority himself. The newly fashioned Bukharan amir sent a letter to Khoqand in which he referred to Irdana Biy as his "son" and, shortly thereafter, ordered the Bukharan army to march against the Yuz tribe in Khojand, Urateppe, and the surrounding areas.[77] Possibly in an effort to keep Bukharan interests from expanding in the direction of Khoqand, there is some evidence to suggest that Irdana Biy struck an alliance with Fazl Biy, the Yuz hakim of Urateppe, and the army of

---

74. Kwangmin Kim, "Profit and Protection: Emin Khwaja and the Qing Conquest of Central Asia, 1759–1777," *Journal of Asian Studies* 71, no. 3 (2012): 603–4.
75. One tael is equal to thirty-seven grams (or 1.3 ounces) of silver of greater than 95 percent purity. If the estimate is accurate, the Qing spent some 1.8 million pounds, or 900 tons, of silver on the conquest of Xinjiang. Kim, "Profit and Protection," 611–12 and note 4.
76. See James Millward, *Beyond the Pass: Economy, Ethnicity, and Empire in Qing Central Asia, 1759–1864* (Stanford: Stanford University Press, 1998); Kim, *Borderland Capitalism*.
77. MT, 381.

Khoqand was dispatched westward to aid in the defense of the city. According to Mulla Avaz Muhammad, unbeknownst to Irdana Biy, an individual identified as Muhammad Amin Biy Hissari betrayed Irdana by falsely warning Fazl Biy that the Khoqandi forces intended to occupy Urateppe and keep it for themselves. It is not possible to determine whether this accusation was true, but it effectively undermined the alliance and left the army of Khoqand exposed.[78] Other sources lend some credence to the theory that Irdana had ulterior motives by suggesting that he had actually established an alliance with Bukhara and the two powers aimed to attack the Yuz jointly.[79] In either case, when Irdana Biy's army arrived at Urateppe, they were routed, and the Yuz troops reportedly built a great minar (tower) from the skulls of the dead soldiers of Khoqand, with the head of the Ming commander placed on top.

Hakim Khan reports that, following this loss, Irdana Biy returned to Khoqand and dedicated himself to tending to the needs of his state. Several years later, Irdana again raised the army of Khoqand and, this time quite deliberately, unleashed it against Urateppe. The two armies met on the banks of the Aq Su River, and ultimately Khoqand was victorious. Irdana took the opportunity to issue a punitive punishment on the Yuz for their past treachery. The Yuz tribe fled, but the Ming hunted them down. Irdana himself is reported to have personally killed eighteen of the Yuz noblemen from horseback, and stopped his assault only when, as his arm grew tired, the nineteenth swing of his sword missed its mark and nearly removed the head of his own horse. With that, he ordered his troops to kill the remaining captives and erect minars from their skulls.[80] The irony of the situation was not lost on Irdana, who ordered that a minar be built of 1,000 (Uz. *ming*) skulls of the Yuz (one hundred); assuming a similar poetic license, Hakim Khan reported that "the Aq Su (White Water) ran red with their blood."[81]

Irdana enjoyed a number of considerable successes during his reign, but he is best known for having established an official relationship with the Qianlong emperor

---

78. TJN, f. 28b.
79. Beisembiev suggests that Khoqand and Bukhara enjoyed a peaceful relationship at this time and that they had in fact joined forces against Urateppe. AIKC, 13. In support of this interpretation, he cites A. Mukhtarov's *Ocherk istorii Ura-Tiubinskogo vladeniia v XIX v.* (Dushanbe: Nauka, 1964), 18–20.
80. Schuyler relates a different and less reliable version of these events. According to his information, Khoqand and Bukhara established an alliance, and the battle, in which the army of Khoqand is said to have killed some 20,000 Bukharan troops and made minars of their skulls, took place during the long reign of Narbuta Biy (1770–99). Schuyler's temporal placement of this event is obviously mistaken as the Bukharan troops were led by Amir Muhammad Rahim Biy, who died in 1758, during the reign of Irdana Biy (1751–52, 1753–63). Narbuta Biy would have been at the most nine years old. Schuyler, *Turkistan*, 1:339.
81. MT, 382.

after the Qing conquest of Altishahr brought the Manchu empire to the borders of the Ferghana Valley. This represented an achievement that no state based in China had been able to accomplish since the Tang (618–970), and it also represented the sudden presence of a military superpower in a politically fragmented region. Referencing Qing records, Tôru Saguchi notes that, "In the ninth month of 1759, General Chao-hui sent his officers to Irdana Biy of Khoqand, and to the towns of Marghilan, Andijan, and Namangan and to the Adigene tribe of the Kyrgyz, asking them to become Qing tributaries."[82] In her work in these and other Qing records, Newby provides the following excerpt from a letter that Irdana Biy dispatched to the Qing,

> Irdana respectfully greets the general of His Majesty's troops. The emperor's bounty is great and the people are content. When we heard that the Qazaqs and the Qirghiz had received the summons we looked forward to your arrival. Now that the imperial guard and his men have come our joy is boundless. I am sending trusted envoys with a message and hope they will be allowed to travel to the capital. We await your instructions.[83]

The following year, Irdana dispatched his hakim of Andijan, Toqta Muhammad Biy, on the first of many Khoqandi ambassadorial missions to Beijing.[84] Gifts included an exceptional white horse in 1760 and a white falcon in 1762.[85]

Qing records pertaining to the empire's official relationship with Khoqand seem to suggest a Qing colonial foothold in the Ferghana Valley; however, more recent analyses have demonstrated that the relationship was actually quite vague, and deliberately so. Most obviously, Khoqand's official relationship with the Qing did not result in any real loss of authority for Khoqand. Rather, both sides found the relationship to be useful in their own ways. The Qianlong emperor's ability to claim that he was receiving "tribute" missions from beyond the Tian Shan had currency in Beijing, insofar as it demonstrated considerable territorial expansion and projected

---

82. Tôru Saguchi, "The Eastern Trade of the Khoqand Khanate," *Memoirs of the Research Department of the Toyo Bunko (The Oriental Library)* 24 (1965), 49. Here and below I have slightly altered Saguchi's system of transliteration to conform to contemporary practices.
83. Newby, *The Empire and the Khanate*, 25 and note.
84. Newby, *The Empire and the Khanate*, 25. Additional insight into Irdana's motivations and the facsimiles and English-language translations of two diplomatic correspondences he dispatched to the Qing court in 1760 can be found in Takahiro Onuma, Yayoi Kawahara, and Akifumi Shioya, "An Encounter between the Qing Dynasty and Khoqand in 1759–1760: Central Asia in the Mid-Eighteenth Century," *Frontiers of History in China* 9, no. 3 (2014): 384–408.
85. Saguchi, "The Eastern Trade," 50.

the image of great power and centralization. The Qing therefore deliberately chose to present Irdana's missions as an indication of Khoqand's "submission" to the Qing, which explains why the Qing records report them as such.[86] For his part, Irdana found that he could use a powerful ally such as Beijing to advance his efforts to assert his authority in the local political environment while also improving Khoqand's commercial relationship with China. At the most basic level, such a relationship would strengthen his hand in the Ferghana Valley and enable him to reap the benefits of taxing a more active transit trade in Chinese goods.[87]

The relationship provided a number of tangible benefits, but it also imposed certain limits. For example, there is some evidence that Irdana early on tried to assert equal footing with the Qianlong emperor by adopting the title of khan. The evidence regarding this matter is dubious, however, and even if it should be accurate, his efforts clearly failed.[88] He further claimed the right to extend his rule over the Adigine Kyrgyz, and, as discussed below, the Qing put an end to that effort as well. Nevertheless, at the time the Qing did recognize Irdana as the greatest among his own, Central Asian equals.[89] Khoqand did not yet exist as anything resembling a centralized power in the valley. But in the years ahead, Irdana and his successors would be able to use their relationship with the Qing to great effect in pursuit of that goal. From Khoqand's perspective, that would have been a desirable outcome, and establishing an official relationship that included accepting a position that the Qing could present to their own constituencies to be subordinate was part of a logical strategy to achieve that outcome.

Even as Irdana was establishing this relationship, other anxieties conspired to undermine it. Shortly after 1762, reports began circulating that the Qing were planning another massive invasion of territories even farther to the west, intending to target Turkestan and Samarqand. In the wake of the massive campaigns of the previous decade, fear spread across the region that territories west of the Tian Shan would soon be confronting Chinese armies. According to the account penned by Choqan Valikhanov, the famous Kazakh scholar and captain in the Russian imperial army, Irdana responded along with Fazl Biy in Khojand and several Kyrgyz "sultans"

---

86. Newby makes this point, and it is confirmed in Onuma et al., "An Encounter," 385.
87. As discussed earlier, this policy was a successful one and Irdana Biy's successor, Narbuta Biy, continued to maintain a close relationship with the Qing and used it to great effect. Kim emphasizes the importance of this trade in the gradual rise of a more centralized power in Khoqand. Kim, *Borderland Capitalism*, 106.
88. Newby, *The Empire and the Khanate*, 32–33; Onuma et al., "An Encounter," 403; Saguchi, "The Eastern Trade," 55.
89. Saguchi, "The Eastern Trade," 50.

by issuing a call requesting support from a new, but also considerable power in the region: Ahmad Shah Abdali, the founder of the Indo-Afghan Durrani Empire (dynastic rule stretched from 1747 to 1973).[90] A former commander in the Persian army, from Nadir Shah's death in 1747, Ahmad Shah had established himself as the ruler over what had been Nadir Shah's eastern territories.

By 1762, Ahmad Shah's realm stretched from Khurasan to the Indus River, and from the Arabian Sea nearly to the Amu Darya. His young Durrani administration was ideally situated to reap the benefits of developing and mediating the quite substantial overland trade between India and its neighbors to the north and west.[91] Ahmad Shah issued a command to stop all commerce with the Qing, and his Afghan forces arrived in the region late in 1763, taking up a position between Khoqand and Tashkent. By that time, however, it had already become clear that the Qing campaign would not materialize. The Afghan troops made their way back southward to renew their struggles against the Sikhs in Kashmir, and Khoqand was more than happy to resume regular relations with their new Qing neighbors.[92]

In her study of Qing relations with Khoqand, Laura Newby confirms that Khoqand's alliance with the Qing had no real implications in terms of Khoqand's autonomy. Put simply, there were no taxes imposed on Khoqand, there were no Qing officials stationed in the valley, there was no Qing oversight of Khoqand's administration, and throughout its existence the relationship remained quite vague and open for negotiation.[93] While the Qianlong emperor used Khoqand's "tribute missions" to enhance his own prestige at home, Irdana Biy deliberately and strategically did whatever possible to improve Khoqand's access to Chinese markets. In the coming years, as the agricultural and commercial economy of Xinjiang grew, this developed into an important revenue stream. Khoqand was able to augment its military power, substantially strengthen its political position in the valley, and challenge Bukhara's commercial and military dominance in the region.

The inhabitants of the valley benefited greatly from these developments. Khoqand dispatched as many official ambassadorial missions to China as the Qing would allow: they sent forty-eight of these between 1762 and 1821.[94] As was

---

90. See Chokhan Valikhanof, *The Russians in Central Asia . . .* , trans. John and Robert Michell (London: Edward Stanford, 1865), 189–90. See also Chokan Valikhanov, *Sobranie sochinenii v piati tomakh* (Alma-Ata, 1962), 2:316. This event is also discussed in Onuma et al., "An Encounter," 385.
91. Jos Gommans, *The Rise of the Indo-Afghan Empire, c. 1710–1780* (Leiden: E. J. Brill, 1995), 89.
92. Newby, *The Empire and the Khanate*, 34–35 and notes.
93. Newby, *The Empire and the Khanate*, 27–29.
94. Cf. Saguchi, "The Eastern Trade," 51; S. A. M. Adshead, *Central Asia in World History* (London: Macmillan, 1993), 196–97.

customary, the gifts that the Qing sent back to Ferghana always far exceeded the value of the "tribute" sent to China. More important, merchants attached to the official ambassadorial missions were permitted to trade tax-free in Chinese markets along the mission's route, and their Qing patrons even paid for their lodging and transport costs.[95]

Qing archival records indicate that the official gift exchanges and the accompanying ambassadorial trade were substantial and profitable for the Shahrukhid rulers. But the trade conducted by the growing communities of "Andijani" merchants (primarily Turkic Muslims from the Ferghana Valley) was much greater in value and much more important for the economy of Khoqand as a whole. For their part, the Andijanis used their relationship with the Qing to develop a commercial network that involved thousands of individuals occupying communities in urban centers across the new Qing territory of Xinjiang.[96] They served as import and export agents, owned land (in small amounts), and traded with local Turkic Muslims, Indian merchants, and the many Chinese merchant groups that rapidly extended their own interests into Xinjiang.[97] It was this last group, the Chinese merchant families, that represents the most tangible evidence of the structures that linked the fate of Xinjiang, and through it Khoqand, with the commercial economy of China's eastern seaboard. It is important to stress both that the Andijanis' trade was very profitable for Khoqand, and also that the sustained presence of their commercial network in Xinjiang even into the Russian colonial era represents another important mechanism through which Central Asians remained connected to globally integrative patterns. As the Chinese economy absorbed immense amounts of New World silver through its eastern seaboard, its growth and transformation was felt far to the west in Xinjiang, and even farther in Khoqand.[98] It did not stop there. In 1820, even as Khoqand struggled against Bukhara for regional dominance, Baron von Meyendorf traveled from Orenburg to Bukhara where he found Khoqandi merchants to be among the dominant commercial groups in local markets there as well.[99]

---

95. Newby, *The Empire and the Khanate*, 48–50.
96. Newby, *The Empire and the Khanate*, 45–50, 64–66.
97. Kim, *Borderland Capitalism*, 73; Millward, *Beyond the Pass*, 113–52. For a recent survey of literature on the role that commerce played in Qing imperial expansion, see C. Patterson Giersch, "Commerce and Empire in the Borderlands: How do Merchants and Trade Fit into Qing Frontier History?" *Frontiers of History in China* 9, no. 3 (2014): 361–83.
98. This is a central thesis developed in Kim, *Borderland Capitalism*. Kim examines the role that Qing fiscal policies played in the rise of a capitalist economy in Xinjiang during this period.
99. Baron von Meyendorf, ed., *A Journey from Orenburg to Bokhara in the Year 1820*, tr. Captain E. F. Chap-

Some commodities that were traded between Khoqand and Xinjiang in this period were locally produced and locally consumed, but the overwhelming majority represented a transit trade that connected producers and markets in Central Asia, China, Russia, and India, and, through further mediation, beyond. Goods produced locally in the Ferghana Valley included fruit, paper, and silk. Chinese silk and porcelain came from the other direction, though both were overshadowed by large amounts of medicinal rhubarb and tea. The tea trade was already substantial in the late eighteenth century, and it grew to be considerably more so as tea became an increasingly popular beverage in European markets.[100] In the nineteenth century, Russians reportedly consumed millions of kilograms of tea per year, and, although there were multiple means by which tea reached Russian markets, Khoqandi merchants took an aggressive role as mediators in that trade. Revenue from this trade enabled Khoqand to advance multiple other state-building initiatives. As some of the resources retrieved from this trade were directed to religious endowments (waqfs, *awqāf*) across the valley, it also fueled the khanate's growing religious infrastructure.

The Khoqandi chronicles present one particular view of Irdana Biy's political motivations and aspirations. Looking elsewhere, one finds additional evidence to complicate that image. For example, Qing sources report that, in the wake of a series of Kyrgyz attacks against Khoqandi caravans traveling to Kashgar, in 1762 Irdana Biy launched a campaign against the Adigene Kyrgyz noble Hajji Biy and annexed the vilayat of Osh, including the cities of Osh and Uzgen.[101] But like Irdana, Hajji Biy had also established a relationship with the Qing. Hajji Biy appealed to the Qing emperor, who responded by ordering Irdana Biy to return control over that vilayat to Hajji Biy. Although it is highly unlikely that Irdana had any intention to press on and occupy Kashgar, the Qianlong emperor reprimanded Irdana and made it clear that any effort to expand in the direction of Qing territory would meet with a harsh response:

> Why don't you give a thought to the large numbers of Qing troops stationed in Yarkand, Aqsu and Khotan when you plot to invade and occupy Kashgar? Do you really think you can defend Kashgar, even if you are quite lucky enough to take

---

man (Calcutta: Foreign Department Press, 1870), 35, 42. Meyendorf observed no merchants from China or Kashgar, which suggests that Khoqandi merchants, or Andijanis, were mediating that trade.

100. Newby, *The Empire and the Khanate*, 129–35. For an Uzbek study on this trade, see A. A. Makhkamov, "Rol' Kokanda v chainoi torgovle Rossii so Srednei Aziei v kontse XIX–nachale XX veka," ÖIF 7 (1990): 43–46.

101. Newby, *The Empire and the Khanate*, 30–31; Ploskikh, *Kirgizy i Kokandskoe Khansvto*, 88–107. For further elaboration on the complexities of the matter, see Onuma et al., "An Encounter," 393–95, 403–4.

Kashgar? Once determined, the powerful Qing army could sweep both Khoqand and Andijan in a matter of a few days. It will not be too early to regret.[102]

To be sure, the Qianlong emperor did not claim, or even aspire, to exercise authority over Khoqand as he did over Kashgar. Qing historiography has moved beyond the notion that the Qing administration functioned in accordance to a strictly defined tribute system, or that participating in what the Qing sources describe as a tribute mission entailed accepting Qing sovereignty or suzerainty.[103] Rather, embassies and gift exchanges were tools in a sort of diplomatic toolbox on which the Qing could draw to manage their relations with distant powers both within, and beyond, their frontier.[104] Officially, the Qing recognized an administrative distinction between far western city-states such as Tashkent, Andijan, Osh, and Khoqand, each of which the Qing considered to be an "outer vassal" (*waifan*), and the populations of Xinjiang, which, along with Tibet and Mongolia, the Qing considered to be an "inner vassal" (*neifan*).[105] While this may seem to imply a clear distinction between the waifan and the neifan, Newby finds that, in fact, there was no such clear distinction. Rather, comparing the two, she finds that:

> The ritual and regulations surrounding the missions were almost identical and the whole question, therefore, of what it meant to be an "inner vassal" as opposed to an "outer vassal" ... was at best a hazy concept during much of the Qing. As scholars have continued to unravel the tribute system, to grapple with the relationship between tribute and tax, and the relative importance of trade, diplomacy and ritual in Qing foreign relations, one point becomes clear: the tribute mission and accompanying ritual did not define the nature of the relationship, or shape policy, but rather as James Hevia has shown, it was a medium for constructing power relations.[106]

---

102. Saguchi, "The Eastern Trade," 56.
103. Saguchi, "The Eastern Trade," 9–10. Newby finds the "tribute" mission to be "an empty and misleading term to apply to the conduct of foreign relations during the Qing period."
104. For an overview of recent studies on Qing policies regarding non-Han ethnic groups during the period of their expansion into Xinjiang, Mongolia, and Tibet, see Dittman Schorkowitz and Chia Ning, eds., *Managing Frontiers in Qing China: The Lifanyuan and Libu Revisited* (Leiden: E. J. Brill, 2016).
105. Newby, *The Empire and the Khanate*, 3 and note.
106. Newby, *The Empire and the Khanate*, 9 and notes. Observing certain limits to his argument, Newby cites James Hevia, *Cherishing Men from Afar: Qing Guest Ritual and the Macartney Embassy of 1793* (Durham: Duke University Press, 1995), 21, 128. She also cites Pamela Crossley, *A Translucent Mirror: History and Identity in Qing Imperial Ideology* (Berkeley: University of California Press, 1999), 332–33.

A NEW UZBEK DYNASTY, 1709–1769 — 47

One must therefore question what the Qing language of subordination meant to Khoqand, and similar waifan powers. Despite Qing rhetoric implying the contrary, the Khoqand chronicles suggest that it meant very little.[107]

That is not to say that Khoqand's relationship with the Qing had no meaning. To the contrary, in the context of the 1760s, in the wake of the Qing conquest of Xinjiang, Khoqand viewed the Qing as a dominant force in the region: one that could quite effectively use alliances, offers of military support, and commercial incentives as leverage to achieve their goals. The Qing Governor-General ordered Irdana to withdraw his forces, which he did, and Osh was returned to its previous hakim.[108] The official relationships that the Qing established created opportunities for the Qing to exert leverage. Despite repeated threats to do so, after their initial conquest of Altishahr the Qing would never dispatch such a substantial force into the region. To use force was unnecessary. The Qing found that the projection of their power was all the legitimacy they needed to achieve the stability in the region that they desired.

Irdana Biy's conflict with Hajji Biy Adigene also sheds light on another important factor in the history of the region. Khoqand's relations with the Kyrgyz would remain conflicted over the years, with periods of collaboration punctuated by Kyrgyz "riots and rebellions" directed against their Uzbek neighbors.[109] Ploskikh's argument that the Kyrgyz were critical players in regional politics, aiding both the Uyghur and Uzbek powers in their efforts to resist Qing imperialism, strikes a rather flat, nationalistic tone. Efforts to resist the Qing were marginally successful at best, and it seems reasonable to suggest that something more than Kyrgyz determination kept the Qing from marching across the Tian Shan.[110] But Ploskikh's study does provide a lengthy account of the Kyrgyz role in the early history of Khoqand, from their struggles alongside the Ming against the Jungars in the 1740s through their submission to Khoqand in the 1760s. Khoqand's offers of assistance in claiming superior pasture for Kyrgyz herds in the eastern parts of Ferghana, near Andijan and the Chui Valley, drew large numbers of Kyrgyz from the eastern slopes of the Tian Shan. Kyrgyz and Sarts, both Turks and Tajiks, settled in close proximity to each other, as their descendants remain today.

---

107. Newby notes, for example, that the Kazakhs submitted to the Qing, but that they were already subjects of the Russians. On the ground, such matters could change on a day-to-day basis. Newby, *The Empire and the Khanate*, 28–29.
108. Newby, *The Empire and the Khanate*, 32–33; Schuyler, *Turkistan*, 1:338.
109. This literature is summarized in detail in Ploskikh, *Kirgizy i Kokandskoe Khansvto*, 16–68.
110. Ploskikh, *Kirgizy i Kokandskoe Khansvto*, 78–88.

By and large, Irdana Biy's reign was a prosperous one. He suffered a devastating loss to the Yuz. But he also annexed a number of vilayats, briefly occupied Tashkent in 1765 until it was retaken by Ablay Khan, and directed resources to expanding and beautifying his capital city of Khoqand.[111] When he died in 1769, Irdana Biy left a somewhat larger and stronger state, a diplomatic relationship with the Qing that would prove critical to the future of Khoqand, five daughters, and no sons.

A NEW STATE IN A TIME OF CRISIS

A series of notable developments occurred in the half century following Shah Rukh Biy's successful bid to establish Uzbek Ming rule in the central and western portions of Ferghana Valley. The Shahrukhid lineage wrenched political authority from the Chadak Khojas, negotiated three successful transfers of power within the family, and eliminated one potential threat in the form of Baba Bek, who had been foisted onto the throne as a Jungar puppet. The Ferghana Valley also received a large number of migrants from Samarqand, Altishahr, the Pamirs, and other locations that had suffered during the Kazakh occupations of the region and other disruptive conflicts.

Khoqand was spared the destruction and destabilization that followed Nadir Shah's invasions in 1737 and 1740. Indeed, one could argue that it was precisely because Nadir Shah did not invade the Ferghana Valley that the Shahrukhids were well positioned to take advantage of the conflict and devastation elsewhere in their centralization efforts. But the valley was not so far removed from other crises that unfolded during this period. In 1745, the Jungar invaded and besieged the new Shahrukhid capital of Khoqand, and they returned several times over the next decade; the Uzbeks struggled against the Kyrgyz; and Khoqand suffered a devastating loss to the neighboring Yuz, whose state-building aspirations mirrored their own. Indeed, looking back over the first fifty years of its existence, the formative victory over the Chadak Khojas is monumental only insofar as the Uzbek amirs obstructed the khojas' efforts to develop their own state. At Irdana's death, in 1769, Khoqand had managed to survive the unpredictable, unstable environment of the first half of the eighteenth century. But it remained a proto-state, a small and loosely connected constellation of city-states that in all meaningful ways can be distinguished only in terms of its geography from the Keneges in Shahrisabz and the Yuz in Urateppe and Khojand.

---

111. TS, f. 22a–b; TJT, fols. 21b–22a; Jin Noda and Onuma Takahiro, *A Collection of Documents from the Kazakh Sultans to the Qing Dynasty* (Tokyo: University of Tokyo Research Center for Islamic Area Studies, 2010), 119.

Geography is important, however, and whether he knew it or not, in the wake of the Qing conquest of Altishahr, Irdana Biy's ability to establish an official relationship with the Qing would soon prove invaluable to Shahrukhid efforts to establish themselves as the sole power in the valley. Within a few years, merchant groups from Ferghana were exploiting Khoqand's relationship with the Qing by expanding their network in Kashgar and extending it beyond. During the long reign of Irdana Biy's nephew and successor, Narbuta Biy (1770–99), Khoqand began to mint its own currency. He and his successors established patronage networks, expanded irrigation agriculture, and developed a military that could both protect the valley and extend Khoqand's boundaries over Tashkent and far into the steppe. On his deathbed in the city of Khoqand in 1769, this would have seemed a dream to Irdana.

Two
CRAFTING A STATE, 1769–1799

DURING THE REIGN of Irdana Biy, Khoqand was little more than a city-state, one of several in the Ferghana Valley. Khoqand had escaped the worst of the destruction brought about by the Kazakh occupation of neighboring regions in the 1720s and the Persian invasions of 1737 and 1740. But it suffered at the hands of the Jungar Qalmaqs and only managed to repel them with the aid of the Yuz. Khoqand's position began to change in a measurable way following the Qing conquest of the Jungars and subsequent annexation of Altishahr, which together constituted the new and very large western Qing territory of Xinjiang. Irdana Biy and others in the region welcomed the Qing presence as, from their perspectives, it offered a much-needed opportunity for stability as well as potentially lucrative economic opportunities. Irdana Biy had planted the seeds for something grand, but he died before he could have known whether his efforts would bear fruit.

The degree to which Khoqand's relationship with the Qing could serve as an engine for growth and development in the Ferghana Valley became clearer during the nearly three-decade-long reign of Irdana's nephew, Narbuta Biy. From his ascension to the throne in 1770, Narbuta Biy dispatched as many "tribute missions" to Beijing as the emperor would permit. The total value of the actual gifts exchanged was never terribly substantial; for Narbuta, the real value of these official missions to the Qing court in Beijing was in the tax-free trade rights granted to Khoqand's ambassadors. The missions returned with large amounts of valuable merchandise, which equipped Narbuta with vital resources to support his state-building efforts. Far more important was securing permission for Khoqand's Andijani merchants to expand their presence and activities throughout Xinjiang. In an effort to strengthen the commercial economy of Xinjiang, the Qing encouraged the Andijani merchants with low tax rates, and through their efforts Khoqand mediated a vibrant transit trade between the Russian and Qing empires. The activities of the Andijanis represented one important means by which Khoqand connected with the larger global economy.

Expansion into Qing markets brought Narbuta's government an important source of revenue. Khoqand was able to increase the size and strength of its military, which it used to expand its authority and territory throughout the valley. That revenue was also used to develop patronage networks among the tribal and religious elite. As more people moved into the valley from the surrounding areas, Narbuta Biy also began new initiatives to expand irrigation agriculture. This created arable land on which he could settle migrant populations, and his control over water resources gave him leverage over populations throughout the valley as well as increased tax revenue. By the time of his death in 1799, Narbuta had transformed Khoqand from the greatest of the city-states in the valley into a real capital. Foreign wealth streaming into the region had a sustained and tangible impact on the rise of Khoqand.

TANISTRY

Several decades ago, Joseph Fletcher borrowed the concept of tanistry from Celtic history and applied it to Central Asian history. He found tanistry to be both critical to understanding the political mechanisms associated with Turco-Mongolian succession struggles, and at the same time "too often overlooked" in its application to those struggles. Fletcher defines the term as follows:

> Put briefly, the principle of tanistry held that the tribe should be led by the best qualified member of the chiefly house. At the chief's death, in other words, the succession did not pass automatically, in accordance with any principle of seniority such as primogeniture, but rather was supposed to go to the most competent of the eligible heirs.[1]

---

1. Joseph Fletcher, "The Mongols: Ecological and Social Perspectives," *Harvard Journal of Asiatic Studies* 46, no. 1 (1986): 17.

In practice, tanistry assured that in succession struggles the will of the people, or more precisely the people's tribal leadership, superseded the wishes of the previous ruler who had died. Having been favored by a highly regarded but now-passed ruler may have worked to an individual's advantage in the ensuing competition. But many factors were at play in a succession struggle and being named heir apparent by no means guaranteed a successful elevation to the throne. The end result was quite often a bloody and destructive competition among a number of viable candidates, all of whom aimed to establish alliances and win over supporters as they undermined, or eliminated, their opponents. Fletcher applied this to the Mongols, but it is no less relevant in discussions of many other Turco-Mongol political bodies, including Khoqand.

At the beginning of his reign in the early 1750s, one of Irdana Biy's cousins, 'Abd al-Rahman, had been conspiring against him in competition for the throne of Khoqand. 'Abd al-Rahman was a son of the recently deceased Shahrukhid ruler, 'Abd al-Karim Biy (d. 1750), and was married to Irdana's sister Oyjan Oyim. Irdana emerged victorious in the ensuing struggle. 'Abd al-Rahman realized that his failed attempt to take the throne put his life in jeopardy and so he took his family and fled to the fortress of Chahar Kuh, just fifty miles south of Khoqand.[2] For seven years, 'Abd al-Rahman was effectively independent of Khoqand and de facto ruler of Chahar Kuh, a clear indication of the limits of Irdana's power at the time.

As Irdana became more secure in his position, he convinced 'Abd al-Rahman to return to Khoqand with an offer of forgiveness and a high post in the palace. In Hakim Khan's account of the events that followed, this detente brought a welcomed harmony to the Shahrukhid family, but it created angst among others in the administration who perceived 'Abd al-Rahman's return as a threat to their ruler and to their own upward mobility. More precisely, two of Irdana Biy's nobles, Idris (or Iris) Quli Biy and 'Abd al-Rahman Bahadur, are said to have conferred with each other and concluded that it was too dangerous to permit Irdana to "keep a serpent under his arm" such as his newly rehabilitated and highly ambitious cousin. Late one night, they snuck into 'Abd al-Rahman's living chambers and killed both him and Oyjan Oyim.

Accounts presented in other sources suggest that Hakim Khan, who was born in 1803, or roughly fifty years after the event, delivered a whitewashed version of these events and that it was in fact Irdana Biy himself who had ordered the murder of his

---

2. MT, 383; TJN, f. 29a. "Chahar Kuh," our contemporary Chorku, is a small city a few miles south of Isfara, in Tajikistan. Drawing his information from other sources, Beisembiev places 'Abd al-Rahman in "the fortress of Isfarayin," AIKC, 296.

sister and brother-in-law.³ This interpretation is supported by the fact that there is no indication that Irdana Biy punished either Idris Quli Biy or 'Abd al-Rahman Bahadur even for the murder of his own sister. Instead, Irdana appears to have rewarded them by appointing them to two of the highest posts in the military. In later years, both advanced into even higher positions in the government administration.⁴

As Hakim Khan was himself a member of the Shahrukhid family, it seems likely that he sought to protect Irdana's reputation by pinning the responsibility for the murder elsewhere. This apparent manipulation aside, his account of the event remains valuable. Hakim Khan reports that when Oyjan Oyim's mother, Oychuchuk Oyim, learned of her daughter's murder, she first fainted and then flew into an uncontrollable rage, screaming, crying, and tearing the hair from her head.⁵ Having buried two husbands, both rulers of Khoqand, she was now married to the venerable sufi leader Ishan Ortuq Khoja, and she had become more widely known as Keneges Oyim, a *laqab* (nickname) that highlights both her social status and the importance that the Ming-Keneges alliance continued to represent in Khoqand. Recovering her senses, she located her daughter's twelve-year-old son, Narbuta (b. ca. 1751), who was still alive and unharmed.⁶ She brought her grandson to look at his dead parents and asked him if he knew who had been responsible. He whispered the names of the culprits through his tears, and Oychuchuk Oyim carefully swore him to secrecy on the matter. She then buried her daughter and son-in-law and quickly departed Khoqand, taking Narbuta to Shahrisabz, where the Keneges hakim Bek Nazar Biy welcomed her and awarded her control over part of her father's estate.

One can be quite certain that Oychuchuk Oyim had revenge in mind several years later when she deposited her son Hakim Khan (the grandfather of our chronicler by the same name) with the khojas in Dehbid, near Samarqand, and took her grandson Narbuta to Urateppe.⁷ The city's hakim Fazl Biy Yuz welcomed her and gave her a place to live as she began a lengthy correspondence with Irdana that culminated with the mutual agreement that she would send Narbuta back to Khoqand, and that he would be protected and safe. On his arrival, Irdana appointed his nephew to the post of hakim of Muimubarak (Qarateppe at the time), east of

---

3. AIKC, 296.
4. AIKC, 47, 296.
5. MT, 383.
6. Although he is known throughout the chronicles primarily as Narbuta, his given name was 'Abd al-Hamid. AIKC, 490.
7. MT, 384.

Marghilan in the central part of the valley. One year later, in 1769, Irdana Biy suddenly became sick and died. Irdana had fathered five daughters but had no son to compete as his heir.[8]

Irdana's immediate successor to the throne in Khoqand was his younger cousin Sulayman Biy, whose father Shadi Biy (another son of Shah Rukh) died as a young man in a hunting accident. The Khoqand chronicles provide little insight into the specific events, conspiracies, and details of the accused incompetence that rendered Sulayman Biy's reign so short and ineffective, but the information they do provide supports the applicability of Fletcher's tanistry thesis. The primary architects of Sulayman Biy's elevation to the throne had been none other than Idris Quli Biy, who served at the time as hakim in Marghilan, and ʿAbd al-Rahman Bahadur, who served as hakim in Khojand.[9] Both had feared impending retribution for their role in the murder of Narbuta Biy's parents, and on learning of Irdana's death they rushed to Khoqand to ensure that Sulayman Biy and not Narbuta Biy would be the successful candidate, despite the fact that Sulayman Biy was apparently ill prepared for the challenges that he faced.

One can only imagine the immense pressures that Sulayman Biy encountered as unnamed and unknown conspirators undermined his authority at every turn, rapidly engineering his fall in order to shift favor to other candidates. Realizing that dissension was too great and their efforts had failed, three months after Sulayman Biy had been placed on the throne, Idris Quli and ʿAbd al-Rahman Bahadur agreed to have him killed, and at this they were successful. In the meantime, the Uzbek tribal aristocracy had become united behind Narbuta Biy and in 1770 they summoned, and finally coaxed, the eighteen-year-old grandson of ʿAbd al-Karim to come to Khoqand and take his place on the throne.[10] For their part, Idris Quli and ʿAbd al-Rahman Bahadur appear to have recognized that they had no option but to side with the

---

8. TS, f. 22a–b; TJT, fols. 21b–22a.
9. MT, 385; TJN, f. 31a–b.
10. MT, 385; TJN, f. 31b; TS, fols. 23a–24b. There is some confusion in the sources as to when Irdana Biy died and Narbuta Biy ascended the throne. Because of this, at different places in his work Beisembiev advances both 1763 and 1770 as the year of Narbuta Biy's ascension. See AIKC, 13, 490. Hakim Khan states that Irdana Biy ruled for ten years, which would place his death in 1763 rather than 1769. Niyazi states that Narbuta was fourteen years old when he ascended the throne, which would place the event around 1765. This is contradicted by other sources, including documentary evidence in Qing records indicating that Irdana Biy lived late into the 1760s, and Kazakh documentary records that have him fighting a battle with Ablay Khan in 1767. Cf. Newby, *The Empire and the Khanate*, 45–46; Noda and Takahiro, *A Collection of Documents*, 119. Taking all available information into consideration, the most convincing explanation is that Irdana Biy died in 1769, and, following Sulayman Biy's short reign of several months, Narbuta Biy ascended the throne in 1770.

FIG. 2.1 Urateppe, Market Square.
Turkestanskii Al'bom, 1865–72, Library of Congress, Prints & Photographs Division, LC-DIG-ppmsca-14820.

majority and hope that Narbuta would forgive them for their roles in the death of his parents. He did forgive them, and after he was elevated as ruler of Khoqand, Narbuta Biy was married to Idris Quli's niece, Ming Oyim, whose children would include both 'Alim Khan (r. 1799–1811) and 'Umar Khan (r. 1811–22), arguably the two most influential rulers in the khanate's history.[11]

Even ascending to the throne with a substantial amount of support, Narbuta was not immune to the centrifugal tendencies inherent to political transition. The early years of Narbuta Biy's long reign (r. 1770–99) were occupied with suppressing rebellions orchestrated by family members and other powerful groups, especially the Yuz tribe, who were persistently jockeying for increased influence in the region. In this area, the chronicles deliver far more information than is useful, weaving a dramatic narrative of Narbuta Biy's bravery as he fought his way through a near endless series of valorous victories and excruciating defeats.

To briefly summarize, upon ascending the throne, Narbuta Biy appointed one of his two half-brothers, Shah Rukh Biy (named after the progenitor of their line),

11. MT, 386; TJN, f. 32a.

to serve as hakim of Tura Qurghan. He appointed his other half-brother, Hajji Bek, to serve as hakim of the critical outpost of Khojand, which he promptly lost to Yuz forces in nearby Urateppe. Narbuta led a successful campaign to recover Khojand, taking Urateppe along with it and forcing the Yuz to retreat westward to Jizzakh.[12] Narbuta Biy then appointed Idris Quli as hakim of Urateppe, though he soon lost it to the Yuz who pursued him into the valley, caught up with him near Namangan, and shot him. Idris Quli died three days later in captivity.[13] The Yuz pillaged as far as they could make it into the valley, eventually withdrawing back to Khojand.

Several years later, after the Yuz leader Fazl Bek had died and his son Khudayar Biy was killed in battle, Narbuta Biy was able to assert a firmer grip over Khojand. Meanwhile, farther to the west, the Manghit Amir Shah Murad (r. 1785–1800) had ascended the throne in Bukhara and he led his army eastward to Urateppe. Narbuta Biy's uncle, Hakim Khan (again, grandfather of the chronicler by the same name), had now relocated to Khoqand and he served as Narbuta Biy's ambassador to Bukhara. Hakim Khan negotiated a truce that left Khojand in Khoqand's hands, where it would generally remain for the duration of the khanate's history.[14] Conflict with both the Yuz and the Manghit over Urateppe and Jizzakh was recurrent throughout Narbuta's reign and after.

RELATIONS WITH THE QING

From almost immediately after the Qing conquest of Xinjiang, Khoqand benefitted from Qing fiscal policies in the region. The Qing conquest itself had begun as a calculated move to eliminate the Jungars from the Qing frontier. The Qing did not perceive Xinjiang as a territory from which they could extract great amounts of wealth as taxes. Rather, maintaining it would be an expense: the price the Qianlong emperor was willing to pay for securing peace and stability on his western frontier. Over time, Qing policies resulted in a dramatic improvement in the commercial economy and agricultural production across the region.

The Qing administration in Xinjiang governed indirectly through local Turkic Muslim begs (a Turkic noble), and they used financial incentives to secure loyalty and local supplies for Qing troops stationed in the region. The incentives that the

---

12. MT, 389–90.
13. MT, 392.
14. MT, 396.

Qing provided include financial stipends, land grants, and, more important, access to water resources, as well as control over large numbers of peasant farmers who the Qing assigned to work their land and improve agricultural production.[15] Kwangmin Kim finds that this model was generally a success, and, for more than a century, from the Qing conquest in the late 1750s to the 1860s, the begs who collaborated with the Qing became the "undisputed power holders in eastern Turkestan."[16] Over time, Qing policies in Altishahr enabled the transformation of vast tracts of wilderness into large and productive commercial farms.[17]

The begs of Xinjiang were content to permit the Qing to claim the region as long as the Qing honored their part of the bargain by promoting trade in the region, providing financial incentives to the local nobles, and giving them ample authority to rule according to their own laws and traditions. From one decade to the next, the Qing pumped silver into the region in exchange for horses and other livestock, cotton cloth, and raw cotton (both purchased and collected as tax from local farmers). The Qing administrators granted local elite control over lucrative mining areas as well, and each year many tons of jade flowed eastward from the hills surrounding Yarkand and Khotan, along with other goods produced locally and brought into the region from elsewhere. This was augmented by the *xiexiang*: an annual redistribution of wealth in the form of silver from provinces that enjoyed a surplus to those that the Qing found to merit additional support, such as Xinjiang. Millward's figures suggest that, already by 1795, the Qing were diverting some 845,000 taels of silver to Xinjiang each year.[18] This figure would reach into the millions in later years. At the same time, Qing fiscal policies also encouraged the flow of silver into Altishahr in the hands of private Chinese merchants, whose arrival in the region followed closely behind the military.

In exchange for their loyalty, local elites could become extraordinarily wealthy. Kim identifies individuals in control of commercial interests that included many thousands of acres of farmland, along with the labor to work that land, and jade mines that boasted production levels reaching as high as fifty tons per year. One Turkic noble is identified as having been capable of producing wealth for commercial investments that exceeded 6,000,000 tael of silver.[19] The Qing set tax rates exceptionally low to encourage foreign traders, and what taxes the Qing did collect

15. Brophy, *Uyghur Nation*, 65 and note 34; Kim, *Borderland Capitalism*, 73.
16. Kim, *Borderland Capitalism*, 47.
17. Kim, *Borderland Capitalism*, 7.
18. Millward, *Beyond the Pass*, 58–61.
19. Kim, *Borderland Capitalism*, 7.

were in local currency, which the state then used to pay locals to transport their goods. The system was designed to strengthen the economy of the region and, as it did, make the nobility more dependent on their relationship with the Qing. Kim summarizes:

> The begs' efforts set the oasis economy on the path of unprecedented economic growth. Arable land doubled during Qing rule, even using a conservative measure. In 1772, land under cultivation was recorded as 3.4 to 3.5 million mu. By the 1850s–60s, that had expanded to 6.8 million mu. The actual figure was larger, though, because the official number excluded land belonging to the religious facilities (*mazārs* [shrines], *khanqas* [Sufi meeting places], *madrasas* [Islamic schools], and mosques), bestowed as religious endowments (*waqf*)—a prominent portion of property holdings in oasis society. During the same period, the oasis population increased more than threefold, again using a conservative measure. While the population estimate of 1772 stood at a little under 200,000, it rose to 1,015,000 in the 1850s–1870s.[20]

For Khoqand, the economic development of Xinjiang between the mid-eighteenth and mid-nineteenth centuries provided opportunities that would be difficult to overstate. The generally strong diplomatic relations between Khoqand and the Qing equipped Khoqand with access to those resources, and it also represented a lucrative form of trade in and of itself. In the years immediately following the Qing conquest of Kashgar, Irdana Biy sent four embassies to Beijing. Khoqand's ambassadors delivered an assortment of luxurious and rare gifts to the Qianlong emperor, including the finest horses from the region and several hunting birds. Newby notes that the emperor was so fond of one particularly striking white hawk that he had the Italian Jesuit missionary and Qing court artist Giuseppe Castiglione paint it.[21] In return, Irdana received generous gifts from the Emperor as well as permission for those who accompanied the embassy to trade within the Qing realm tax-free.

In the early years, these "tribute missions" were a form of political pageantry, insofar as they were intended to be very public affairs that both parties used to project an image of power. The embassies drew attention as they passed from one

---

20. Kim, *Borderland Capitalism*, 10–11 and notes. Kim discusses the development of this system from 1759–1825 in chapter 2. The statistical figures demonstrating growth in Xinjiang's population and the amount of arable land are detailed in the appendices.
21. Newby, *The Empire and the Khanate*, 45. Castiglione's painting is reproduced on the cover of Newby's book.

Qing city to the next, and the envoys were treated royally at every stop along the way to Beijing. For his part, Irdana used such official displays to his own advantage in regional politics. Qing recognition of Khoqand's legitimacy as physically displayed through the gift exchanges enabled Irdana Biy to elevate his status above other Uzbek tribal powers in the valley.[22] With his ascension to the throne in 1770, Narbuta Biy inherited Khoqand's relationship with the Qing, and he fully embraced it. One of Narbuta Biy's first acts as the new ruler of Khoqand was to dispatch a mission to Beijing charged with delivering gifts and relaying to the emperor his intention to honor Khoqand's established relationship with the Qing Empire.

THE OFFICIAL MISSIONS

Even a cursory glance at Henry Howorth's 1880 treatment of Central Asian history exposes it as unreliable, marred by errors, and a rather poor example of Orientalist scholarship. Nevertheless, his study includes an exceptionally interesting account of one of the four missions that Narbuta Biy dispatched to Beijing, as relayed through an Afghan ambassador that the Durrani ruler Zaman Shah (r. 1793–99) sent to Narbuta Biy's court in 1794. The ambassador's report suggests that the pomp that accompanied Irdana's envoys in the 1760s had dissipated, but that the substance of the relationship remained firmly intact.

> The representative of Khokand was met at the Chinese frontier by a carriage, shaped like a box, drawn by two horses, and as it was wintry-cold they put a hot stone before him to warm him, while the carriage itself contained all necessary food and drink. He dined *en route*, while he stayed to sleep at some post station . . . It took him a month and a few days to reach Peking from the frontier. He was admitted to an audience in the palace, whose grandeur greatly surprised him; the walls and ceiling being coated with gold and glass, and in the midst was a kiosk, also richly gilded and glazed. He prostrated himself in the prescribed way, and then saw a hand issue from the top of the kiosk and heard a voice speaking in "the Turkish of Kitai," which said, "The Emperor deigns to ask, does my son Narbuteh bi enjoy good health and contentment?" The envoy prostrated himself again, and replied, as he was told, "Narbuteh has no other wish than to satisfy the behests of his majesty." Afterward the emperor gave him presents for the khan to the value of ten laks of rupees [1,000,000

---

22. Newby, *The Empire and the Khanate*, 45–47.

rupees], which were put into the carriage in which he once more returned to Khokand.²³

A million rupees would be a royal gift indeed, but there is good reason to doubt that the value of the gifts that the Qianlong emperor dispatched to Narbuta reached anywhere near that level. In fact, in her investigation of the Qing imperial records regarding these gift exchanges, Newby finds that the value was actually quite modest. These records show that in 1792, Narbuta dispatched a mission to the Qianlong emperor with gifts that included two horses, several bolts of satin cloth and camel felt (each bolt consisted of approximately forty feet of cloth), and several articles of clothing made from fox pelts. In return, Qianlong gave Narbuta thirteen bolts of silk and satin cloth, a small number of porcelain and glass dishes, several jars of tea, and assorted other items including 100 taels (or *liangs*) of silver, equal to a little more than eight pounds, or approximately 350 rupees.²⁴ It would take considerable imagination to conclude that the value of this gift exchange approached 1,000 rupees, much less 1,000,000. As Newby concludes, "the prime financial motive for the missions lay not in the gift-exchange, but the profits to be made from trade."²⁵

There were two additional and much more important components to this "official" trade relationship. The first of these pertains to the Andijanis, Khoqandi merchants who took up residence in Altishahr and mediated transregional trade between that region and the Central Asian markets to the west. They will be addressed shortly. The second and more immediate element of Khoqand's trade with the Qing is that the tribute missions sent to Beijing included both official diplomats as well as Khoqandi merchants, to all of whom the Qing emperor granted the courtesy of free travel and transport between the *karun*—Qing border outpost located to the northwest of Kashgar—and his palace in Beijing. The travelers were also provided lodging in

---

23. Henry H. Howorth, *History of the Mongols: From the 9th to the 19th Century*, pt. 2, div. 2 (London: Longmans Green and Co., 1880), 818. The same account is reproduced in French translation from the original Persian in 'Abd al-Karim Bukhari, *Histoire d l'Asie Centrale par Mir Abdoul Kerim Boukhary...*, trans. Charles Schefer (Paris: Ernest Leroux, 1876), 282–83. For elaboration, see Newby, *The Empire and the Khanate*, 46–47 and notes. Newby observes that the original Persian account is found in the *Tārīkh-i Ahmad*, an Afghan history of the Durrani state from 1750 to 1797. See Schefer's appendix III for a discussion of this source. Citing Beisembiev, she cautions that some Khoqandi sources use the Indian numerical designation of a lak to refer to 10,000 rather than its traditional 100,000.

24. This is according to the weight of the 1774 silver rupee, minted with 164.74 grains of pure silver per coin. P. Kelly, *The Universal Cambist and Commercial Instructor: Being a Full and Accurate Treatise on the Exchanges, Monies, Weights, and Measures, of all Trading Nations and their Colonies...*, 2d ed. (London, 1821), 1:94.

25. Newby, *The Empire and the Khanate*, 48.

Beijing free of charge for as long as forty days and the right of tax-free trade in Qing markets.

This privilege was extremely profitable, and seems to have constituted the major motivation for Khoqand to dispatch as many missions to Beijing as the emperor would permit. Newby references documents pertaining to a mission from 1809, for example, which had amassed eighty-eight cartloads of merchandise by the time it had reached Hami on the return trip. The merchants were carrying tea, silk cloth, ceramics, and other goods that weighed in at nearly 70,000 pounds.[26] Returning attention to the mission Narbuta had dispatched in 1794, if one were to take the magnitude of this tax-free official trade into consideration, it seems much more plausible that Narbuta might have been in a position to reap a return that reached into the hundreds of thousands of rupees. In terms of explaining the confusion in the Afghan ambassador's report, it seems likely that the ambassador simply conflated the gift exchange and the official trade. This is perhaps not so surprising given that Narbuta Biy attached no small measure of importance to his diplomatic relationship with the Qing, and it is reasonable to expect that he would have had a vested interest in encouraging such exaggerated reports, or at least not going out of his way to correct them or limit their circulation.

This revenue stream had multiple implications for Khoqand. Most important, prosperity in the Ferghana Valley drew more people from the surrounding areas, which prompted Narbuta Biy to begin new initiatives to expand irrigation agriculture. This created arable land on which he could settle migrant populations, and his control over water resources gave him leverage over those peoples while also increasing taxation revenue. These policies exploited the Valley's agricultural potential, they drew waves of migrants to the Valley over the years, and they represent the early establishment of the irrigation infrastructure that would eventually give rise to the cotton boom of the late nineteenth and early twentieth centuries. Isenbike Togan has rightly suggested that this trade actually represented the engine behind a sort of "silent revolution" within the Uzbek Ming polity. That is to say, by the end of Narbuta's reign, the revenue Khoqand attained through its relations with the Qing had enabled it to transform from the highly decentralized framework that had dominated the Central Asian political arena in the first half of the eighteenth century into something more powerful and grand.[27]

---

26. Newby, *The Empire and the Khanate*, 48–49. Newby references Qing sources that estimate the weight of the cargo at 53,000 *jin*, roughly equal to 68,900 pounds.

27. Isenbike Togan, "A Silent Revolution in 19th Century Central Asia," in *Change and Constancy: Historical Perspectives on the Way to Social Transformation*, conference proceedings (Beijing: Beijing Forum, 2011), 148.

The official trade was not without its limitations. While Khoqand aimed to send embassies as often as possible, the Qing aimed to limit their frequency to once every three to five years. According to Qing administrators in Kashgar, in the half century between 1759 and 1809, Khoqand sent twenty-three missions to Kashgar, only a fraction of which were permitted to continue on to Beijing. Those that were denied permission to do so remained in Altishahr, where they were allowed to trade at an agreeable tax rate but not granted the right to tax-free trade.[28] Comparing these figures with other Qing records, Newby finds that between 1760 and 1811, Khoqand was permitted to send nine envoys all the way to Beijing while an additional sixteen envoys and auxiliary traders were denied permission to travel onward but were allowed to remain in Altishahr. The number of envoys dispatched appears to have increased dramatically between 1809 and 1821, a period that roughly overlaps with the reign of 'Umar Khan (r. 1811–22). During those twelve years alone, some twenty-three envoys made their way eastward to Kashgar, and several were permitted to continue on to Beijing.[29]

However, the most important objective of Khoqand's ambassadorial missions to the Qing court was neither the gift exchange nor the proceeds from the official tax-free trade in Qing territories. Far more important was securing permission for several thousand Khoqandi merchants to expand their network in urban and rural markets throughout Xinjiang. Not only did the Qing grant the Andijanis access to Xinjiang, in an effort to bolster the commercial economy of the region, Qing policies actively encouraged the "Andijani" merchants with low tax rates. Over time, these same Andijanis found themselves well placed to take up a mediatory position in the growing transit trade between the Russian and Qing empires.[30]

THE ANDIJANIS

The Qing conquest of Altishahr created opportunities for Khoqand that no power in the Ferghana Valley had enjoyed since the Tang era, a millennium earlier. To be sure, merchants from the Ferghana Valley had been active in Altishahr since long before the Qing annexed the region in 1759. Indeed, Andijanis appear to have been present in Altishahr during the seventeenth- and eighteenth-century period of khoja

---

28. Saguchi, "The Eastern Trade," 51.
29. Saguchi, "The Eastern Trade"; Newby, *The Empire and the Khanate*, 49 and note.
30. The "Andijanis" were identified as such possibly because of the historical importance of that city, in contrast with the quite recent establishment of Khoqand.

rule in the region.³¹ At present there is little known about the magnitude of their presence during these earlier years.³² But the fact that significant numbers of Andijanis appear in Qing records almost immediately after the Qing conquest strongly suggests that they were reasonably widespread in Altishahr under the khojas, too. Saguchi cites Qing records dating to 1760 indicating that, already by that time, "with peace restored in Kashgharia, merchants are constantly coming in from the Buruts (Kyrgyz), Khoqand, Andijan and Marghilan."³³

Two years later, Andijani merchants are identified alongside Kyrgyz pastoralists as sellers of livestock to Qing administrators in Yarkand, an important commercial center for Xinjiang's trade with the mountainous countries to the south and, through them, India.³⁴ Soon thereafter, Andijani merchant communities were established in virtually every important urban center—Osh, Aqsu, Kashgar, Yarkand—and they reached many rural markets as well. In these early years, the Qing permitted the Andijanis to circulate freely throughout Altishahr and to extend their trade northward as far as Ili, though they were not permitted to make their way farther eastward to the markets in Qomul, Turfan, Qarashahr, or Kucha.

These limits aside, the Qing imposed a new series of policies designed to promote this trade. Prior to the Qing conquest of the region, local Muslim merchants were taxed at a rate of 10 percent, while foreign merchants were taxed at 5 percent for the total volume of their trade. In an effort to encourage the growth of the commercial economy, the Qing dropped these rates to 5 percent on local Muslims and a quite reasonable 3.33 percent for foreigners on the total value of their imports.

As was customary throughout the region, the foreign communities answered to an *aqsaqal* (elder) who supervised the community and served as an intermediary between his people and the state. The first appointment of an aqsaqal to supervise the Andijani merchants in Qing territory was made in Yarkand already in 1762. Within ten years the number of Andijani merchants in that city had increased to such an extent that the hakim found it necessary to appoint a second aqsaqal.³⁵ By the 1820s,

---

31. Saguchi, "The Eastern Trade," 67.
32. During the sixteenth and earlier in the seventeenth centuries, while Bukhara ruled over the Ferghana Valley, the merchants who predominantly mediated trade with Altishahr were identified as Bukharans. See Gulchekhra Sultonova, "Torgovye otnosheniia mezhdu Bukharskim i Yarkendskim khanstvami v XVI–nachale XVII veka," *Bulletin of IICAS* 11 (2010): 40–48.
33. Saguchi, "The Eastern Trade," 68.
34. Millward, *Beyond the Pass*, 145.
35. Newby, *The Empire and the Khanate*, 66.

Qing records document some 1,446 Andijanis in the city of Ili alone, with a comparable number occupying the other cities of Altishahr.[36]

As the number of Andijani traders increased, so did the magnitude of their trade. Echoing the northern Kiakhta trade with Russia, Qing records document a steady flow of large amounts of Chinese rhubarb passing along the southern routes as well.[37] Some of this remained in local markets, where it was valued for its ability to produce a deep yellow dye, but the vast majority was traded onward to markets farther to the west where it was valued (incorrectly, it would seem) for its medicinal attributes as a gentle purgative.[38] Qing records identify individual merchants responsible for transporting shipments of several hundred, or even several thousand pounds of rhubarb and growing quite rich in the process. The evidence of a vital trade along southern routes does not undermine the well-documented importance of the Russo-Qing Kiakhta Treaty of 1727 in establishing a northern route; however, it does complicate the portrayal of the Qing westward trade as seen from the perspective of the official trading outposts. Later events add additional emphasis to this very point.

Already in the 1760s, the Andijanis played a central role in the rhubarb trade. This expanded dramatically toward the end of Narbuta Biy's reign, most notably from 1785–92, when a diplomatic conflict with Russia led the Qing to close off Russian access to the precious root and suspend the Kiakhta trade. During these seven years, with the northern route closed and under careful watch, Chinese merchant-smugglers flooded markets in Ili and Altishahr with rhubarb, and the Andijani merchants were all too eager to profit by smuggling it westward into the valley, from where caravan traders could transport it onward to Russian trading outposts along the Irtysh River. Saguchi references Qing documents suggesting that, during this period, "more than 10 million chin (or "jin," a weight equaling 13,000,000 pounds) of rhubarb were found privately traded in Sinkiang by Muslims from Andijan and other places . . . Shrewd (Chinese) merchants brought rhubarb from China to Sinkiang, and sold it through Andijan merchants to Russia for large profits."[39] To be sure, the Andijanis

---

36. Saguchi, "The Eastern Trade," 85.
37. For a discussion of the northern route, see Morris Rossabi, "The 'Decline' of the Central Asian Caravan Trade," in *The Rise of Merchant Empires*, ed. J. Tracy (Cambridge: Cambridge University Press, 1990), 368.
38. Erika Monahan, "Locating Rhubarb: Early Modernity's Relevant Obscurity," in *Early Modern Things: Objects and Their Histories, 1500–1800*, ed. Paula Findlen (London: Routledge, 2013), 228, 240; Matthew Romaniello, "True Rhubarb? Trading Eurasian Botanical and Medical Knowledge in the Eighteenth Century," *Journal of Global History* 11, no. 1 (2016): 3–23.
39. Saguchi, "The Eastern Trade," 76.

FIG. 2.2 Caravan.
Turkestanskii Al'bom, 1865–72, Library of Congress, Prints & Photographs Division, LC-DIG-ppmsca-14344.

were not the sole traffickers in rhubarb from Xinjiang, but Saguchi does identify them as the most important.

The commercial interests of Andijani merchants were of course not limited to rhubarb. Most of their business interests appear to have involved orchestrating a mediatory trade in a variety of merchandise among markets in China, Russia, and India. Caravans of horses and camels moved opium, Indian textiles, silks and satins, indigo and other dyes, chemicals, paper, and much, much more across the mountain passes between the Ferghana Valley and Altishahr. Over the course of the eighteenth and nineteenth centuries, tea eclipsed rhubarb as a cash crop, and Andijani merchants reportedly moved hundreds of thousands of pounds of tea in the official trade—and they smuggled that much again—each year.

The considerable magnitude of the unofficial trade, what the Qing considered to be smuggling, makes it difficult to venture anything approaching a precise estimate of the magnitude of Andijani trade in Qing markets. According to the Qing governor of Ili, the Khoqandi merchants in his area were exceptionally shrewd at smuggling and dealing in prohibited goods, and he estimates that between 1805 and 1807 (several years after the Kiakhta suspension was lifted) they smuggled some 1.3 million pounds of tea from Ili alone.[40] Trading in saltpeter was prohibited, but because Khoqand placed a great value on acquiring it to make gunpowder (*phūr*), Andijani merchants were heavily involved in smuggling that alongside other contraband articles as well.[41]

Recognizing the magnitude of this trade and its impact on the development of the Khoqandi state does not require a survey of every commodity that Andijani merchants dealt in as they recreated, in some ways, a more modern version of the ancient Sogdian merchant network. To summarize rather simply, the Andijanis supplied Altishahr with horses and other livestock, an assemblage of articles produced within the region, Siberian furs, and an array of other Russian merchandise and European manufactured goods, all of which enjoyed high demand in markets throughout China. In exchange, along with tea, rhubarb, and other merchandise, large amounts of Chinese silver also passed westward. Summarizing the outflow of silver through Xinjiang into Khoqand to roughly 1820, one Qing report alleges that the military had "appropriated hundreds of millions of *liang*" for maintaining troops in the region, but that all of this silver had flowed into the hands of "alien merchants" trading in the region who received silver in exchange for "fur and other insignificant goods" only to take that silver westward, out of the empire. This affirms Saguchi's conclusion that, "Chinese silver, thus brought to the Uzbek countries from China through Eastern Turkistan in the 18th and 19th centuries, played an important role in international commerce in Central Asia and provided Khoqand with one of the economic foundations for its development into a khanate."[42]

WATER AND THE RISING STATE

In the middle of the eighteenth century, the Shahrukhid dynastic family asserted a dominant position over three additional territorial possessions: Andijan, Namangan, and Marghilan. Each of these represented a semi-autonomous *beglik*, an Uzbek word that might be roughly translated into English as a fiefdom, or city-state. As the ruler of the beglik of Khoqand, Irdana Biy was recognized as the senior Shahrukhid leader, but in effect he was the greatest among equals. In 1770, Narbuta Biy ascended the throne in Khoqand in the same position. Drawing on the revenue retrieved from Khoqand's diplomatic relations with the Qing, he was able to enhance his military

---

40. Saguchi, "The Eastern Trade," 83.
41. Saguchi, "The Eastern Trade," 77.
42. Saguchi, "The Eastern Trade," 77–80.

strength and develop patronage networks. This secured the loyalty of Khoqandi nobles and enabled him to stabilize his rule and considerably expand Khoqand's authority both in its control over its subordinate begliks and in the number of begliks it claimed. Narbuta Biy did much to enhance Khoqand's infrastructure, but his greatest achievement during his long reign was to bring the disparate begliks of the Ferghana Valley under the umbrella of Khoqand in a lasting way, incorporating them all into vilayats, or provinces, of what would soon become the Khanate of Khoqand.

Early on, Narbuta Biy tightened Khoqand's grip over the city of Osh, which the Qianlong emperor had in 1762 forced Irdana to return to the Kyrgyz. The Adigene Kyrgyz had long been Khoqand's neighbor to the east, and while they had aligned themselves with the Qing throughout Irdana Biy's reign, Narbuta Biy took advantage of the loose grasp that the Qing held over the area to convince, or coerce, the Kyrgyz around Osh to shift their allegiance to Khoqand. In the 1780s, he extended Khoqand's authority over other Kyrgyz populations in the valley and into the Tian Shan, groups that would add considerable strength to Khoqand's growing military.[43]

Managing the relationships of various groups of subjects with disparate and often conflicting interests took considerably more effort than simply forcing submission and then trusting that they would remain loyal and obedient. Writing more than a century ago, the Russian ethnographer Vladimir Nalivkin observed that one of the central problems that confronted the rulers of the khanate during this period was a persistent tension, occasionally rising to open and violent conflict, among the populations in the valley who based their living on farming and those who lived a nomadic, or semi-nomadic, lifestyle. One of the most effective ways that the Shahrukhids resolved these conflicts was by imposing a sedentary lifestyle among some of the nomadic groups in the valley, transforming Qipchaqs, Kyrgyz, and other nomads into farming populations. But as more nomads became settled farmers and more people—both nomads and sedentary populations—migrated into the valley, arable land grew scarce. This precipitated another major development that began to take shape during the reign of Narbuta Biy: the need to expand irrigation agriculture in the Ferghana Valley. From this period forward, the image one encounters in descriptions of the valley begins to shift as Khoqand gradually engineered the transformation of wilderness and open pasture into irrigated farmland.

Narrative sources report that, during the latter part of the eighteenth century, the semi-nomadic Kyrgyz in the southeast zone of the Ferghana Valley were irrigating some agricultural lands for cultivation during the summer, and the Qipchaqs

---

43. Ploskikh, *Kirgizy i Kokandskoe Khansvto*, 93.

did much the same along the Naryn River in the area of Uch Qurghan.[44] Compared to the irrigation networks that the Sarts had developed along the plains, these projects were small, poorly managed, and often abandoned as the Kyrgyz prioritized the pastoral-nomadic aspects of their economy. Quite often, at the end of their summer stay in the valley, the Kyrgyz would plant winter wheat, for example, which they would then leave alone and return to harvest in the spring only to find that some "enterprising Sarts" had in the meanwhile occupied that land and claimed it as their own.[45] Such circumstances led to considerable interethnic friction in the region.

Toward the end of Narbuta's reign, the growing number of Kyrgyz, Sarts, and other populations who had been settled in the southeast portions of the valley were suffering water shortages. Narbuta recognized that their loyalty to Khoqand depended on their ability to prosper as farmers in his domain, and he responded by orchestrating larger canal-building projects in that region. This included a large canal stemming from the Qara Darya River, which at that point had not yet had any significant amount of irrigation water drawn from it.[46] The seven-mile-long Uch Qurghan Ariq (an *ariq* is an irrigation canal) was also excavated in this period.[47] Already during the late eighteenth century, water rights in the Ferghana Valley had serious political implications. Michael Thurman explains that, by this time:

> the flows of the Isfayram, Aq Bura, and Aravan Rivers had been almost entirely diverted to irrigation, much of it in the low-lying foothills. Upon retaking Osh, Narbuta Biy placated the aristocracy of the town by granting them exclusive rights to the use of the Aq Bura River in drought years. This severely reduced flows to Andijan, and in response the population of the area was periodically mobilized to widen and deepen the Andijan Say Canal, the first large scale irrigation structure to appear under the khanate.[48]

---

44. Michael Thurman, "Irrigated Agriculture and Economic Development in the Ferghana Valley Under the Qoqand Khanate" (MA thesis, Indiana University, Bloomington, 1995), 12 and 60, note 22. See S. Jalilov, *Farghana Vadiysining sugharilish tarikhidan (XIX–XX asr bashligi)* (Tashkent: Fan, 1977), 29–30. See also the classic treatment by V. V. Bartold, "K istorii orosheniia Turkestana," in V. V. Bartold, *Sochineniia* (Moscow: Nauka, 1965), 3:97–233. For a survey of Bartold's work on Khoqand, see K. F. Shamsiev, "Voprosy istorii Kokandskogo Khanstva v trudakh V. V. Bartol'd," ÖIF 3 (1986): 51–55.
45. Thurman, "Irrigated Agriculture," 12.
46. Thurman, "Irrigated Agriculture," 12.
47. Thurman, "Irrigated Agriculture," 10 and 59, note 18.
48. Thurman, "Irrigated Agriculture," 12–13.

As migrant populations arrived from Kashgar and the surrounding Pamir and Tian Shan ranges, the population of the valley grew and agricultural production grew along with it. This was especially so along the right (northern) bank of the Syr Darya, which had a lower grade and was therefore easier to irrigate from the river. The left (southern) bank of the Syr Darya suffers from a higher grade, and so constructing canals that could extend irrigation into that part of the valley took considerably more effort. Until the completion of the Great Ferghana Canal in 1940, irrigation in the southern Valley was largely dependent upon drawing water from snowmelt draining down the northern slopes of the Pamir-Alay into alluvial fans. This was achieved most effectively in the southeastern part of the valley and the areas directly south of Khoqand. It is for that reason that, throughout the history of the khanate, the Kyrgyz and other semi-nomadic populations were the principle occupants of the south-central stretches of the valley.

Prior to Narbuta Biy's efforts to expand irrigation networks in the northern parts of the valley, many of the cities that would later become major urban centers were much smaller. Namangan, for example, is today home to more than 400,000 people, making it the second largest city in modern Uzbekistan. But it was little more than a village until the end of the eighteenth century, when canals were dug to divert water from the Padsha Ata River through multiple canal networks to the city's outlying areas.[49] This process began during the reign of Narbuta Biy, and it expanded during the nineteenth century with more and larger canals diverting water to more locations. The expansion of irrigation in the Ferghana Valley, as elsewhere in the region, would continue through the Russian imperial and Soviet eras, and even to the present day.

In addition to settling nomadic groups, Narbuta used water as a way to settle migrant farming communities and maintain a degree of leverage over those communities. Khoqand asserted the authority to determine which groups had access to which water supplies and how much water each group could access. At the same time, the settled populations themselves were responsible for expending the labor to create and maintain their own canals. Larger irrigation projects called for the use of corvée-style labor to excavate trunk canals out of which many smaller canals could divert water to different settlements. In all of these cases, the Khoqand-appointed *mirab* (irrigation official) was the person responsible for overseeing the fair and equitable distribution of the state's water from irrigation canals to the farmers. The mirab was therefore an extremely important post in Khoqand's civil administration,

---

49. Thurman, "Irrigated Agriculture," 10.

and the degree to which they were actually "fair and equitable" would be a reasonable question to ask.

Another feature of Narbuta Biy's reign was his effort to stabilize tensions among the Uzbek tribal nobility and the religious elite, both sufis and 'ulama alike, through a policy of strategic marriage alliances. Whether motivated by genuine piety or an effort to appear pious in the eyes of the religious, Narbuta Biy's greatest construction project was the grand (and still operational) Madrasa-i Mir in Khoqand, and he arranged for his five daughters to be wedded to important religious figures.[50] In doing so, he was publicly ensuring that the next generation of Shahrukhid leadership would have a favorable bias toward religious institutions, their objectives, and their leadership. Further contributing to Khoqand's growing legitimacy in the region during this period, Narbuta Biy established an accord with Bukhara that officially recognized Khoqand's legitimate position as an Islamic state in Central Asia, and he became the first ruler in Khoqand to mint his own coins, the *pūl* or *fulūs*, a small copper coin of little value.[51] In an effort to characterize the prosperity that Narbuta Biy's subjects enjoyed during his reign, Niyazi repeats popular traditions that food was abundant and affordable, and, while it is most certainly an exaggeration, that one could buy an entire sheep for just one fulūs.[52]

Beyond such tales, the general strength of Narbuta Biy's reign is more convincingly demonstrated in the events surrounding an attempted coup that his half-brother Hajji Bek staged near the end of the eighteenth century. Hajji Bek had served as hakim of various cities, including Marghilan, Khojand, and Tura Qurghan, after Narbuta Biy's other half-brother Shah Rukh died and left that post vacant. Serving as governor did not satisfy Hajji Bek's ambitious nature and, as Narbuta Biy was

---

50. TJN, f. 38a.
51. Narbuta Biy only minted copper coins, though silver coinage was introduced under his son and successor 'Alim Khan. Babadjanov suggests that Narbuta Biy's earliest minting dates to 1776–77, while Kočnev places it in 1770–71. Babadjanov, *Kokandskoe Khanstvo*, 116; Boris D. Kočnev, "The Last Period of Muslim Coin Minting in Central Asia (18th–Early 20th Century)," in *Muslim Culture in Russia and Central Asia from the 18th to the Early 20th Centuries*, ed. Michael Kemper, Anke von Kügelgen and Dmitriy Yermakov (Berlin: Klaus Schwarz Verlag, 1996), 439.
52. TS, f. 25a. Howorth (again, incorrectly) claims that Narbuta Biy did not mint his own coins (Howorth, *History of the Mongols*, 817). Examples of the three varieties of copper coins that Narbuta had minted are on display at the Historical Museum in Qoqand, and described in the Museum's publication, *The Kokand Khante [sic] Coins Catalogue, from the Funds of Museum* (Kokand, 2001). See also S. Kh. Ishankhanov, *Katalog monet Kokanda, XVIII–XIX vv.* (Tashkent: Fan, 1976). Additional information, descriptions, and images of later gold coins collected by the American diplomat, Eugene Schuyler (1840–90) during his visit to Russian Central Asia in 1873 can be found in Charles C. Torrey, *Gold Coins of Khoḳand and Bukhārā* (New York: American Numismatic Society, 1950). See also the discussion in AIKC, 13.

growing older, Hajji Bek launched a bid to take the throne for himself. According to Niyazi, Hajji Bek gathered support from the Qurama tribe that occupied the territories southeast of Tashkent.[53] From there he gained support from the hakims of Tura Qurghan and Andijan among other Uzbek elites, and then made his way to Besh Ariq, just outside of Khoqand, where he began assembling an army to put Narbuta's capital under siege. Ultimately, however, the coup failed. While it appears that the loyalty of the nobility was up for sale, the general population refused to follow their opportunistic leaders into rebellion and risk the peace, stability, and prosperity they had come to enjoy.[54] Hajji Bek withdrew and Narbuta Biy generously forgave his half-brother. A few years later, Narbuta's son, 'Alim, would not afford his uncle the same kindness.

As Khoqand grew larger and more powerful during the second half of the eighteenth century, a similar process was unfolding nearby in Tashkent. There, the local aqsaqals grew concerned that Bukhara and Khoqand would take notice of their city's rapidly increasing importance as a center of trade with the Russian steppe fortresses to the north and struggle to take the city for themselves. With that in mind, the aqsaqals accepted a Kazakh with Chinggisid ancestry by the name of Bahadur Farman to enter the city and serve as hakim and defender.[55] Mulla Avaz Muhammad reports that, after Bahadur Farman's death, factions supporting four different khojas struggled for power and Tashkent descended into an intense civil war. By 1784, another Kazakh of Chinggisid ancestry, Yunus Khoja, emerged victorious and Tashkent's status was rapidly restored.[56]

Yunus Khoja established himself as a serious power broker in the region: he utilized the increased resources of his vilayat to subdue the Kazakh populations in the steppe, and he freely delivered sanctuary and assistance to several rebellious political refugees from Khoqand, including Narbuta Biy's half-brother and scourge, Hajji Bek. The population of Tashkent had also grown significantly over the years, as prosperity had transformed it from a modest regional town of some 30,000 into a major commercial center of 80,000.[57]

---

53. TS, f. 25b. The Qurama were a conglomeration of at least six different tribes, including both Uzbeks and Kazakhs. Their composite nature is indicated in the very word *qurama*, which literally means something stitched together of different pieces. Beisembiev, "Migration," 37.
54. TS, fols. 27a–29b.
55. MT, 394; AIKC, 119.
56. TJN, f. 35b. For Tashkent's recovery, see Jeff Sahadeo, *Russian Colonial Society in Tashkent, 1865–1923* (Bloomington: Indiana University Press, 2010), 14 and notes.
57. Sahadeo notes that a Russian geographer visited the city and found it to be home to 40,000 male residents (so presumably 80,000 male and female). Azadaev similarly finds the population of the city in the middle of the nineteenth century to have been 80,000 people. See Sahadeo, *Russian Colonial*

Undeterred, Narbuta Biy sent a terribly unsuccessful expedition against Tashkent, which resulted in the deaths of thousands of his soldiers and the capture and execution of some seventy Khoqandi nobles.[58] Shortly thereafter, in 1799, Narbuta Biy suddenly died. While his nearly three-decade-long reign ended on a sour note, considered as a career it had been exceptionally successful. Narbuta was the first of the Shahrukhids to extend his control over the entire Ferghana Valley, he strengthened Khoqand's commercial and agrarian economies, and he had effectively prepared the ground for Khoqand to emerge from its chrysalis. During the course of his life, Narbuta Biy had five sons and five daughters from multiple mothers. His eldest son, Muhammad Amin was born of a Qalmaq mother and had predeceased him, leaving 'Alim as the oldest living male child. Next oldest was his daughter, Oftab Oyim, the chronicler Hakim Khan's mother, and then her younger brother 'Umar.[59] These three children were all born from Ming Oyim, the niece of the Ming noble Idris Quli Biy, and all would play important roles in the future of the khanate.

THE EMERGING STATE

In the early years of his reign, Narbuta Biy benefitted from the invisible hand of his Keneges grandmother, Oychuchuk Oyim, the widow of two Shahrukhid rulers who even from afar wielded considerable influence in Khoqandi politics. Having fled to Shahrisabz with Narbuta under her arm in the wake of his parents' murder, Oychuchuk Oyim painstakingly negotiated her grandson's return to Khoqand and appointment as hakim of Muimubarak. When Irdana Biy died the following year, Narbuta's greatest enemies leveraged their political capital to hoist Sulayman Biy onto the throne. Their temporary success ended three months later in a very public failure. Idris Quli and 'Abd al-Rahman Bahadur then had little choice but to join the chorus of Uzbek amirs and support Narbuta's elevation to the throne. At least in terms of political tensions internal to the family, with his grandmother's aid Narbuta began his reign with a comparatively firm footing.

This placed him in a good position to maximize the benefits made available through Khoqand's close relations with the Qing. The Qing viewed Xinjiang in this period not as a source of revenue, but as a necessary expense: liberal fiscal policies designed to benefit local Turkic Muslim elite and the injection of large amounts of

---

Society; see also F. Azadaev, *Tashkent vo vtoroi polovinie XIX veka* (Tashkent: Nauka, 1959), 29.
58. MT, 404.
59. MT, 401.

silver into local economies were the price the Qianlong emperor was willing to pay for peace and stability on his western frontier. Khoqand benefitted greatly from Qing policies. Narbuta dispatched several embassies to Beijing and while he received generous gifts in return, these were far outweighed by the profits from the tax-free trade that the accompanying merchants were able to conduct on his behalf. Still more important was the revenue retrieved from the several thousand Andijani merchants who extended their reach deeper into the commercial economy of Xinjiang and mediated the transregional movement of Chinese silver, tea and rhubarb, Indian cottons and dyes, Russian furs and manufactured goods, and much more.

Narbuta's administration invested this revenue wisely, developing patronage networks among the Uzbek amirs and the religious elite on the one hand, and expanding irrigation agriculture within the Ferghana Valley on the other. This marks the early establishment of the social contract that would secure the loyalty of both the religious and tribal elite, and place the Shahrukhid leadership at the intersection of the valley's many different political interests. As the population of the valley grew larger, demand for arable land increased. In response, Narbuta exploited the valley's wilderness and abundant water to maintain political order and bring greater prosperity. From this period on, the landscape of the valley gradually transformed as new and expanded irrigation networks brought more and more land under the plow. This equipped Narbuta with leverage over his settled subjects, and it also enabled him to expand his military forces to some 20,000–30,000 soldiers, which he used to extend Khoqand's reach and authority across the entire Valley. Narbuta Biy also normalized relations with his Bukharan neighbors and began minting his own coinage. Considered together, these factors contributed to Narbuta Biy's success in transforming his realm from a loose collection of semi-autonomous city-states under the umbrella of Khoqand into a fledgling state. This process would be advanced considerably during the reigns of his two sons, 'Alim (r. 1799–1811) and 'Umar (r. 1811–1822).

Three
THE KHANATE OF KHOQAND, 1799–1811

NARBUTA BIY'S LONG and successful reign was a gentle prelude for greater things to come. The next stage of Khoqand's development began more abruptly during the short, tumultuous, and transformative reign of Narbuta Biy's son, 'Alim, who initiated his fierce efforts at centralization by directing a dreadful series of purges against all who opposed him, or whom he feared may eventually do so. During his short twelve-year reign, 'Alim would also revolutionize Khoqand's army by emphasizing a reliance on new gunpowder weaponry, establish a new military corps whose loyalty was linked directly to him, defend the valley from an invading Kazakh army, conquer Tashkent, and begin the expansion of Khoqand's territory into the steppe. Following his adoption of the lofty title of "khan," his reign also marks the official transformation of his domain from a collection of city-states to the larger, more centralized, and much more powerful Khanate of Khoqand. 'Alim Khan's reign was a period of radical transformation in Khoqand's politics and position within the region, and such periods often produce both winners and losers. He himself would not be counted among the winners.

'ALIM ẒĀLIM

At the time of Narbuta Biy's death in 1799, support for his successor was divided among his brother Hajji Bek and two of his sons, Rustam Bek and 'Alim, born of two different mothers. Rustam Bek had been his father's chosen successor and he also enjoyed widespread support among some of the Uzbek tribes and Sarts (a name broadly applied to settled Turks and Tajiks). But the extent of his support was limited as his mother was not a member of the Ming.[1] There is some evidence to suggest that Narbuta Biy's bias in favor of Rustam may have actually prompted 'Alim to preemptively kill his father and claim the throne for himself, but that evidence is not definitive.[2] In any event, at least partly because Ming Oyim proved to be the more influential of Narbuta Biy's widows, her son 'Alim was able to draw more support and successfully claim the throne in Khoqand.[3] 'Alim appointed Rustam Bek hakim of Kanibadam and, soon thereafter, congratulatory embassies arrived in Khoqand from Bukhara and Khiva, and even from Yunus Khoja in Tashkent.[4]

In his economic policies, 'Alim followed in his father's footsteps in encouraging the expansion of irrigation agriculture in the valley. During the early years of his reign (1800–1803), 'Alim ordered workers to dredge the Yangi Ariq ("New Canal") near Namangan. When the project was started, the Yangi Ariq channeled between forty-seven and fifty *tegirman* (an amount equal to about 300 cubic feet of water per second) into fifty-five smaller channels that serviced sixteen settlements.[5] Work on this project continued through his reign and, when finished, conscripted farmers and other workers had widened and deepened the canal, and extended it so that ninety-six smaller canals branched off of it. In describing the magnitude of just this project, Thurman notes:

> The most impressive of these branches was the large Mutagan Ariq, which linked the Yangi Ariq with areas near Zarkent and Ghirvan. At the confluence of the Yangi Ariq and the Chartaq Say, a dam 51 meters wide and 5 meters high regulated flow between the two rivers. These measures boosted the carrying capacity of the Yangi Ariq to 250 tegirmans. This project facilitated the cultivation of an estimated 43,600 hectares (168.3 square miles) of newly irrigated land, and improved water supply to 19,600 hectares (75.7 square miles) of previously irrigated land.[6]

---

1. TS, f. 31a–b. Some sources identify his mother as Kyrgyz, others as Yuz. AIKC, 225.
2. AIKC, 291.
3. MTF, fols. 27a–27b; TS, f. 30b.
4. TJT, f. 23a.
5. Thurman, "Irrigated Agriculture," 13. Each *tegirman* ("mill wheel") equals a flow of 6.25 cubic feet per second, "i.e. enough water to turn a mill wheel" (Thurman, 53).
6. Thurman, "Irrigated Agriculture," 13–14.

Recalling that the total area of the almond-shaped Ferghana Valley is roughly 8500 square miles, this single project expanded or brought new irrigation services to approximately 2.87 percent of the valley's total area. The project was ambitious, and it is important to emphasize that this was only one of multiple similar projects launched in the late eighteenth and early nineteenth centuries. Many of these were small and localized, but several were even larger in scope than the Mutagan Ariq.

As a stark contrast to Babur's fifteenth-century depiction of the Ferghana Valley as a wilderness paradise, by the time the Russian Empire dissolved the khanate in 1876, well over half of the valley was irrigated and cultivated.[7] Reporting on his travel through the region in 1873, the American diplomat Eugene Schuyler found the agricultural economy of the khanate to be exceptionally strong. He observed the extensive networks that Khoqand had put in place over the years and noted the recent completion of two particularly large irrigation systems—the Khan canal and the Mussulman Qul canal.[8]

The totality of these initiatives gradually, but substantially, expanded the magnitude of Khoqand's irrigation agriculture and provided multiple political and economic benefits. Not the least of these were increasing agricultural revenues for the treasury—which under 'Alim began to mint silver coinage for the first time—and providing the Shahrukhids with a mechanism to exert leverage over large segments of the population.[9] Access to water is at the heart of agricultural communities' livelihood, and Khoqand deliberately and strategically used its ability to exercise control over who did, and did not, enjoy that access as a way to enhance its centralized authority.

At the same time, the official trade accompanying embassies between Khoqand and Beijing suffered during 'Alim's reign, and between 1801 and 1809 the Qing completely refused permission for envoys to continue on to the capital.[10] This was partly a result of 'Alim's inappropriate use of the word *dost* (friend) in reference to the Qing emperor in his early diplomatic correspondence, which suggested his intention to claim equal status to the emperor. It may also have stemmed from 'Alim's largely successful efforts to assert Khoqand's authority over the Kyrgyz tribes in the Tian Shan. Perhaps the most important factor was the aggressive stance that 'Alim took in his relations with the Qing in events unfolding in Xinjiang. As Newby notes, fifty

---

7. See the map in Thurman, "Irrigated Agriculture," 52.
8. Schuyler, *Turkistan*, 2:55–56.
9. Babadjanov, *Kokandskoe Khanstvo*, 119 and note 2.
10. Newby, *The Empire and the Khanate*, 62. 'Alim sent missions in 1804 and 1807, but they were denied permission to continue on to Beijing.

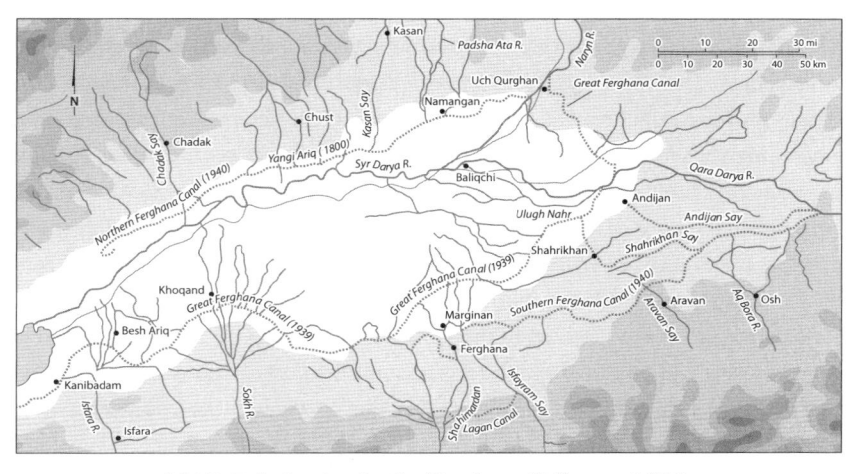

MAP 7 Irrigation in the Ferghana Valley ca. 1876.

Map by Bill Nelson based on "Main Rivers and Irrigation Canals in the Ferghana Valley," in Jonathan Michael Thurman, "Modes of Organization in Central Asian Irrigation: The Ferghana Valley, 1876 to Present" (PhD diss., Indiana University, 1999), map 2, 293.

years earlier the Qianlong emperor only needed to issue simple threats to influence policy on the ground in Khoqand. But by the early nineteenth century, it had become quite clear that Qing policies were tilted toward managing a peaceful hold over the region, and another large-scale Qing invasion was unlikely.[11] Having at last received an apology for the "discourteous tone" that 'Alim had used in his earlier correspondence, the Qing finally permitted an embassy in 1809.[12] The merchants took full advantage of the opportunity, and when they returned to Khoqand, they did so with eighty-eight carts loaded with Chinese merchandise in tow.

'Alim's aggressive stance disrupted diplomatic relations but it does not seem to have done anything to undermine Khoqand's commercial position within Xinjiang. The Andijani merchants remained the largest foreign commercial presence in the region, and they continued to dominate the movement of merchandise westward into the valley. This was largely a product of the combination of two concomitant developments: the commercial opportunities for foreign merchants that Qing fiscal policies provided and the restrictions that the Qing imposed on their own subjects, which made it difficult for them to conduct trade beyond the boundaries of the empire.[13] The

---

11. Newby, *The Empire and the Khanate*, 70–72.
12. Newby, *The Empire and the Khanate*, 61 and note.
13. Newby, *The Empire and the Khanate*, 64; Millward, *Beyond the Pass*, 23–24.

Andijani merchants eagerly exploited their mobility by establishing partnerships with local commercial interests. Political friction with the Qing would develop into a much greater problem in later years, but Khoqand would continue to benefit from Qing policies in the region even into the 1850s, strategically using diplomacy to assert greater authority over the Andijanis and other foreign merchants in Altishahr.[14]

In terms of more domestic matters, 'Alim was acutely aware that claiming the throne was an achievement but retaining it would be a much greater challenge. From the first days of his rule, 'Alim encountered widespread resistance across the valley. He hastily arranged for his sister Oftab Oyim to marry the influential and austere Ma'sum Khan, who was then appointed to occupy the post of hakim in Isfara. Unfortunately, that post was held by Boibuta Bahadur, a Qalmaq who had been one of Narbuta Biy's more reliable amirs. Boibuta Bahadur had not supported 'Alim, and so when he learned of 'Alim's intention to replace him with his new brother-in-law, he refused to vacate his post. 'Alim responded by leading a campaign against him, and soon thereafter he launched a widespread series of purges that included his half-brother Rustam Bek, his uncle Hajji Bek, virtually all of the amirs and khojas who had supported them, and numerous others.[15]

'Alim did not stop there. Following a pattern set by many aspiring monarchs who struggled to overcome entrenched nobility, he expanded his purges to include many of his late father's administrators. Under Narbuta Biy the religious orthodoxy had grown influential in Khoqand, and now 'Alim found that they obstructed his efforts to centralize power.[16] He targeted religious leaders, both 'ulama and sufis, senior military officers, and even members of the Shahrukhid family. Those who escaped execution were expelled to Bukhara, or elsewhere.[17] It was not without good cause that he earned the ignominious nickname 'Alim Ẓālim ('Alim "the Tyrant").[18]

Some insight into the circumstances underpinning these purges is found in the events surrounding the death of the Ishon Buzurg Khoja, a descendant of the celebrated Naqshbandi Lutfallah Chusti (d. ca. 1571). In recognition of his ancestral heritage in Chust, and also because Buzurg Khoja's son was married to one of Narbuta Biy's daughters, upon his ascension to the throne, 'Alim had appointed Buzurg Khoja hakim of Chust. Soon thereafter, for reasons that likely stemmed from 'Alim's

---

14. Newby, *The Empire and the Khanate*, 67.
15. MT, 402–3; TS, f. 31a–b. Niyazi reports that his own father, Mulla 'Ashur Muhammad, was among those who fled Khoqand at that time.
16. TJT, f. 48a; TS, 45b.
17. TS, f. 31a–b; MT, 403.
18. MTF, f. 27a–b. For a full listing of references, see AIKC, 291.

plummeting popularity during the purges, Buzurg Khoja staged a revolt of his own and his troops began pillaging areas around Khoqand.[19] 'Alim dispatched an "army of four flags" against the khoja, but they were defeated and each of the four commanders (*sardars*) was captured. 'Alim then placed his brother, 'Umar, in charge in Khoqand and personally led the campaign to suppress this new theocratic threat in Chust. Buzurg Khoja fled, first to the Kyrgyz and then to Tashkent, where he sought refuge and support from the Kazakh hakim, Yunus Khoja.[20]

Viewing this as a great opportunity, Yunus Khoja conspired with Buzurg Khoja to run a campaign into the Ferghana Valley and take Khoqand for himself. He sent Buzurg Khoja back to Chust while he led an army of Kazakhs eastward into the valley. For his part, Buzurg Khoja arrived home to a lukewarm reception from a population that had suffered and grown tired of the futility of his rebellion. The people recognized that Khoqand had grown in strength over the previous decades and that 'Alim was now in a much stronger position than his predecessors had been. Buzurg Khoja was captured and delivered to 'Alim, who welcomed him, met with him in private conversation, and indicated that all would be forgiven. 'Alim then ordered to have Buzurg Khoja secretly executed later that evening.[21]

Soon thereafter, 'Alim received word that Yunus Khoja was leading an army of some 80,000 troops into the Ferghana Valley.[22] 'Alim dispatched a rider to Khojand to enlist the support of a particularly talented Tajik commander named Rajab, originally from Badakhshan, whom 'Alim would later appoint hakim of Khojand.[23] As Yunus Khoja led his army through Qurama territory on their way into the valley, 'Alim and his sardars prepared the Khoqandi force to meet him head on. Meanwhile, Rajab led his army across the Syr Darya, so that he might approach the Kazakh forces from behind, opening a second front in the battle and blocking the Kazakhs if they should try to retreat.[24]

As the three armies faced off near the city of Ghurumserai, Rajab positioned his troops and strategically placed one hundred snipers under cover.[25] Rajab's troops

---

19. MT, 404; AIKC, 113.
20. MT, 405–6.
21. MT, 406–7. The perpetrator of the murder was the hakim of Andijan, Malla Diwan Beg.
22. TS, f. 48a; MT, 407; TJD, f. 25a; MTF, f. 34a–b. The troops included Kazakhs and others from the vicinity of Tashkent.
23. Sources identify Rajab by other title as they changed over the years, including Rajab Diwanbegi and Rajab Qushbegi. Cf. MT, 407; TS, f. 48b; AIKC, 220.
24. TS, f. 49a; MT, 408; TJT, fols. 25b–26b.
25. TS, f. 49b. Recall that rifles were reserved for snipers. A well-made musket was accurate only to about 150 yards.

rushed forward from behind while 'Alim's soldiers advanced against the Kazakhs from the other side of the river. Yunus Khoja's army was decimated. When the battle was finished, dead Kazakh soldiers were piled "like bundles of sticks" and the water of the Syr Darya "ran red with blood."[26] Yunus Khoja escaped with a few of his commanders, but his military had been destroyed, and all of their weapons, tents, and other supplies were now in Khoqand's possession.[27] Rajab was the real hero of the battle and as a reward he was elevated into the position of Commander of the Army (Amir-i Lashkar). Soon thereafter, 'Alim assembled all of the men of state and produced in front of them a new *dafter* (a record-keeping book). He then publicly reassigned the remaining nobility to new positions in the state, indicating that he had ended his purges.[28]

This was a welcome policy change, but it did not end 'Alim's brutality or his efforts to increase his control over powerful interest groups in Khoqand, including the Uzbek tribal aristocracy as well as the sufi leadership. In terms of the latter, 'Alim was himself a devoted sufi and student (*murīd*) of the Yassavi Sheikh Hazrat Maulavi Namangani. Over time, he had grown concerned that some of those who claimed to be sufis, or the sons of sufis, were in fact imposters and that they were guilty of earning a dishonest living through false piety.[29] He extended this suspicion beyond just the sufi orders to the Islamic institutions at large. He therefore launched a series of initiatives designed to strengthen Islamic practices in Khoqand. He banned the use of amulets and other religious innovations, including the popular Central Asian tradition of tying knots on branches of isolated trees and venerating them as holy. Those members of the 'ulama who failed to meet his standards were punished. At the same time, he instituted an examination for all sufis in Khoqand, and those who failed were branded as charlatans and forbidden from taking on students.[30] These new regulations were popular among some but they caused consternation and alarm among others. Some suggest they may even have nearly brought an end to 'Alim's life.[31] The story regarding the attempted assassination is as follows.

In the evenings, after the final (*'ishā*) prayer, 'Alim would often host a group devotional ceremony (*zikr* or *dhikr*) in his palace.[32] According to the account favored

---

26. MT, 408; TS, f. 50b.
27. MT, 408.
28. TS, f. 31a–b.
29. MT, 424.
30. Dubovitskii and Bababekov, "The Rise and Fall," 33.
31. For one such view, see Susanna S. Nettleton, "Ruler, Patron, Poet: 'Umar Khan in the Blossoming of the Khanate of Qoqan, 1800–1820," *International Journal of Turkish Studies* 2, no. 2 (1981): 132.
32. MT, 425.

by Niyazi, one evening, deeply entranced while chanting his zikr, one of the participants suddenly thrust a knife into ʿAlim's side. The would-be assassin failed to achieve his goal. He was stopped just as he prepared to stab ʿAlim a second time and he was captured, beaten, and interrogated, but with no results. The event was clearly premeditated, though the perpetrator was quickly killed and he took any explanation for the specific circumstances that led him to commit his crime to his grave.[33]

Writing several decades earlier, Hakim Khan presents a more detailed account of these events, one that sheds some light on ʿAlim's character and temperament, and helps to explain some of the difficulties that he would soon encounter in his reign. In describing the zikr, Hakim Khan explains,

> Among those who regularly attended was a young man who would become so entranced that he would even foam at the mouth. ʿAlim became convinced that he was nothing more than a charlatan faking his religious devotion. One day in the middle of the *zikr*, several of the *murīds* achieved ecstasy and some fell to the ground. This young man fell in front of ʿAlim, and his exaggerated behavior made ʿAlim certain that he was only pretending. ʿAlim grabbed him and hauled him into a small corridor outside of the room, where he began to punch the man in his head. As he was suffering this beating the man pulled a small knife from his shoe and in the ensuing struggle he stabbed ʿAlim a total of eighteen times before ʿAlim struck him in his right arm with a sword. Before long, other *murīds* came to the corridor and, after several of them were wounded, a dwarf known as Kichkina Khan ("Little Khan") observed that the man's right arm was wounded, grabbed the knife in his left hand, and forced the man to the ground.[34]

This account produces a very different narrative than the version Niyazi presents. Rather than a calculated assassination attempt motivated by a desire to exact revenge on ʿAlim for some unknown tyrannical offense, it appears here that the attack was provoked primarily by the ruler's suspicious and abusive nature. The attacker pulled out his knife and stabbed ʿAlim not as a premeditated effort to kill him, but because he feared for his life.

Adding credence to Hakim Khan's account is that, following the attack, ʿAlim spent the next forty days resting a short distance south of the palace at the home of his sister and brother-in-law, Maʿsum Khan, Hakim Khan's parents. Between visits with his

---

33. TS, fols. 45b–47b.
34. MT, 424–27.

doctors, 'Alim is said to have enjoyed the abundant shade and richly stocked fruit trees and flowers in Ma'sum Khan's garden, as well as the company of his young nephew, Hakim Khan.[35] It seems reasonable to suggest that the circumstances surrounding the attack would have been among the topics that the uncle and nephew discussed.

MILITARY REFORMS

From early in his reign, 'Alim began to reform his military. Under Narbuta Biy, Khoqand's army of irregulars, referred to as the Qaraqazan (Black Scorpion), had grown to between 20,000 and 30,000 Uzbek troops and had been paid predominantly by rights of pillage.[36] This force had generally proven effective within the valley, but 'Alim recognized that the older patronage-based military institutions that his father had inherited from Irdana would hinder his own centralization efforts. Military technology had improved dramatically over the preceding century, and 'Alim aimed to take advantage of those developments. If he was to lay the foundation for Khoqand to achieve its full potential, he needed a well-supplied standing army armed with muskets, cannons, and gunpowder, as well as training in how best to use them. Financing these reforms would require additional resources, and, stretching the limits of Islamic law (*shari'ah*) and the patience of the 'ulama, he imposed new supplementary (*bida'*) taxes on his subjects.[37]

Taking a page from Ottoman history, 'Alim set aside the long-held tradition praising the martial skills of Turks over Tajiks. He devised a different military model that drew on his Tajik subjects in the Pamir-Alay and emphasized loyalty and technology over the strategies that his father's military had employed. With this in mind, he established a special standing army of musketeers called the Gala Bahadur that consisted of between 10,000 and 20,000 extremely loyal "slave soldiers," nearly 6,000 of whom were identified as "Ghalcha," or Tajik mountain troops (Kohistanis) from the Pamirs.[38] Speaking highly localized Persian dialects nearly incomprehensible

---

35. MT, 428.
36. Beisembiev, *Tarikh-i Shahrukhi*, 67.
37. TJN, f. 39a. The results of 'Alim Khan's disregard for shari'ah is discussed in Babadjanov, *Kokandskoe Khanstvo*, 362–75.
38. Cf. TS, fols. 32a–38a, 62b; MT, 428; TJN, fols. 39a–b, 56b. According to Niyazi, the Ghalcha were divided into two parts: one was comprised of troops from Qarategin and Khayaji, and the other with troops from Darvaz, Badakhshan, Kulab, Hissar, Roshan, and Shughnan. At first, some 3,700 Ghalcha troops came from Qarategin, and only 500 troops arrived from the other locations. These were sent back to the mountains and they returned with 1,700 more. TS, fols. 32b–33a. Niyazi provides abun-

even to Tajik speakers in the plains, and removed from their mountain homeland to the Ferghana Valley, the Ghalcha were utterly dependent on, and vehemently loyal to, 'Alim Khan.[39] This was the Sipāh-i Jadīd, or the "New Army," and it existed alongside the Sipāh-i Kuhna, or the "Old Army," which included another 30,000 soldiers.[40]

Niyazi reports that the Tajiks were put through a program of extensive military training, during which the soldiers each received a monthly stipend and the state provided their clothing, horses, and other necessities.[41] Because of their heritage as Tajik farmers, and despite their training, the Uzbek soldiers mocked and ridiculed the Ghalcha, labeling them "donkey jockeys unfamiliar with the work of horses" and "good only for digging in the dirt."[42] 'Alim's Uzbek commanders were also dismissive of the Tajiks' military potential and initially even refused to work with them. This changed after the Uzbek amirs recognized that 'Alim's mind could not be swayed and that leadership over the Ghalcha would actually be a highly desirable post. Offers to assume such a position were declined: these soldiers were vehemently loyal to 'Alim, and he personally would lead them into battle.[43]

After a full year of training, in late 1806, the Ghalcha were ready for the battlefield. In a bold public display, 'Alim donned Tajik clothing and, on December 25, 1806, mounted his horse and led the Ghalcha against Urateppe, which had fallen into the hands of Amir Haidar of Bukhara (r. 1800–1826). The Gala Bahadur took heavy fire as they approached the city and unleashed catapults and artillery against the defenders. Wherever 'Alim went, he was surrounded by 1,000 Tajik troops who protected his every move. In just a few hours, the Gala Bahadur breached the city walls and, drawing their swords, fought their way inside. In less than an hour, the Manghit

---

dant information on the subject, and his assessment seems to be reliable as his own grandfather was from Kohistan. Beisembiev, "Migration," 37.

39. On the Ghalcha as an ethnic category, see Daniel Beben, "The Legendary Biographies of Nāṣir-i Khusraw: Memory and Textualization in Early Modern Persian Ismāʿīlism" (PhD diss., Indiana University, 2015), 251–53. Beben notes that the origins of the term are obscure, but that "the most likely explanation is that the term is a Turkified rendering derived from the old-Iranian term *ghar*, or 'mountain,' reflected as well, for example, in the name of the region of Gharjistān in present-day northern Afghanistan, to which is appended the Turkic adverbial suffix–*cha*." See also Robert Barkley Shaw, "On the Ghalcha Languages (Wakhi and Sarikoli)," *Journal of the Asiatic Society of Bengal* 45 (1876): 139–278. On the use of Ghalcha slaves as agricultural labor in Xinjiang, see Kim, *Borderland Capitalism*, 104.

40. AIKC, 777. According to Beisembiev, the Sipāh-i Kuhna could grow as large as 100,000 troops if necessary.

41. TS, fols. 33a–34a.

42. TS, f. 34b.

43. TS, f. 35b.

FIG. 3.1 Urateppe.

Turkestanskii Al'bom, 1865–72, Library of Congress, Prints & Photographs Division, LC-DIG-ppmsca-14816.

advance troops had surrendered.[44] In a single day, the Ghalcha had won a rapid and decisive victory, extending Khoqand's territory to the west and clearly establishing Khoqand's credentials as a military power in the region. Some 3,000 enemy troops were killed in the battle and a host of the Bukharan ruler's Manghit amirs had been captured. 'Alim was preparing to have the amirs and captured soldiers executed, but Hakim Khan reports that his father, Ma'sum, convinced him to spare their lives and imprison them instead, arguing that while killing them would enrage Amir Haidar for a few days, imprisoning them would extend his rage long into the future.[45]

The Tajiks pillaged Urateppe, after which 'Alim appointed a new hakim to govern over the city.[46] Fearing that Khoqand's army would continue onward to Samarqand, which at the time was in Manghit hands, Amir Haidar ordered two of the city's gates to be covered with earth as a defensive measure.[47] Soon thereafter, Amir Haidar led

---

44. TS fols. 35b–36a.
45. MT, 412.
46. TS, fols. 37b–38a; MTF, fols. 29a–30b.
47. TS, fols. 38b–39b.

a campaign that aimed to retake Urateppe, but with the support of the population, the Khoqandi hakim, Qadam 'Inaq, resisted. The population was compensated for all they had lost, and, while Khoqand's efforts to continue on to Jizzakh failed, Urateppe was, for now, in Khoqand's hands. The Ghalcha were rewarded with a lengthy furlough and promised that, when they were recalled to service, they would be equipped with even better artillery.[48]

Two key factors contributed to the Ghalcha corps' success in battle. First was their vehement loyalty to 'Alim Khan, whose unwavering and paternalistic support seems to have fostered an exceptionally strong and stable esprit de corps that propelled the troops into battle. Second was their access to, and training in, an array of new military technologies and strategies, which available accounts indicate they used to great effect. In the grand scheme this was a minor victory, so minor in fact that many of the chroniclers neglected even to include it in their accounts. As a member of a Tajik military family, Niyazi seems to have fixated on it, perhaps because of the novelty of a relatively small army of Tajiks running such a successful campaign against Urateppe, a city of considerable size. Khoqand would not be able to hold on to Urateppe. In fact, Hakim Khan reports that 'Alim put the city under siege no fewer than a dozen times.[49] But the battlefield success of this cadre of Kohistani farmers is a good illustration of how Central Asian warfare had changed since Nadir Shah's invasions six decades earlier.

Over the next few years 'Alim focused his efforts on further consolidating his authority, suppressing rebellions, and other affairs of state. He cautiously returned patronage to the religious elite, whom he hoped to appease with the construction of a new religious school in Khoqand, known as the Madrasa-i 'Ali.[50] Militarily, he regained control over all of the vilayats of the valley and he reasserted his authority over Khojand. 'Alim continued to shower support on his Ghalcha corps, and it did not take long before his favors began to elicit a degree of jealousy among his other soldiers. In the wake of their victory over Urateppe, for example, 'Alim sought to reward the Ghalcha by granting them wives from the area around Khoqand. The Tajiks appreciated the gesture, but it upset tribal elders as well as his Uzbek amirs.[51] 'Alim's advisors warned him against his implementation of such lopsided policies, but he remained certain that the loyalty and skill of his Ghalcha corps would insulate him from any potential retribution. The Ghalcha were the cornerstone of his plans

48. TS f. 45a; MTF, f. 31a.
49. MT, 419.
50. TS, f. 81b.
51. MT, 428–29.

to centralize his control, and, for the time being, his faith and his fate remained in good hands.

In January 1807, 'Alim and his commanders agreed that, with Tashkent having just suffered a severe loss in both manpower and artillery, weapons that were now in Khoqand's possession, it would be prudent to press their advantage.[52] When 'Alim announced his intention to run a campaign against Tashkent, his religious leadership—both sufis and 'ulama—objected. 'Alim was determined to move forward anyway, and he placed his younger brother 'Umar in charge of the campaign.

'Umar's army traveled with a substantial artillery train of camels and carts. As he approached Tashkent from the south, he divided this into two forces that surrounded the Qurama territories from opposite sides.[53] One after another, villages and small towns submitted, and as the Khoqandi amirs moved forward, they folded the Qurama manpower into their army, using young men as soldiers and others as supplementary labor to build defensive covers and the tall siege structures (*sarkūb*) that enabled Khoqand's snipers to target people inside walled cities from above.[54] Before long, Tashkent vilayat was in Khoqand's hands, and the city stood alone.

A short time after Yunus Khoja's failed invasion of the Ferghana Valley, he contracted tuberculosis and died.[55] Yunus Khoja's eldest son, Sultan Khoja, had been elevated as hakim of Tashkent in his place, and he was in that position as 'Umar led his army across the Syr Darya and put Tashkent under siege.[56] The Khoqandi army dug in, building its defenses and siege structures. Days turned into weeks, and, with nobody allowed in or out, food became scarce and reports began to circulate that the city dwellers were reduced to eating bark from trees and staying alive by consuming sheep blood, an affront to Islamic dietary laws.[57]

Facing a rebellion among his own starving people, Sultan Khoja decided to capitulate. But as he prepared to turn himself over to 'Umar, he was convinced to engage the Khoqandi forces directly in one final effort at victory. The Tajik troops had meanwhile planted explosives underneath the city walls and positioned themselves high up in siege structures. All at once the Khoqandi forces began an offensive, with

---

52. TS, f. 53a–b. Babadjanov places Khoqand's conquest of Qurama and Tashkent one year earlier, in 1806. Babadjanov, *Kokandskoe Khanstvo*, 119. Bregel places it in 1809, EIr, s.v. "Central Asia vii, in the 12th–13th/18th–19th Centuries," 5:197.
53. TS, f. 55a.
54. TS, fols. 57a–59b.
55. Muhammad Salih places Yunus Khoja's death in 1808, TJT, f. 39a. Drawing on other sources, Beisembiev places it in circa 1805, AIKC, 520.
56. MT, 415.
57. TS, f. 60a; MTF fols. 39b–41a.

snipers unleashing one volley after another as the explosives reduced the city walls to dust, creating such a cloud that "one could not tell if it was day or night."[58] Victorious, 'Umar had a number of Tashkenti amirs executed, Sultan Khoja was captured, and he appointed Sultan Khoja's younger brother Hamid Khoja to the position of hakim, serving on behalf of 'Alim in Khoqand. The victory celebration had barely concluded before it became clear that, despite his promise of loyalty, Hamid Khoja would be no more pliable than his brother had been.[59]

'Umar then engineered a solution that would more firmly place Tashkent in Khoqand's hands. Outside of the walled city of Tashkent was a secondary fortress known as Niyaz Bek, which served to protect the city's water supply.[60] 'Umar led a battalion of 500 Khoqandi soldiers to the fortress, and after a lengthy battle with substantial losses on both sides they forced the defenders to withdraw, leaving Niyaz Bek, and Tashkent's water supply, in Khoqand's hands.[61] Hamid Khoja dispatched an ambassador to 'Umar and announced his submission.

Upon learning of his brother's victory, 'Alim personally traveled to Tashkent with a number of Khoqandi dignitaries and they spent a month celebrating in the city.[62] The brothers then returned to Khoqand where 'Alim installed 'Umar as hakim of Marghilan (the post customarily assigned to the heir apparent) and arranged for his marriage to Mahlar Oyim (1792–1842), the daughter of the hakim of Andijan who would later earn her own fame as the celebrated Uzbek poetess Nadira. Shortly after the wedding, Mahlar Oyim became pregnant with the couple's first son, Muhammad 'Ali ("Madali" Khan, r. 1822–42).

It is difficult to identify precisely when 'Alim Biy became restyled as 'Alim Khan. With only a few exceptions, chroniclers tend to identify him as 'Alim Khan from the moment he ascended to the throne.[63] Numismatic evidence provides some insight. Where the earliest coinage minted during his reign identifies him as 'Alim Bek, silver coins dating to 1806/7 are stamped with the name 'Alim Khan.[64] Muhammad Salih suggests that it was in the wake of Khoqand's victory over Tashkent that 'Alim became the first of the Shahrukhid lineage to claim the title of Khan of Khoqand.[65]

---

58. TS, f. 62a.
59. MT, 416.
60. AIKC, 706.
61. MT, 417; MTF, f. 39b.
62. TJT, f. 39b.
63. Niyazi quite deliberately refers to him as amir or padshah through the bulk of his reign. See TS, f. 55a.
64. Babadjanov, *Kokandskoe Khanstvo*, 119. The coins are stamped with the year 1221 in the Hijri calendar, which ended on March 10, 1807.
65. TJT, f. 39b. Beisembiev seems to agree. AIKC, 14, 291. Citing Bartold and "Abdoul Kerim Boukhary,"

Complicating matters further, Muhammad Salih also notes that ʿAlim Khan was the first Shahrukhid to refer to himself as "Baburi," indicating a claim that the Shahrukhids' dynastic line emanated from Zahir al-Din Muhammad Babur: again, a Timurid prince whose mother was a Chinggisid princess and who was himself born in the Ferghana Valley in 1483.[66] For several reasons, the widely accepted notion that ʿAlim devised this fictive kinship to claim a Chinggisid ancestry and justify his adoption of the title of Khan are problematic, and they will be put under closer scrutiny in the next chapter.

At the same time, there is merit in Newby's efforts to link ʿAlim Khan's decision to claim a higher title to his deliberate effort to stake out a more aggressive position in Khoqand's relations with the Qing. ʿAlim's early diplomatic communication with the Qing had been overly familiar, referring to the emperor as "friend," for example.[67] Although the Qing dismissed out of hand any effort on the part of Irdana Biy to adopt the title of Khan in the 1760s, now some fifty years later, ʿAlim Khan was in a much stronger position to lay claim to the loftier title.[68]

A STEPPE TOO FAR

It is here that the trajectory of Khoqand's history would take an abrupt turn. Wedged between Khoqand and Bukhara, Tashkent was the gateway to the steppe, and, by the end of the eighteenth century, it had grown to represent an important independent power in the region. Previous Shahrukhid rulers had directed their commercial interests eastward toward China and focused their military campaigns either within the Ferghana Valley itself or to the southwest, against Khojand and Urateppe, two cities situated dangerously close to the valley's only exposed entrance. ʿAlim Khan retained a strong interest in Khoqand's commercial affairs in Xinjiang. But as Khoqand's political relations with Beijing faltered, ʿAlim Khan

---

Nettleton suggests that ʿAlim claimed the title of Khan already in 1801–2. Nettleton, "Ruler, Patron, Poet," 135 and note. However, ʿAbd-al Karim Bukhari's account relies heavily on oral tradition and much of what he presents is inaccurate, unreliable, and should be used with caution. See Schefer's notes in his introduction to Bukhari, *Histoire d l'Asie Centrale*, iii. See also Newby, *The Empire and the Khanate*, 61 and note 47.

66. TJT, f. 23a.
67. Newby, *The Empire and the Khanate*, 61–62 and notes.
68. Eckart Schiewek has located an archival record held in Kazan that indicates Narbuta also claimed the title of khan. The record in question dates to January 8, 1799, or very near the end of Narbuta's life. Personal communication, July 2017.

directed his attention elsewhere, and this led to Khoqand's annexation of Tashkent.[69]

Tashkent was a great prize, but 'Alim Khan perceived even greater opportunities farther to the north. By the time of his reign, Khoqand's northward trade through Tashkent had grown to become a critical aspect of the state economy, and 'Alim Khan recognized that Khoqand's benefits from this relationship could be greatly enhanced if he could continue his territorial expansion in that direction. In 1809, he dispatched his newly appointed hakim of Tashkent, a Kazakh named Sarimsaq Tura, into the steppe with orders to take the city of Turkestan (historically known as Yas) and the surrounding areas in the southern steppe for Khoqand.[70]

Sarimsaq Tura's hard-won victory over Kazakh defenders created the basis for a new steppe vilayat—one that would soon stretch up the Syr Darya to the fortress of Aq Masjid and extend eastward across the steppe to the Qing border.[71] Celebrating his victory, Sarimsaq Tura sent ninety camels loaded with gifts to Khoqand. In response, 'Alim confirmed Sarimsaq's right to rule over the Qipchaq Steppe, and, across this vast area, the *khutba* (Friday sermon) was read in the name of 'Alim Khan.[72] Excepting only Tamerlane himself, that victory marked the first time a sedentary power in Central Asia had extended its authority northward into the steppe in the nearly six centuries since Chinggis Khan led the conquest of the Khwarezmian Empire in 1220. Whereas Tamerlane achieved his victory with nomadic soldiers, 'Alim Khan had achieved his with gunpowder.

Soon thereafter, 'Alim Khan's ambition outgrew the willingness of his nobility and even his most loyal Ghalcha corps to follow him. As the winter of 1810–11 was already upon him, 'Alim Khan grew determined to expand his authority even farther into the steppe and he ordered his army to prepare to march to Tashkent. Ma'sum Khan and other close advisors had grown concerned that popular support was shifting in favor of his brother and that powerful interests were developing conspiracies to overthrow 'Alim Khan. Ignoring his advisors, 'Alim Khan assembled his army and, providing a powerful incentive for his troops to succeed, a caravan of 300 camels loaded with merchandise to be sold in the Russian markets.[73] When the army of Khoqand arrived in Tashkent, 'Alim Khan ordered them to continue on to Chimkent.

---

69. Newby, *The Empire and the Khanate*, 60–62, 67–68.
70. Sarimsaq Tura was the uncle of Muhammad Salih, the author of the *Tārīkh-i jadīdah-i Tāshkand*. AIKC, 247.
71. TS, f. 44a. The Russians renamed the town Perovsky after the Russian general who conquered it in 1853. Since 1926, it has been known as Kyzyl Orda, or Red Fort.
72. TJT, fols. 43b–46b.
73. MT, 431; TS, f. 64b; MTF, f. 42a.

The Ghalcha marched into the wintry, frozen steppe, and they held Chimkent under siege for twenty days while he stayed safely behind in Tashkent. The Ghalcha kept the city surrounded, but they suffered as they did. The cold was so severe that they could not even hold the metal of their muskets.[74]

'Alim Khan had overplayed his hand. In the wake of his purges and in response to his unrelenting efforts at exerting centralized authority, religious and tribal leaders from nearly every part of the khanate's administration had already begun to favor his younger brother, 'Umar. With his Ghalcha corps out of reach in the frozen steppe to the north, several of his amirs convinced 'Umar to join them in carrying out a coup. In the middle of the night, 'Umar and his co-conspirators departed for Khoqand, where the rebels planned to announce that 'Alim Khan was dead and that 'Umar would replace him as Khan. 'Alim Khan was left behind in Tashkent with his Ghalcha corps two days away.

Upon learning of his brother's actions, 'Alim Khan recalled his loyal amirs and Ghalcha troops to Tashkent with the intention of leading them back to Khoqand to reassert his control over the capital. But he watched his popularity deteriorate as the frozen Tajik soldiers plodded their way back into Tashkent, many having lost fingers, hands, and feet to frostbite in the frozen steppe.[75] 'Alim Khan sought to ameliorate their suffering by distributing among them the 300 camel loads of goods that he had intended to take to Russia.[76] He then ordered Sarimsaq Tura and other amirs to be executed for their complicity with the rebellion.[77] But his efforts to reclaim authority were insufficient, and, Niyazi reports, every night another 1,000 Tajik soldiers deserted 'Alim and rushed to Khoqand to join 'Umar.[78] Two days after Sarimsaq Tura was executed, 'Alim Khan led those who had remained loyal on the long march to Khoqand.

'Alim's reign, and his life, came to an end on the road to Khoqand. More troops deserted their khan as they crossed the cold mountain passes southeast of Tashkent.[79] As his support dwindled, 'Alim Khan came to realize that defeat was at hand. He considered departing the region entirely and going on the hajj, but he decided instead to make his way to Khoqand and place himself at his brother's mercy, hoping that he might be permitted to live out his days engaging in spiritual pursuits at a sufi hostel (*khanaqah*).[80] But peaceful retirement was not to be his fate. Again, what

---

74. TS, f. 65a.
75. TJT, f. 49b; TS, fols. 65b–67b.
76. TS, f. 67b.
77. TS, f. 49a; AIKC, 247.
78. TS, f. 69a.
79. TS, f. 69a.
80. MTF, f. 44a–b.

follows is an abridged version of Hakim Khan's account of the events surrounding his uncle's death. While these are clearly the dramatized recollections of a boy, Hakim Khan was present at the time and he provides the only first-hand account of the events that transpired surrounding his uncle's death. Hakim Khan recalls that,

> on his way back to Khoqand, 'Alim Khan tried to pass the Red Bridge (*kizil kubrūk*) at Panghaz, but the locals were well armed and they refused to let him pass. At this time, 'Alim was accompanied by 200 women in his harem and only 40 loyal troops. Of his advisors, only Ma'sum remained loyal; all his other amirs had deserted him. Ma'sum advised 'Alim to flee to Khojand and seek refuge with the hakim there. 'Alim refused, and he ordered his son Shah Rukh to return to Tashkent and take the position of hakim for himself. 'Alim and his entourage continued onward down the cold, wet, and muddy road. It took two days to get across the mountains and into the valley. On the third day, the group arrived at Badam Chashma.
>
> 'Umar had ordered his troops to keep a watchful eye on this route, and late at night they encountered 'Alim and his harem. Recognizing that an attack was imminent, Ma'sum secretly made his way to 'Umar's amirs, informed them of their situation and intent, and begged them to let the women and children live. Sometime in the middle of that night, a man snuck into Hakim Khan's tent, put his hand over the seven-year-old boy's mouth, and told him to keep quiet. It was 'Alim Khan. He kissed his nephew's forehead and told him goodbye, and then he and five soldiers slipped away on horseback, leaving the harem behind.
>
> 'Alim had decided to try and make his way back to Khoqand where he would ask for 'Umar's mercy. But 'Umar had meanwhile dispatched multiple bands of soldiers to locate his brother. It was a small cadre of ten Qipchaq soldiers loyal to 'Umar that encountered their former khan. These men had earned a reputation as extraordinarily brave soldiers, so much so that no Uzbek could match them. It was just such Qipchaqs who had a century earlier killed the ruler of Bukhara, 'Ubaydullah Khan (d. 1711).
>
> The Qipchaqs surrounded 'Alim, and as they approached him he drew his sword and fought alone. 'Alim Khan had already cut off two of their heads when one Qipchaq wounded him with his spear. 'Alim pulled the spear from his enemy's hands and, using that same spear, killed that soldier and two others. Fearing for their lives, the other five began to flee when one soldier, armed with a musket, shot 'Alim Khan. The bullet pierced his armor as if it were onionskin. 'Alim Khan fell to the ground covered in blood, dead.[81]

---

81. MT, 437–46. Additional information can be found in Babadjanov, *Kokandskoe Khanstvo*, 117–37.

Setting aside Hakim Khan's dramatic embellishments, it seems reasonable to conclude that 'Alim had advanced ahead of his harem, that he reached Altiqush, just three or four miles north of Khoqand, and that he was ambushed and killed in January 1811.[82] 'Umar is said to have received the news of his brother's death with great sadness. The amirs responsible publicly begged 'Umar's forgiveness. They loudly announced that they knew 'Umar did not want them to kill his brother, that 'Alim Khan's death was a terrible tragedy, and that their intent all along had been to convince him to return to Tashkent so he could govern over the khanate's northern vilayat in the Qipchaq Steppe and leave Khoqand to 'Umar.[83]

Other aspects of the accounts detailing this event strongly suggest that, if there was any expression of sadness on 'Umar's part, it was a deliberate fiction intended for public consumption. Most obvious is that at the same moment 'Umar and his amirs were reputedly crying over the terrible tragedy of 'Alim Khan's death, 'Umar himself dispatched a fast rider to Tashkent with instructions to have two of his amirs there locate his eighteen-year-old nephew Shah Rukh and kill him. This was accomplished.[84] 'Umar Khan had his brother's bloody clothes put on display in the bazaar so that all could see that 'Alim was dead, and that the transfer of power was complete. 'Umar then issued an order that 'Alim Khan's body be carried through the streets of Khoqand and placed to rest in the Dakhm-i Shahan, the mausoleum of the Shahrukhid royal family, where it remains today.[85]

KHOQAND BECOMES A KHANATE

Almost from his ascension to the throne in 1799, 'Alim focused his efforts on centralizing his power and elevating his position from that of a "greatest among equals," such as his father had been, to one more akin to an absolute monarch. Throughout

---

82. AIKC, 532. Although the sources uniformly agree that 'Alim Khan was killed as he approached Khoqand, there has been some debate and confusion regarding the year in which it happened. Newby's research in the Chinese records suggests that 'Alim Khan ruled until 1811. Niyazi reported that 'Umar Khan succeeded his brother during the winter and in the year 1225 A.H. As the first day of the first month of 1226 A.H. corresponds to January 26, 1811, it seems most likely that 'Alim Khan was killed sometime before that date in January 1811, and not in 1810 as has most often been suggested. See TS, f. 72a; Newby, *The Empire and the Khanate*, 32, 60, 68; Clifford Edmund Bosworth, *The New Islamic Dynasties: A Chronological and Genealogical Manual* (New York: Columbia University Press, 1996), 295.
83. TJN, f. 55a.
84. MT, 445.
85. MTF, f. 46a; TJT, f. 49b; TS, f. 71b.

his reign, 'Alim Khan continued his father's efforts to promote the expansion of irrigation agriculture in the valley and, although his arrogance damaged diplomatic relations with Beijing, Andijani merchants were permitted to continue on with their activities in Xinjiang. But the defining feature of his reign was revolutionary change, not continuity. Whereas Narbuta Biy had carefully balanced patronage among multiple constituencies, 'Alim Khan's preferred to deal with the remnants from his father's administration and other influential figures who posed a real or perceived threat to his centralization efforts with execution and exile. His brutality brought results, but it also earned him a lasting legacy as 'Alim Ẓālim.

At the same time, 'Alim instituted military reforms that contributed to the transformation of Khoqand into a more centralized, and much more powerful khanate. The cornerstone of these reforms was the establishment of the Gala Bahadur, a standing army of some 10,000 "slave soldiers," all of whom were loyal directly to 'Alim and all of whom were paid not through rights of pillage, but from the treasury. Taking advantage of Khoqand's recent annexation of Tajik realms and the trust 'Alim placed in several of his new Tajik amirs, roughly 6,000 of these soldiers comprised a special corps of Kohistani Tajik troops known as the "Ghalcha." Following extensive military training in battlefield exercises and the use of gunpowder weaponry and artillery, the Ghalcha proved to be highly capable on the battlefield. This extremely loyal and well-trained force gave 'Alim the confidence to continue centralizing his control over the state. The strength of his military enabled him to repel Yunus Khoja's efforts to invade the Ferghana Valley, and then to launch his own invasion and annexation of Tashkent in 1807.

The revolutionary transformation of the Khanate of Khoqand in such a short period of time was a remarkable achievement. But it had come at a great cost in terms of a persistent resentment for 'Alim Khan's purges, a deep suspicion of his objectives, and a profound lack of trust in his leadership. The sufi khojas were dismayed by his execution and persecution of many religious figures. The Uzbek amirs shared those grievances, and their animosity toward 'Alim was compounded by his doting paternal patronage of the Tajik Ghalcha troops. Thus, in January 1811, with 'Alim Khan in Tashkent and his loyal Ghalcha corps camped in the frozen steppe outside of Chimkent, 'Alim Khan's younger brother 'Umar and the Khoqandi nobility launched a coup. 'Alim Khan's death followed soon thereafter.

The historical record presents 'Alim Khan as arrogant, mean-spirited, coldhearted, and perhaps even befitting the label of tyrant. But in terms of his legacy, he can be credited with considerable territorial expansion, implementing important military and monetary reforms, and significantly strengthening the centralized power of his state. He can also be credited with preparing the ground for the celebrated reign of his brother, 'Umar, who would draw on new modes of legitimacy and engineer a cultural efflorescence that would be celebrated long into the future. While 'Alim would be reviled as 'Alim Ẓālim, his younger brother would be remembered as 'Umar Khan, *jannat-makān*, a beloved ruler who "Resides in Paradise."

Four
A NEW "TIMURID RENAISSANCE," 1811–1822

IN JANUARY 1811, as 'Alim Khan made his way across the frozen mountain passes southeast of Tashkent only to meet his death a few miles outside of Khoqand, his younger brother 'Umar sat on a flat platform draped in white felt (*āq kigīz*), and, as one of his supporters read aloud the Sura al-Fath ("The Victory," Sura 48 in the Qur'an), 'Umar was elevated as the new khan of Khoqand (r. 1811–22).[1] It had been 102 years since 'Umar Khan's great-great-grandfather Shah Rukh had himself been elevated to the leadership of the Ming tribe in a similar āq kigīz ceremony.[2] Now, in the wake of 'Alim Khan's twelve-year reign, the Khanate of Khoqand was in 'Umar's hands and it was positioned to reach its greatest heights.

'Umar Khan proved to be much more politically astute than his older brother. From the earliest days of his reign, 'Umar presented himself as the antidote to his brother's tyranny. 'Umar disbanded his brother's Ghalcha corps; welcomed back to Khoqand those whom his brother had exiled; developed a court culture in Khoqand designed to mimic the achievements of the great Timurid Renaissance; and crafted a new model for legitimacy that had broad appeal across multiple constituencies, including both tribal and religious groups. On the one hand, these achievements secured 'Umar Khan's legacy by shaping his presentation in the chronicles as the

---

1. TS fols. 72b–73a; MTF, f. 46b.
2. The chronicles indicate that his elevation involved the Mongol āq kigīz ceremony. With no contemporary source to corroborate this claim, it is possible that it was a later invention.

wise, pious, and benevolent poet-ruler who gave rise to the greatest cultural efflorescence in the khanate's history. On the other hand, careful scrutiny of available sources exposes this narrative as a carefully constructed fiction. 'Umar Khan was guilty of employing the same types of violence and brutality as his brother. But in an effort to enhance his claims to legitimacy, 'Umar's chroniclers took care to document and broadcast his cultural and other achievements, and conceal the rest.

Like his brother, 'Umar was an accomplished military commander. But he was even more astute as a politician and in the wake of his brother's tyranny, 'Umar's charm and charisma earned him abundant good will. In his *Tā'rīkh-i Turkistān*, Mulla 'Alim Makhdum Hajji describes 'Umar as "endowed with a charming disposition, a quick and clever judgment, social morality and goodness."[3] 'Alim had fallen because of his heavy-handed methods, brutality, and harsh disposition. 'Umar deliberately fostered an image of himself as the polar opposite. Among his first acts as khan was to dispatch an ambassador to Bukhara to announce to all those who had fled Khoqand during his brother's purges that they would be welcome to return home.[4] Rajab Diwanbegi, the hero in Khoqand's victory over Yunus Khoja's Kazakh invasion of the valley, had already made his way from Bukhara to Shahrisabz when he learned of 'Alim Khan's death.[5] He was among the first to take advantage of the opportunity to return home, where he was welcomed on his arrival and awarded a position in 'Umar Khan's government.[6]

Even today 'Umar remains celebrated for his genteel manner and the cultural achievements of his court. These achievements were real and notable, but they were also deliberately orchestrated for public consumption. In reality, 'Umar could match his brother's brutality when he found it necessary or beneficial to do so. One need only recall that 'Umar was a central participant in the coup that toppled his brother's reign, and he had ordered his brother's murder as well as the murder of his nephew, Shah Rukh, in Tashkent. 'Umar dealt with other potential sources of conflict with no less brutality. 'Alim Khan's uncle, 'Idris Quli Biy, presented the most immediate threat. He had accompanied 'Umar on his flight from Tashkent to take the throne in Khoqand and now, with the support of two other nobles who were also involved in the coup, he conspired to do the same to 'Umar.[7] But when Rajab Diwanbegi was informed of the plan to place 'Idris Quli on the throne, he elected to side with 'Umar,

---

3. Mulla 'Alim Makhdum Hajji, *Tā'rīkh-i Turkistān* (Tashkent, 1915), 53. Cited in Nettleton, "Ruler, Patron, Poet," 134. For more on the *Tā'rīkh-i Turkistān*, see KI, 115.
4. TS, f. 74a; MTF, f. 46b. The ambassador is identified as Muhammad Nur Khoja Tajiki.
5. AIKC, 220.
6. TS, f. 74b.
7. Niyazi identifies Mumin Bek and Qaytaqi Bahadur as the other principle conspirators.

who quickly rounded up the conspirators and had them summarily executed.[8]

In military matters 'Umar was also no more generous than his brother. The Uzbek poet Dilshad is said to have written the following condemnation of 'Umar Khan's actions in the wake of yet another campaign against the unfortunate inhabitants of Urateppe in 1818. The accuracy of the figures she provides is clearly questionable, but she was an inhabitant of Urateppe and claims to have witnessed events after Umar Khan's victory:

> All the prisoners were herded into the square of Chor-su. People whispered that on that day 13,400 people had been taken prisoner. The amir of Ferghana himself, Amir Umar Khan, despite being a scholar and great poet, had mercy on neither the scholars nor poets of this oppressed people.[9]

Looking back from the vantage point of several decades later, the chronicles present 'Umar Khan's reign as a stark contrast to the tyrannical purges of 'Alim Khan before him and the unbridled excesses of his son Muhammad 'Ali after him. However, Babadjanov correctly concludes that it is more accurate to regard 'Umar Khan as an urbane and charismatic master of "political intrigue," or perhaps public relations, than the mythologized figure one encounters in the chronicles of his reign, and in scholarly treatments as well.[10] His deliberate effort to present himself as the counterpoint to his brother's tyranny through carefully staged pageantry and strategic history writing has effectively manipulated the optics of his reign and misled many who have taken the accounts in the chronicles at face value.[11]

More careful analysis suggests that 'Umar also was not the model Islamic ruler that historians have often presented him to be. In addition to various behavioral tendencies that one would be more inclined to attribute to his brother, he was reputedly fond of smoking and, according to his nephew's account, his premature death in 1822—he was only some thirty-six years old—was brought about in no small part due to excessive drinking.[12] One should take care not to accept such accounts uncritically. Hakim Khan's narrative of the events surrounding his family's history is deeply personal and, while it provides remarkable insight into the dynamics of the

---

8. TS, f. 74a; MT, 446; MTF, f. 47a.
9. Dubovitskii and Bababekov, "The Rise and Fall," 33. The original is found in A. Mukhtarov, *Dilshod i ee mesto v obshchestvennoi zhizni tadzhikskogo naroda v 19–nachale 20 veka* (Dushanbe, 1969), 296–97.
10. Babadjanov, *Kokandskoe Khanstvo*, 145.
11. Babadjanov singles out Nettleton, "Ruler, Patron, Poet," as one such example. For another, more recent example, see Paul Georg Geiss, *Pre-Tsarist and Tsarist Central Asia: Communal Commitment and Political Order in Change* (London: RoutledgeCurzon, 2003), 149.
12. MT, 546.

Shahrukhid rulers, it is also very likely to have been shaped by his own experiences. It is entirely possible, for example, that 'Umar Khan's alcohol consumption was actually quite moderate, and that Hakim Khan's assessment was exaggerated and, one might speculate, informed by a vindictive or even puritanical mind-set that he adopted after his exile and pilgrimage to Mecca, or by some other motivation. Looking ahead, one could suggest the same for his treatment of Jahangir Khoja's weakness for opium and also Madali Khan's infamous substance abuse, discussed below. But at least in terms of 'Umar Khan, it would be just as reasonable to suggest that the incorporation of alcohol into his court culture was consistent with his effort to emulate Timurid court culture, which famously permitted and at times, one might argue, even encouraged the consumption of wine.[13]

Another important facet of 'Umar's new approach to governance was restoring the trust of the Uzbek tribes through the immediate dismissal of the Ghalcha conscripts from 'Alim Khan's new army, the Gala Bahadur.[14] 'Alim had invested considerable resources into arming and training his Ghalcha slave-troops, and he relied on their loyalty to provide the protection he needed to advance his highly aggressive political reforms. We will never know how the history of Khoqand would have unfolded if 'Alim had been able to continue down that path. Instead, 'Umar favored the gentler, more stereotypically Timurid approach of governing through multiple constituencies, and his coup was successful at least partly because he was willing to restore the Uzbek tribes to their privileged military positions and dismiss the Ghalcha. The Uzbek tribal aristocracy rewarded him with their determined loyalty, and they maintained the momentum of 'Alim's conquests by expanding the boundaries of the khanate far to the north. Military successes went a long way toward consolidating 'Umar Khan's legitimacy in the eyes of his subjects and other political powers in the region. But 'Umar advanced a number of other initiatives that were at least as important in this regard.

LEGITIMACY IN A GOLDEN CRADLE

In her study on legitimacy in the post-Chinggisid Bukharan Amirate, Anke von Kügelgen illustrates in fine detail how the Manghit leadership used history writing

---

13. For a discussion of this theme, see Stephanie Honchell, "The Story of a Drunken Mughal: Alcohol Culture in Timurid Central Asia" (PhD diss., The Ohio State University, 2014), 79–92.
14. TS, f. 73b. According to Niyazi, while the Ghalcha corps was dissolved, those Tajiks who were especially skilled soldiers were retained in the Gala Bahadur.

as a way to identify a set of values and craft a historical narrative that equipped them with the legitimate right to rule as the amirs of Bukhara.[15] Some years earlier, Yuri Bregel advanced a similar argument regarding the production of the great history of Khwarezm that the historians Munis and Agahi assembled in early nineteenth-century Khiva.[16] One could say the same about history writing in Khoqand. The histories of Khoqand that have survived were all written for deliberate purposes, and the official chronicles that were written with the patronage of the Shahrukhid family betray an effort to present a carefully shaped vision of the past in support of their claim to legitimacy in Khoqand. Toward the end of his reign, 'Umar Khan himself patronized the authorship of the earliest chronicles of Khoqand, first the *'Umarnāma* and soon thereafter the *Shāh-nāma-i 'Umar-khānī*, to achieve precisely that objective.[17] At the same time, the Ming claim to legitimacy in Khoqand exhibits a number of unique qualities, and it merits further investigation.

For roughly a century after Shah Rukh Biy was elevated as the principal leader of the Ming, his dynastic descendants governed only as the biys of Khoqand. As observed in the previous chapter, 'Alim Khan appears to have been the first in his line to adopt the title of khan, which he seems to have done near the end of his reign in the wake of his victory over the Chinggisid ruler Yunus Khoja's sons in Tashkent and Khoqand's annexation of that city. From that point to the end of their reign in 1876, the Shahrukhids would retain the title of khan, although individual rulers would place a greater emphasis on other terminologies of kingship when it suited their purpose (e.g., amir, sultan, or even evoking the Mughals as padshah). But 'Umar Khan found that consolidating his brother's elevation of Khoqand as a khanate would require more than just adopting new regal terminology. He required a mechanism that would permanently place the legitimate right to rule over the Ferghana Valley in the hands of the Shahrukhids.

As Chinggisid legitimacy in Bukhara teetered and then collapsed during the first half of the eighteenth century, the Uzbek amirs across the region began looking elsewhere for successful models of leadership. The most successful of these models by far was the legacy left by Amir Timur, or Tamerlane, and his Timurid descendants.

---

15. Anke von Kügelgen, *Die Legitimierung der mittelasiatischen Mangitendynastie in den Werken ihrer Historiker* (Istanbul: Orient-Institut; Würzburg: Ergon-Verlag, 2002). Published in Russian translation as *Legitimatsiia Sredneaziatskoi dinastii Mangitov v proizvedeniiakh ikh istorikov (XVIII–XIX vv.)* (Almaty, 2004).
16. See especially the subsection "The work" in Bregel's introductory essay to Shir Muhammad Mirab Munis and Muhammad Riza Mirab Agahi, *Firdaws al-Iqbāl: History of Khorezm*, trans. and ann. Yuri Bregel (Leiden: E. J. Brill, 1988), xxv–l.
17. For a full discussion of Khoqand's historiography, see Beisembiev's KI.

Timur himself was a Turkic Muslim born in Shahrisabz, and he launched multiple large and successful campaigns across a territory that stretched from Delhi to Ankara, and from Isfahan deep into the Qipchaq Steppe. He defeated his adversaries and brought an extraordinary amount of wealth to his capital of Samarqand, which he adorned with great architecture.

Timur remains recognized as one of the most successful military commanders in the history of the region. In the fifteenth century, his heirs excelled as patrons of the arts and the sciences, leaving their own proud legacy in Islamic statecraft. In the sixteenth century, Timur's descendants gave rise to the great Mughal Empire, which flourished into the eighteenth century and which is still referred to in Central Asia as the Baburid Empire after its Central Asian founder. In the context of the eighteenth-century Bukharan crisis, it was this legacy, Ron Sela convincingly argues, that made Timur such a compelling alternative to the Chinggisids and propelled the creation of the *Tīmūr-nāma* literary genre, apocryphal stories that elevate Timur's personal achievements to mythological levels.[18]

At the turn of the nineteenth century, the Shahrukhids in Khoqand also looked to the Timurids to anchor their claim to legitimacy. They were not alone: Ibrahim Biy, the Keneges hakim of Shahrisabz, also appears to have claimed a Timurid ancestry.[19] From the early eighteenth century, the Manghit in Bukhara connected their reign to Timur in other ways as well, such as by incorporating a pilgrimage to the enormous grey-blue marble slab known as the Kök Tash or "Heavenly Stone" that had been part of Timur's throne as part of the political ritual for their coronation ceremony.[20] The ceremony involved spreading a white felt rug across the Kök Tash, the same āq kigīz derived from earlier Mongol traditions, and then elevating the newly enthroned ruler.

The Shahrukhids went even farther by crafting a mythological dynastic history that directly linked their own lineage to Babur himself. Doing so anchored their dynasty with a long tradition of political legitimacy in the Ferghana Valley, it enabled them to claim a genealogical connection with the wealth and power of

---

18. Ron Sela, *The Legendary Biographies of Tamerlane: Islam and Heroic Apocrypha in Central Asia* (Cambridge: Cambridge University Press, 2011).
19. Beisembiev cites Muhammad Salih on this point. See AIKC, 29.
20. Ron Sela, "The 'Heavenly Stone' (Kök Tash) of Samarqand: A Rebels' Narrative Transformed," *Journal of the Royal Asiatic Society* 17, no. 1 (2007): 29–30. Sela notes that the ornately carved stone was moved to its present location, the courtyard of the Gur-i Amir, Timur's mausoleum in Samarqand, only in the 1950s or 1960s. The Kök Tash should not be confused with the large slab of jade that serves as Timur's cenotaph. See Sela, "The 'Heavenly Stone,'" 22, 28.

Babur's heirs in India, and it linked their bloodline with Timur and the great legacy of the Timurid Renaissance in Central Asia. According to this history, the Uzbek Ming ruler Shah Rukh himself was a descendant of Babur's son, named Altun Beshik, who, when he was a baby, was tucked away in a golden cradle (*altun beshik*) and left behind in the Ferghana Valley prior to Babur's departure for Kabul and India. Laying claim to a Timurid lineage equipped the Shahrukhids with a compelling vision for political legitimacy that would appeal to virtually all constituencies across their realm.[21]

The existence of this legend has long been known—Nalivkin wrote about it in his history of Khoqand well over a century ago—but only in recent years has it received close and critical attention.[22] Most analyses have attributed the propagation of this legend to a Shahrukhid effort to justify their claim to rule as the Khans of Khoqand by linking their lineage with Chinggis Khan through Babur's mother, a Chinggisid princess. That explanation is unconvincing for several reasons, not the least of which is that during the six centuries that had unfolded since Chinggis Khan died in 1227, Chinggisid legitimacy passed only through his male descendants.[23] The Altun Beshik legend has come down to us in multiple variants—a number of which differ substantially—yet every one of them presents an entirely male dynastic history that links Shah Rukh with Altun Beshik and, through him, with Babur. In no variant of the legend does the lineage pass through a woman, nor is there a variant that continues the genealogy through Babur's mother to Chinggisid Khan. Additionally, the chroniclers themselves exhibit a clear emphasis on linking the Shahrukhids to Timur, and not Chinggis Khan: Muhammad Salih, for example, dismissively refers to the Manghits in Bukhara as the *nā'yib* or deputies to Amir Timur, while emphasizing that the Shahrukhids were of his own lineage.[24]

The discussion here does not offer a comprehensive comparative analysis of the multiple versions of the Altun Beshik legend codified in the chronicles.[25] It is well

---

21. Sela references this precise motivation in his introduction. See Sela, *The Legendary Biographies*, 17–18.
22. Nalivkin, *Kratkaia istoriia*, 47–51.
23. See. Timur K. Beisembiev, "Legenda o proiskhozhdenii kokandskikh khanov kak istochnik po istorii ideologii v Srednei Azii: po materialam sochinenii kokandskoi istoriografii," in *Kazakhstan, Sredniaia i Tsentralnaia Aziia v XVI–XVIII vv.* (Alma-Ata, 1983), 94–105; Beisembiev, *Ta'rikh-i Shakhrukhi*, 83–84; Babadjanov, *Kokandskoe Khanstvo*, 306–38; Bababekov, *Qōqan Tarikhi*, 20–22; Sela, *The Legendary Biographies*, 17–18.
24. TJT, f. 53b.
25. An attempt to provide such a discussion can be found in the chapter, Scott C. Levi, "The Legend of the Golden Cradle: Babur's Legacy and Political Legitimacy in the Khanate of Khoqand," in *History of Central Asia in Modern Medieval Studies: In Memoriam of Professor Roziya Mukminova*, ed. D. A. Alimova (Tashkent: Yangi Nashr, 2013), 102–18. However, that attempt fails to capture certain key

established that the legend is contrived, and so there is no benefit to be found in testing it for historical accuracy. The variations one finds in the existing versions of the legend clearly suggest that the story circulated orally and passed to codified text at different times. What follows is intended to provide only a short summary of the legend that highlights several features relevant to the present discussion.

Nearly all versions of the Altun Beshik legend begin with the narrative of Babur delivering his first son to the people of the Ferghana Valley as he abandons his homeland in the wake of his loss to the Shibanid Uzbeks. From there, accounts diverge. Some indicate that Babur dressed the baby in silk and golden clothing and carefully tucked him away in a golden cradle, which he then placed under a tree out in the wilderness.[26] In the version of the legend Muhammad Fazl Bek presented, Babur ordered one of his companions to stay behind and watch over the baby from a distance until the cradle should be discovered, at which time he was to report back to Babur. Most versions tell that, after some time, people from three (or four, or five) Uzbek villages (or tribes) happened upon the child. They happily claimed responsibility for him, and they divided Babur's inheritance between them. In Muhammad Fazl Bek's version, the Turghavut claimed the baby, the Saray claimed the clothing, and the Chingit claimed the cradle.[27] A Turghavut woman is reported to have named him Altun Beshik and raised him as her own.[28] Muhammad Salih relays a slightly different version, in which Babur is said to have personally named the child Altun Beshik, and also to have handed the baby over to the elders of five tribes, the Ming, Changinat, Pilakhan, Saray, and Turghavut, announcing: "Sardars, I am going to Khurasan and India and I leave behind my eight-month-old son. Perhaps my heirs will someday be necessary for you."[29] As an oral tradition, the legend appears to have exhibited considerable flexibility insofar as it appears to have been modified to incorporate those communities that were most important to Khoqand's political composition at any given point in time. Most of the versions are variants of this typology.

Mulla Avaz's account is notable in that it presents two different versions of the Altun Beshik legend and, while they are no less manufactured than other versions,

---

aspects of the legend's production and so the analysis it provides requires revision here. The most significant revision is in shifting the temporal placement of the legend's codification from the reign of Alim Khan to the reign of 'Umar Khan. This is in response to Aftandil Erkinov's convincing argument in favor of doing so, discussed below.

26. MTF, fols. 11a–15a; TJT, fols. 12a–14b.
27. Bababekov lists the Ming, Kirk, Qipchaq, and Qirghiz as the four groups who take responsibility for the baby. Bababekov, *Qōqan Tarikhi*, 21.
28. Tirghava is a village near to present-day Khoqand.
29. TJT, f. 12a.

the fact that they are steeped in actual historical events gives a sense of the effort that the Shahrukhids exerted to make the legend more believable.[30] Although nearly all versions begin with Babur leaving Altun Beshik alone in the Ferghana Valley, one of the variants he presents also differs in that it begins roughly a century later, in India, shortly after the death of Emperor Akbar in 1605. What follows is an abridged version with the parenthetical addition of dates and other information:

> At that time, a group of amirs threw their support behind the rebellious Sultan Khusrau (or Khusrau Mirza, 1587–1622), the eighteen-year-old son of the newly crowned Emperor Jahangir (Shah Selim, "Sahib Qiran Sani," r. 1605–27). At roughly this time, the group of rebellious amirs took Muhammad Muqim (b. Muhammad Hakim [1554–85] b. Humayun Shah [1508–56] b. Zahir al-Din Muhammad Babur [1483–1530]) to Kabul in the hope of taking the city, and eventually extending their control over the rest of the Mughal Empire and elevating Muhammad Muqim to the throne.[31] This plan was never realized, however, as Jahangir entered Kabul in 1607. The Timurid heir Muhammad Muqim and his close associate Mulla Zaman fled Kabul for Khurasan.
>
> From there, the fugitives continued on to Bukhara where the Toqay-Timurid ruler Wali Muhammad Khan (r. 1605–11) b. Jani Muhammad Khan (r. 1599–1603) welcomed them. Muhammad Muqim is then said to have spent three years in Bukhara before he succumbed to his desire to conquer the Ferghana Valley, the birthplace of his great-grandfather Babur. Muqim Khan prepared an army to unleash against the valley and return it to Timurid hands, but luck was not with him. In the ensuing battle, Muqim Khan was injured—stabbed but not killed—and he and his followers fled the battle into the valley and reached the village of Turghavah.
>
> It was at this time that Muqim Khan's pregnant wife, Sharaf al-Nisa Begim bint 'Ali Khan, delivered her child and died during childbirth. The mother was buried in Turghavah, and a conference of the amirs concluded that the child should be dressed in golden-embroidered clothing and left in the village, entrusted to two maidservants of two of Mulla Zaman's most trusted men, while the rest of the entourage made their way eastward to Kashgar in the hope of finding a physician to heal Muqim Khan's wounds. They aimed to put together an army in Kashgar and

---

30. TJN, fols. 17a–18a.
31. Muhammad Hakim was indeed a son of Humayun through Machuchuk Oyim. See Annette Beveridge, trans., *The History of Humayun: Humayun-Nama by Gul-Badan Begum* (reprint; New Delhi: Atlantic Publishers, 1989), 62–65. Further investigation in the Indian chronicles has yielded no evidence that he had a son named Muhammad Muqim.

return to take Andijan and, from there, the rest of the Ferghana Valley. But on Monday, the first day of the month Zia al-Hijjah 1019 (February 14, 1611), Muhammad Muqim died near the city of Osh. He was buried there and his followers dispersed in all directions.

At this point in his narrative, Mullah Avaz shifts to a different account of the Altun Beshik legend.[32] The author repeats that Muhammad Muqim had lost an important battle and had left behind "a son for whom Allah wanted to make a great state." Whereas Mullah Avaz previously related that four people were left in Turghavah to tend to the baby, here his account takes a different turn:

> The child was left alone in Buzghavah and was then discovered by four people belonging to four different nomadic tribes: the Ming, the Yuz, the Qipchaq, and the Kyrgyz. These wanderers recognized the elegantly dressed baby as a Baburid, and they took him to a village where he was raised under the common authority of all four tribes, and given four names: Altun Beshik, Humayun, Amir Elli, and Tangri Berdi Sultan.[33] As the boy grew to adulthood he was well educated in the art of hunting and he became famous among the Uzbeks and other nomadic tribal peoples (*aymokiya*) in the valley. Altun Beshik's senior wife was Qutli Khanim, the daughter of a leader of the Uzbek Ming tribe. They had a son who was named Tangri Yar Sultan (some accounts "Islamized" this name and instead called him Khuda Yar Sultan), and it was through him that Altun Beshik's lineage passed. When this boy was six years old he met with the Sufi Sheikh, Khoja Ahmad Kasani (1461–1542, known as Makhdum-i A'zam), who prophesied that the boy's descendants would forge a great dynasty.[34]

Over the next five generations, the senior position in the family passed from Tangri Yar Sultan to Yar Muhammad Sultan to Abu al-Qasim Khan to Sultan Asil, who served as senior family member for thirty-two years and left the leadership of the Ming to his son Shah Mast Bek, whom his Turkic subjects referred to as Chamashbek. Here, Mulla Avaz presents the story, mentioned in chapter 1 in the context of Shah Rukh's rise to power, that Chamashbek was a disciple of Lutfallah Chusti, a revered sufi sheikh who had left Samarqand for the Ferghana Valley. It was Sheikh Lutfallah Chusti who, Beisembiev observes, was said to have foretold that

---

32. TJN, fol. 18a.
33. TJN, fol. 18b.
34. TJN, f. 19a.

Chamashbek's descendants would some day be rulers over the Ferghana Valley.[35] In this version of the story, it would be four more generations before the leadership passed to Shah Rukh Biy, the son of 'Ashur Muhammad, who was twenty-seven years old when he defeated the khojas of Chadak.

There are numerous obvious inconsistencies in these accounts, one of which is the periodization of these two lineages: Muhammad Fazl Bek gives only 145 years for the leadership to pass through eleven generations from Altun Beshik (presumably born c. 1502) to Shah Rukh Biy (r. ca. 1709–21), while Muhammad Salih gives the same process a full 200 years to pass through twelve generations, and Mulla Avaz traces it through only ten generations.[36] Still, this is a surprisingly minor variation, which is indicative of the considerable attention that was devoted to the legend in official literature. The motivations for such attention are clear. First, it seems reasonable to expect that the Shahrukhids sought to enhance believability by incorporating elements from Shah Rukh's actual lineage, which they then creatively linked to Babur. This enabled the Shahrukhids to appropriate the cultural currency attached to Babur's Timurid ancestry, his own regal legacy in the Ferghana Valley, and also the very real achievements of the Timurid Emperors—Babur's "other descendants"—in India.[37] From the time of Akbar's reign, the magnificence of Babur's Indian Empire was very well known throughout Central Asia, and it was especially valued in Babur's own Ferghana Valley.

These key features of the legend are now well established, but dating the origin of the legend with any precision is another matter. The fact that Muhammad Salih referenced 'Alim Khan's propensity to refer to himself as "Baburi" at first glance seems a clear indication that the Altun Beshik legend was codified during his reign.[38] But recalling that Muhammad Salih wrote his account sometime after 1862, more than fifty years after 'Alim Khan's death, there is good reason to approach the information he presents with a measure of caution. It is possible that 'Alim Khan did indeed refer to himself as "Baburi," though it is equally possible that the suggestion that he did so was a later invention. In either case, one must distinguish between propagating a poorly defined popular tradition that seeks to link the Shahrukhid family with Babur on the one hand, and the creation of a very specific and detailed legend deliberately crafted to add credence to that linkage on the other.

---

35. AIKC, 14.
36. See the chart in Levi, "The Legend of the Golden Cradle," 115–16.
37. See Aftandil Erkinov, "Les Timourides, Modèles de Légitimité et les Recueils Poétiques de Kokand," in Écrit et Culture en Asie Centrale et dans le Monde Turko-Iranian, X–XIX Siècles, ed. Francis Richard and Maria Szuppe (Paris: Association pour l'avancement des études iraniennes, 2009), 285–330.
38. TJT, f. 23a. I have argued as much in the past. See Levi, "The Legend of the Golden Cradle," 108.

The first written account of the Altun Beshik legend is found in Mirza Qalandar Mushrif Isfaragi's *Shāh-nāma-i 'Umar-khānī*, which 'Umar Khan commissioned and which was completed circa 1822.[39] Babadjanov regards the earliest contemporary account linking the Shahrukhids with Babur to be 'Abd al-Karim Fazli Namangani's *'Umar-nāma*, a poem written shortly before the *Shāhnāma* was completed.[40] In Babadjanov's analysis of the *'Umar-nāma*, he finds no mention of Altun Beshik; rather, the genealogical connection between the Shahrukhids and Babur is presented simply as fact. He interprets this as the earliest evidence of an attempt to create a genealogical link to Chinggis Khan.[41]

Digging deeper, Aftandil Erkinov finds that, while oral traditions suggesting that the Ming had a Timurid ancestry may have circulated earlier, firm evidence of the propagation of that myth can be dated to the reign of 'Umar Khan even prior to the authorship of the *'Umar-nama*. A specialist in literary history, Erkinov has analyzed 'Umar Khan's poetry, which he authored under the pen name (*takhallūs*) of Amīrī. In the preface to the *Dīwān-i Amīrī*, Erkinov located a couplet, written in Chaghatai, in which 'Umar Khan himself declared:

> My rosebush is the offspring of a tree from Timur Kuragan's garden . . .
> The young tree of my creation is a new plant from the lawn of Babur Sultan.[42]

Erkinov's research suggests that 'Umar Khan had been dissatisfied with Fazli Namangani's *'Umar-nāma* precisely because it did not do enough in terms of establishing his legitimacy. He therefore found it necessary to commission Mushrif to do more than just simply allude to the genealogical connection: he ordered Mushrif to craft a convincing story that fleshed out the historical circumstances behind that connection.[43] In determining just how Mushrifi managed to achieve this goal, Erkinov located and worked through a collection of manuscripts that had been in

---

39. Aftandil Erkinov, "Fabrication of Legitimation in the Khoqand Khānate under the Reign of 'Umar-Khan (1225–1237/1810–1822): Palace Manuscript of 'Bakhtiyār-nāma' Daqāyiqī Samarqandi as a Source for the Legend of Altun Bīshīk," *Manuscripta Orientalia* 19, no. 2 (2013): 4 and note 8.
40. Babadjanov, *Kokandskoe Khanstvo*, 314–15.
41. Babadjanov argues that 'Umar Khan advanced a corresponding effort to link his ancestry to Sayyids, or descendants of the Prophet Muhammad, but that they refused to acknowledge him as such and his attempt failed. See the discussion in Babadjanov, *Kokandskoe Khanstvo*, 338–52.
42. Erkinov, "Fabrication of Legitimation, 4 and note 17. Erkinov cites the *Dīwān-i Amīrī*, copied in 1818–19, and located within the *Muhabbat-nāma*, held at the Istanbul University Library (Tur. 5452), f. 351b. A less elegant variant translated from a different text can be found in Nettleton, "Ruler, Patron, Poet," 138.
43. Erkinov, "Fabrication of Legitimation," 5. Citing Beisembiev, Erkinov observes that leaving a child behind, such as Babur is said to have done with Altun Beshik, is a common Turkic literary device.

'Umar Khan's private library.[44] One of these volumes, a copy of a medieval text known as the *Bakhtiyār-nāma*, includes no fewer than ten variants of stories that all revolve around a plot involving a boy who is lost and then eventually grows to become a ruler. While that fact in and of itself does not constitute the proverbial smoking gun, in his comparative analysis of the two texts, Erkinov finds "many identical plot points" and sufficient additional evidence to support the conclusion that this very manuscript was the inspiration for creating the Altun Beshik legend as it was presented in the *Shāh-nāma-i 'Umar-khānī*.[45] While the oral tradition of the Shahrukhid's genealogical connection to Babur may predate 'Umar Khan's reign, one can state with reasonable confidence that the Altun Beshik legend itself was a deliberate product of his court.

From the beginning of the nineteenth century, the Altun Beshik legend became widely accepted and incorporated as a key part of the Shahrukhid ruling ideology.[46] At the same time, the legend does not stand alone as the only means that the Shahrukhids used to advance their claims to legitimacy. In the wake of 'Alim Khan's tyrannical reign, 'Umar Khan turned to a faithful adherence to the more practical matters of the Timurid political legacy, crafted not so much by Timur himself as by his own son and heir who, perhaps coincidentally, was also named Shah Rukh (r. 1409–47). These include providing fair and just governance, patronizing Islamic religious institutions as well as art and culture, and doing so simultaneously and through multiple constituencies.[47] Such an approach gave rise to the Timurid Renaissance in the fifteenth century, and the Timurid prince Babur and his own heirs quite famously embraced similar methods in developing their own court culture in India.[48] Now, at the beginning of the nineteenth century, it served 'Umar Khan quite well, too.

A CULTURAL EFFLORESCENCE

The Altun Beshik legend was an important facet of 'Umar Khan's claim to legitimacy, but it was not enough only to claim a familial connection with the Timurids. If 'Umar was going to put any weight on that claim, he needed to recreate the Timurid court

---

44. Erkinov, "Fabrication of Legitimation," 9.
45. Erkinov, "Fabrication of Legitimation," 9.
46. Beisembiev, "Legenda," 95.
47. Scott C. Levi, "The Ferghana Valley at the Crossroads of World History, 1709–1822," *Journal of Global History* 2, 2 (2007), 230–31.
48. Lisa Balabanlilar, *Imperial Identity in the Mughal Empire: Memory and Dynastic Politics in Early Modern South and Central Asia*, London: I. B. Taurus, 2012; Stephen F. Dale, "The Legacy of the Timurids," *Journal of the Royal Asiatic Society* 3d ser., 8, 1 (1998), 43–58; Dale, *The Muslim Empires*, 71.

in his own realm or, more correctly, the image of the Timurid court that in the eighteenth century had come to inform popular understandings of what it was that made the Timurids preferable to the Chinggisids. With this goal in mind, 'Umar set out to transform his government from his brother's military enterprise into a more urbane institution, one that replicated the Timurid Renaissance in Herat during the celebrated reign of Sultan Husayn Baiqara (r. 1469–1506). He and his courtiers would prove their worth by echoing in Khoqand the achievements of such literary giants as 'Abd al-Rahman Jami (1414–92) and, of course, 'Alisher Nava'i (1441–1501).[49] 'Umar himself, writing as Āmirī, claimed to be second only to Nava'i in his skills: a dramatic exaggeration to be sure, but a comparison that was intended to demonstrate his Timurid ancestry and bolster his claims to legitimacy.[50] His efforts to achieve these goals are richly documented in the effusive treatments that his contemporary poets, or at least those who relied on him for their livelihood, and even much later chroniclers showered on him and his reign.

From his ascension to the throne in 1811, 'Umar generously offered patronage to artists, poets, historians, educators, and other scholars, many of whom had earlier fled his brother but now flocked to the khanate in large numbers. At the same time, he publicly mollified the religious orthodoxy through several initiatives: he eliminated those taxes that his brother imposed and that were not condoned by Islamic law; he returned the 'ulama to positions of real authority in his administration; he financed the construction of multiple Islamic institutions; and he appointed the austere Ma'sum Khan, who had remained loyal to 'Alim Khan even to the end, to serve as his Shaykh al-Islam, chief religious authority, advisor and moral compass for his court. The khanate's growing number of madrasas filled with students studying grammar, logic, philosophy, religion, debate, jurisprudence, and Qur'an commentary.[51]

In a further effort to contrast himself against his brother, at least in some contexts 'Umar early on deemphasized the designation of khan in favor of the Perso-Islamic padshah, or simply shah. This appears to reflect a desire both to be associated with the Mughal padshahs and also to bolster his claim to legitimacy through religious

---

49. See Aftandil Erkinov, "Imitation of Timurids and Pseudo-Legitimation: On the Origins of a Manuscript Anthology of Poems Dedicated to the Kokand Ruler Muhammad Ali Khan (1822–1842)," tr. by Jürgen Paul, Graduate School Asia and Africa in World Reference Systems, Martin Luther University, Halle-Wittenberg, Working Paper No. 5, 3; Aftandil Erkinov. "Les Timourides," 285–330.

50. Aftandil Erkinov, "Umarkhon tuzdirgan 'Muhabbatnoma' she'riy majmuasi tarikhiy man'a sifatida," in M. Iskhakov, ed., *Markaziy Osiio tarikhi: man'ashunoslik va tarikhnavislik izlannishlari, ilmiy to'plam*, Toshkent, 2009, 217–23; Aftandil Erkinov, "Noiob Qu'liozma Izidan," *Moziydan Sado* 44, 4 (2009), 20–21.

51. TJT, f. 51b.

means, which he further advanced by claiming to be the "savior of the state and *sharī'ah* [Islamic law]."⁵² Similarly, 'Umar's official seals and his coinage indicate that, almost upon his ascension to the throne in 1811, he assumed the decidedly Islamic titles of *amīr al-muslimīn* and *imām al-muslimīn* (Commander, or Leader of the Muslims).⁵³ This enhanced his efforts to draw legitimacy from a carefully articulated persona as a just and pious Islamic ruler who, as a staunch defender of Islamic law, claimed both "spiritual as well as secular authority."⁵⁴ It also contrasted with his Bukharan neighbor Amir Haydar's adoption of the still more ambitious title of *amīr al-mu'minīn*, the caliphal Commander of the Faithful, which he had printed on his own coins.

The contest for greater legitimacy among the Bukhara Manghit amirs and the Khoqand Ming khans reached the international stage as well. Komatsu Hisao finds that, in an effort to consolidate his own position, 'Umar Khan sent an embassy to Istanbul for the express purpose of appealing to "the Sultan-Caliph" to recognize his authority, to provide military support, and also to place Khoqand's status as an Islamic state higher than that of the Bukharan Amirate.⁵⁵ The gifts that 'Umar Khan's ambassador delivered to the Ottoman Sultan Mahmud II (r. 1808–39) included a manuscript, the *Muhabbat-nāma* (The Love Letter), which included the full collection of poetry written by the Timurid master of Chaghatai belles lettres, Alisher Nava'i, as well as 'Umar Khan's own *dīvān* (a collection of poems).⁵⁶ Ultimately, the Ottoman Sultan recognized the legitimacy of 'Umar Khan's rule independent of Bukhara, but he politely demurred from granting 'Umar either the military assistance he requested or the higher status he desired.⁵⁷ According to Hakim Khan, the Sultan designated 'Umar

---

52. See the discussion on 'Umar Khan's efforts to appear as a just and pious Islamic ruler in Babadjanov, *Kokandskoe Khanstvo*, 362–75.
53. MT, 452. Erkinov, "Fabrication of Legitimation," 7; Kočnev, "The Last Period of Muslim Coin Minting," 440. The title is a deliberate deviation from the caliphal title, *amīr al-mu'minīn*, "Commander of the Faithful." Erkinov's ability to place it already in 1811/12 challenges the interpretations by Nalivkin and Bartold, and more recently Beisembiev, Vohidov, and Babadjanov, who have argued that it was a later innovation.
54. Kočnev, "The Last Period of Muslim Coin Minting," 440.
55. Komatsu Hisao, "Khoqand and Istanbul: An Ottoman Document Relating to the Earliest Contacts between the Khan and Sultan," *Asiatische Studien, Études Asiatiques* 40, no. 4 (2006): 968. As noted in chapter one, contrary to the title of Hisao's valuable essay (and contrary to the Ottoman vizier's own statement on the matter), this was not, in fact, the earliest contact between these two powers. Recall that ninety years earlier the Shahrukhid ruler 'Abd al-Rahim Biy dispatched an embassy to Sultan Mahmud I (r. 1730–54), although that event did occur in 1730, ten years before the capital was established at Khoqand.
56. Aftandil Erkinov, personal communication. The *Muhabbat-nāma* is held at the Istanbul University Library, Ms. No. T 5452. See also Hisao, "Khoqand and Istanbul," 972.
57. Hisao, "Khoqand and Istanbul," 970–71. See also Hisao's annotated translation of the Ottoman decree, 978–81.

khān-i khānān (khan of khans) and sent him gifts that included a sword, two pistols, two watches, two pairs of binoculars, and an outfit made of Turkish silk.[58]

Nettleton relays a story that apparently circulated in Khoqand in later years and further articulates the distinction between the reigns of 'Alim and 'Umar as they took shape in popular memory. At some point in his reign, 'Alim Khan is said to have tried to impress the 'ulama by setting aside funds to finance the construction of a new mosque and madrasa. The construction materials had been purchased and gathered, when an Ishan convinced 'Alim not to go forward with his plans as it violated the tenet that "holy places may not be built with unjustly acquired means." Fearing what might happen if he should disregard the warning, 'Alim Khan instead used the materials to construct a fortress. This left it to 'Umar, who ruled "in accordance with God's law," to oversee the construction of religious institutions and earn the blessings that would come from doing so.[59]

That tradition provides the backdrop for two great building projects that 'Umar financed during his reign: the Jama' Masjid, or congregational Friday Mosque of Khoqand, and a grand madrasa as well.[60] At the ceremony launching the construction of the Jama' Masjid, it was said that 'Umar himself had gathered all of the 'ulama and literati and announced to them: "Any of you who can claim never to have strayed from the *sunna* (path or example) of the Prophet are invited to come and place the cornerstone brick." When nobody stepped forward, he placed the brick himself.[61] On completion of the madrasa, 'Umar is said to have proudly declared that he had "provided bountiful aid and support for professors and teachers . . . so that in the madrasas, from the tumult of the traffic of students of learned sciences, there was inspired dialogue in lofty discussion; and in the elementary schools was a hubbub from the great number of children for recitation of lessons."[62]

Following the example that his father set, 'Umar Khan also financed the construction of additional mosques and madrasas as part of his considerable and sustained patronage to the 'ulama. The effects of these policies had a lasting impact on the religious infrastructure in the khanate. In 1829, one visitor to Khoqand reported that there were 100 mosques in that city alone and some 400 across the khanate.[63]

---

58. MT, 532–33.
59. Cited in Nettleton, "Ruler, Patron, Poet," 133 and note.
60. TS, f. 81a. Muhammad Fazl Bek states that it was begun in his sixth year, MTF, f. 50a.
61. MTF, f. 50b.
62. *Kitab-i Dewan-i Āmir-i Fārghanā* (Tashkent, 1901), 4; "Āmirī," in *Dewan* (Tashkent, 1972), 3. Cited in Nettleton, "Ruler, Patron, Poet," 134 and note.
63. N. I. Potanin, "Zapiski o Kokandskom khanstve khorunzhago Potanina," *Vestnik Imperatorskogo Russkogo geograficheskogo obshchestva*, pt. 18, no. 2 (1856): 281. Cited in Nettleton, "Ruler, Patron, Poet," 135 note 37.

FIG. 4.1 Exterior Prayer Hall of the 'Umar Khan Mosque.
Author photo.

Additional insight into his motivations are provided by Niyazi, who suggests that his efforts earned him the goodwill of a number of religious leaders who, when called on, were all too willing to issue legal decisions (*fatwas*) in support of his actions.[64]

Construction was not limited to religious institutions, of course. 'Umar's administration continued to advance efforts to develop even more expansive irrigation networks, bazaars, caravanserais, and more. 'Umar himself ordered the Yangi Ariq extended to a length of more than eighty miles, and he added the new Khan Ariq as well as the Shahrikhan Say, which irrigated some 40,000 hectares, or more than 150 square miles and, Thurman notes, "remained the largest irrigation structure in the Ferghana Valley until 1940."[65] The Shahrikhan Say was constructed at least partly to support 'Umar Khan's efforts to encourage settlements around Shahrikhan, literally "The City of the Khan," a city that 'Umar himself established as a regal retreat in the eastern part of the valley in 1815/16.[66] In just the years since 'Alim Khan ordered the Yangi Ariq dug in 1800–1803, these three large-scale irrigation projects alone had expanded irrigation agriculture over roughly 10 percent of the Ferghana Valley.

64. TS, fols. 81b–82a.
65. Thurman, "Irrigated Agriculture," 14–15.
66. AIKC, 16.

The Shahrukhids' expansion of irrigation agriculture in the Ferghana Valley was a pragmatic solution to problems associated with managing conflict among an ethnically diverse and more densely populated region. But one could also argue that the Shahrukhids' agrarian policies represented yet another way that they sought to emulate the achievements of the fifteenth-century Timurids. In her own work on the fifteenth-century Timurids, Maria Subtelny demonstrates that Sultan Husayn Baiqara himself had quite deliberately used irrigation agriculture to appease multiple conflicting constituencies while simultaneously averting a growing fiscal crisis by expanding his agrarian tax base.[67] The results were extraordinarily successful for the fifteenth-century Timurid state, and Subtelny demonstrates how late Timurid policies gave rise to the great plantation-style agricultural estates of Khoja Ahrar (1404–90) and his descendants in and around Samarqand. The Timurid court of Herat was so clearly a model for 'Umar Khan that it seems reasonable to suggest he had much the same in mind for Ferghana.

The maintenance and progressive expansion of irrigation networks was the primary means that the Shahrukhids used to develop their agricultural economy and tax base, but it was not the only one. Russian colonial records from later in the nineteenth century suggest that it was at roughly this same time that Khoqand began welcoming Indian traders and financiers into the Ferghana Valley. For more than two centuries Indian merchant communities had been active in neighboring Bukharan territories, and I have elsewhere examined their role as long-distance traders and moneylenders deeply engaged in financing the agricultural economy.[68] Evidence of Indian merchant activity in the Ferghana Valley during the seventeenth and eighteenth centuries is lacking. But Russian records indicate that Indian merchants were ubiquitous in the Ferghana Valley by the 1860s, and they appear to have begun extending their reach into the khanate in the early nineteenth century. In a petition submitted in 1878 to the Russian Governor General Konstantin von Kaufman, thirteen Indian merchants signed a letter claiming that "more than seventy years ago people from our community came to this region in small groups to pursue business."[69] In subsequent decades their numbers grew, as did their involvement in the khanate's agricultural economy. Official records from the 1870s identify Indians

---

67. Maria Subtelny, *Timurids in Transition: Turko-Persian Politics and Acculturation in Medieval Iran* (Leiden: E. J. Brill, 2007).
68. For the most recent treatment, see Scott C. Levi, *Caravans: Indian Merchants on the Silk Road* (Gurgaon: Penguin, 2015). Other publications on this theme are listed in the bibliography.
69. Central State Historical Archive of the Republic of Uzbekistan, fond I-1, opis' 11, delo 39, lists 53–54. For further discussion, see Scott C. Levi, *The Indian Diaspora and Its Trade, 1550–1900* (Leiden: E. J. Brill, 2002), 250–58.

as owners of large amounts of immovable property, including shops, houses, caravanserais, and farmland.

As a patron of the arts, 'Umar Khan's court sponsored dozens of poets, and his own work earned him a place among their ranks. While much of the poetry produced at 'Umar Khan's court exhibits genuine artistic merit, one also finds sycophantic efforts that seem to have impressed the chroniclers but today appear rather saccharine. In 1821, a selection of 629 poems authored by some seventy court literati were codified in a single text, the *Majmū'a-i shā'irān*. The majority of these poems are intended to compliment 'Umar through imitation or shower praise on him, even going so far as to directly compare him to Sultan Husayn Baiqara.[70] The poet Sultan Khoja (d. 1834/35), a native of Samarqand who became famous in Khoqand under the *takhallus* of Adā, provides a poignant example:

> *If Adā's words (verses) are excelling over Nawā'ī, what is astounding in that?*
> *Since who is higher—shah 'Umar or sultan Husain Bāiqarā?*[71]

The following is an example of 'Umar Khan's own poetry, taken from his *dīvān*.[72]

Qašïŋğa tegüzmägil qalamnï,
Bu xat bilä buzmağïl raqamnï.

Butxānalar ičrä heč tarsā,
Bir körmädi sen kibi sanamnï.

'Āšiqlarïŋğa tarahhum etgil,
Köp aylama javr ilä sitamnï.

Naqši qadamïŋ muyassar olsa,
Naylay bu jihanda jāmi Jamnï.

---

70. Erkinov, "Imitation of Timurids," 6–13.
71. *Majmū'a-i shā'irān*, IVAN Ms. No. 7510, f. 121b, cited in Erkinov, "Imitation of Timurids," 11. The translation belongs to Erkinov. This was not the only such anthology to emanate from 'Umar's court, see Nettleton, "Ruler, Patron, Poet," 137.
72. 'Umarkhon (Amiriy), *Devon: Üzbek tilidagi she'rlar* (Tashkent: Fan, 1972), 251–52. Additional published examples of 'Umar Khan's poetry can be found in Zebo Qobilova, *Amiriy sher'iiati* (Toshkent: Fan, 2010).

Köŋlüm qušï tāyiri harimiŋ,
Sayd etmä kabutari haramnï.

Tā bevatan olmasun köŋüllär,
Zulfuŋdïn ayurma peču xamnï.

La'lïŋ ğamïdïn közüm tökär qan,
Behuda kečürmägil bu damnï.

Yoluŋda ğubāri rāh boldum,
Bašïmğa yetürmädïŋ qadamnï.

Sen yārdïn özgä kimgä dermen,
Köŋlümdägi dard ilä alamnï.

Bir kāsa šarābi arğuvāniy,
Pāmāl qïlur hujumi ğamnï.

Iqlimï vafā Amiridur-sen,
Ey šah, bu gadāğa qïl karamnï.

Do not let a pen touch your eyebrow,
Do not ruin the writing with a new line.

Devotees in idol temples
Have never seen a beauty like you.

Have mercy on those who are in love with you,
Do not torture them more.

If it was easy to make a picture of your footsteps,
What use would the goblet of Jam have for me?

The bird of my soul is the bird of your sanctuary,
Do not hunt down the sacred dove.

Do not make hearts lose their homeland,
Do not make the curls disappear from your locks.

The sorrow your ruby lips caused made my eyes shed bloody tears.
Do not let this moment pass in vain.

I became dust on the road for you,
And you still did not touch my head with your feet.

Without you, my beloved, how else could I make disappear
The sorrow and anxiety from my heart.

A gobletful of dark red wine,
Defeats the attacks of sorrow.

You are the Amir of the country of faithfulness,
Have mercy, please, on this beggar of yours.[73]

Although their own impressive contributions are notably absent from the *Majmū'a-i shā'irān*, women were also an important part of the literary court culture in Khoqand. The most famous of Khoqand's women poets was Nadira, the *takhallus* of none other than 'Umar Khan's principle wife, Mahlar Oyim (1792–1842), who authored some 10,000 verses and produced a dīvān of her own that included some 136 poems in Chaghatai Turkic and another 44 in Persian.[74] In addition to her creative work, Nadira and other elite women participated at 'Umar's court in multiple ways, including establishing waqfs in support of madrasas and other educational institutions. Among the madrasas these women financed, two were named in honor of women: one after Narbuta Biy's wife, and another after one of his daughters.[75] The following is an example of Nadira's poetry, taken from her dīvān.[76]

---

73. I attribute the selection of this poem, its transcription in Chaghatai, and its translation into English to Dr. Benedek Péri, who generously permitted its inclusion here.
74. Nettleton, "Ruler, Patron, Poet," 137.
75. Nettleton, "Ruler, Patron, Poet," 137–38.
76. The original is found in Aziz Qayumov, *Nodira (Ghazallar)* (Tashkent, 1958), 9. The poem is also available in the Uzbek publication by Mahbuba Qodirova, *Uvaisii, Nodira* (Toshkent: Fan, 1993), 141. For additional published treatments of Nadira's poetry, see Makhuba Kadyrova, *Nadira, Ocherk zhizni i tvorchestva* (Tashkent: Fan, 1967.) For more on the history of Urateppe, see the classic study by Akhror Mukhtorov, *Istoriia Ura-Tiube (konets XV–nachalo XX vv.)* (Moscow, 1998).

Tiyradur subhi našātïm, sāqiyā, keltir šarāb,
Šāmi hijrān zulmatïda jāmi maydur āftāb.

Mahi tābān yüzligim, har lahza yād etsäm seni,
Dudi bağrïmdïn čïqar ot ičrä tüšgän-dek kabāb.

Band etib zulfïŋ arā köŋlimni āzād etgäniŋ,
Quš učurgan-dek erür bağlab ayağïğa tanāb.

Kāš-ki āhïm nasimïdïn taharruk äyläsä,
Yār-kim ruhsārïğa gul bargïdïn salmïš niqāb.

Hajr āšubï balādur-kim, anï tašvišïdïn,
Qatrayi simāb yaŋlïğ köŋlim äylär iztirāb.

Šād erür ul šāhi davrān vaslï birlä xātirïm,
'Ayš davrānïğa saldï davri gardun inqilāb.

Bevafālar-dek seni hargiz farāmuš äylämäs,
Nādira, yādïŋnï äylär tā dami yavmulhisāb.

I am in a dark mood in the morning. Cupbearer bring some wine!
In the darkness of a lonely night wine is our sun.

My moon-faced beloved, I remember you every second.
My heart emits black smoke. It has fallen on a fire like a piece of kebab.

You bound my heart with your locks and then you told me to go.
It is like making a bird fly with its feet bound.

I wish that the wind of my sighs moved my beloved
Who had covered his/her face with a veil of rose petals.

The sorrow of separation tortures me.
This pain makes me feel like
A drop of pure mercury. My heart aches.

My mind was happy with the memories of my union
with the shah of our times,
The time of happiness was disturbed by the turn of fate's wheel.

I will never forget you, not like the unfaithful ones.
Nadira will remember you until judgment day comes.[77]

Nurten Kılıç-Schubel has directed attention to women's education in this period. Questioning notions of pervasive illiteracy beyond the elite, Kılıç-Schubel has observed that there was a much more widespread culture of women writing in the Ferghana Valley than just those who wrote at 'Umar's court in Khoqand, and many of these were most decidedly not the political elite. Arguably more talented than Nadira, and certainly more interesting than her, was Dilshad (1800–1905/6), who authored the poem, excerpted above, chastising 'Umar for orchestrating the 1818 massacre in her hometown of Urateppe. Having survived that horrific event, she and several thousand other residents of Urateppe were marched into a life of captivity in the Ferghana Valley. Her autobiographical *Tārīkh-i muhājirān* (History of the migrants) documents this event, which initiated a very long lifetime of writing.[78]

It is important to emphasize that there may be good reason to question the historical veracity of Dilshad's account as her work and interpretations would have been shaped by her own biases and agendas. This is especially so later in life, when she would have been writing as a subject of a Russian imperial administration that was overtly hostile to the Khoqand khans it had displaced and had a vested interest in disparaging them. Nevertheless, her accounts provide a powerful counterbalance to the obsequious treatments penned by 'Umar Khan's chroniclers. To an extent, these same chroniclers make certain observations that support Dilshad's perspective, such as Hakim Khan's own report that, after one failed attempt to take Urateppe, 'Umar ordered his troops to burn the wheat fields "so that only dirt and mud remained" as

---

77. I attribute the selection of this poem, its transcription in Chaghatai, and its translation into English to Dr. Benedek Péri, who generously permitted its inclusion here.
78. For further discussion, see the chapter by Nurten Kılıç-Schubel, "Writing Women: Women's Poetry and Literary Networks," in *Horizons of the World: Festschrift for İsenbike Togan*, ed. İlker Evrim Binbaş and Nurten Kılıç-Schubel (Istanbul: İthaki Publishing, 2011), 405–40.

FIG. 4.2 Women's Section of the Khan's Court.
Turkestanskii Al'bom, 1865–72, Library of Congress, Prints & Photographs Division, LC-DIG-ppmsca-14912.

a punishment to the resistant population.[79] In her study of women's writing in this context, Kılıç-Schubel presents a remarkable anecdote from Dilshad's work. The setting is placed not long after the captives from Urateppe arrived in Khoqand, with Dilshad being escorted into 'Umar Khan's private chamber:

> I was brought into the presence of the khan by one of his harem. He was wearing his bedclothes. There was a table between me and him and there was a pomegranate on it. The khan at first treated me well, but in my eyes he was still an oppressor and an executioner. Then he showed me a pomegranate and said, "Hey you, poet daughter of a Tājik, compose a poem. He said, "What do you say of this pomegranate?" I said, "You filled it with the blood of young girls."[80]
>
> 'Umar was naturally incensed, and he punished young Dilshad by giving her

---

79. MT, 479. Hakim Khan reports that he next withdrew to Khojand, "where he rested with local girls."
80. MT, 411–12.

away as a slave. As fortune would have it, the recipient of his gift was also from Urateppe; he took pity on Dilshad and helped her escape the palace.

Nadira and Dilshad represent only two of the many women poets who flourished in the Khanate of Khoqand. Just a few of the many others include Jahan Atun Uvaysi, Mu'azzam, Anbar Atin, and Mahzune, all of whom were highly productive.[81] Kılıç-Schubel finds that women writers emerged "from all walks of life," and, while some enjoyed court culture and made their impact through both artistic production and patronage, others drew their experiences from "poverty and displacement rather than privilege."[82] What is perhaps most fascinating is that these women writers, all of them, were well educated in the Persian and Chaghatai literary cultures, as well as the more classical styles of Islamic education. Their numbers were significant, and the literary culture that they produced and participated in was vibrant and widespread throughout the Ferghana Valley, and beyond.

'Umar Khan was not the progenitor of this literary culture, and he did not revolutionize women's education in nineteenth-century Central Asia. The active engagement of women in the public sphere has a long history in Central Asia irrespective of their activities in the Khanate of Khoqand.[83] But an analysis of this literature does suggest that 'Umar Khan and his court can be credited with continuing to promote women's education and using it as part of his larger effort to appear as a just, cultured, benevolent and, above all, "Timurid" monarch.

TERRITORIAL EXPANSION

'Umar Khan shaped Khoqand's court culture to mimic the Timurids. At the same time, he also aimed to demonstrate the merits of his Timurid ancestry through military expansion. In addition to Khoqand itself, at the time of his reign the khanate consisted of at least nine additional vilayats: Marghilan, Namangan, Shahrikhan,

---

81. I am grateful to Donohon Abdugafurova for bringing the work of Anbar Atin ("Otin") to my attention.
82. Kılıç-Schubel, "Writing Women," 405.
83. For more on sedentary women's history in the Ferghana Valley, see Vladimir Nalivkin and Maria Nalivkina, *Muslim Women of the Fergana Valley: A 19th-Century Ethnography from Central Asia*, ed. Marianne Kamp and trans. Mariana Markova and Marianne Kamp (Bloomington: Indiana University Press, 2016). Although the Nalivkins' observations were recorded during the Russian imperial period, they hold clear relevance for the pre-imperial period as well.

Chust, Khojand, Andijan, Qurama, Tashkent, and Navad.[84] 'Umar's first concern was to ensure that the valley remained protected from Bukharan incursions, and he no doubt had that in mind when, in 1813, he dispatched Khoqand's forces to Shahrisabz in support of Keneges efforts to remain independent of Bukharan rule.[85] With that achieved, he next directed his attention northward, to the steppe.[86]

Khoqand's campaigns to the north hinged on maintaining control over Tashkent, which 'Umar himself had led his brother's forces to victory over several years earlier. Should Khoqand lose that key city, supply lines would be broken and his possessions in the steppe would be isolated and unprotected. With that in mind, 'Umar personally returned to Tashkent to consolidate his control there through the generous distribution of gifts, hosting banquets and feasting with his subjects, and executing those "few trouble makers" whom he feared may pose an immediate or potential threat.[87] Following a successful visit, he returned to Khoqand and soon thereafter continued to pursue his brother's vision for a new vilayat in the steppe.

In 1815, 'Umar dispatched an army to conquer the city of Turkestan ("the Fortress of Hazrat Sultan Yasavi").[88] The campaign was a resounding success, and it placed not just the city of Turkestan, but also the Yasavi shrine and the surrounding areas all in Khoqand's hands. 'Umar appointed a new hakim for Turkestan and held a grand celebration at the Yasavi shrine. 'Umar himself is said to have offered a sacrifice of seventy sheep at the event, enough to fill the enormous bronze cauldron that still dominates the shrine's *kazandyk* (great hall).[89] As the army returned southward, they were feted in the streets of Tashkent with a celebration and parade.[90]

In the wake of that victory, during the later years of 'Umar's reign and also under his son, Muhammad 'Ali Khan (r. 1822–42), Khoqand expanded its control over virtually all of what is today southern Kazakhstan and Kyrgyzstan. Khoqand aimed to protect this new vilayat against Kazakh tribes and the encroaching Russians by developing a chain of fortresses over the more than 600-mile line that stretched from

---

84. MT, 521.
85. AIKC, 16.
86. MT, 449–51. 'Umar's early successes in the north may be partly attributed to the fact that, in 1812, Russia was fully occupied with Napoleon's invasion and was therefore in a poor position to aid its Kazakh allies.
87. TS, fols. 74b–76b; MTF, 49a.
88. Rajab Qushbegi appears to have commanded this army, although the sources contradict each other on this matter. Cf. TS, f. 76a, MTF, 49a.
89. Nettleton, "Ruler, Patron, Poet," 132. As Hakim Khan describes the event, the great cauldron at the Yasavi shrine was filled with the meat of seventy-three sheep, but 'Umar provided only eighteen of them. MT, 452.
90. TS, f. 78a.

FIG. 4.3 Turkestan, with Yasavi Mausoleum.
Turkestanskii Al'bom, 1865–72, Library of Congress, Prints & Photographs Division, LC-DIG-ppmsca-12197.

Aq Masjid eastward to the Ili River.[91] Located on the banks of the Syr Darya near the Aral Sea, Aq Masjid was an especially important possession as it enabled Khoqand to assert control over trade routes leading to Russia not just from Khoqand, but also from Bukhara and Khiva. These territorial acquisitions were greatly beneficial to Khoqand, just as they were devastating losses for those Kazakhs who had long benefitted from taxing the trade that passed through their territories in the southern steppe. For the past century, the Kazakhs had worked with Russian interests to achieve their goals in the area. Now, Janet Kilian observes, "the Kazakhs' fractured khanates could no longer benefit from economic control over those cities, and Kazakh society transformed into a different kind of nomadism with different motives to ally with Russia against their common enemies."[92] This alliance would eventually undermine Khoqand's hold over its steppe territories, and much more

91. AIKC, 15.
92. Janet Marie Kilian, "Allies and Adversaries: The Russian Conquest of the Kazakh Steppe" (PhD diss., George Washington University, 2013), vi, 3–6.

than that as well. The expanding Russian Empire would soon subsume them all, but the legacy of Khoqand would, in some ways, continue. Indeed, many of the Khoqandi steppe fortresses would eventually transform into the medium and large cities that dominate urban life in southern Kazakhstan and northern Kyrgyzstan today.[93]

'Umar Khan enjoyed less success in his struggles against his Bukharan neighbors. That conflict centered on Urateppe, which remained largely independent but was at that time allied with Bukhara. This fanned 'Umar's fear that Amir Hydar would take advantage of Khoqand's focus on the steppe to use it as a staging ground for an invasion of the valley. Again, it is neither possible nor desirable to describe here even the major Khoqandi campaigns waged against Urateppe. To do so would weigh down the present discussion with an endless string of artillery barrages and gunfire "so heavy the bullets came down like rain," sniper assaults, siege engines, and the use of explosive devices to breach walls that were being fortified to make them stronger and more suitable to defend against artillery.[94] In the end, Khoqand would prove unable to launch a campaign against Bukhara, primarily because the two forces were of comparable strength and the Khoqandi army could not move with confidence past Jizzakh.[95] With their persistent focus on military and political matters, the chronicles make it quite clear that siege warfare, stronger fortresses, and the advancement of artillery and other gunpowder weapons had made military advancements in the sedentary zone a slow, plodding affair dominated by infantry troops. By the turn of the nineteenth century, the day of the lightning-fast nomadic cavalry was effectively gone and the Military Revolution was at last in full swing in Central Asia.[96]

---

93. AIKC, 15.
94. For example, see MT, 521; MTF, f. 52b.
95. MT, 521–27. 'Umar learned of a rebellion in Bukhara and seriously considered campaigning there to take over the city. He elected not to because he could not ensure that his rear would remain safe from potential attacks emanating from Urateppe and Jizzakh.
96. The scholarship on the early modern Military Revolution is abundant. For the most comprehensive introduction to the field affects, see Geoffrey Parker, *The Military Revolution: Military Innovation and the Rise of the West, 1500–1800*, 2nd ed. (Cambridge: Cambridge University Press, 1996). For the debate surrounding the application of the term within Europe, see Clifford J. Rogers, ed., *The Military Revolution Debate: Readings on the Military Transformation of Early Modern Europe* (Boulder, CO: Westview Press, 1995). For the importance of approaching the Military Revolution as a collaborative process involving European, Asian, and other powers, see Ágoston, *Guns for the Sultan*; Richard M. Eaton and Philip B. Wagoner, "Warfare on the Deccan Plateau, 1450–1600: A Military Revolution in Early Modern India?" *Journal of World History* 25, no. 1 (2014): 5–50; Geoffrey Parker and Sanjay Subrahmanyam, "Arms and the Asian: Revisiting European Firearms and Their Place in Early Modern Asia," *Revista de Cultura* (Macau), 26 (2008): 12–42. For the introduction of gunpowder weaponry into Central Asia in the eighteenth century, see Holzwarth, "Bukharan Armies," 273–354.

Military superiority was important, but it was not always enough to ensure victory. In the wake of Khoqand's victories in the steppe, the Bukharan-appointed hakim of Urateppe, Mahmud Khan Tura, had sensed that the khanate's power in the region was on the rise, and he dispatched a letter to 'Umar Khan announcing his desire to change his allegiance in favor of Khoqand.[97] 'Umar was ecstatic, and just six days later he arrived at the gates of Urateppe in front of an army of 10,000 Khoqandi troops. Entrance to the city was granted to a group of ambassadors, followed by 'Umar Khan himself. Mahmud Khan Tura formally capitulated and showered 'Umar with gifts. 'Umar returned to Khoqand confident that Urateppe was in his hands, but soon thereafter Mahmud Khan reneged and shifted allegiance again in favor of Bukhara.[98] 'Umar then returned to Urateppe, Mahmud Khan again capitulated, and this time 'Umar took him captive and brought him back to Khoqand. Conflict with Bukhara seemed imminent, and 'Umar looked to the now senior Tajik commander, Rajab Qushbegi (formerly Rajab Diwanbegi), to settle the matter.[99]

Rajab had repeatedly proven himself a talented soldier and able administrator. At the beginning of 'Alim Khan's reign he had quite literally saved the khanate by coming to 'Alim's aid in repelling Yunus Khoja's army of Kazakh troops from Tashkent. That earned him the position of Amir-i Lashkar, but only until 'Alim Khan's purges motivated Rajab to flee to Bukhara. Following his return to Khoqand in 1811, 'Umar elevated him as Rajab Diwanbegi and appointed him hakim of Tashkent and its environs, a position that placed him in charge of some 400,000 Kazakhs and in which he served until 1816.[100] It was Rajab who led 'Umar's campaign against Turkestan, and in the wake of that victory he was elevated yet again, as Rajab Qushbegi.

With Mahmud Khan Tura removed from his post, 'Umar now appointed Rajab Qushbegi to the critical post of hakim of Urateppe and charged him with defending it against the coming Bukharan attack. But when Muhammad Rahim, the Bukharan Ataliq, arrived and put the city under siege with a combined force of Manghit and Yuz soldiers, Rajab was incapable of mounting an effective defense. After several days, he withdrew back to Khoqand and left Urateppe once again in Bukharan hands. 'Umar Khan's attack of Urateppe in 1818, which resulted in the terrible devastation that Dilshad's poetry depicts, appears to have been a punitive answer to this loss.

---

97. MT, 527; AIKC, 416–17. Mahmud Khan was related to Amir Hydar and served as hakim of Urateppe for some twelve years.
98. MTF, fols. 53a–54a; MT, 449.
99. MT, 457–60.
100. AIKC, 220.

Events surrounding this particular instance underline the importance of Urateppe in the power struggle between Khoqand and Bukhara, and also the historical 'Umar Khan rather than the mythologized literary figure. Rajab Qushbegi's loss infuriated 'Umar Khan, and he seems to have suspected that Rajab gave up too easily and may even have conspired with Muhammad Rahim, a man with whom Rajab had been close during his years of exile in Bukhara and who now assumed the position of hakim of Urateppe. 'Umar nearly killed Rajab right then and there, but as Rajab was sixty-six years old and nearing the end of his service, 'Umar was convinced not to act on his emotions. Soon thereafter, an unnamed conspirator capitalized on Rajab Qushbegi's weakened stature by drafting a letter in Rajab's name and sending it to 'Alim Khan's surviving son in Qarategin (modern Tajikistan), promising him the throne if he would return to Khoqand.[101] 'Umar learned of the letter and confronted Rajab, who maintained that he had nothing to do with it. 'Umar publicly forgave him, but then several days later, he ordered Rajab to escort Irnazar Diwanbegi from his post in Qurama to a higher position as hakim of the vilayat of Turaqurgan and Namangan.[102] Irnazar Diwanbegi strangled Rajab Qushbegi in the middle of the night and then tossed his body into the cold waters of the Syr Darya River.[103]

KHOQAND'S BRIEF GOLDEN AGE

In the wake of his victory over Yunus Khoja's heirs in Tashkent, 'Alim Khan established Khoqand as a khanate. This broke six centuries of precedent clearly set by the Chinggisid *yasa* (law) and respected by Amir Timur and his Timurid heirs that the right to rule as a khan was restricted to descendants of Chinggis Khan as traced exclusively through his male lineage. 'Alim Khan's decision to adopt that title illuminates an important period of transition in Central Asian political culture. This is especially so in the Ferghana Valley where the Uzbek Ming Shahrukhid "khans" began to claim a genealogical link to Babur, and through him to Timur. The Shahrukhids' claim to a Timurid ancestry became a cornerstone of their claim to legitimacy.

The Altun Beshik legend was crafted during 'Umar Khan's reign to advance the plausibility of that claim. The legend exists in multiple variants, none of which exhibit any concern with the Chinggisids and all of which trace the family's ancestry back

---

101. MT, 509.
102. MT, 511.
103. MT, 511–12. Several slaves assisted him in the murder of Rajab.

through an exclusively male lineage to Babur, the last Timurid ruler in the Ferghana Valley and the founder of the great Mughal Empire. This enabled the Shahrukhids to attach their claims to legitimacy to Timur and his Timurid heirs, whose Turkic-Muslim heritage, steeped in local tradition, loomed large in the popular culture of the time. While the accounts presented in the *Tīmūr-nāma* literature bear little resemblance to reality, their popularity in the eighteenth century illustrates that in the public imagination Timur had transformed from the historical conqueror into a legendary folk hero. The material presented here only adds to the body of evidence that Sela marshals in support of his argument that, in the context of the eighteenth-century Bukharan crisis, the Timurid legacy had risen to eclipse even the legacy of Chinggis Khan himself.

At the same time, the Shahrukhids advanced other means to bolster their claims to legitimacy. Religious legitimacy mattered as well, and the Altun Beshik legend folds in tales of the *barakat* (blessings) of both Makhdum-i Azam and Sheikh Lutfallah Chusti, two exceptionally important religious icons whose approval carried a substantial amount of cultural currency in the valley. Military expansion mattered, too, as did the development of a court culture that emphasized literary and artistic production, alongside the patronage of multiple religious and tribal constituencies. Khoqand's subjects meanwhile continued to enjoy a vibrant commercial economy based on the continuation of trade with Qing markets and growing trade with Russia through Tashkent, and the expansion of irrigation agriculture and the agrarian economy within the Ferghana Valley. As the khanate strengthened, 'Umar Khan and other Khoqandi elite, both men and women, financed the construction and operation of many hundreds of mosques, madrasas, sufi hostels, and other pious foundations across the valley, many of which serviced small localized populations while others were truly quite grand.

One should not forget, however, that the historical 'Umar Khan was a more complicated historical figure than the pious, benevolent, even-handed, and fair-minded Islamic ruler that the chroniclers present. A careful reading of the sources exposes him as fully capable of employing the same brutality as his brother and the same tendency toward excess as his son. While he governed with greater sensitivity to his constituencies, the codified image of his court was in essence a carefully crafted propaganda intended for public consumption.

One should also be careful not to overstate 'Umar's role in the development of Islamic culture in the valley. In the eighteenth and nineteenth centuries, rulers across Central Asia endeavored to attract religious scholars and literati to their courts, and they also directed substantial patronage to mosques and other Islamic institutions. Even within the smaller arena of the Ferghana Valley, investment in religious institutions had become commonplace already during the reign of 'Umar's father, Narbuta Biy. Nevertheless, 'Umar Khan's eleven-year reign has come to represent the golden age in the history of the Khanate of Khoqand: the renewal of the Timurid Renaissance, which would be lost again all too soon.

Five

A NEW CRISIS, 1822–1844

WHEREAS 'UMAR KHAN has gone down in history as the greatest ruler of Khoqand, his son and successor Muhammad 'Ali, or Madali Khan, is attributed with squandering all that his father achieved. Both representations suffer from a degree of hyperbole: much as 'Umar was not the paragon of Islamic virtue that his chroniclers present him to be, Madali Khan was something more than a morally bankrupt buffoon. He is undeniably guilty of excesses and poor judgment. But throughout his twenty-year reign Khoqand grew to its greatest size, annexing the full extent of the southern steppe. He also expanded Khoqand's territory deep into the Pamirs and, working alongside the Afaqi Khojas, greatly enhanced Khoqand's commercial reach in Qing territory.

One cannot escape the conclusion that it was Madali Khan's unwillingness, or perhaps inability, to conceal his debauchery and provide charismatic leadership that led to his downfall. While populations across the region were fully capable of rising up and casting off much greater powers than Khoqand, his people would refuse to come to his aid in the face of a Bukharan invasion. With his own army choosing flight over fight, Madali Khan's reign, and his life, ended in 1842. Within just a few weeks, these same Khoqandis would evict the Bukharans, further demonstrating their own agency in the matter. Nevertheless, the damage was done, and for a multitude of reasons, many of which had nothing to do with Madali Khan's troubled reign, Khoqand would never fully recover.

MADALI KHAN

In late 1821 'Umar Khan fell ill and on January 12, 1822, at approximately thirty-six years of age, he died in bed.[1] Ma'sum Khan, brother-in-law to 'Umar and Sheikh al-Islam for Khoqand, gathered the amirs and, together, they agreed that 'Umar Khan's fourteen-year-old son Muhammad 'Ali, known to all as Madali, would succeed his father. Ma'sum instructed his own son, Hakim Khan, to fetch his cousin from the harem. Surrounded by his family and his amirs, Madali was placed on the *āq kigīz* (white felt) and elevated as the new Khan of Khoqand.

At this point, Hakim Khan's account of the inner workings of the court become exceptionally important as he and Madali Khan had been raised together and throughout their adolescence the two cousins were, based on Hakim Khan's telling, very close friends. Hakim Khan's *Muntakhab al-tawarikh* is replete with personal stories of the two cousins' adventures and escapades, inviting comparisons with the likes of Huckleberry Finn and Tom Sawyer. Just a few of the many examples include month-long hunting trips with 'Umar Khan, using falcons and dogs to hunt for quail and wild birds in the fall, and then for lions and gazelles in the winter; stealing tobacco from 'Umar Khan and then earning his profound gratitude by generously gifting him some when he had run out in the midst of putting Jizzakh under siege; getting lost in the wilderness; getting drunk and chasing after an enemy soldier on horseback; flirting with girls; and jabbing thorns into the rear ends of horses to make the horses jump and cause the pretty women in 'Umar's harem to fall to the ground, giving Hakim Khan and Madali the opportunity to lay their hands on the women as they helped them back onto their horses.[2] 'Umar Khan scolded the pair for this last infraction, which resulted in many scrapes and several broken bones. One escapade that led to a considerably harsher ending for the two involved Madali falling in love with his father's new wife, the exceptionally beautiful young Khan Padshah.[3]

It was Mahmud Khan Tura, the deposed Bukharan hakim of Urateppe, who first told 'Umar of the remarkable beauty of Khan Padshah, a descendant of Khoja Ahrar on her father's side (as was Mahmud Khan himself) and Makhdum-i Azam on her mother side. 'Umar was interested, and Mahmud promised that he would deliver her to him in exchange for an official governmental position in Khoqand. 'Umar

---

1. MT, 546.
2. MT, 467–68, 471, 498–99, 526, 538.
3. MT, 489.

agreed, and two senior women were dispatched to speak with Khan Padshah's father, Sayyid Ghazi Khoja, about arranging a marriage. The khoja refused to agree on the grounds that, at approximately fifteen years old, she was still a child. 'Umar's advisors pressured him to be patient, but without even having seen her, 'Umar had grown obsessed and he sent one of his officials to convince Sayyid Ghazi to surrender his daughter. Visibly distressed and no doubt fearing for his life, the khoja eventually relented and gave his permission. Two days later, the girl was brought to 'Umar's palace at his royal retreat in the city of Shahrikhan, and the two were married in an opulent ceremony.[4] For reasons one can only guess, 'Umar became ill that night and, reportedly, did not consummate the marriage.[5] The two were married for two years and four months before 'Umar passed, and though Madali later made much of the fact that the marriage was not consummated on the wedding night, it is difficult to believe that it was not consummated at all.[6]

Some months after the wedding, Madali and Hakim Khan were visiting in the harem and Khan Padshah offered to serve them tea. She was just a few years older than he was and no doubt lonely and happy to have some company. The three had spent time together in the past, but Hakim Khan recalls that it was then that Madali began to fall in love with his father's wife. Recognizing the gravity of the offense, Hakim Khan berated his cousin, warning him that he had "fallen onto the road of the devil" and that "nobody does this, not Muslim, not *kafir*."[7] But nothing could be done: Madali was in love, and after 'Umar Khan's death in 1822 the newly enthroned khan took his father's widow into his own harem. Throughout Hakim Khan's lengthy treatment of his best friend and cousin's reign, where the scribe spells out Madali's name, it is followed by the shameful epithet of *modarzan* (mother-wife).

The reason for Hakim Khan's animosity toward his cousin is not difficult to ascertain. For two decades Hakim Khan and his father had enjoyed an exceptionally close familial relationship with both 'Alim Khan and 'Umar Khan. This had incited jealousy among some amirs, but Ma'sum Khan's austere manner and evenhanded ways had earned him sufficient trust among his brothers-in-law to offset threats and challenges. With a fourteen-year-old boy serving as the khan of Khoqand, that was all about to change, and very quickly.

It is important to stress that Hakim Khan's account of Madali Khan's reign and the factors that led to its undoing is exceptionally detailed, very personal, and,

---

4. MT, 489–94, 512–18.
5. MT, 517.
6. AIKC, 174.
7. MT, 541.

considering the terrible conflict that drove the two cousins apart, firmly biased against Madali Khan. Hakim Khan's account focuses a great deal of attention on his cousin's shortcomings and failures, much more than other chroniclers. This may be partly because Hakim Khan was quite close to Madali Khan and so he had considerably more firsthand information about the ruler's behavior. But there may be other reasons that also merit consideration. Hakim Khan may, for example, have adopted a more puritanical view toward alcohol consumption after he completed the hajj, and that may have shaped his narrative in some ways. One might also reasonably expect his account to exhibit a certain degree of animosity toward a cousin, former friend, and ruler who had treated the author and his father badly. Nevertheless, Hakim Khan's account is much more than a vindictive excoriation. Other chroniclers corroborate Hakim Khan's most serious claims regarding Madali Khan's excessive drinking and problematic behavior, their impact on his reign, and their deleterious effect on the Khanate of Khoqand.[8]

From the outset, Madali appears to have turned his attention to enjoyment over statecraft. Ma'sum Khan's efforts to advise him fell on deaf ears, and they were met with hostility by the other amirs who in 1823 convinced Madali Khan to release him from service and be rid of him by sending him on the hajj.[9] Madali Khan also removed Hakim Khan from Khoqand, though initially he did so by assigning him to a very desirable government position as hakim of Namangan and Turakurgan.[10] Not long after, Madali Khan grew suspicious that a coup was in the works, and knowing what his cousin could tell others about his personal life, he ordered Hakim Khan removed from his post, and then imprisoned.[11] Hakim Khan spent four months as a captive, after which he and roughly one hundred other Khoqandi nobles were ordered to leave the Ferghana Valley.[12] Several were killed en route, while others were permitted to travel out of the khanate and find new residences elsewhere. Many fled to Shahrisabz which, as an independent power in the region, had come to serve as a neutral refuge of sorts for nobles who found it necessary to flee Khoqand and Bukhara.[13] Hakim Khan would eventually settle there himself, but first he traveled by caravan

---

8. Whereas Niyazi's account often differs markedly from Hakim Khan's account, he also chastises Madali Khan for permitting liquor, prostitutes, and gambling in the palace. See TS, f. 99a–b.
9. MT, 554; AIKC, 426–27.
10. MT, 553.
11. MT, 557–62.
12. MT, 562.
13. On the role that Shahrisabz played in the circulation of elite among urban centers in the region, see Eckart Schiewek, "À propos des exilés de Boukhara et de Kokand à Shahr-i Sabz," in *Boukhara La Noble*, ed. Pierre Chuvin, Cahiers d'Asie centrale, no. 5. Tachkent, 1998, 181–97.

northward to Shamai (modern Semipalatinsk), and then on to Omsk, which he described as "a big and beautiful city" with a vibrant commercial economy. He found the Irtysh River to be grand and heavily trafficked by boats that brought merchants and their goods to the region from "all seven climes" of the Earth, drawing an impressive traffic from Central Asia itself.[14]

It was shortly after his arrival in Omsk, in 1824, that Hakim Khan personally met with "The Padshah of Russia," Tsar Alexander I (r. 1801–28).[15] The tsar had made a long overland journey to his Siberian outpost along the Irtysh, and Hakim Khan watched him arrive in a grand procession of six carriages, three silver and three gold, and each of which was pulled by sixteen horses. The tsar removed his fur hat upon greeting the welcome party, and Hakim Khan was struck to find his skin tone so light that it resembled "the color of wheat."[16] As a foreign dignitary, Hakim Khan was invited to observe the Russian military exercises, and he reported that, despite the deaths of several soldiers, the size of the Russian military force and their artillery greatly impressed the local nobles who had assembled for the event. He found the Kazakhs to be less impressive.

During the short time that they were together, Tsar Alexander took an interest in Hakim Khan. Communicating primarily through a translator, although Hakim Khan had also taken advantage of his time in Orenburg to learn some Russian, the two spoke late into the evening one night, and the tsar wished to learn as much as possible about Bukhara and Khoqand.[17] Tsar Alexander even invited Hakim Khan to accompany him back to St. Petersburg, but he politely demurred as he was determined to make his way to Mecca instead. Before his own return to Petersburg, the tsar gave Hakim Khan a diamond ring and other gifts, as well as a letter granting him the right to travel freely across all of Russia.[18] The chronicler then made his way westward to Astrakhan and then crossed the Caspian Sea southward as he made his way to Syria, Iraq, Iran, and Mecca. Having completed his pilgrimage, Hakim Khan returned to Bukhara disguised as a sufi, and eventually settled in Shahrisabz.[19]

Khoqand's northward expansion proceeded rapidly throughout these years. By the time 'Umar died in 1822, Khoqand had annexed Chimkent, Turkestan, and Auliya Ata (known as Dzhambul/Jambul from 1938, and Taraz from 1997), and he had

---

14. MT, 584, 592–93.
15. MT, 599–605.
16. MT, 599.
17. MT, 591, 602.
18. MT, 605.
19. MT, 694.

FIG. 5.1 Khoqandi Cannon, in the Museum Collection of Khudayar Khan's Ark.
Author photo.

overseen the establishment of the fortress at Aq Masjid. During Madali Khan's reign, Khoqand established new fortresses at Merke, Karakol, Pishpek (modern Bishkek, established in 1825), Toqmaq, and at the location where, in 1854, the Russians would build Vernoe (Almaty). By 1834, the Issiq Kul region of modern Kyrgyzstan was completely enveloped within Khoqand.[20] Basing his work on an Ottoman report of the region in 1832, Jean-Louis Bacqué-Grammont charts the borders of the khanate across the Ili River and even to the southern shores of Lake Balkhash.[21]

In the 1830s, Khoqand ran campaigns southward as well, asserting control deep into the Pamirs over Qarategin, Darvaz, and Shughnan in what is today Tajikistan,

---

20. On Khoqand's rule over the steppe in this period, see T. K. Beisembiev, "Vysshaya administratsiya Tashkenta i yuga Kazakhstana v period Kokandskogo Khanstva: 1809-1865gg," in *Istoriko-kul'turnye vzaimosvyazi Irana i Dasht-i Kipchaka v XIII–XVIIIvv* ed. M. Kh. Abuseitova and Safar Abdullo (Almaty: Dayk-Press, 2004), 291–313.
21. Jean-Louis Bacqué-Grammont, "Tûrân, une description du khanat de Khokand vers 1832, d'après un Document Ottoman," *Cahiers du Monde Russe et Soviétique* 13, no. 2 (1972): 19, 203–4.

and annexing Roshan and Wakhan.[22] The commander who oversaw these campaigns is identified in the chronicles as Lashkar Qushbegi, a former Chitrali military slave under 'Umar Khan whose earlier victories had placed the southern steppe territories in Khoqand's hands.[23] Madali Khan justified his annexation of the Pamir territories as an attempt to capture his cousin, Ataliq Khan, a surviving son of 'Alim Khan and a potential claimant to the throne.[24] Additional evidence suggests other, more tangible motivations may also have been at play.

Lashkar Qushbegi's campaigns in the Pamirs reached as far as Sariqol, modern Tashqurghan in Xinjiang, which at that time had been a Qing possession for decades.[25] With Sariqol in his hands, Madali Khan was in a position to tax traders making their way from Badakhshan and even Kashmir to Yarkand.[26] Considered in the wake of Khoqand's wars in Kashgar, discussed below, these acquisitions reflect a Khoqandi effort to outmaneuver Bukhara by asserting control not only over those trade routes leading northward to the Russian outposts on the Irtysh, but also the routes leading eastward to Xinjiang, and southward to Kashmir.[27] In the 1830s, the Khanate of Khoqand was in command of the most important commercial arteries in the region, and it had grown to rival Bukhara in population and far exceed it in size.

Central Asian trade with Russia had grown dramatically since Russia began establishing its Siberian fortresses along the Irtysh.[28] Between the mid-eighteenth and mid-nineteenth centuries, Khoqand's trade with Russia increased by more than ten times. Much the same can be said for Bukhara, and trade from both capitals passed through Tashkent, a Khoqandi possession that served as the gateway into the steppe. In 1834, a Khoqandi official named Khoja Bahadur Khan passed through Bombay en route to Mecca and reported to W. H. Wathen, Persian secretary to the government of India in Bombay, that

> The Kokan merchants meet those of Bokhara at Tashkend, and forming one body,

---

22. Cf. TS, f. 96a; AIKC, 15; Bregel, *Atlas*, map 31, 62–63. Bregel's treatment of Khoqand's northern expansion is substantially more conservative than Bacqué-Grammont's.
23. LA, 31/f. 17a and note 71.
24. AIKC, 16.
25. Newby, *The Empire and the Khanate*, 202–5. This should not be confused with the other Tashqurghan, historic Khulm, in modern Afghanistan.
26. Newby, *The Empire and the Khanate*, 205.
27. Newby, *The Empire and the Khanate*, 205.
28. This is addressed throughout the volume and discussed in detail in part two, "Spaces of Exchange," of Monahan's *The Merchants of Siberia*, 105–206.

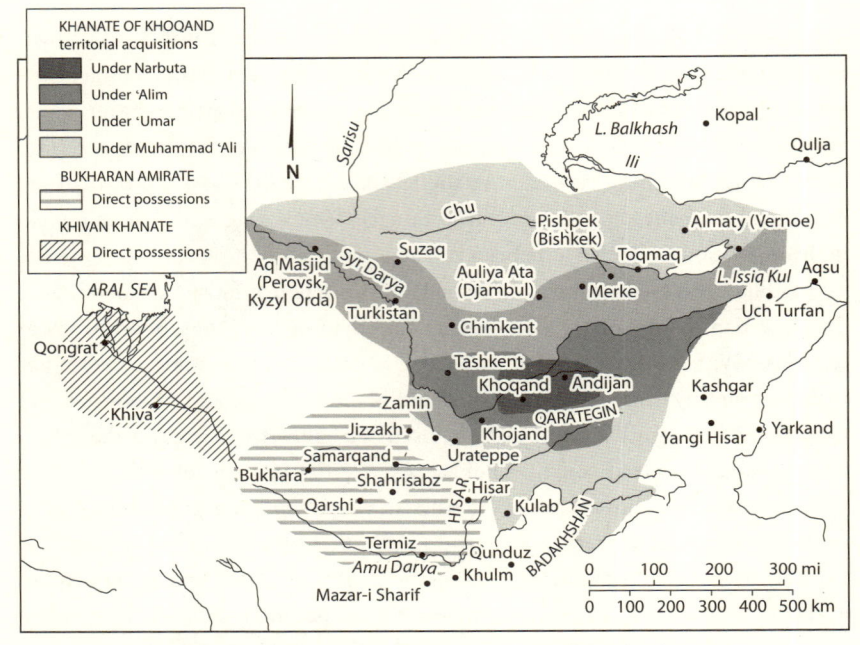

MAP 8 Khoqandi Expansion through Madali Khan's Reign.

Borders for this map are based on a careful analysis of available sources, information available in AIKC, Map 31 in Bregel, *An Historical Atlas*, 63, and the map of Khoqandi expansion presented in Jean-Louis Bacqué-Grammont, "Tûrân, une description du khanat de Khokand vers 1832," *Cahiers du Monde Russe et Soviétique* 13, no. 2 (1972): 196–97. Map by Bill Nelson.

they proceed via Turkistan through the Steppes occupied by the Cossacs, part to Omsk, and part to Orenburg. The productions of China, raw silk, camlet, and cotton yarn, are taken to Russia, and returns are made in furs, gun barrels, and locks, cutlery, Russian leather, and other Russian manufactures.[29]

This report highlights the central importance of Tashkent at the time. But one should not lose sight of the fact that Central Asian merchants mediated a

---

29. W. H. Wathen, "Memoir on the U'sbeck State of Kokan, properly called Khokend, (the Ancient Ferghana) in Central Asia," *Journal of the Asiatic Society of Bengal* 3, no. 32 (1834): 377. For interesting discussions on this theme with additional references, see D. A. Makeev, *Rossiisko-vostochnye torgovye sviazi na rubezhe Srednevekov'ia i Novogo vremeni (XVI–pervaia chetvert' XVIII veka)* (Vladimir: VIT-print, 2013); G. A. Mikhaleva, "O role Orenburga v razvitii torgovykh sviazei Rossii so sredneaziatskimi Khanstvami (vtoraia polovina XVII–nachalo XIX veka)," ÖIF 8 (1977): 43–45.

transit-trade in all varieties of merchandise produced both locally and in distant locations, and in demand in both local and foreign markets. For example, this report elsewhere emphasizes the principle importance of tea, which was transported by horses, each of which could carry between thirty and forty bricks over the mountain passes to Khoqand.[30] But it fails to reference the role Khoqandi merchants played in the quite substantial and highly profitable opium trade, supplying the narcotic to local markets as well as those in Qing and Russian territories.[31] Indian textiles, Chinese tea, rhubarb, porcelain dishes, silks, Siberian furs and leather, European manufactured goods, slaves from Persia and elsewhere, tens of thousands of horses and other livestock, Russian weapons, Indian dyes, tobacco, rice, both fresh and dried fruits—all of these goods and more passed across the trade routes and across the steppe.

In the nineteenth century, saltpeter for gunpowder was another key import commodity, and one finds additional insight into the military history of the period in the observation that Sariqol alone was said to have paid annual taxes to the Qing that included 1,700 *jin*, or more than one ton, of saltpeter.[32] Sariqol was not the only regional supplier of saltpeter at the time, but its ability to supply the Khoqandi military with a ton of saltpeter each year does help explain Madali Khan's willingness to provoke the Qing emperor by wrenching that city from his control.

THE RETURN OF THE KHOJAS

The Qing conquest of Altishahr in 1759 removed the khojas from power in Kashgar, but it did not eliminate them. After defeating the Jungar, the Qing armies moved southward into Altishahr having been provoked by the opportunistic actions of Burhan al-Din and Khoja Jahan, two of the Afaqi khojas who had earlier allied with the Qing against the Jungars and then cast off that alliance in an attempt to assert their authority over the region. Both khojas were eventually killed, and, while Khoja

---

30. Wathen, "Memoir on the U'sbeck State of Kokan," 377.
31. David Bello, "Opium in Xinjiang and Beyond," in *Opium Regimes: China, Britain, and Japan, 1839–1952*, ed. Timothy Brook and Bob Tadashi Wakabayashi (Berkeley: University of California Press, 2000), 141; David Bello, *Opium and the Limits of Empire: The Opium Problem in the Chinese Interior, 1729–1850* (Cambridge, MA: Harvard University Asia Center, 2005), 171–221.
32. See R. H. Davies, *Report on the Trade and Resources of the Countries on the North-Western Boundary of British India*, comp. Sir Robert Montgomery (Lahore: The Government Press, 1862), 347 and note; Newby, *The Empire and the Khanate*, 202, 204, and notes.

Jahan left no children, Burhan al-Din had at least four sons who fled southward into the mountains. In 1763, the Qing were able to pressure Sultan Shah, a ruler in Badakhshan, to turn over three of these young men, along with other family members. They were dispatched to Beijing, where they were allowed to live out their days in a tightly controlled exile. The fourth son, an infant named Sarimsaq, escaped the Qing, and his descendants would eventually become the focal point for anti-Qing resistance in Altishahr.[33]

Newby has painstakingly traced the life and career of Sarimsaq from his infancy, when his fleeing family placed him in the hands of a retainer who took the child into the Pamirs and then on to Qunduz, in what is now Afghanistan. Twenty years later, during the reign of Narbuta Biy, the young man somehow made his way northward to Samarqand, and then Shahrisabz and Urateppe. At some point during this period, the Qing learned of Sarimsaq's existence and grew interested in his activities. Qing sources indicate that he had initiated communications with local powers in Altishahr in the hope that he might convince them to help him raise funds and the popular support necessary to displace the Qing from the region. The Qing grew concerned that the khoja's dynastic charisma may outweigh the prosperity that their fiscal policies offered, and in 1789, the emperor dispatched a letter demanding that Narbuta Biy extradite him. Narbuta refused to do so, citing legal restrictions forbidding him from releasing a coreligionist, but he remained careful not to antagonize his Qing neighbors whose fiscal policies in Altishahr brought great benefits to him, too. Thus, when Sarimsaq launched a campaign from Shahrisabz to take Kashgar in 1797, Narbuta not only refused to support him—he dispatched his own force to stop Sarimsaq in his tracks.

For their part, the Qing did offer Sarimsaq the opportunity to return to his ancestral homeland with assurances that he would be treated well and provided a title and a place in the administration. But Sarimsaq demurred in favor of the security of Narbuta Biy's realm. He knew that Narbuta Biy's ongoing efforts to strengthen his authority depended on the support of the khojas, and the khojas wielded substantial influence in Khoqand. Extraditing one of their own to a non-Muslim foreign power was not an option, and so for Sarimsaq the Ferghana Valley served as a safe haven of sorts.[34] He appears to have lived out his days in Khoqand, free and safe, but hemmed in and denied the opportunity to try his hand at retaking Kashgar.[35] In later years, others would enjoy greater success in pursuing that dream.

---

33. Newby, *The Empire and the Khanate*, 54; Millward, *Eurasian Crossroads*, 96.
34. Newby, *The Empire and the Khanate*, 55–57.
35. Newby, *The Empire and the Khanate*, 60.

A NEW CRISIS, 1822–1844 — 137

The most successful of these was Sarimsaq Khoja's second son, Jahangir Khoja, who was born circa 1787/88, while his father was living under Narbuta Biy's protection.[36] Jahangir Khoja appears to have launched his first attempt to retake Kashgar from the Qing in 1814, though the historical record includes some discrepancies here. Newby cites Qing sources indicating that 'Umar Khan claimed responsibility for halting the adventurer in Marghilan, before he was able to leave Khoqandi territory, a service for which he requested Qing permission to tax Khoqandi traders in Qing territories. That request was denied at least in part because, at that time, the Qing still had doubts that Sarimsaq Khoja had fathered any children.[37]

This stands in contrast to Hakim Khan's account, which suggests that Jahangir Khoja secretly fled Khoqand in the middle of the night with a Khoqandi noble named Haqq Quli and forty soldiers.[38] Hakim Khan reports that he himself was charged with waking 'Umar Khan in the middle of the night to alert him of Jahangir Khoja's flight. 'Umar then ordered a group of soldiers to pursue them, but they were too late.[39] By the time Jahangir Khoja reached Kashgar, he and Haqq Quli were at the head of a force of 540 Kyrgyz soldiers.[40] They put the Qing citadel of Gulbagh under siege, but the Qing forces were heavily armed and too strong. As it became clear that the siege would fail, the Kyrgyz troops panicked and fled, followed by Jahangir Khoja and Haqq Quli. According to Hakim Khan, at that time the Kashgaris had no idea that Jahangir Khoja was among the invading force and he theorizes that, had they known, they most certainly would have done everything possible to aid him in his struggle to unseat the Qing.[41] This event was either too minor to merit notice in the Qing records, or perhaps it was recorded as only a brief skirmish with a small Kyrgyz force. The Qing administration appears to have had no idea that 1814 marked Jahangir Khoja's first attempt to take Kashgar and force the Qing from Altishahr.

Jahangir Khoja made his way westward back across the Tian Shan. Soon after he reached Andijan he was called to meet with 'Umar Khan at his hunting grounds. Trembling with fear of what punishment awaited him for having put Khoqand's

---

36. Newby, *The Empire and the Khanate*, 73; AIKC, 148.
37. Newby, *The Empire and the Khanate*, 73. Further insights can be found in chapter 3, "The 'Holy Wars' of the Uprooted, 1826–30," in Kim, *Borderland Capitalism*, 90–125.
38. MT, 484. My own English translation of Hakim Khan's detailed account of the events surrounding Jahangir Khoja's invasion and conquest of Altishahr can be found in Scott C. Levi and Ron Sela, eds., *Islamic Central Asia: An Anthology of Sources* (Bloomington: Indiana University Press, 2010), 274–80.
39. MT, 485.
40. MT, 494.
41. MT, 495.

relations with the Qing in jeopardy, he was ushered into 'Umar's tent. On a plate in front of the two men were several skewers of goose kabobs. 'Umar instructed the khoja to eat one, and when he did 'Umar asked whether the salt was as good as the salt in China. Jahangir Khoja meekly apologized for his actions, and after some discussion 'Umar laughingly forgave him, welcomed him back, and offered him the robe he was wearing at the time.[42] In the end, 'Umar seems to have blamed the escapade on Haqq Quli, who did not receive the same measure of forgiveness. It is possible, and perhaps even likely, that, as Jahangir Khoja's presence went unnoticed, 'Umar Khan sought to use the event to his advantage. He falsely suggested to Beijing that the attack would have been more serious had he not halted Jahangir Khoja in Marghilan and then requested enhanced taxation privileges as a reward. Regardless, the event makes clear that, while 'Umar Khan was careful not to provoke the Qing, expediency required that he also respect the demands and desires of the khojas so as not to upset the delicate balance of support at his court.

Roughly six year later, in 1820, Jahangir Khoja would again try his luck at taking Kashgar, slipping away from 'Umar Khan and riding eastward into the mountains. By the time he came down on the other side he had some 300 soldiers with him.[43] This time he and his followers let it be known that the grandson of Burhan al-Din Khoja had returned to Kashgar, and they began to draw local support for their cause. Jahangir Khoja's forces advanced and killed a number of Qing troops, but the Qing forces were again too numerous and he was forced to retreat even before he reached the gates of Gulbagh. He then returned to Khoqand, and this time 'Umar Khan put him under house arrest so he could not flee again.[44]

Over the next few years several developments would add considerable loft to Jahangir's claims over Kashgar. 'Umar Khan's death in 1822 and the elevation of Madali Khan to the throne was one factor. Although Madali also desired to keep Jahangir Khoja from venturing into Qing territory, he proved incapable of doing so. Another factor was a growing culture of hostility toward Qing rule in Kashgar itself. Newby notes that one indication of this animosity is the circulation of rape narratives at that time, with young Muslim women suffering at the hands of oppressive Qing administrators.[45] A third factor is Jahangir Khoja's access to supporters in the form of large numbers of Kyrgyz as well as migrant communities who had

---

42. MT, 497.
43. Newby, *The Empire and the Khanate*, 84.
44. MT, 528–31.
45. Newby, *The Empire and the Khanate*, 85–86.

taken refuge in the mountains and who saw him as a charismatic leader able to produce miracles.[46]

Jahangir Khoja's position strengthened year by year until he could no longer be restrained. One Qing source suggests that it was "courtesy of an earthquake" that Jahangir Khoja escaped. But Hakim Khan, who was present at court at the time, does not link the two events.[47] Rather, it seems that it was some time after the earthquake, which Hakim Khan dates to 1822/23, that Jahangir Khoja again fled Khoqand, this time traveling southward into the Alay Mountains and eventually making his way eastward across the Pamirs to Sariqol, where he spent the next few years quietly building support.[48]

Jahangir Khoja's followers periodically engaged Qing forces, but Jahangir Khoja remained out of sight as he amassed resources and made alliances until, in July of 1826, he led a more carefully orchestrated campaign against the Qing with a force of 500 Kyrgyz and Khoqandi troops.[49] Such a small army had little chance in direct conflict, but he hoped that, with some advance notice, it would be enough to ignite a popular uprising. Jahangir Khoja led his troops to Artush, where they visited the tomb (*mazār*) of Satuq Bughra Khan, the tenth-century Qarakhanid ruler and convert to Islam, and the tombs of Jahangir Khoja's ancestors as well.[50] The Qing learned of the khoja's arrival and dispatched an overwhelming force of their own from Gulbagh, including more than a thousand soldiers. Jahangir's forces were routed; hundreds were killed and hundreds more fled. Jahangir Khoja survived by climbing into a tomb and remaining there through the following day as the Qing troops scoured the area looking for him.[51]

At the time, the Qing maintained an estimated 42,000 soldiers across all of Xinjiang, fewer than 5,000 of which were stationed within Altishahr.[52] Concern for Jahangir's actions in the region had motivated the Qing to dispatch additional troops from the border posts (*karun*) into Altishahr. But unbeknownst to himself, Jahangir Khoja's gamble had paid off. The Qing commanders rapidly found themselves at a critical disadvantage when popular support for Jahangir Khoja began to swell by the

---

46. Kim, *Borderland Capitalism*, 109–11.
47. Newby, *The Empire and the Khanate*, 85–86; MT, 569.
48. MT, 569.
49. The most thorough treatment of the khojas' campaigns against the Qing in Kashgar is found in Newby, *The Empire and the Khanate*, 95–123.
50. MT, 570; Newby, *The Empire and the Khanate*, 95; Millward, *Eurasian Crossroads*, 109–10.
51. MT, 570.
52. Newby, *The Empire and the Khanate*, 96.

FIG. 5.2 Satuq Bughra Khan Shrine in Artush.
T. D. Forsyth, *Report of a Mission to Yarkund in 1873, under Command of Sir Thomas Forsyth* (Calcutta: Foreign Department Press, 1875), 81.

thousands. First, some 6,000 *ghazis* (fighters for the faith) arrived from one nearby settlement, and another 12,000 from Kizil Su soon joined them. As support flooded in, the Qing troops were overwhelmed: soldiers and merchants were slaughtered, and those who survived quickly fled. Jahangir Khoja, who to this point had remained in hiding, was finally located, placed on horseback, and the amirs of Kashgar led him into the city. Jahangir Khoja ordered the Qing-appointed hakim to be executed and then assumed his position on the throne.[53]

As word circulated that a khoja had returned and taken Kashgar, the popular revolt grew even more rapidly. The Qing citadel of Gulbagh, adjacent to Kashgar, was well defended and it remained in place, but Qing fortresses in Yangi Hisar, Yarkand, and Khotan fell in rapid succession. This placed western Altishahr in Jahangir Khoja's hands, and rebellion broke out to the east in Aqsu as well.[54] Underlining popular support for Jahangir Khoja are stories of treasure arriving from across the region, including bricks of gold, chests filled with precious stones, and much, much more: so much that, according to Hakim Khan, "it could cover the head of a twelve-year-old

---

53. MT, 571–72.
54. MT, 577; Millward, *Eurasian Crossroads*, 112.

boy."⁵⁵ One family from Yarkand is said to have given him 600 slave soldiers dressed for battle to aid in his struggle to regain his ancestral domains.⁵⁶ Qing fiscal policies had produced considerable wealth for certain nobles over the preceding decades and now some of them were eager to use those resources to push the Qing from the region, or at least to make sure that Jahangir Khoja should look favorably on them if he should succeed. Rather than the elite, Kwangmin Kim suggests that many, if not most, of the soldiers appear to have been from lower social classes. Kim finds that the rebel soldiers came from the ranks of "displaced farmers, runaway slaves . . . renegade merchants and disgruntled Kirghiz tribesmen" who felt themselves to be losers rather than winners in the Qing restructuring of the agrarian regime and commercial economy.⁵⁷ Whether they were nobles or slaves, Jahangir Khoja's supporters hoped for something new, and they hoped that a return to khoja rule would bring it to them.

Prior to the beginning of his campaign, as Jahangir Khoja was working to build support, he issued an invitation to Madali Khan to join forces and bring the army of Khoqand to Kashgar himself with the offer of sharing the financial rewards. Madali had no intention of following Jahangir Khoja into battle. But learning of his remarkable success, he seems to have grown jealous, and then he decided to take Jahangir up on his offer. With visions of treasure in mind Madali hastily led his own army eastward across the passes. But on his arrival, he found the situation quite different than he had expected. Jahangir Khoja had no need of Khoqandi support. Rather, he was now in a position of authority, elevated in stature, and in charge of an army much larger than the one Madali had at his disposal.

Still, Jahangir offered Madali the opportunity to try his luck against the Qing. For five days Madali Khan held Gulbagh under siege. His army managed to blast through one section of the citadel's walls and three time launched efforts to advance inside, but each effort met with staunch resistance, failure, and retreat.⁵⁸ After spending less than two weeks at Kashgar, Madali Khan returned to Khoqand. He now claimed for himself the title of *ghazi*, a fighter for the faith, due to his struggle against the Qing, but he left behind a thousand troops and many of his retinue who opted to take up service for Jahangir Khoja.⁵⁹ Soon after Madali withdrew, Jahangir Khoja's

---

55. MT, 575; Nalivkin, *Kratkaia istoriia*, 127–28; Newby, *The Empire and the Khanate*, 98.
56. MT, 575; Newby, *The Empire and the Khanate*, 98.
57. Kim, *Borderland Capitalism*, 91. That the popular revolt drew followers from across social ranks casts some doubt on Kim's effort to cast the rebellion as part of a larger class struggle. For Kim's treatment of the khoja wars, see 90–125.
58. TS, f. 89a–b.
59. MT, 553, 576.

forces successfully took Gulbagh and he proudly dispatched a notice of his victory to Khoqand.[60] Qing troops in the fortress are said to have been so despondent that they chose to kill themselves, or each other.[61] The 300 or so who did survive were taken captive and enslaved.[62]

Jahangir Khoja had taken western Altishahr in a period of just a few months, but his hold would not last. Hakim Khan attributes his failure to his lack of statecraft experience, placing trust in the wrong people and avoiding those who spoke truthfully to him, and substance-abuse problems. For several years, it seems, Jahangir Khoja had been addicted to opium, and with no limit on his proclivity to indulge, his attention rapidly shifted toward the pursuit of pleasure rather than preparing for the inevitable Qing return.[63] Of course the Qing did return, and with an army of 36,000 troops drawn from garrisons in the north and east.[64] Nine months after Jahangir Khoja had ascended the throne rich beyond his dreams he fled into the Alay Mountains, but he found no refuge there.[65] Qing forces captured him, marched him back to Kashgar, and then sent him to Beijing. In June 1828, the Qing emperor ordered Jahangir Khoja's body sliced into pieces, a punishment known as *ling chi* that was reserved for the worst criminal offenders. His severed head was put on public display.[66]

With their victory secured, the Qing began an investigation to review their policies in an attempt to identify the factors that led to what was in essence a very expensive popular revolt that had cost the Qing more than 11,000,000 taels of silver to put down.[67] The ensuing evaluation of Qing policy resulted in a shift in their presence in the region, and in Qing relations with Khoqand as well. Millward summarizes:

> The review resulted in major changes, including an increase in troop levels in Kashgaria and a punitive boycott on Khoqandi trade. Using moneys confiscated from Khoqandi merchants and local Jahangir supporters, the Qing rebuilt its westernmost

---

60. TS, f. 90b.
61. MT, 577.
62. Newby, *The Empire and the Khanate*, 97. Newby suggests that this may also have given rise to new layers of conflict and competition among the Afaqi and Ishaqi Khoja lineages.
63. MT, 529–30, 578.
64. Newby, *The Empire and the Khanate*, 101.
65. Hakim Khan dates this to February or March of 1826. Relying on Qing records, which are likely to be more accurate on this matter, Newby dates it to 1827. See MT, 579; Newby, *The Empire and the Khanate*, 101.
66. Newby, *The Empire and the Khanate*, 119.
67. Millward, *Beyond the Pass*, 63.

cities and constructed stronger fortifications behind high tamped earth walls at some remove from the old Muslim quarters of the towns. Chinese merchants then located their shops and houses in between the old and new cities, on land the government now rented to them. The lingering effects of this pattern of settlement are still visible today in Kashgar, where as one proceeds east from the old town around the Id Kah (Id Gah) Mosque the neighbourhoods become newer and more heavily inhabited by Han residents. Notably, the Qing took no measures for the defence of the native Uyghur sections of these cities.[68]

The wall built around the new citadel, or Yangi Gulbagh, measured more than twenty feet high and thirty feet thick. Mirroring developments that had unfolded across the globe in response to the gunpowder age, Yangi Gulbagh was designed to withstand heavy artillery.[69] The new reliance on such fortifications in Kashgar represents a significant innovation in the Qing imperial presence in the region.

Farther to the west, Jahangir Khoja's campaign would leave a lasting legacy. In addition to publicly demonstrating that the Qing were vulnerable to popular uprising, he had altered the nature of Khoqand's relations with the Qing. Because of his success, Khoqand had transitioned from using its relationship with the Qing as an engine for economic growth to supporting and even participating in a jihad that aimed to displace the Qing. In the short term, this had a chilling effect on diplomatic ties, and it led the Qing to impose severe (though temporary) restrictions on the ability of Andijani merchants to travel, trade, and reside in Altishahr. In 1828, as Madali suffered a loss against Urateppe to the west, the Qing enforced trade sanctions against Khoqand and began expelling Andijani merchants who had lived in Altishahr for less than ten years. Qing officials confiscated merchandise, especially tea and rhubarb, and the Qing economic policies that had long encouraged the transit trade through Altishahr to the Ferghana Valley were revoked. The Qing special commissioner dispatched to the region, Nayancheng, offered to discuss a reversal of these policies but only in exchange for Jahangir Khoja's family, including his young son, Buzurg Khoja.[70] These efforts came to naught.

So it was with little to lose and much to gain that, just three years after Jahangir Khoja was executed, Madali Khan enlisted Jahangir's older brother, Yusuf Khoja, to lead another jihad against the Qing. Hakim Khan suggests that the initial idea for the jihad came not from Madali, but from Yusuf himself, who had recently made his

68. Millward, *Eurasian Crossroads*, 112.
69. TS, f. 92a; MTF, f. 59a. Niyazi gives the figures as twelve *gaz* high and fifteen *gaz* thick.
70. Newby, *The Empire and the Khanate*, 122, 124–37, 135–36, 148–49.

way to Khoqand from Shahrisabz. Madali was reluctant to provoke the Qing as he was no doubt keen to end the trade sanctions and restore the relationship that had for decades brought so much wealth into Khoqand. However, he looked more favorably on the expedition when Yusuf Khoja promised him that, if their combined forces should take Kashgar, he would turn all of the treasure over to Madali Khan. Madali assembled his amirs and their troops and officially placed Yusuf Khoja at the head of the army, with Haqq Quli in the position of real responsibility as Amir-i Lashkar, accompanied by Muhammad Sharif Ataliq Mingbashi and the highly accomplished Lashkar Qushbegi.[71] Madali himself accompanied them as far as Osh, and then he returned to Khoqand, leaving Yusuf Khoja and the Khoqandi amirs to lead a force of some 30,000 to 40,000 troops eastward to Kashgar.[72]

For three months, the Khoqandi force would try once again to unseat the Qing from Altishahr, but even with such a substantial invasion force their efforts were in vain. The Khoqandi army found the Qing defenses protecting the new Gulbagh cantonment to be too strong to breach even with heavy artillery. The Khoqandis tried to dig under the walls to blast their way in, but as they approached Yangi Gulbagh the Qing defenders on the wall doused them in naphtha and set them ablaze.[73] The Khoqandi troops then abandoned the citadel and instead made their way into the Muslim neighborhoods in Kashgar, which they cruelly sacked.

Thus, where Jahangir Khoja's arrival provoked a widespread popular uprising and a celebrated, if temporary, victory among those who welcomed the return of khoja rule in the region, Yusuf Khoja's campaign encountered resistance and failed to topple even a single Qing fortress.[74] In examining the reason for this failure, Newby rightly observes that "the strong Khoqandi presence in the leadership of the army left the Altishahris in no doubt that this was primarily a Khoqandi rather than a khoja enterprise."[75] Although many of the locals perceived the khojas to be rightful leaders that would act with their best interest at heart, they viewed the Khoqandis as a foreign power with competing ambitions. The Qing meanwhile mobilized some 40,000 troops in their own defense.[76] With defeat imminent, Haqq Quli delivered an ultimatum to the Qing commander: he would agree to lead his army back to

---

71. MT, 699–700.
72. Estimates regarding the size of the force vary. See Newby, *The Empire and the Khanate*, 154 and note 5.
73. TS, f. 92b; MTF, f. 59a.
74. Millward, *Eurasian Crossroads*, 112. The campaign and all its failures are described in detail in Newby, *The Empire and the Khanate*, 154–60.
75. Newby, *The Empire and the Khanate*, 163.
76. Newby, *The Empire and the Khanate*, 160.

Khoqand if the Qing would agree to stop tyrannizing the Muslim populace.⁷⁷ The Qing naturally agreed, and the jihad was brought to an end.

Madali's army did not return to Khoqand weighted down with carts filled with the gold and silver, precious stones, and other luxurious items that had filled his dreams. They did, however, bring with them a large number of people: Turkic Muslims who took the opportunity to flee Qing rule for Khoqand.⁷⁸ Beisembiev places the figure at between 50,000 and 60,000 people, some 10,000 of whom perished while making the treacherous journey across the mountains.⁷⁹ This would certainly have been reported in Beijing, and it also would have represented a considerable influx of subjects for the khanate, even considering that the total population of Khoqand at the time had grown to number some 3,000,000 people.⁸⁰ One wonders if the returning army may also have absconded with the cannon on display at Khudayar Khan's fortress in Khoqand today, engraved with Chinese characters that translate: "Undefeatable Divine Cannon."

The most important result of Yusuf Khoja's jihad was the Qing decision to reverse their foreign policy vis-à-vis Khoqand. The primary motivation for doing so was expediency. In fact, the Qing had never profited in any meaningful way through taxing the exportation of goods from Xinjiang and so this new arrangement represented no real loss for the Qing treasury. But the Qing defense of the region had been extremely costly, amounting to some 8,000,000 ounces of silver, or more than 220 tons, as well as immense loss of manpower and material resources.⁸¹ Reflecting on the efforts to restore khoja authority in the region, it was clear at least to some at the Qing court that punitive policies and sanctions had alienated critical local interests. This created dangerous opportunities that even a small power such as Khoqand could exploit to great effect.⁸² With that in mind, the Qing forgave those Kashgaris who had supported the Khoqandi invasion, they lifted the trade sanctions against Khoqand, they compensated the Andijani merchants for their confiscated property and other losses, and, most remarkably, they granted Andijanis and other foreign traders the privilege of trading tax-free in Altishahr.⁸³ Madali Khan was even granted

---

77. MTF, f. 60a.
78. MT, 700.
79. Beisembiev, "Migration," 38.
80. Beisembiev, "Migration," 38. Roughly two-thirds of Khoqand's population at this time was sedentary. Beisembiev notes that at least some of these migrants were settled in a new village called "Kashghar-Qishlaq" in the eastern region of the valley, near Osh.
81. Millward, *Eurasian Crossroads*, 113.
82. Newby, *The Empire and the Khanate*, 167–73.
83. Millward, *Eurasian Crossroads*, 113.

146 — A NEW CRISIS, 1822–1844

FIG. 5.3 Qing Cannon, in the Museum Collection of Khudayar Khan's Ark.
Author photo.

FIG. 5.4 "Undefeatable Divine Cannon."
Author photo.

the right to place his own Khoqandi *aqsaqals* (community elders) in the region to collect taxes from Andijani merchants on his behalf—a privilege that his father ʻUmar Khan had tried, and failed, to secure for himself.[84]

Khoqand asserted the right to collect taxes from other foreign merchants as well, including merchants from Kashmir and Badakhshan, although their basis for advancing that claim was dubious.[85] While Khoqandi aqsaqals appear to have actually collected such taxes, they do not appear to have done so with the blessings of the Qing. Newby's skepticism regarding this matter is supported by two official letters that Khoqand dispatched to the Qing in the wake of the 1847 Jihad of the Seven Khojas, discussed below. The analysis of these letters demonstrates that Khoqandi taxation privileges in Altishahr would remain a point of negotiation for years to come, and the ability of Khoqand to exercise its claim would depend on which power had the stronger hand in the region at the time.[86] Granting Khoqand favorable trade conditions, as was done in 1832, was again recognized as the price the Qing would have to pay for peace in Xinjiang. For the time being, Chinese tea, rhubarb, silver, and more continued to flow westward into, and through, the Ferghana Valley.

This did not bring about an end to khoja efforts to reestablish their reign in Altishahr. As discussed in the next chapter, others would launch small campaigns in the 1840s and 50s.[87] But generous Qing fiscal policies eroded the khojas' popular support, and over the next several decades none would have the success that Jahangir Khoja enjoyed in 1827.[88] That would change, but, rather than the khojas, it was the Khoqandi commander Yaʻqub Bek who in 1865 would lead the most successful Khoqandi invasion of Kashgar, and the rest of western Altishahr.

84. Newby, *The Empire and the Khanate*, 192–99; Millward, *Eurasian Crossroads*, 114.
85. Newby refutes Fletcher's earlier argument that this represents China's "first unequal treaty," preceding the Opium Wars by more than a decade. She peels away the layers of historical interpretation that led some to conclude that Khoqand enjoyed extraterritoriality in Altishahr. Qing interpretations were quite different and did not include any form of extraterritoriality or the right to tax foreign merchants other than those from Khoqand. Newby, *The Empire and the Khanate*, 192–99. At the same time, others have found some compelling reasons to argue that what the Khoqandis enjoyed did indeed constitute extraterritoriality. See Pär Kristoffer Cassel, *Grounds of Judgement: Extraterritoriality and Imperial Power in Nineteenth-Century China and Japan* (Oxford: Oxford University Press, 2012), 44–45 and notes. For Khoqandi aqsaqals collecting taxes (2.5 percent to Muslim merchants and 5 percent to non-Muslims), see Millward, *Beyond the Pass*, 101.
86. For the original Turkic-language letters and a Chinese-language analysis of their contents, with a short English summary, see Takahiro Onuma, Yasushi Shinmen, and Yayoi Kawahar, "Reconsidering the 1848 Khoqand Documents Stored at the National Palace Museum," *Tohoku Gakuin University Review, History and Culture* 49 (2013): 1–24.
87. See also the discussion, "Invasions of Seven Khōjahs," in Tōru Saguchi, "Kashgaria under the Chʻing Rule," *Acta Asiatica* 34 (1978): 76–78.
88. Saguchi, "Kashgaria under the Chʻing Rule," 115.

THE BUKHARAN INVASION

Over the course of his reign, Madali Khan had earned a dubious reputation for engaging in questionable behavior, and doing so quite publicly. Accusations included (though were not limited to) gambling, excessive consumption of alcohol, and maintaining an illicit relationship with Khan Padshah, the young woman who had been married to his own father.[89] While marrying one's own father's widow was permitted and even common among the ruling Mongols, such traditions were considered abhorrent by the Muslims of early modern Central Asia. Though some Central Asian Hanafi legal interpretations permitted the modest consumption of wine, drinking to excess in a public setting was clearly forbidden.[90] Hakim Khan reports that Madali Khan also enlisted two women and charged them with identifying attractive girls for his harem. In cases where a girl's father was able to pay a sufficiently high price, the women permitted the girl to stay with her family. In cases where they were not able to produce sufficient wealth, the girls were taken and deposited in the palace for Madali's personal enjoyment.[91]

Stories about such matters circulated throughout the valley and beyond, and as time went on his closest advisors came to realize that, despite prosperity and territorial expansion, support for his reign had begun to waver. In an effort to reverse this trend, one of Madali's most trusted confidants, Haqq Quli, agreed to approach the khan and address these growing concerns. He did so twice, both times unsuccessfully, and after the second request Madali grew suspicious of his motives and ordered him to be executed by beheading.[92] Madali sought to secure the support of the religious elite by financing the construction a grand new madrassa in his capital, which Niyazi reports was completed in 1837.[93] Even this was not enough. With fear of an impending coup growing, Madali then sent his younger brother, Sultan Mahmud Khan, into exile in Shahrisabz.[94] Whether or not Sultan Mahmud had genuinely been conspiring to take the throne from his brother remains unknown, but Madali's actions effectively put him in a position to do just that, and with powerful support.

---

89. MT, 701–3.
90. For a discussion of Central Asian Hanafi legal interpretations regarding alcohol consumption, see Honchell, "The Story of a Drunken Mughal," 16–32.
91. MT, 701.
92. MT, 703.
93. TS, f. 96a.
94. Hakim Khan had retired to Shahrisabz following his international travels, and it was there that he would have learned of the earlier events that unfolded following his departure from Khoqand.

A NEW CRISIS, 1822–1844 — 149

FIG. 5.5 Madali Khan Madrassa.
Turkestanskii Al'bom, 1865–72, Library of Congress, Prints & Photographs Division, LC-DIG-ppmsca-14909.

In one last, feeble attempt to restore his reputation, Madali appealed to the 'ulama to approve his relationship with his beloved Khan Padshah. The overwhelming response was that *sharī'ah* provided no way to legitimize a relationship with a woman who had been married to one's own father. Madali eventually found two mullahs who were willing to grant their approval, and against the recommendations of his advisors, the two were married.[95] As word of their union spread, popular opinion of Madali's leadership sank from disapproval to disgust. News of these events soon reached Sultan Mahmud Khan in Shahrisabz, who then reached out to Amir Nasrallah (r. 1827–60) in Bukhara for assistance.[96] Soon thereafter, Nasrallah dispatched an ambassador who delivered a message accusing Madali of violating the sharī'ah for his own pleasures and demanding that he bring the marriage to an immediate end.

---

95. MT, 710–12. Hakim Khan reports that Madali Khan's decision enjoyed the support of his drinking and gambling friends, one of whom suggestion that, "Of course it is permissible; you were born with a penis when you came out of your mother, right?" Madali is said to have found this argument to be convincing and rewarded the man by appointing him to the official governmental rank of "Sardar of Pigeons and Games." MT, 712.
96. MT, 713.

For seven decades, Khoqand had been on a steady trajectory of expansion. From his ascension in 1770, Narbuta Biy brought the entire valley under the authority of Khoqand. His older son and successor, 'Alim Khan, had both defended Khoqand from Yunus Khoja and his Kazakh soldiers, and then taken Tashkent from those same forces. 'Umar Khan furthered his brother's efforts and effectively began the process whereby Khoqand would establish a series of fortress towns to govern over the southern steppe. From his ascension to the throne in 1822 and throughout the 1830s, Madali Khan oversaw the later stages of Khoqand's northward expansion into the steppe, which placed Khoqand in control over a territory that stretched from the Aral Sea to the borders of Xinjiang, and southward even to Wakhan in the Pamirs. At the same time, Khoqand had again managed to assert control over Urateppe.

On the face of it, Khoqand was at its greatest strength and positioned to become stronger. But important constituencies that Madali depended on were growing disaffected. In addition to those he offended with what they perceived to be immoral behavior, there is also evidence to suggest that Madali had financed his military successes partly with funds that he had unjustly appropriated from Andijani merchants. During the 1830s, Qing reports suggest that these merchants also grew disaffected and increasingly looked to Altishahr as a more predictable environment for their work.[97] The evidence suggests that from 1840 Madali, blind to his weakening position at home and armed with a strong military, aimed to follow his good fortune in Altishahr and the steppe by shifting his sights westward, toward Bukhara. But it was here that Madali Khan's luck would run out, depleting the fortunes of his state and the Shahrukhid legacy along with it.

In 1840, during the eighteenth year of his reign, Madali Khan's army occupied the small settlement of Peshaghar, situated between Urateppe and Jizzakh, and began to construct a fortress there.[98] Khoqand had occupied this territory once before, in the 1810s, and Madali aimed to develop it for use as a launching point for additional westward campaigns, which he would achieve at Bukhara's expense. Beisembiev notes that Madali had even worked to reclaim the desert wasteland between Khojand and Urateppe in an effort to make the land arable and prepare it for larger settlements.[99]

Madali next set his sights on Jizzakh. The revenue he stood to gain from a victory over Jizzakh was by no means substantial. According to the figures presented by the British agent Alexander Burnes, when it was in Bukharan hands in the early 1830s,

---

97. Kim, *Borderland Capitalism*, 129–30.
98. TS, f. 96b; AIKC, 559.
99. AIKC, 16.

FIG. 5.6 Jizzakh, Grand Bazaar.
Turkestanskii Al'bom, 1865–72, Library of Congress, Prints & Photographs Division, LC-DIG-ppmsca-14824.

the treasury received only some 8,000 tilā (gold coins) in annual tax revenue from Jizzakh, less than the 12,000 tilā collected from Qarshi but more than the 6,000 tilā collected from Ghijduvan.[100] But a victory over Jizzakh would open access for Madali Khan to continue farther into the Zerafshan Valley, and beyond. And so, armed with ambition and overconfidence, Madali and a small cohort rushed headlong into battle, intending to take Jizzakh from its Manghit defenders.[101] He quickly failed, retreated to Urateppe, and then made his way back to Khoqand.[102] Just one month after he appointed his hakim in Peshaghar and returned to Khoqand, the Bukharan army arrived and demolished what had been built of the fortress.[103] Soon thereafter Amir Nasrallah and Madali Khan met at Zamin and conferred with each other for two hours. The two sides reached a truce, and Jizzakh remained in Bukharan hands.[104]

Madali had skirted disaster for the time being, but on his return to Khoqand he

---

100. Alexander Burnes, *Travels into Bokhara* . . . (London: John Murray, 1834), 2:369–70.
101. MT, 715. Hakim Khan suggests that he was drunk.
102. MT, 715.
103. TS, f. 96b.
104. TS, fols. 96b–97a.

was confronted by demands that he must divorce Khan Padshah, which he dismissed out of hand. Soon thereafter, he learned that Nasrallah was leading an exceptionally large force against Urateppe, and that its leadership included his own brother, Sultan Mahmud Khan.[105] Urateppe quickly fell to the Bukharans, and Nasrallah issued a demand that Madali also turn over Khojand, Qurama, Tashkent, and all of Khoqand's territories in the Dasht-i Qipchaq as well. Without even waiting for a response, the Bukharan forces advanced to take the fortresses at Yom and Zamin. Madali moved to counter the Bukharan invasion at Khojand, but with popular support slipping away he turned control of the city over to Amir Nasrallah, who soon thereafter appointed Madali's own brother as the city's new hakim.[106] With Nasrallah threatening invasion of the valley and pressuring Madali to arrange a meeting, Khoqand descended into a popular revolt; even Khan Padshah fled the palace to her father's residence.[107]

With the political climate in Khoqand growing increasingly tense, Madali exchanged multiple ambassadors with Nasrallah and managed to convince him that he would mend his ways. Nasrallah agreed to withdraw, and Madali Khan's mother, Mahlar Oyim, worked to repair her two sons' relationship. Echoing her late husband's pronouncements at the time of 'Alim Khan's death, she convinced Madali to announce that he would divide the realm with his brother: Madali would retain control over Ferghana and the Pamirs, while Sultan Mahmud would assume authority over all of Khojand, Urateppe, Tashkent, and the Dasht-i Qipchaq.[108] The plans were well laid out, but they would not come to fruition. In no time at all Madali had returned to his well-established behavioral patterns, and when they heard that the support of his own military officials was wavering, the Bukharan army returned as well.

The Bukharan military again marched toward the valley, and, as it reached Khojand, the army of Khoqand came out to meet it. The Bukharan forces were well prepared and emboldened by reports that many in the Khoqand camp welcomed their arrival, while the Khoqandi forces suffered a lack of both leadership and resolve. As the Bukharan troops advanced, Madali Khan's troops began to scatter. Many fled, and others hoped to escape what was rapidly becoming a massacre by jumping into the Syr Darya River, only to drown instead. Those who remained loyal were slaughtered. Eventually, a small number of battle-worn and battered soldiers made their

---

105. MT, 717; TS, f. 98b.
106. MT, 721; MTF, f. 62b.
107. MT, 720–21; TS, f. 99a.
108. MTF, f. 62b.

way back to Khoqand, and word followed that the Bukharan soldiers had entered the valley and were close behind them.[109] Nasrallah himself led the Bukharan forces, taking one village after the next, until they reached Besh Ariq.

Since long before ʿAlim Khan ascended the throne in 1799 and began imposing sweeping military reforms, Khoqand had been working toward implementing improved military technologies and developing a larger standing army. Hakim Khan estimates the number of soldiers in Khoqand's army at the time of the Bukharan invasion to have reached "close to 100,000" (*qarīb ṣad hazār*).[110] Though that figure may be an exaggeration, it is worth noting that the aforementioned Khoqandi official Khoja Bahadur Khan suggested in his report to Wathen in Bombay that the Khoqandi army could in times of need produce a cavalry force of 50,000, in addition, it would seem, to infantry and irregulars.[111] In the meanwhile, Bukhara's military had also been far from stagnant, and, Holzwarth notes, Nasrallah himself had initiated "a new breeze of modernization" to the Bukharan military during the latter half of the 1830s. Holzwarth considers the implementation of a standing force to have represented "a turning point in the history of Bukhara," as it "enabled the ruler to crush all tribal uprisings and weaken the Uzbek chieftains."[112] Alexander Burnes visited Bukhara at the beginning of that decade and placed the size of the regular army at 24,000 soldiers, some 20,000 of whom were cavalry armed with swords and lances, and 4,000 of whom were infantry troops armed with matchlocks and equipped with forty-one cannons. Like ʿAlim Khan's now-disbanded Ghalcha corps of several decades earlier, these troops were well trained, paid out of the treasury, and further supported by some 50,000 additional militia fighters who could be called to battle when needed.[113]

By the time Nasrallah's conflict with Khoqand began in 1840, Bukhara had effectively implemented "new-style regiments" that included "cannonades fired by 300 *sarbāz*" (literally "those risking the head," specialists in the use of cannon, mortar, and other artillery) as well as matchlock units. The sarbāz units were garrisoned and

---

109. MT, 726.
110. MT, 715. As Hakim Khan had lost all affection for his cousin, he may have been inclined to exaggerate the size of Khoqand's force in order to make Madali appear even more incompetent than he actually was. The figure of 100,000 (again ṣad hazār, and not lak) is confirmed in the critical edition of Hakim Khan's chronicle, Muḥammad ḥakīm Khān, *Muntakhab al-tawārīkh: Selected History*, ed. Yayoi Kawahara and Koichi Haneda (Tokyo: Research Institute for Languages and Cultures of Asia and Africa, 2006), 2:606.
111. Wathen, "Memoir on the Uʾsbeck State of Kokan," 372.
112. Holzwarth, "Bukharan Armies," 328.
113. Burnes, *Travels into Bukhara*, 2:372. Cited in Holzwarth, "Bukharan Armies," 328.

trained in European-style military traditions, and these forces proved very effective in Bukhara's victory at Peshaghar.[114] In his visit to the region in 1841–42, Nikolai Khanykov reported that their numbers included some 1,000 soldiers armed with flintlock muskets as well.[115] In essence, it was the effectiveness of the sarbāz troops against Khoqand in 1840 that led Nasrallah to increase his emphasis on them, and, Holzwarth notes, the advantage they provided was "decisive in the capture of a number of fortresses on the Kokand border." On its return, Nasrallah's army employed some 1,000 sarbāz troops equipped with eleven cannons and two mortars in the conquest of Zamin and Khojand.[116]

It is tempting to attribute the Bukharan victory to superior weapons technology, and the Bukharan accounts do suggest that Nasrallah's reforms in the second half of the 1830s equipped his forces with a significant field advantage over Madali's military. Military technology, however, is only part of the story. Even with this field advantage, Bukhara's new-style military was incapable of defeating the considerably less powerful Keneges in Shahrisabz. Furthermore, contrary to what one Persian envoy suggested, Khoqandi forces had long been acquainted with cannons, mortars, artillery troops, and techniques for storming fortresses.[117] 'Alim Khan had several decades earlier implemented reforms quite similar to those of Nasrallah, although during the early years of 'Umar Khan's reign, certain aspects of those reforms were derailed in favor of policies that would earn him the loyalty of the traditional Uzbek power structures. The Ghalcha corps, the centerpiece of 'Alim Khan's reforms, was dismissed. But 'Umar and Madali both appreciated the importance of arming their troops with more technologically current weaponry, and over several decades their investment had paid off in terms of Khoqand's remarkable territorial expansion.

Considered in context, it seems highly unlikely that Nasrallah would have enjoyed such successes had Madali been able to provide the leadership necessary to bring his khanate's full resources to bear in its own defense. The city of Khoqand alone had grown to an estimated 100,000 people, by some reports surpassing the city of Bukhara in population and boasting 100 madrasas and 500 mosques.[118] But popular opinion was firmly pitched against Madali Khan, and when faced with a serious

---

114. Holzwarth, "Bukharan Armies," 331.
115. Nikolai Khanykov, *Opisanie Bukharskogo khanstva* (St. Petersburg, 1843) 181. Cited in Holzwarth, "Bukharan Armies," 331.
116. Holzwarth, "Bukharan Armies," 332, 333.
117. Holzwarth, "Bukharan Armies," 332.
118. Wathen, "Memoir on the U'sbeck State of Kokan," 372.

contest, such as that which the Bukharans presented, many of his commanders chose to flee rather than defend the khanate's morally bankrupt leadership. With the Bukharans advancing on the capital, Madali had no choice but to send word to his brother, Sultan Mahmud, that he wished to abdicate the throne lest the khanate be lost entirely. Hoping to rally popular support and save the khanate, Sultan Mahmud made his way to join his brother in Khoqand.[119]

Sultan Mahmud Khan arrived in Khoqand in 1842, but it was too small a gesture to reverse public opinion, and too late to be of any use. The Bukharan army entered Khoqand and fought its way through the streets to the heart of the city, eventually reaching the Madrasa-i Khan.[120] The army of Khoqand was defeated, and the Bukharan troops pillaged everything they could get their hands on. The treasury was emptied, the palace was pillaged, the women and children of the harem were taken, and even the mosques were stripped of carpets, books, and clothing.[121] Sultan Mahmud Khan fled and was captured in Shahrikhan, and both he and Madali Khan's son, Muhammad Amin, were marched in front of Amir Nasrallah and executed. Madali Khan's mother, Mahlar Oyim, the celebrated poetess Nadira, was also captured and killed.[122] Madali himself was captured near Marghilan, and he too was brought in front of Amir Nasrallah, who ordered him to be executed by beheading.[123]

Khoqand was emptied of all who had served as state administrators. The 'ulama, sufi sheikhs, and even the skilled workers were taken to Bukhara. Amir Nasrallah himself remained in Khoqand for thirteen days, after which he appointed Ibrahim Parvanachi Manghit, who in 1840 had governed as the Bukharan hakim of Urateppe, to serve as the hakim of Khoqand. The Bukharan Amir then returned home.[124] In addition to wealth and property, Nasrallah took Madali's beloved Khan Padshah back to Bukhara with him and, for two months, she "belonged" to him until he tired of her and had her executed as well.[125]

Khoqand was left in Bukharan hands, but Nasrallah's grasp was weak. After just ten weeks, Ibrahim would be forced to flee for his life and Khoqand would again be back in Shahrukhid hands. In the end, the Khoqandi people themselves had been the key agents in orchestrating Madali Khan's fall; the Bukharan army was simply the instrument that they had used to achieve that goal. Still, the occupation would

119. MT, 727–28.
120. TS, f. 99b.
121. TS, f. 100a; MT, 728–29.
122. TS, f. 100a; MT, 730.
123. TS, f. 100b; MT, 731.
124. MTF, f. 63b; AIKC, 30.
125. AIKC, 174.

leave a lasting legacy as, for reasons not yet apparent, it sent Khoqand from a long, sustained trajectory of growth and territorial expansion into a downward spiral from which it would never recover.

KHOQAND AT THE CROSSROADS

Where the chroniclers have tended to gloss over 'Umar Khan's faults in an effort to present him in as fair a light as possible, quite the opposite has been true for his son and successor, Muhammad 'Ali Khan. To an extent, they had good reason to do so. From the time Madali ascended the throne as a young man of fourteen, he dispensed with his father's administrative diplomacy. Where 'Umar Khan provided access and patronage to multiple key constituencies, Madali Khan forced formerly trusted advisors and family members into exile, or had them executed. In a sense, he could be said to have followed in the footsteps of his uncle, 'Alim Khan, but even that comparison falls short. 'Alim had deliberately applied brutality to achieve greater centralized authority, whereas Madali simply surrounded himself with sycophants and scoundrels. He was prone to substance abuse, gambling, and other sorts of problematic behavior, and, while his father may have engaged in some of the same activities, Madali was not interested even in shielding his indiscretions from the public eye. Popular opinion shifted against him, and his legacy would ultimately be secured through his decision to ignore sharī'ah and even his most trusted advisors by taking his late father's young wife Khan Padshah into his own harem, marrying her, and refusing to submit to the demands of the 'ulama that he divorce her.

Despite his character flaws and questionable leadership skills, Madali Khan was able to secure a number of remarkable accomplishments during his two decades on the throne. His support for the khoja invasions of Altishahr was a gamble that easily could have ended worse than it did. Jahangir Khoja was executed in Beijing, but Madali had also put Gulbagh under siege, and, while he failed miserably, he did escape back to Khoqand with his life. The subsequent restrictions that the Qing placed on Khoqandi merchants in their territory prompted Madali to enlist Yusuf Khoja for another attempted overthrow of the Qing. In this case, Madali seems to have played his cards right. The Khoqandi invasion failed to achieve even a single victory in the region, but the Qing recognized that their punitive policies created an environment that would likely encourage future invasions and popular rebellions, the suppression of which represented a significant expense in wealth and resources.

In the end, Madali failed to annex Kashgar, but he managed to secure tax-free trading privileges and other rights in Xinjiang.

Madali Khan also oversaw Khoqand's greatest territorial expansion. By 1840, the khanate extended through Tashkent deep into the steppe, where Khoqand maintained a series of fortresses that stretched eastward from Aq Masjid to the borders with the Qing. Control over the southern steppe equipped Khoqand with a measure of authority over the Kazakh and Kyrgyz nomads in the area, as well as control over the trade routes linking sedentary Central Asia with the Russian fortresses on the Irtysh River. Madali Khan's armies also expanded Khoqand's territory southward into the Pamirs, where they reached as far as Wakhan. For a few short years, virtually all of Central Asian trade with Qing possessions in Altishahr passed through Khoqand.

A careful analysis of Khoqand's territorial expansion in the early nineteenth century indicates that Madali Khan governed a territory that extended over some 250,000 square miles, roughly the size of the state of Texas in the United States and substantially larger than France and even Ukraine in Europe.[126] Although still smaller than Altishahr, over the four decades since Narbuta Biy's death in 1799, Khoqand had increased in size by a factor of thirty. Khoqand's population continued to expand as well, as large numbers of migrants made their way into the valley, including tens of thousands who came from Altishahr. By the end of his reign, Madali Khan ruled over some 3,000,000 subjects, a population three times greater than the total population of Altishahr a decade later.[127] It is not difficult to imagine why the Bukharan Amir Nasrallah would have become uncomfortable with Khoqand's rapid territorial expansion and improved access to resources.

Khoqand's military strength had grown substantially during the early decades of the nineteenth century, but the same was true for the Bukharan Amirate, especially

---

126. See Map 8. I conducted the calculation using Google Maps technology and the MAPS.ie program (http://www.maps.ie/distance-area-calculator.html). Bacqué-Grammont's map suggests that Khoqand included virtually all of Semirech'e and additional northern territories, and that it was therefore considerably larger than can be supported by available sources. At the same time, a similar exercise using Bregel's Map 31, which estimates the borders of Khoqand in the year 1834, results in a slightly smaller area of approximately 230,000 square miles. This difference is attributed to the fact that Bregel's map does not credit Khoqand with a significant amount of territory north of the Chu River and Lake Issiq Kul that Khoqand claimed later in the 1830s. Cf. Bacqué-Grammont, "Tûrân, une description du khanat de Khokand," 196–97; Bregel, *An Historical Atlas*, 63.

127. Kim, *Borderland Capitalism*, 201 (appendix A). According to Kim's statistics, which he breaks down by oasis, the total population of Eastern Turkestan during the period stretching between the 1850s and 1870s was barely over 1,000,000 people. His calculation is based on the assumption of seven people per household. The estimate for Khoqand is found in Beisembiev, "Migration," 38.

following Amir Nasrallah's military reforms of the 1830s. When Madali Khan showed signs of encroaching on Bukharan territory, first in 1840 with his establishment of a new fortress at Peshaghar, he provoked a rapid Bukharan response. Nasrallah's forces demolished that fortress and leveraged Madali's dismal popularity to extend Bukharan control eastward to Khojand, and ultimately into the valley itself. In 1842, Madali Khan's army was defeated, the Bukharans occupied the city of Khoqand, and Madali himself was captured and executed, as were his son, brother, mother, and many others.

It is tempting to attribute this loss to Bukhara's superior military strength. But such an explanation seems unconvincing when one considers that Khoqand itself had demonstrated considerable success on the battlefield, that Bukhara had been unable to conquer the much smaller city of Shahrisabz, and that popular rebellions such as the one that emerged in support of Jahangir Khoja could unseat a power as great as the Qing. Rather, there appear to be two equally important principal factors behind the Bukharan victory: first, that Madali had lost legitimacy in the eyes of his people; and second, that many of his administrators and advisors themselves feared his increasingly capricious, dangerous, and perhaps even paranoid behavior. 'Umar Khan had masterfully articulated a Timurid-style social contract that promised at least to project an image of a just and pious Islamic rule to multiple constituencies. Under Madali, the military commanders and their troops were unwilling to risk their lives in defense of a ruler whom they found to be reprehensible and in whom they had little faith. The Bukharan victory was a devastating loss for the Shahrukhids, but it was a loss that elements of the Khoqandi military had effectively engineered. Just ten weeks after Nasrallah entered Khoqand, his hakim was evicted from the valley and the khanate was back in Shahrukhid hands.

Six

CIVIL WAR, 1844–1853

IN 1842, AFTER two decades of remarkable territorial expansion and continued development of Khoqand's agricultural infrastructure, a Bukharan invasion brought Madali Khan's reign to a violent end. Khoqand was considerably larger than Bukhara and it boasted a formidable military, but the regime suffered a crisis of legitimacy. By the time of Madali Khan's reign, the Shahrukhids had established a claim to legitimacy that rested on two pillars: their (albeit fictive) Timurid ancestry and their role as the rightful upholders of Islamic law. Madali Khan's unconcealed debauchery combined with his blatant disregard for *sharī'ah* broke the social contract on which Shahrukhid legitimacy was based. His escapades were well known, but taking his father's widow Khan Padshah as his own wife was the last straw. Furthermore, those involved in governance were understandably concerned by his increasingly unpredictable and even tyrannical tendencies.

Learning of the extent to which Madali Khan had fallen out of public affection, the Bukharan Amir Nasrallah recognized an opportunity to eliminate an expansive and threatening neighbor and greatly enhance his own power and prestige in the process. Nasrallah's invasion was a resounding success but it would not be a lasting one. He had occupied the capital, executed Madali Khan, and appointed his own hakim (governor) in his place. But the Khoqandi people had used Bukhara to engineer a regime change, and they had no intention of accepting Bukharan authority on a permanent basis. Within a matter of ten weeks, the Bukharans were forced from the valley and the Khoqandis began making plans for the future of their khanate.

The final period of the khanate's existence stretches some thirty-four years, from Madali Khan's death in 1842 to the Russian annexation of the khanate on February 2, 1876. This period witnessed repeated efforts to achieve stability through the implementation of policies that had proven successful in the past: elevating a suitable Shahrukhid ruler; diverting resources to strengthen the military; expanding the agricultural base; using access to water to retain the loyalty of settled groups; and balancing patronage among tribal groups, settled farmers, and religious constituencies. In some ways, this period exhibits continuity with well-established patterns in the valley. Irrigation canals brought water to more land, the population continued to expand, and, excepting periodic disruptions, trade flourished along both latitudinal and longitudinal axes. One of the more striking commercial developments toward the end of this period is an increase in the production of cotton, grown in the valley as a cash crop for export to Russia's industrializing markets.[1]

However, as Khoqand's infrastructure grew stronger, the khanate also suffered political crises and rising ethnic tensions: Uzbeks, Qipchaqs, Sarts, and Kyrgyz all vied for influence and control over the throne to protect their own interests in what was becoming an increasingly precarious regional environment. There were three primary causal factors behind this crisis: the weakening Qing grasp over Xinjiang, the Russo-Kazakh alliance to the north, and the southward movement of the Russian imperial frontier. The Russian army captured Aq Masjid in 1853 and established a fortress at Vernoe (Almaty) the following year. After that, the Khoqandi steppe fortresses would fall in quick succession, ending three decades of Khoqandi control over the steppe.

FINDING A NEW FOOTING

In 1842, with Madali Khan dead, Ibrahim Parvanachi Manghit sat on the throne in Khoqand as the Bukhara-appointed hakim and his brother, Karim Berdi Zinbardar, served as hakim of Andijan and Marghilan. Nasrallah had returned to Bukhara victorious, but far from accepting Bukharan sovereignty, the Khoqandi leadership

---

1. Askarov et al., eds., *Istoriia Uzbekistana*, vol. 3: *XVI–pervaia polovina XIX veka* (Tashkent: Fan, 1993), 228. Although significant for Central Asian markets, the total amount of cotton imported overland to Russian markets remained a small percentage of the total Russian consumption. See Sven Beckert, *Empire of Cotton: A Global History* (New York: Alfred A. Knopf), 345–46.

representing the Ming, Sarts, Qipchaqs, and Kyrgyz gathered to plot a course of action.[2] Relations among these parties would grow increasingly divisive in the coming years, but facing crisis they agreed to put their support behind another member of the Shahrukhid lineage, Sher 'Ali (c. 1790–1844), one of three sons of Narbuta Biy's younger brother, Hajji Bek.

In the wake of Hajji Bek's death, which Narbuta Biy's son 'Alim Khan had ordered, Sher 'Ali's family had fled Khoqand to seek refuge among the Kyrgyz in the Talas Valley.[3] Now, with the future of the khanate uncertain, the Khoqandi nobility invited Sher 'Ali to return and take his place on the throne. He did so, at the head of a force of several thousand soldiers.[4] Muhammad Fazl Bek summarizes the events surrounding his return as follows.

> In the year 1258 AH (1842 CE), Sher 'Ali Khan b. Hajji Bek b. 'Abd al-Rahman Bek b. 'Abd al-Karim Khan was installed as khan by the traditional *āq kigīz* (white felt) ceremony. Word soon arrived that the Bukharan amir was planning another campaign against Khoqand. Sher 'Ali Khan called a meeting of the elders, who decided that they would strengthen the city's defenses by building a wall. Men were brought in from the neighboring villages, and, after forty days, when the wall was half done, news arrived that the amir was coming with an army. People from the nearby villages heard of this and many sought refuge in the city, while others fled. Those who remained bolstered the city's defenses by digging a moat and building barricades around the areas of the city not yet protected by the wall.
>
> Advance troops from Bukhara reached the Ghazi Gate and pillaged the surrounding villages, but the people of Khoqand fought hard against the Manghits. On seeing the moat, the wall, and the city's other defenses, the Bukharan troops understood that Khoqand had marshalled considerable resources to build such a wall in a month and a half. The Bukharan amir commanded his troops to attack from the unfinished portion of the city's defenses. They unleashed volleys from their muskets and rifles, but the Khoqandis returned heavy fire and the Bukharans were unsuccessful. On the fourth day of the siege, the amir ordered his troops to attack from the direction of Muimubarak Gate, but they failed to breach Khoqand's defenses. They tried again from the direction of the river, but the Khoqandis fought with determination, and many Manghit soldiers were killed.

---

2. MTF, f. 64b. Ibrahim Parvanachi's career in the Bukharan government stretched into the 1860s. Various sources identify him by ranks that he held at other times, including Ibrahim Diwanbegi and Ibrahim Dadkhwah. AIKC, 30, 370.
3. AIKC, 277.
4. MTF, f. 64b; TS, f. 101b; MK, f. 133a.

The amir grew upset and ordered his troops to attack from Tokai Teppe, on the eastern side of the city near Marghinan (Marghilan) Gate. As there was no wall yet built at that location a few of the Bukharan soldiers were able to enter the city, but the Khoqandi people had lined up large carts to provide cover and they pushed the Bukharan troops back. According to Niyazi, the amir began to realize that his campaign would lead to failure. He had earlier been able to defeat Khoqand because the people had let him. But with Madali Khan gone, they fought hard to regain their autonomy.

Over just a few days, this situation began to become precarious for the Bukharan amir. At that time, the Bukharan army included some military commanders who had earlier fled Khoqand. As the Bukharan troops failed to defeat Khoqand, a number of these individuals began to shift their allegiance, abandoning Bukhara for Khoqand. Realizing that he would soon find himself in a dangerous and potentially lethal position, the Bukharan amir ordered his army to withdraw and return to Bukhara.[5]

Muhammad Fazl Bek assembled his account decades after the fact. But drawing on a number of chroniclers who were alive at the time, his treatment of these events echoes the conclusion advanced above: Bukhara's victory over Khoqand was not a product of Bukharan military superiority. Rather, it was a determined effort on the part of the Khoqandi nobility to engineer the fall of their ruler. Despite Madali Khan's military successes and the size and strength of his state, he had lost legitimacy in the eyes of his people. Now, just a few months after suffering a devastating defeat, the Khoqandi forces proved quite capable of mustering a defense sufficiently strong to repel a determined Bukharan army.[6]

With his capital secure, Sher 'Ali turned his attention to restoring Khoqand's control over the khanate's other territorial possessions. According to Niyazi, Sher 'Ali Khan promptly dispatched a messenger to Tashkent demanding that the city be returned to Khoqand.[7] The hakim was Muhammad Sharif, a Khoqandi noble who had served as a military commander under both 'Umar Khan and Madali Khan, but who had since switched loyalty to Amir Nasrallah. Muhammad Sharif refused to submit, and so Sher 'Ali Khan commanded his second oldest son, Malla Bek, to join his own brother-in-law, the seasoned Kyrgyz military commander Yusuf Mingbashi, and lead a campaign against Tashkent.[8]

---

5. TS, f. 106a–b.
6. MTF, fols. 65a–66b. Muhammad Fazl Bek's narrative relies heavily, though not exclusively, on Niyazi. See TS, fols. 101a–7b.
7. TS, fols. 108a–9a.
8. Beisembiev notes that Malla Bek's given name was Muhammad Yar Khan, though he is uniformly referred to as Malla Bek in Khoqandi sources. "Malla" itself can mean either "red-haired" or "blond." AIKC, 461 and note.

Camping on the outskirts of the city, Malla Bek sent agents to the *aqsaqals* (elders) of each *mahalla* (neighborhood) within the city walls asking them to support Khoqandi efforts to retake the city. It was already too late when the hakim learned of the conspiracy: the aqsaqals arranged for a city gate to be opened during the night, and the Khoqandi forces entered under cover of darkness. The Khoqandi troops made their way through the city streets, they faced off against the hakim's army at the Chirchik, River, and the hakim's forces were overrun. Defeated, Muhammad Sharif begged forgiveness and requested permission to remain hakim in Tashkent, serving on behalf of Khoqand rather than Bukhara.[9] Malla Bek refused. He took Muhammad Sharif back to Khoqand and replaced him with Sher 'Ali Khan's eldest son, Sarimsaq Biy.[10]

On their way back to Khoqand, Malla Bek led his army to Khojand and, on their arrival, Amir Nasrallah's hakim, Khoja Qalan Juybari, turned his city over without a fight. Back in Khoqand, Sher 'Ali Khan graciously welcomed the khoja, and the two began to form a close relationship that culminated some years later with the marriage of Sher 'Ali's son, Khudayar, to the Khoja's daughter. At the same time, Sher 'Ali Khan had Muhammad Sharif locked in a metal cage and tortured. He was eventually killed, ripped to pieces by an angry mob.[11]

This exceptionally harsh treatment of Muhammad Sharif is partly attributable to his failure to willingly return Tashkent to Khoqand, but other factors were also at play. During Madali Khan's twenty-year reign, Muhammad Sharif had been honorifically referred to as the Khan's Father (Khan Atāsī).[12] Considering the debauchery that Muhammad Sharif had enabled, the price that it had cost the Khoqandi people, and the ignominious end of Madali Khan's reign, it seems reasonable to conclude that Sher 'Ali Khan's torture and execution of Muhammad Sharif was a well-orchestrated public spectacle, the primary purpose of which was to distance himself and his reign from that of his predecessor.

In a matter of months, Sher 'Ali Khan had reasserted Khoqandi control over much of the territory that was lost during the tumultuous 1842 Bukharan invasion. But his good fortune would quickly change. The centrifugal forces and uncertainties inherently associated with periods of political transition combined with fears that Bukhara might return in force to propel a rapid rise in tensions among the Tajik, Kyrgyz, and Qipchaq peoples and terminally undermine Sher 'Ali Khan's reign. At the heart of the problem was that he himself had been raised among the Kyrgyz, and so any act

---

9. TS, f. 115b.
10. TS, f. 130b; MTF, f. 69b; AIKC, 232.
11. TS, f. 117b; MTF, fols. 67a–70a; AIKC, 398.
12. AIKC, 398.

or decision that appeared to favor them was met with deep suspicion from his other constituencies. One Qipchaq commander in particular, Musulmanqul Mingbashi, conspired to assert his independent control over the Qipchaq populations in the valley's south-central pasturelands, doing so at the great expense of the Kyrgyz who also occupied the region.[13] At the same time, a Tajik commander, Shadi Mingbashi, was serving as hakim of Marghilan and inflicting no end of pain on the Qipchaq populations in his vilayat.[14] After multiple battles and considerable loss, the rebellious Tajik commander Shadi Mingbashi orchestrated the defeat and murder of Sher 'Ali Khan's Kyrgyz brother-in-law, Yusuf Mingbashi. Sher 'Ali Khan responded coolly, and appealed to all parties to set aside their grievances for the interest of the state. The Qipchaq commander Musulmanqul then deceived Sher 'Ali Khan into arranging a meeting with his Tajik counterpart. The purpose for the meeting was ostensibly to negotiate a peace, but in reality it was an ambush that culminated in Shadi Mingbashi's murder. In the short term, Musulmanqul emerged victorious and the Qipchaqs had achieved the most influential position in the khanate.[15] Musulmanqul's treachery in achieving this goal and his partisan bias in the years that followed would have lasting and severely disruptive implications.

Thoroughly disaffected, the Kyrgyz in the area of Uch Qurghan and Alay put the city of Osh under siege.[16] At this, Musulmanqul once again claimed loyalty to Khoqand, and he led a substantial army of Qipchaq soldiers into the mountains to suppress the Kyrgyz rebellion.[17] The Khoqandi forces were in Osh for just two days when news reached him that the late 'Alim Khan's son Murad—who had three decades earlier fled Ferghana during 'Umar Khan's reign—had now returned at the head of some 200 troops. This small force somehow made their way into Khoqand, and, on August 16, 1844, they killed Sher 'Ali Khan and elevated Murad as the new khan.[18] Sher 'Ali Khan had ruled for little more than two years before he was laid to rest in the Shahrukhid mausoleum, the Dakhm-i Shahan.

Acting quickly, Musulmanqul dispatched spies to Khoqand and led his army westward to Namangan, where Sher 'Ali Khan's third son, thirteen-year-old Sayyid Muhammad Khudayar (ca. 1830–1881), born of his younger wife, was serving as

---

13. MTF, fols. 70a–71a. According to one source, Musulmanqul was given his name because his appearance was so ugly it was feared that if he were not named Muslim he might otherwise become an infidel, AIKC, 424.
14. TS, fols. 121a–123a; MTF, f. 71b; AIKC, 258.
15. MTF, fols. 72a–73a.
16. MTF, fols. 74b–75a.
17. MK, f. 134a. According to Umidi, Musulmanqul's army included 20,000 soldiers.
18. TS, f. 131b; MTF, f. 75a–b; AIKC, 421–22.

hakim. The spies reached Musulmanqul's encampment on the banks of the Naryn River and reported that Murad enjoyed no support within the city and that the aqsaqals of Khoqand would approve the installation of Khudayar in his place. Musulmanqul ordered a few of his closest advisors to fetch Khudayar and there, in the field, Musulmanqul placed the boy on a white felt rug and the military commanders elevated him in an ad hoc āq kigīz ceremony. Khudayar joined the army and returned to Khoqand. The Qipchaq troops met with little resistance as they entered through the Urgench Gate, and, as they made their way to the arc, they killed or captured as many Kyrgyz as they could find. Having served as the Khan of Khoqand for little more than one week, Murad Khan was executed.[19] In 1844, at approximately thirteen years of age, Khudayar Khan was placed on a white felt rug a second time and elevated to the position of khan by a more formal āq kigīz ceremony, this time in the Shahrukhid fortress in his ancestral capital of Khoqand.[20]

In selecting Khudayar to succeed his father, Musulmanqul passed over his two older brothers, Malla and Sarimsaq, both of whom were born of Sher 'Ali Khan's senior wife, Suna Oyim, and both of whom had a stronger claim to the throne than their younger brother Khudayar. Musulmanqul's decision to sidestep the more likely candidates in favor of Khudayar appears to have been a deliberate move to enhance his own power at court. Upon Khudayar's elevation, Musulmanqul used his authority as the khan-maker to assume a supervisory position over the affairs of state until his young protégé should mature sufficiently to take matters into his own hands. Musulmanqul's authority was enhanced by arranging the marriage of his daughter to Khudayar, a union that gave Musulmanqul additional leverage as the young ruler's father-in-law. But consolidating this arrangement required the support of Khudayar's oldest brother Sarimsaq, hakim of Tashkent vilayat.[21] To achieve that goal, Musulmanqul required diplomatic assistance, and for that he turned to the highly regarded leader of the Naqshbandiya-Mujaddidia sufi order in Khoqand, Miyan Khalil, also

---

19. MTF, f. 75b; MK, f. 134b. According to some traditions, Musulmanqul personally killed Murad Khan. Estimates for the number of days Murad was on the throne vary between eight and eleven. AIKC, 421.
20. TS, f. 133a; MTF, f. 76a–b; MK, f. 134b; AIKC, 178–79. Sources suggest that Khudayar was as young as twelve and as old as fifteen at the time of his ascension. The most detailed scholarly survey of Khudayar Khan's reign is found in the first chapter of Nabiev, *Iz istorii Kokandskogo Khanstva*, 29–95. Nabiev's work and the accompanying documents, produced in facsimile and Russian-language translation with notes, provide a considerable amount of interesting information regarding Khudayar Khan. However, Nabiev's treatment of this period in Khoqand's history is marred by his focus on a small set of documents that pertain to the khan's own properties and his determined effort to portray Khudayar Khan as an exploitative and despotic feudal lord.
21. AIKC, 232.

known as Muhammad Khalil Sahibzadeh, or Hazrat Sahibzadeh.[22]

Born in Peshawar, Miyan Khalil had long ago made his way to the Ferghana Valley and served the Shahrukhids in a number of high government posts. Most famously, he served as Khoqand's ambassador to Russia in 1841–42, a responsibility that involved a lengthy conversation with Tsar Nicholas I (r. 1825–55).[23] In 1846, Musulmanqul dispatched him again, this time to Tashkent, with the intention of enticing Sarimsaq Biy to return to Khoqand and pay his respect to his younger brother. Despite Miyan Khalil's assurances that Sarimsaq would be permitted to return to his post in Tashkent, Musulmanqul had secretly arranged for Sarimsaq Biy to be reassigned as hakim of Baliqchi, a remote post in the eastern stretches of the Ferghana Valley where the Qipchaq tribes were the dominant force. Three months later, Musulmanqul arranged for him to be killed. This infuriated Miyan Khalil and sent fear through the Khoqandi leadership, but it removed any threat that Sarimsaq may have posed to Musulmanqul's control over Khudayar Khan's reign.[24]

Since installing Khudayar Khan in 1844, Musulmanqul effectively marginalized his young son-in-law while building an administration that advanced the interests of the Qipchaq tribes at the expense of Sarts and Kyrgyz. He appointed loyal Qipchaq nobles to high military and government positions, and across the valley Sarts in particular complained that Qipchaqs had driven them from their farmland and restricted their access to much-needed irrigation canals.[25] Matters came to a head as Khudayar Khan came of age and began to strive to assert himself into Khoqandi politics. He had spent the early years of his life among the Kyrgyz, and he looked to

---

22. His full name was Hazrat-i Miyan Fazl Khalil. TS, fols. 134b–36b; MTF, f. 76a–b; AIKC, 164. Miyan Khalil and other religious figures employed as diplomats for Khoqand have attracted some scholarly attention. See Sherzodhon Mahmudov, "Muhammad Khalil Sakhibzade, The Leader of the Naqshbandia-Mujaddidia in Khoqand Khanate and his Embassy Activity," Kyrgyz Respublikasy Osh Mamlekettik Universiteti, *Arashan gumanitardyk institutunun ilimiy jurnaly* 17–18 (2015): 175–78. For an essay on the role of influential sufis in Khoqand's diplomatic exchanges with India, including Miyan Khalil, see Sherzodhon Mahmudov, "The Role of Sufis in Diplomatic Relations between the Khoqand Khanate and India," in *Sufism in India and Central Asia*, Nasir Raza Khan (New Delhi: Manakin Press, 2017), 39–52. For an analysis of the literature on the Naqshbandiya Mujadidiya, see JoAnn Gross, "The Naqshbandīya Connection: From Central Asia to India and Back (16th–19th Centuries)," in *India and Central Asia: Commerce and Culture, 1500–1800*, ed. Scott C. Levi (New Delhi: Oxford University Press, 2007), 232–59.

23. For a recent Uzbek-language study of all Khoqandi diplomatic relations with Russia, see Nosirjon Topildiev, *Qo'qon Khonligining Rossiia bilan diplomatic aloqalari tarikhidan (XIX asr–1876 yilgacha)* (Tashkent: Fan, 2007).

24. TS, f. 136a; MTF, f. 77a; AIKC, 232.

25. Thurman, "Modes of Organization," 35.

them and to the Sarts for support.

The process of wrenching power away from the Qipchaqs was bitterly contested, and before long the Qipchaq leadership began a series of uprisings across the valley that resulted in widespread devastation, including the deaths of a number of influential sufis and religious leaders.[26] This tilted popular opinion away from Musulmanqul and, as Khudayar Khan's efforts gradually bore fruit, Musulmanqul began to suffer dissension among his followers. With his power in the valley in tatters, Musulmanqul and a number of loyal Qipchaq nobles launched a campaign to take Tashkent for themselves. The Qipchaqs entered the city, but they were unable to hold it and were forced to withdraw.[27] With this loss, Musulmanqul seems to have determined that his best course of action would be to try to unite the Qipchaqs through bold leadership by organizing a large-scale campaign against Khoqand. The Qipchaqs made their way eastward with the army of Tashkent in pursuit and Khudayar Khan's brother Malla Bek leading the Khoqandi forces in defense of their capital. By all descriptions, the battle was horrendous: troops and bystanders went deaf from the sound of heavy artillery, guns, and bombs; the ground was soaked with blood from the mutilated bodies of Qipchaqs and Sarts; Musulmanqul fled, and Khoqand was victorious.

Three days after this battle, Khudayar Khan launched another campaign that aimed to end the Qipchaq threat for good. Relying heavily on Sarts, his settled populace, Khudayar Khan himself led the Khoqandi army eastward to Bilqillama Lake, near Baliqchi.[28] The Qipchaq tribes were again defeated and elected to cut their losses, submit to Khoqand, and turn over Musulmanqul.[29] Khudayar Khan took his father-in-law captive and forced him to watch as one after another Qipchaq noble was killed in front of him. Then, on November 2, 1852, Musulmanqul was publicly executed, hanged on the road to Khoqand.[30]

In his treatment of the events that followed the Qipchaq defeat, Niyazi generously suggests that Khudayar Khan had intended to restrict his punishment to the Qipchaq nobility but that the rest of the population in Ferghana was less forgiving. Mulla Yunus presents a less apologetic treatment in his *Ta'rikh-i 'Alimquli Amir-i lashkar*, a history of the Qipchaq commander 'Alimqul who was de facto ruler of Khoqand in

---

26. TS, f. 141b; MTF, f. 81a.
27. Niyazi provides a detailed account of the campaign, TS, fols. 142a–150a.
28. AIKC, 552.
29. TS, f. 150a–b; MK, f. 135a–b; MTF, fols. 85a–86a.
30. TS, f. 151a; MK, f. 135a–b; MTF, f. 86a.

later years.³¹ Reflecting on these events from his home in Andijan, where he wrote his history in 1902/3, Mulla Yunus recalls:

> By sunrise we had already arrived at the stream [running] near the palace gates. The Qipchaqs were also gathered there for a greeting ceremony at the palace. At that moment Badavlat ordered his warriors to draw their sabres, load their muskets and kill the Qipchaqs wherever they could be found. With loud cries both the mounted and foot soldiers broke into the citadel together, shouted at the Qipchaqs who were sitting at the table of food in the khan's presence, caught them, took them out and killed them. On that day all of the Qipchaqs in Khoqand except for the children of Utambay Mingbashi and Nar Muhammad Qushbegi were slaughtered; no one was left alive.³²

Over the next several months, a genocidal wave spread across the valley as Sarts purged Qipchaqs by the thousands.³³ Once that was brought to an end, with Khudayar Khan in firm control of the throne in Khoqand and his older brother Malla Bek serving as hakim in Tashkent, it must have appeared that at last, a full ten years after the Bukharan invasion, Khoqand had finally found firm footing. Nothing could have been farther from the truth.

RUSSIAN EXPANSION: THE VIEW TO THE NORTH

As Khudayar Khan was fully occupied with his father-in-law Musulmanqul, Russian forces were at the same time advancing southeastward from Fort Raim (Raimskoe ukreplenie), established in 1847 near the northeastern shores of the Aral Sea. In July 1852, apparently unprovoked, the Russian general Count V. A. Perovskii (1795–1857)

---

31. As discussed in the Note on Sources, Beisembiev establishes that the author of this chronicle, which lacks a signature and was previously considered to have been anonymous, was Mulla Mirza Yunus Jan Tashkandi, a subordinate of 'Alimqul and younger contemporary to Ya'qub Bek, LA, 2–4.
32. LA, 36–37/fols. 24b–25a.
33. The tradition circulates today that, during this period, Sarts would approach strangers in the bazaar, point to a pile of wheat, and ask the stranger to identify it. If the response was *gandom*, the Tajik word that the Sarts used, the person was safe. But if the person answered *boldoi*, the word for wheat the Qipchaqs favored, they were killed. According to Umidi, some 10,000 Qipchaqs were purged in this period, MK, f. 136a. Beisembiev suggests that the figure was higher, with 5,000 Qipchaqs killed just in the city of Khoqand and another 7,000 killed elsewhere in the valley, LA 37, note 102. Others place the total number as high as 20,000. Cf. Newby, *The Empire and the Khanate*, 232; Dubovitskii and Bababekov, "The Rise and Fall," 36.

dispatched one of his subordinates, Colonel Blaramberg, to run a reconnaissance mission to Aq Masjid to ascertain Khoqandi strength at the fortress. At that time, the Khoqandi commander of Aq Masjid was none other than Ya'qub Bek (b. 1820, Badaulat, "The Fortunate One"), the famous Tajik amir whose career would later take him to Kashgar. Blaramberg arrived to find the fortress at Aq Masjid missing its commander as Ya'qub Bek had been recalled to Tashkent to take up a leadership role in Khudayar Khan's fight against Musulmanqul.[34] Apparently, Blaramberg took the initiative, and, acting with neither orders nor proper siege artillery, he attacked Aq Masjid.

On receiving word of the Russian siege, Ya'qub Bek hastened back to his fortress at the head of a Khoqandi army. The Russians had in the meanwhile made little headway in their siege as their weaponry was not up to the task. The walls were strong, an estimated four fathoms (twenty-four feet) thick and six fathoms (thirty-six feet) high, and the Russian shells made little impact.[35] Ya'qub Bek's timely arrival, along with a lucky cannon shot fired from the fortress that struck and destroyed the Russian field guns, ended the initial siege of Aq Masjid.[36] The Russians withdrew, defeated but determined to recover the upper hand rather than suffer a permanent loss of prestige—a valuable commodity in steppe politics.

Perovskii himself prepared for the campaign the following year, and he personally led a larger force armed with proper siege artillery through the miserable wasteland, struggling against air thick with biting gadflies and mosquitoes. On July 2, 1853, Perovskii arrived outside the fortress, where he initially accepted an invitation from the Khoqandi commander of the fortress, 'Abd al-Wali, to negotiate a peace between the two powers. On reaching the fortress unarmed, however, Khoqandi sources themselves declare that the Khoqandi commander "conducted himself in a treacherous way, sent all the marksmen to the fortress wall . . . and after the command to 'Fire in volleys!,' fired at the Russians."[37] The effort to kill Perovskii failed, and from a safe distance he composed the following letter to the Khoqandi commander:

> From the Governor-General of Orenburg to the Commander of the Fortress of Ak-Mechet.
>
> By order of my Sovereign, the Emperor of all the Russias, I have come to take

---

34. LA, 35/fols. 22a; AIKC, 511–12.
35. Valikhanof, *The Russians in Central Asia*, 346.
36. LA, 35/f. 23a.
37. LA, 39/f. 28a–b.

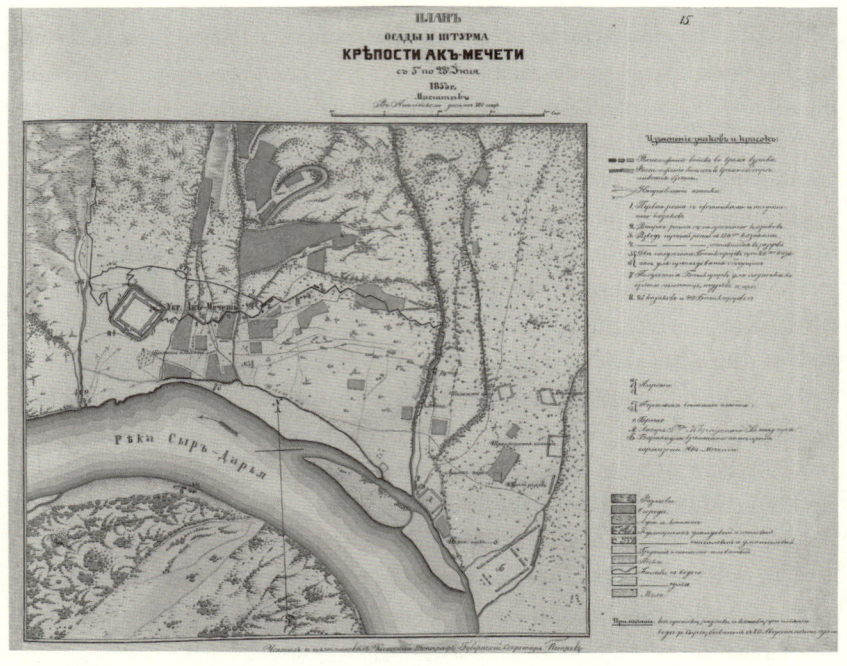

FIG. 6.1 Russian Plan for the July 1853 Conquest of Aq Masjid/Ak Mechet.
Turkestanskii Al'bom, 1867–72, Library of Congress, Prints & Photographs Division, LC-DIG-ppmsca-15112.

Ak-Mechet, erected by the Kokanians on Russian territory for the purpose of oppressing the Kirghizes [*sic*, Kazakhs], subjects of His Imperial Majesty.

Ak-Mechet is already taken, although you are inside it, and you cannot fail to perceive that without losing any of my men, I am in a position to destroy every one of you.

The Russians have come hither not for a day, nor yet a year, but for ever. They will not retire.

If you wish to live, ask for mercy; should you prefer to die in Ak-Mechet, you can do so; I am not pressed for time, and do not intend to hurry you. I here repeat that I do not come to offer you combat, but to thrash you until you open your gates.

All this I would have told you on the first day of my arrival, when I approached the walls of your fortress unarmed, had you not traitorously opened fire on me, which is not customary among honourable soldiers.[38]

---

38. Valikhanof, *The Russians in Central Asia*, 348–49.

Perovskii then prepared for the siege, and, though he encountered fierce resistance, the Russians inflicted a devastating defeat on Khoqand.[39] Choqan Valikhanov describes:

> After the first alarm at midnight, the troops were to commence issuing in parties from the trenches, and their gradual withdrawal was to continue until the second alarm. Before dawn, at three in the morning, on the discharge of three rockets, the remaining soldiers were to abandon the works, and a company would occupy the covered trenches. All the men would then be stationed 300 fathoms from the point where the mine would explode. After this, at half-past three, when three rockets would be discharged in rapid succession, the mine would be sprung, and the storm would immediately commence.
>
> All these arrangements were punctually carried out. At three o'clock, in the grey light of dawn, the earth shook, and a black mass of earth was hurled into the air, falling down in two confused mounds on the ground. Dense clouds of dust enveloped the fortress, and piercing shrieks arose from behind the walls. The mine was sprung most successfully; the part blown up presented an opening more than ten fathoms broad . . .
>
> Five minutes had hardly elapsed after the explosion, and the shrieks and cries of the women and children had not yet subsided, when the Kokanians were already at the breach, and though exposed to a severe fire of grape, poured heavy discharges of musketry at the batteries and Russian storming columns . . .
>
> Twice the Russians rushed to the assault but were vigorously repulsed each time, and driven into the ditch; it was only after the third attempt that the Kokanians were forced to retreat, and the Russians, reinforced by another company, occupied all the walls and opened fire from their guns on the garrison inside. The assault lasted altogether twenty minutes, and by half past 4 A.M. of the 8th of August, the fortress was in the hands of the Russians.
>
> The defence of the Kokanians at the breach, and at all points, was most desperate. Notwithstanding that Muhamed-Vali, the commandant, who had upheld the spirit of the garrison, was killed at the commencement of the storm, all his subordinates showed the same determined spirit, and were killed to a man. Two hundred and thirty bodies were counted in the ditch and inside the fort, which proves that the struggle, though short, was exceedingly severe.[40]

---

39. TS, f. 152b. See also M. L. Iudin, *Vziatie Ak-Mecheti v 1853 godu kak nachalo zavoevaniia Kokandskogo Khanstva* (Moscow: Izdatel'stvo Vladimira Bolasheva, 1917).
40. Valikhanof, *The Russians in Central Asia*, 354–56. Writing several decades later, Mulla Yunus provides a

FIG. 6.2 Ruined Gate of Aq Masjid, Interior of Fort Perovsk.
Turkestanskii Al'bom, 1867–72, Library of Congress, Prints & Photographs Division, LC-DIG-ppmsca-09957-00013.

The chronicler Niyazi, who tends to be generous in his treatment of Khudayar Khan, found Khoqand's loss of Aq Masjid to be so shameful that, Morrison suggests, he deliberately dated it to three years later, thus making it coincide with a rebellion that Khudayar Khan's brother Malla orchestrated in 1856 and excusing Khudayar Khan for Khoqand's failure to deal effectively with the Russian attack.[41] Despite Khoqand's concerted efforts to retake Aq Masjid, the Russians retained it, renamed it Fort Perovsk, and from that new forward outpost asserted their control over the abysmally hot and thoroughly unpleasant lower courses of the Syr Darya.

---

generous description of the Russian treatment of the women in the wake of their victory, LA, 39–40/ fols. 28b–29a.

41. See the chapter, "This particularly painful place: The failure of the Syr-Darya line," in Alexander Morrison, *The Russian Conquest of Central Asia: A Study in Imperial Expansion*, forthcoming. I am grateful to the author both for providing me with drafts of his chapters and for granting me permission to reference them here.

In 1847, the same year that Fort Raim was established to the west, Russia constructed another fortress some 500 miles to the east at Kopal, in Semirech'e. In 1854, one year after taking Aq Masjid, Russian troops moved southward from Kopal, crossed the Ili River, and established a new fortress which Tsar Nicholas I decreed should be named "Vernoe" ("Faithful") on the border of Khoqandi territory, at a location the Khoqandis referred to as Qurghan Almati.[42] Having established these two forward outposts, the Russian fortifications in the steppe at the time formed the shape of a great horseshoe, with a wide gap between Aq Masjid and Vernoe and Khoqandi control reaching northward through the middle as far as the Chu River. Khoqand was under siege from the north.

Continued Russian expansion into Central Asia was planned, but delayed by the Crimean War (1853–56). But even with Russia's distraction during these years, the introduction of this new political dynamic into the region added layers of complications to Khoqand's relationships with its Kyrgyz and Kazakh subjects and neighbors. These complications would first undermine Khoqand's authority in the steppe, and then everywhere else. From 1847 on, more than anything else, it was the Russian presence and its continued expansion in the region that disrupted the political environment of the khanate. Khudayar Khan launched a variety of efforts to recover lost territory. His methods were at times quite harsh, but they were intended to quell uprisings that Russia had put in motion.

The crisis that began to unfold in Khoqand had multiple implications at both the local and regional levels. Fearing what was to come from Russia, Khudayar Khan hoped that Great Britain might welcome an appeal from a potential Central Asian ally in the ongoing cold war (the Great Game) between those two imperial powers. With that in mind, on February 28, 1854, Khudayar Khan drafted a letter and dispatched an Afghan ambassador to deliver it to the Commissioner of Peshawar for the (soon to be dissolved) East India Company. The following is an excerpt from that letter, which was delivered to its recipient some six months later.

> Remembering our old friendship therefore, and looking on the two states as one, I have despatched the trusty Shahzadah Sooltan Mahomed to enquire after the prosperity of your government, and to ask your advice as to the best possible way of keeping at a distance these blackguard (*budmash*) Russians, and in short to freely communicate the state of things here, and ask your council [*sic*] in full reliance on your good will and friendship. He will then return to us with your communications.

---

42. See Bregel, *Atlas*, map 31, 62–63.

And my reliance on your friendship is such that I confidently hope that you will send one or two persons of . . . skill and wisdom in the arts of chemistry, and of the smelting of metals, with instruments of mining; and also a few military engines and weapons which might be the means of expelling this tribe of evil-doing Russians, who are always subverting order. By so doing you will prove your sincerity and increase our mutual friendship.[43]

But for all theND surrounding the Anglo-Russian Great Game and British aspirations in extending their colonial possessions into Central Asia, in fact the British demonstrated no interest in becoming entangled in Khoqand's struggle against Russia. It is, however, worth noting that a small number of Indian Muslim soldiers did take up the ambassador's call for help against Russia.

Many volumes have been written on Russian objectives in Central Asia, and there is no benefit in providing a full analysis of all the many factors that informed Russian colonial expansion into Central Asia.[44] It may be both useful and relevant, however, to clarify a couple of key points. In an incisive essay on the subject, Alexander Morrison advances a successful effort to dismiss two of the more frequently referenced Russian motivations, which, together, continue to constitute "a dominant narrative that refuses to go away."[45] These are the imperialistic ambition of Russian generals eager to take Central Asia before their Great Game adversaries beat them to it on the one hand, and the economically reductionist explanation that Russian industrialists engineered the conquest in an effort to transform Central Asia into a cotton-producing periphery on the other.[46] Although one can locate piecemeal evidence and generations of historiographic approval for both explanations (Lenin himself was keen to lay the Russian conquest of the region at the feet of "big capitalists" in general, and textile manufacturers in particular), Morrison

---

43. For the British summary of this ambassador's visit, see National Archives of India, Foreign, S.C., 24 November 1854, nos. 1–22, "Account of the Khanate of Kokand," 38–40. I am grateful to Alexander Morrison for bringing this report to my attention, and for providing me with his transcript of these records. A slightly later shortened summary of this report can be found in Sodhi Hukm Singh, *A History of Khokand: From the Commencement of Russian Intercourse until the Final Subjugation of the Country by that Power*, ed. Major Charles Ellison Bates (Lahore: Government Civil Secretariat Press, 1876), 4 and note.
44. For recent work on this theme, in addition to Morrison, see Kilian, "Allies and Adversaries."
45. Alexander Morrison, "Introduction: Killing the Cotton Canard and Getting Rid of the Great Game: Rewriting the Russian Conquest of Central Asia, 1814–1895," *Central Asian Survey* 33, no. 2 (2014): 132. The essay introduces a special issue of the journal *Central Asian Survey* on the Russian conquest of Central Asia, several contributions to which are referenced below.
46. For a recent iteration of the latter in a global context, see Beckert, *Empire of Cotton*, 345–46.

demonstrates that neither represented a driving force behind the Russian conquest of the region.[47]

Russia's conquest of Aq Masjid in 1853 and its establishment of Vernoe in 1854 had been undertaken explicitly to advance Russian territory southward into the sedentary zone, a plan that most certainly would have taken shape earlier had it not been delayed by the Crimean War.[48] Later in the 1850s, with that debacle behind them, Russian administrators in Orenburg began to focus attention on achieving a "natural frontier" in the south and debating whether such a frontier should begin, or end, with Tashkent. There was little in terms of resistance.[49] But to appreciate what led Russia to adopt such a perspective, one must look back much farther than just the 1850s. The process of Russian expansion in the steppe must be approached from the perspective of Russian relations with their Kazakh neighbors as they were taking shape already in the early eighteenth century.[50]

More than a century before the victory at Aq Masjid, Russian troops moved southward through western Siberia and established military forts along the Irtysh at Omsk, Semipalatinsk, and elsewhere. Thomas Welsford finds that, even prior to this period, in the sixteenth century, there was in effect no uniform Kazakh Khanate. Rather, khanal authority among the Kazakhs had been a considerably more complicated and diffuse "multiform polity" that poorly reflected the sedentarized model of the Shibanid Uzbeks, against which it has most often been compared.[51] In the early seventeenth century, the Kazakh tribes had come to constitute three more clearly defined separate powers that would become known as: the Kishi (Junior) Zhüz, situated above the Aral Sea in the west; the much larger Orta (Middle) Zhüz to the east, which maintained a contested frontier with the Jungar Khanate until the Qing brought that power to an end in 1757; and the Uly (Senior) Zhüz to the southeast, which controlled the cities in the southern steppe—including Tashkent, until 'Alim Khan's victory over the Kazakhs placed that city firmly in Khoqand's hands.[52]

---

47. Morrison, "Killing the Cotton Canard," 134–35.
48. Morrison, "Killing the Cotton Canard," 135.
49. See Alexander Morrison, "'Nechto eroticheskoe,' 'courir après l'ombre'?—Logistical Imperatives and the Fall of Tashkent, 1859–1865," *Central Asian Survey* 33, no. 2 (2014): 153–69.
50. This is a central argument advanced in Janet Kilian's above-mentioned dissertation, "Allies and Adversaries."
51. Thomas Welsford, "The Disappearing Khanate," in *Turko-Persian Cultural Contacts in the Eurasian Steppe: Festschrift in Honour of Professor István Vásáry*, ed. B. Péri and F. Csirkes (Leiden: E. J. Brill, forthcoming). I am grateful to the author for providing me access to his forthcoming work and permission to reference it here.
52. See Allen J. Frank, "The Qazaqs and Russia," in *The Cambridge History of Inner Asia: The Chinggisid Age*, ed. Nicola di Cosmo, Allen J. Frank, and Peter B. Golden (Cambridge: Cambridge University Press, 2009), 363–79.

The defining features of this long period in Kazakh history include the consolidation of Russian control along the Siberian Line, repeated Jungar-Kazakh wars in the early eighteenth century that culminated in the 1723 Jungar invasion that propelled the Kazakh Barefooted Flight, the stabilization of the eastern frontier following the Qing victory over the Jungars, and then, through the 1830s, Khoqand's expansion northward across much of the territory of the Senior Zhüz and deep into the pastures of the Middle Zhüz. Politically divided and pressured from the north by Russia and from the south by Khoqand, the Kazakh leaders were territorially restricted, militarily overpowered, and struggling against each other to access the pasturelands they needed to keep their animals fed and their people alive.[53]

One well-established strategy that the Kazakhs found useful to overcome the immediate challenges that confronted them was establishing alliances with both Russia and China. The military and logistical support they received in exchange for commercial treaties and assurances of peace could prove decisive in internal conflicts. But Kazakh rulers such as the Middle Zhüz's celebrated Ablay Khan (r. 1771–81) thought little of casting aside such allegiances when they lost their immediate value. Time and again this pattern frustrated the Russians.

From the early nineteenth century, this led the Russian administration to embrace policies that gradually imposed greater control over the Kazakh leadership and the actions of the Kazakh peoples. Politically, the Russians further divided the Middle Zhüz into three separate divisions, each of which was placed under the leadership of a Russian-appointed Kazakh who served as an agent to the Russian government.[54] They also imposed a new judicial system on their Kazakh subjects.[55] These moves provoked resistance, and some Kazakhs launched bold efforts to reassert the authority of the Kazakh khan. The most famous of these was led by Kenesary Kasimov, a Middle Zhüz descendant of Ablay Khan who, for a decade (1837–47), struggled to unite the Kazakhs under his leadership. In the end, Russian forces and their Kazakh allies pushed Kenesary and his Kazakh allies into northern Kyrgyz territories, where the would-be Kazakh khan was captured and killed. Before long those territories would also fall into Russian hands.[56]

---

53. For an excellent study of the ways that tsarist administrators worked to acquire knowledge of the steppe and its inhabitants, highlighting the agency of the Kazakh intermediaries in shaping Russian policies, see Ian W. Campbell, *Knowledge and the Ends of Empire: Kazakh Intermediaries and Russian Rule on the Steppe, 1731–1917* (Ithaca: Cornell University Press, 2017).
54. Bregel, *Atlas*, 62.
55. Virginia Martin, *Law and Custom in the Steppe: The Kazakhs of the Middle Horde and Russian Colonialism in the Nineteenth Century* (Richmond, Surrey: RoutledgeCurzon, 2001).
56. On the relationship between the development of new administrative positions in Kyrgyz governance

One can identify general patterns in the rapidly shifting political alliances and tensions in the steppe. While some in the Junior Zhüz and Middle Zhüz found value in embracing Russian patronage, during the 1820s and 1830s those in the more southern Senior Zhüz were inclined to embrace Khoqand. In her study of this dynamic, Janet Kilian examines how the tensions among Russia, Khoqand, Bukhara, Khiva, and the Qing all influenced Kazakh political dynamics, drawing Russia deeper into steppe politics in the process. Kilian presents Russian expansion into Kazakh territories as a dialectic that was driven during the eighteenth and nineteenth centuries by mutual need. Russia needed Kazakh aid in securing a stable frontier to protect Russian settlements from raids and improve trade with, and through, the Central Asian states to the south. At the same time, Kazakh ambitions in allying with the Russians centered on financial incentives and applying Russia's military strength to enhance their own authority. These alliances were perpetually negotiated, they were easily cast off, and over time they contributed to Russia's transformation into a more European-style colonial power.

Turning to Aq Masjid, Kilian emphasizes that the Russian conquest of that Khoqandi fortress would not have been possible had Kazakh allies not provided all varieties of supplies and animals to transport those supplies, as well as Kazakh labor and guides.[57] In the wake of the Russian victory, Kazakhs in the vicinity of the fortress initially remained loyal to Khoqand and even refused to sell the victorious Russians their animals out of fear that Khoqand would return and retaliate.[58] But once they realized that the Russians were entrenched, their allegiance shifted to favor the Russians. The result was the gradual consolidation of Russian control over the Kazakh zhüzes. It is, however, important to emphasize that the process of Russian expansion through the steppe did not unfold without its hurdles, and Khoqand was arguably the greatest of these.

Looking ahead, later in the 1850s, with the Crimean War behind them and relations with the Qing normalized following the 1851 treaty of Ghulja (Qulja), Russian plans resumed to close the gap that separated Perovsk (the new name for Aq Masjid) and Vernoe. In his study of Russian motivations behind these campaigns, Morrison sets aside the common trope of European colonial objectives to control and civilize the Kazakhs, who were depicted as unenlightened savages and Russia's "most

---

and Russian colonial expansion into the region, see Daniel Prior, "High Rank and Power among the Northern Kirghiz: Terms and Their Problems, 1845–1864," in *Explorations in the Social History of Modern Central Asia (19th–Early 20th Century)*, ed. Paolo Sartori (Leiden: E. J. Brill, 2013), 137–79.

57. Kilian, "Allies and Adversaries," 234.
58. Kilian, "Allies and Adversaries," 235.

inconvenient neighbors" in the Russian chancellor Alexander Gorchakov's infamous Circular, issued in November of 1864.[59] Instead, Morrison identifies more tangible motivations, and he finds that both political and ecological factors played important roles in pressing Russia to expand southward sooner rather than later.[60] Politically, even having lost control over Aq Masjid, Khoqand remained capable of exerting control over the populations that occupied the highly porous territories of the southern steppe. This created difficulties for the Russians' Kazakh allies, nomadic populations whose assistance was critical to the Russians' survival in the steppe, and whose winter pastures rested in Khoqandi territory.[61] Khoqandi forces aimed to extract taxes from these Kazakhs, and they launched repeated raids against both Russian and Kazakh settlements even into the 1860s.

No less important is that, ecologically, the lower Syr Darya was a bleak wasteland, as severely hot in the summer as it was cold and desolate in the winter, and infested by biting flies, mosquitos, scorpions, camel spiders, and tarantulas that made life excruciating for the soldiers posted to that region.[62] To the east, Vernoe was established where Almaty sits today—a lush zone surrounded by forests and mountains, with abundant clean water and ample access to the necessities of life. Already in the 1850s, Valikhanov presciently suggested that:

> Almaty, we are entitled to suppose, will soon become a place of no small commercial importance to all Central Asia. The small Tartar village with a mosque, now forming the southern part of the settlement, gives promise of being developed in time into a large trading town. The geographical position of Almaty, which is mid-way between Kuldja and Kokan, and on the road from Kashgar to Semipalatinsk, justifies us in anticipating that many merchants from the three neighbouring countries will transfer their activity to this point of convergence of the various routes of Central Asiatic commerce. Accordingly, we find that the commercial importance of Vernoé is increasing annually. Trading caravans, which so late as 1856 usually passed by without stopping, now always halt here for traffic.[63]

---

59. Alexander Morrison, "Russia, Khoqand, and the Search for a 'Natural' Frontier, 1863–1865," *Ab Imperio* 2 (2014): 166–67. For a recent study that emphasizes the role that the civilizing mission played among certain Russian imperial elite, see Ulrich Hofmeister, "Civilization and Russification in Tsarist Central Asia, 1860–1917," *Journal of World History* 27, no. 3 (2016): 411–42.
60. Morrison, "Russia, Khoqand, and the Search for a 'Natural' Frontier, 1863–1865," 166–67.
61. Kilian, "Allies and Adversaries," 234.
62. See the chapter, "'This Particularly Painful Place': The Failure of the Syr-Darya Line as a Frontier, 1851–1865," in Morrison, *The Russian Conquest of Central Asia*; Valikhanof, *The Russians in Central Asia*, 344.
63. Valikhanof, *The Russians in Central Asia*, 240.

Perovsk offered no similar amenities. As Aq Masjid, that fortress had been established as Khoqand's farthest western outpost in the steppe. It was maintained for purposes of strategy, exerting control over trade routes, and extracting taxes from Kazakhs. In essence, it was a hardship post. Meat was available, but other food supplies and local resources were lacking, agriculture was possible but difficult, the crops that were grown were insufficient, efforts to settle Kazakhs so that they might increase agricultural production were unsuccessful, and for the Russians to supply the several hundred men garrisoned there was proving to be extremely expensive and a logistical nightmare. Matters were made worse by high livestock mortality rates, repeated Khoqandi attempts to retake the fort, the exploitation of caravan traders who supplied the Russians at exorbitant rates, and the Russians' need to rely on Kazakh allies for help that often proved insufficient.[64] Fort Perovsk was repaired and bolstered with new fortifications in 1858–59, but it could not remain the terminal point of Russian expansion. It was merely a stepping-stone.[65]

After several years of discussion, debate, and analysis, with many views articulated and considered, it was clear that Russia would either need to accept the loss of prestige associated with retreating from Perovsk to Orenburg, or advance from Perovsk. It gradually became clear that the most desirable way to proceed would be to connect the Russian forts at Perovsk and Vernoe by establishing new defenses along the Syr Darya line, and then advance that frontier to a more easily managed and sustainable terminus. Fear that further advancement would stir animosity among the Central Asian khanates was outweighed by the prospect of establishing a colonial foothold in Tashkent and reaping the benefits of the transit trade that passed through that city.[66] In August 1863, Tsar Alexander II approved the plan to proceed in such a way, and it was realized soon thereafter.[67]

In May 1864, Russian forces advanced eastward from Perovsk and westward from Vernoe. The Khoqandi fortresses at Yangi Qurghan and Turkestan fell quickly in the west, as did Toqmaq, Pishpek, Merke, and Aulie Ata in the east. Underlining the importance that current military technology played in the victory, Major General Mikhail Cherniaev wrote to his father that his proud victory at Aulie-Ata "hardly cost us any losses, thanks to the constant rain, which prevented the Khoqandis from using their matchlocks."[68] The Khoqandi commander 'Alimqul's army initially

64. Kilian, "Allies and Adversaries," 235–36; Morrison, "This Particularly Painful Place."
65. Morrison develops this theme in his chapter on the establishment, and failure, of the Syr Darya Line.
66. Morrison, "This Particularly Painful Place."
67. Morrison, "This Particularly Painful Place."
68. Quoted in Morrison, "Russia, Khoqand," 175 and note 32.

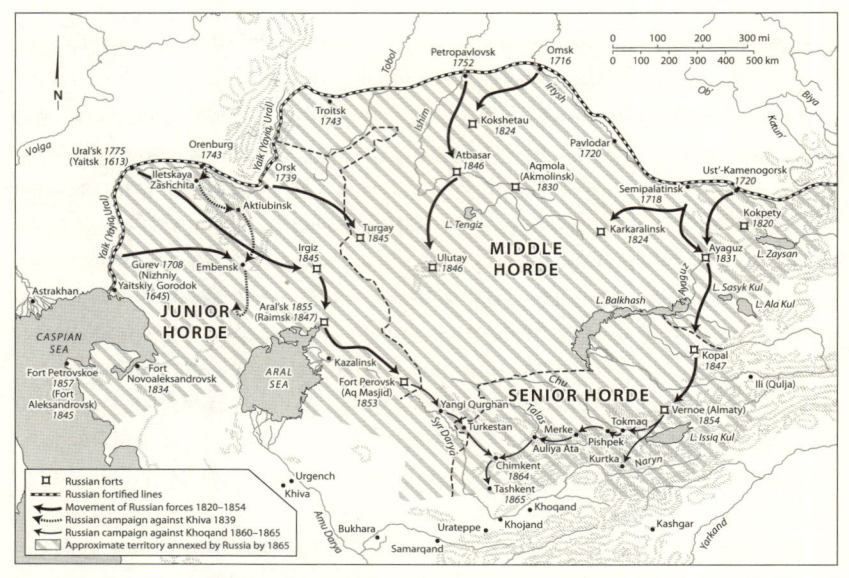

MAP 9 Russian Conquest of Central Asia.
Map by Bill Nelson. Based on the map, "Russian Conquest of the Kazakh Steppe c. 1865," originally drawn by Janet Kilian. Edited and reproduced with Janet Kilian's generous permission.

repelled Cherniaev's forces at Aq Bulaq as they approached Chimkent.[69] But the city's defenses were weakened when 'Alimqul was recalled to Ferghana to defend the capital from a Bukharan invasion—another opportunistic attempt to capitalize on the chaotic political climate in Khoqand at the time. Cherniaev's second campaign to take Chimkent met with success, and with that victory Russia had established its new "Khoqand Line" across the southern steppe, the whole of which was soon thereafter consolidated as a Russian district, subordinate to Orenburg. The often-repeated assertion that Russia had fully subjugated the Kazakh zhüzes by 1848 may be accurate from the Russian perspective. But from the vantage point of Khoqand, Russian control over the Senior Zhüz was secured only in 1864.

Later that fall, Cherniaev launched an embarrassing failed attempt to lead 1500 men to take Tashkent. Admonished, and having received contradictory orders, little guidance and apparently tacit approval from his superiors, Cherniaev resolved to rectify the situation and establish at Tashkent a firm, natural border with Khoqand farther to the south, thereby ensuring that "peace and order be introduced into the

---

69. Morrison, "Russia, Khoqand," 178.

khanate."⁷⁰ Waiting until spring, in May 1865, Cherniaev led a more substantial campaign that secured the Russian conquest of Tashkent.

That is not to say that the Russian conquest of Tashkent should be solely attributed to the ambition and efforts of one general. Cherniaev was one of many important actors in a long and complex historical process that had been unfolding for decades, even centuries, and that balanced multiple objectives with countless contingencies. In the end, it is difficult to disagree with Morrison's conclusion that "Cherniaev determined the timetable, but not the general direction of Russian policy."⁷¹ But with the Russian annexation of Tashkent, Khoqand had been stripped of its most valuable territorial possession. This put in motion a demoralizing wave of insecurity and an opportunistic fervor that would terminally destabilize Khoqand and ensure that Tashkent would be no more a natural border than Aq Masjid had been.

PROBLEMS IN KASHGAR: THE VIEW TO THE EAST

In the wake of Jahangir Khoja's 1826 invasion of Kashgar, the Qing expelled large numbers of Andijani merchants and began experimenting with trade sanctions, higher taxes, and more aggressive policies as a way to tighten their grip on Xinjiang. This resulted in widespread discontent, which Madali Khan exploited in 1830 by launching his own invasion of Kashgar. For reasons discussed in the previous chapter, Madali Khan's invasion failed to provoke the popular uprising that he had hoped it would. But his campaign was sufficient to remind the Qing how precarious their hold over the region truly was. The Qing were able to reassert their control over the region, but only at great expense in both silver and supplies.⁷²

In response, the Qing implemented a rapid return to earlier policies: they agreed to forgive locals who had supported the Khoqandi invaders, they compensated Andijani merchants for their lost merchandise and property, they permitted Andijanis and other foreign merchants the right to trade in Xinjiang free of taxation, and they placed Khoqand-appointed *aqsaqals* in charge of urban markets across the region. This created a predictable and secure commercial environment in the region that would last for the next two decades. As Millward notes, "both powers now shared an interest in border stability and the smooth functioning of commerce."⁷³

---

70. Morrison, "Russia, Khoqand," 183, 188.
71. Morrison, "Russia, Khoqand," 189.
72. Millward, *Eurasian Crossroads*, 113.
73. Millward, *Eurasian Crossroads*, 113–14.

This harmonious relationship came crashing down not long after the First Opium War (1839–42) as a series of rebellions, especially the exceptionally long, disruptive, and extraordinarily costly Taiping Rebellion (1850–64), spread across China.[74] This led to a fundamental Qing fiscal crisis with widespread ramifications across the empire that included bringing an end to the *xiexiang*, the Qing silver stipend, that the local begs in Altishahr had come to depend on. The Taiping Rebellion in southern China had nothing whatsoever to do with Central Asia. But once again, events unfolding far from Central Asia had a direct impact on the region.[75] While they were felt first in Xinjiang, it did not take long for the shock waves to reach Khoqand, too.

In the years after the First Opium War ended, the Qing were initially able to continue transferring silver into Xinjiang at levels that approximated the earlier pattern. Millward's statistics indicate that the *xiexiang* even increased in the 1840s, from just over 1,000,000 taels in 1838 to more than 4,000,000 taels in each of 1846, 1847, and 1848. The dramatic increase over the years reflected Qing efforts to undermine various khoja efforts to provoke rebellion among the very nobility whom the Qing depended on, and who depended on the Qing.[76] But as rebellions took root and spread, and the Qing economic crisis grew in magnitude, the Qing silver surplus disappeared. In 1853, silver shipments to Xinjiang were brought to an end. Millward summarizes:

> After around 1853, many provinces in China proper, particularly those in the devastated Jiangnan, began to default on their stipend obligations, and silver shipments to cities in Zungharia and Altishahr fell gravely into arrears . . . By 1858, Kashgar and Yangi Hisar had received no *xiexiang* (silver stipend) for four years, despite an 1857 attack led by khoja descendants Walī Khan and Tawakkul . . . In Yarkand, as the supply of silver *yuanbao* ingots declined, their price on the local market rose from 300–400 *tänggä* to 1,000 *tänggä* around 1860. Foreign traders in the city knew that the troops of the Qing garrison were no longer receiving their pay in silver, but in local coin. By 1860, according to a Board of Revenue estimate, the outstanding stipends owed Gansu and Xinjiang amounted to between 10 and 20 million taels.[77]

---

74. See Richard von Glahn, *The Economic History of China: From Antiquity to the Nineteenth Century* (Cambridge: Cambridge University Press, 2016), 374–84.
75. See the chapter "Global Crises of Oasis Capitalism, 1847–64," in Kim, *Borderland Capitalism*, 156–83.
76. Millward, *Beyond the Pass*, 61.
77. Millward defines *xiexiang* as "silver shipped from China proper to Xinjiang." Millward, *Beyond the Pass*, 58, 235–36.

Efforts to compensate for the deficit through mining and the introduction of copper coinage failed, and regional treasuries were rapidly drained.[78] The Qing had long used silver to facilitate their rule in the region. The fiscal crisis of the 1850s ground the Qing gears to a halt, and the khojas once again stepped in to try and restore Turkic Muslim rule in Kashgar.

The 1847 Holy War of the Seven Khojas was unsuccessful, but it could in some ways be seen as the initial stages of the uprisings that would eventually supplant Qing rule in Altishahr, albeit temporarily.[79] Newby notes that there remains some uncertainty about the identities of the specific khojas in question, as the sources that have survived often refer to them by different names and titles. But it appears that they were all sons or grandsons of Jahangir Khoja and his two brothers, and they included Katta Tore and two of his sons, as well as Yusuf Khoja, Wali Khan, Tawakkul Tore, Kichik Khan, and possibly also Buzurg Khan, the son of Jahangir Khoja himself.[80]

Katta Tore and his supporters were able to take Kashgar and appoint him the new ruler of the region, but their victory would be short-lived as the Turkic Muslims in Altishahr failed to deliver the widespread support that the khojas hoped they would.[81] Likely explanations are that the flow of Chinese silver into Xinjiang remained strong in the 1840s, and the khojas appeared not as charismatic spiritual figures, but as agents of Khoqand who threatened to undermine regional security. The khojas could rally several thousand troops, but they were incapable of giving rise to the groundswell of support that Jahangir Khoja had enjoyed two decades earlier.

In response to this invasion, some 20,000 families fled Altishahr in fear of an impending Qing reprisal or famine, many making their way westward for Khoqand. Thousands died along the road, and those who did manage to reach the Ferghana Valley found little support under Musulmanqul's regime. Many found no option at all other than to sell their children into a life of slavery for a few paltry coins to keep them alive.[82] Three months after Katta Tore took Kashgar, the Qing had reasserted control over the region and the khojas had returned to Khoqand.[83] A Qipchaq force, most likely dispatched by Musulmanqul, intercepted them as they were en route to Osh. The Qipchaqs placed Katta Tore in captivity and relieved the khojas of the

---

78. Millward, *Beyond the Pass*, 236–37; Kim, *Borderland Capitalism*, 157.
79. Newby, *The Empire and the Khanate*, 223–26. For further discussion, see Kim, *Borderland Capitalism*, 157–61, though Kim's explanations for events in Khoqand differ in a number ways from the interpretations presented here.
80. Newby, *The Empire and the Khanate*, 224 and note.
81. Newby, *The Empire and the Khanate*, 230.
82. Nalivkin, *Kratkaia istoriia*, 168. Referenced in Newby, *The Empire and the Khanate*, 226 and note.
83. Newby, *The Empire and the Khanate*, 225.

silver and other loot that they were carrying back from their brief escapade in Altishahr.

Despite their repeated defeats, the khojas were unwilling to give up their ancestral claim, and their efforts resumed as disaffection with Qing rule spread. In June 1852, Buzurg Khan, Tawakkul Tore, and their followers took advantage of the chaotic climate in the valley following Musulmanqul's execution to launch yet another, failed attempt to invade Kashgar. One month later, Qing troops repelled a similar invasion led by Wali Khan. Attacks continued as the termination of the silver stipend from 1853 exacerbated the widespread discontent in Altishahr and created fertile ground for continued rebellions. Small-scale khoja invasions were launched in 1854, 1855, and 1856, each of which was put down without having given rise to the popular rebellion that the khojas desired.[84] In 1857, Khoja Wali Khan unleashed yet another effort to restore khoja rule in Altishahr, this time on a much larger scale and with highly unexpected results.

In June of that year, Wali Khan passed the Qing *karun* (frontier outpost) with just a few dozen men. As he approached Kashgar that number grew to several hundred. Making their way straight for the city, he and his supporters caught the Qing defenders by surprise, and, the following day, Wali Khan and his followers took the city in the name of Buzurg Khan, son of Jahangir Khoja and the senior member of the family. Within a few days his followers swelled into the thousands, and before long he was said to have commanded an army of 70,000 cavalry soldiers and 4,000 infantry soldiers.[85] By all accounts, from the end of the silver stipend in 1853, the environment in Altishahr had deteriorated to such an extent that a substantial part of the local population was at last willing to throw their support behind the khojas in order to effect regime change.

On the throne, Wali Khan drew support from the extensive Khoqandi presence in the region—at the time Kashgar alone was home to between 4,000 and 6,000 Khoqandis.[86] But his leadership style proved to be exceedingly harsh, even tyrannical, and he quickly fell out of favor among the Turkic Muslims of Kashgar. Specifically, his imposition of dress codes, religious customs, and traditions that were common in Khoqand but alien to the Kashgaris led them to perceive his rule as a foreign occupation, and a much more invasive one than that of the Qing.[87]

---

84. Newby, *The Empire and the Khanate*, 233–34.
85. Newby, *The Empire and the Khanate*, 235–37.
86. According to Newby, Qing sources estimate the number of Khoqandis in Kashgar alone to have been between 4,000 and 5,000. Valikhanov suggests the higher figure of 6,000. Newby, *The Empire and the Khanate*, 237.
87. Newby, *The Empire and the Khanate*, 237–40.

This perception was confirmed by the Kazakh scholar and soldier Choqan Valikhanov, who secretly made his way to Kashgar in the guise of a merchant the following year and found that, rather than representing a return to the celebrated khoja rule of a century earlier, Wali Khan was considered a Khoqandi ruler, and not a very good one at that.[88] That is not to say that the khojas were working on behalf of Khoqand. There is little to support claims that Khudayar Khan himself had supported the khojas in their efforts, although there is also no evidence to suggest that he obediently followed Qing demands to obstruct those campaigns. In any event, Kashgari support for Wali Khan's rule quickly diminished, and some three months after Wali Khan had taken the throne, Qing relief forces arrived and his troops scattered.

Wali Khan would not be the last Khoqandi with aspirations in Kashgar. Already in the following year, shortly after unseating his younger brother in 1858 and taking the throne in Khoqand for himself, Malla Khan dispatched an ambassador to Beijing to affirm Khoqand's relations with the Qing. The ambassador, 'Abd al-Karim, was denied permission to proceed from Yarkand. Angered at this insult and waiting impatiently for instructions from Malla Khan, over the next year 'Abd al-Karim's behavior slid into lecherous debauchery, and he was unceremoniously killed during a brawl with Qing troops.[89] In the interim, it seems that he had worked feverishly to "stir up trouble" and exploit the weakening Qing hold over the region to the advantage of Khoqand.[90] In a letter he had secretly dispatched to Malla Khan, but which the Qing discovered before it could pass beyond the karun, 'Abd al-Karim wrote:

> The Muslims in China all read the Islamic scriptures and look forward to being governed by a ruler like you. Large numbers of Muslims gather at the *mazār* and all through the night they wail and recite the scriptures as they long for your highness. Now we await you, *inshallāh*. It looks as though the region governed by the Chinese is deteriorating day by day. Everyone looks forward to when all the land west of Hami will be under your control.[91]

---

88. Newby, *The Empire and the Khanate*, 237. See the published account, Chokan Ch. Valikhanov, "O sostoianii Altyshara ili shesti vostochnykh gorodov Kitaiskoi provinstii Nan-lu (Maloi Bukharai) v 1858–9 godakh," in Valikhanov's *Sobranie sochinenii* (Alma-Ata: An Kaz SSR, 1962), 2:265–412.
89. For the full account of 'Abd al-Karim's experiences and objectives in Altishahr, see Newby, *The Empire and the Khanate*, 240–46.
90. Newby, *The Empire and the Khanate*, 242.
91. The quotation, translated from Qing records, belongs to Newby. Newby, *The Empire and the Khanate*, 242.

Malla Khan would never achieve that goal, and one after another, the khoja campaigns failed as the charisma of their lineage diminished. But they did open the door for the Khoqandi Amir-i Lashkar, the opportunistic adventurer Ya'qub Bek, to invade Kashgar in 1864, displace the Qing, and rule the region as the Amir of Kashgar until his death in 1877.[92]

TIMES OF TROUBLES

Khoqand never recovered from the Bukharan invasion that ended Madali Khan's reign. Two years later, in 1844, Sher 'Ali Khan had managed to reassert Khoqandi authority over Tashkent, and he appeared to have achieved some success at stabilizing the khanate when 'Alim Khan's son Murad returned from exile, killed him, and usurped the throne. Little more than a week later, Sher 'Ali Khan's Qipchaq commander Musulmanqul returned to Khoqand, killed Murad Khan, placed Sher 'Ali Khan's young son Khudayar on the throne, and then arranged for the new khan to marry his own daughter. In this uncertain environment, Qipchaqs, Kyrgyz, and Sarts struggled against each other for resources and power, and with Musulmanqul asserting his control over his son-in-law and the state, for the next several years the interests of the Qipchaqs won out. Musulmanqul had played the ethnic card for the benefit of his own community, and, with Russian expansion and Chinese fiscal policies destabilizing Khoqand, it could not be unplayed.

Khoqand had thrived for more than a century by balancing the interests of its multiple ethnic and religious constituencies. But during the last three decades of its existence, ethnic conflict grew fierce. Later histories have tended to attribute this to the tyrannical favoritism of the ruling elite, who were indeed guilty of permitting, and even orchestrating, horrific partisan acts. This chapter has argued that the rise in ethnic conflict during these years was a symptom of two principle underlying causes: a growing sense of insecurity stemming from Russian expansion in the north, which became especially severe as Khoqand's steppe fortresses fell beginning with Aq Masjid in 1853; and economic problems associated with the Qing fiscal crisis to the east, which led to widespread rebellions and, also in 1853, the end of the silver stipend that had long ensured the loyalty of Turkic Muslim nobles in Altishahr. It was just months before those events that Khudayar Khan had aligned with the Sarts

---

92. Kim Hodong, *Holy War in China: The Muslim Rebellion and State in Chinese Central Asia, 1864–1877* (Stanford: Stanford University Press, 2004).

to outmaneuver his Qipchaq father-in-law, capture him, and, in November 1852, order his execution. But Khudayar Khan's success did not bring a resolution to the crises that confronted his khanate. From this point forward, Russia's increasingly aggressive presence in the region would ensure that Khoqand's troubled times would continue and that the stable and "natural border" that the Russians had long hoped to reach would always remain over the horizon.

Seven
KHOQAND DEFEATED, 1853–1876

THE LATER RULERS of Khoqand (and indeed Central Asia more generally) often appear in the historical record as despots and exploitative feudal warlords who, if they were not completely incapable of delivering effective governance to their people, had little interest in doing so. As is often the case, one can find evidence to support such a perspective, but that evidence represents only part of the larger picture. The discussion in this final chapter analyzes the Khanate of Khoqand's dramatic collapse from the Khoqandi perspective. In doing so, it identifies multiple contributing factors behind the collapse, and tyranny, despotism, and greed had little to do with it. In fact, the principal force propelling the Khoqandi crisis was actually external to the region. From 1853, as the Russian Empire expanded southward through the steppe, the Russian imperial presence itself became a destabilizing force even beyond the Russian frontier. This created a context of crisis that led ethnic factions within the khanate to seek out opportunities to secure their own interests and, ultimately, terminally undermine indigenous authority in the valley.

Having swept through the southern steppe in just twelve years, in 1865, General Mikhail Cherniaev led the Russian conquest of Tashkent. Cherniaev appears to have intended Tashkent to represent a stable southern border for the Russian Empire. But as was the case in so many other Asian and African states that rose and fell during the Age of Empire, internal conflict within Khoqand deepened as the Russian presence in the region increased. The resulting instability created both the opportunity for Russian colonial expansion into Khoqand as well as a perceived need among the Russian administrators to act on that opportunity in the interest of restoring stability. The Russians defeated the army of Khoqand in 1868, and then in 1876 utterly extinguished the khanate and incorporated the Ferghana Valley into the Russian Empire.

As the history of Khoqand moves beyond all vestiges of early modernity and into Central Asia's Russian imperial period (1865–1918), researchers suddenly have an overabundance of historical sources. Manuscript libraries offer collections of locally produced sources; archival holdings include the expansive Russian state records, correspondence, and legal documents; other libraries boast rich collections of journalists' reports and travel accounts, memoirs, diplomatic records, Russian and Soviet Orientalist scholarship, photographic archives; and researchers can also look to architectural monuments, archeological remains, and a growing body of contemporary scholarship produced both within the region and internationally. There is much work to do on this material, and much that can be done. But here I focus only on the elements needed to complete this study of how globalizing forces shaped the gradual rise, efflorescence, and fall of the Khanate of Khoqand.

KHOQAND DEFEATED

In 1852, Khudayar Khan had appointed his older brother, Malla Bek, to serve as hakim of Tashkent. Mulla Yunus suggests that there had already been considerable friction between the brothers, and that Khudayar dispatched Malla to Tashkent specifically because the young ruler feared his "harsh and impertinent" nature, and wanted him far from Khoqand.[1] The following year brought new challenges: General Perovskii led the Russian conquest of Aq Masjid and the Qing silver stipend ended, after which the khojas launched a series of successive attempts to reclaim Altishahr from the Qing. Whether it was warranted or not, Khudayar Khan is said to have laid the blame for the loss of Aq Masjid on his brother.[2] With the Qipchaq tribesmen disaffected following the execution of Musulmanqul and the realm under siege from the north, Malla Bek defended himself. He and his supporters began to claim that Khudayar Khan was incapable of navigating the challenges that faced Khoqand and that Malla Bek should be placed on the throne instead.[3]

---

1. LA, 38/f. 26b.
2. TS, f. 153a.
3. MK, fols. 136b–37a; LA, 38/f. 27a.

Acting quickly before harsh dialogue could turn into rebellion, Khudayar Khan placed his Tajik commander Ya'qub Bek as hakim of Khojand, and he himself led his army to Tashkent. Malla Bek realized that he was outmatched and had little chance at victory and, dispatching word of his apologies to his brother, fled to Samarqand where Amir Nasrallah welcomed him and offered him sanctuary.[4] Some months later, Khudayar Khan's younger half-brother Sufi Bek, the hakim of Andijan, hosted a great three-month-long *khitān* celebration (*toi*) to honor the circumcision of Khudayar Khan's first son, Nasir al-Din Bek.[5] Amir Nasrallah appointed Malla Bek to serve as the Bukharan ambassador to Khoqand, and he dispatched him to Andijan so he, too, could attend the festivities for his nephew. The two brothers made peace, and Khudayar appointed his older half-brother to serve as hakim of Marghilan.[6]

Several years later, Nasrallah's forces launched yet another campaign against Khoqand. Starting out from Urateppe, in just a few weeks the Bukharan army made its way to Toqai Teppe and then placed Khoqand under siege for two months before successfully taking the city. Again, the deciding factor in the Bukharan victory does not seem to have been an overwhelming military strength. Rather, with the Bukharans approaching, Malla Bek perceived an opportunity to take advantage of ethnic conflict in the valley. Khudayar Khan had relied heavily on the Sarts in his efforts to defeat his Qipchaq father-in-law, Musulmanqul. Malla Bek now exploited this to rally the support of the Qipchaqs and the Kyrgyz against Khudayar, and he then collaborated with Bukhara to force Khudayar Khan to submit and flee.[7] Nasrallah placed Malla on the throne in Khoqand and made his way back to Bukhara. Khudayar Khan's first reign (1844–58) was brought to an end.[8]

Malla Khan's reign began late in 1858 with the appointment of Qipchaqs and Kyrgyz to Khoqandi leadership posts at the expense of the Sarts.[9] Exhibiting his familiar bias and illustrating the ethnic tensions prevalent in the Ferghana Valley at the time, in his description of Malla Khan's three year and four month reign, Niyazi decries that "steppe people were everywhere." His objection to Malla Khan's bias in favor of the Qipchaqs and Kyrgyz is further evidenced in the title of his chapter: "The Events of Malla Khan on the First Day of his Assumption of Power,

---

4. TS, f. 155a; MK, 137b; LA, 40/f. 29b. According to Umidi, this happened in 1856/7.
5. MK, f. 138a; LA, 42/f. 32b; AIKC, 495.
6. MK, f. 138a.
7. TS, fols. 157b–158a.
8. MK, f. 139a.
9. AIKC, 461.

His Misrule, His Bringing of Thieves into his Bed Chamber, and the Ways of Steppe Women."[10]

Other sources give a slightly less unsympathetic perspective. Under Malla Bek's leadership Khoqandi forces tried vehemently to stem Russian expansion, but their efforts did little even to slow the inevitable. The Russians were occasionally held back in the many engagements during these years, but their campaigns were largely successful, immensely disruptive, and they made establishing an effective ruling regime essentially impossible. Following the Russian destruction of the Khoqandi fortress at Yangi Qurghan in the autumn of 1861, the support of Malla Khan's Qipchaq and Kyrgyz troops began to waiver.[11] His own Kyrgyz troops rebelled and killed him, on or about February 25, 1862, and replaced Malla Khan with his nephew Murad Bek, the son of Malla's elder brother Sarimsaq Biy and former hakim of Namangan and Marghilan. Murad Bek now ruled for roughly four months as the Kyrgyz puppet, Shah Murad Khan (r. 1862).[12]

When word reach Khudayar Khan that Malla had been killed, he immediately began preparations to retake Khoqand. Amir Nasrallah died in 1860, and his son and successor, Amir Muzaffar al-Din (r. 1860–86), found greater value in helping Khudayar Khan retake the throne than in trying to build a relationship with the young and inexperienced Shah Murad Khan. Khudayar Khan took advantage of this support and, first traveling northward into the steppe, assembled an army as he made his way to Tashkent, which he took by force.[13] The two armies of Khudayar Khan and Amir Muzaffar then made their way to take Khojand, where Ya'qub Bek was appointed a second time to serve as hakim.[14] The Bukharan forces remained behind and Khudayar Khan advanced into the valley and recovered Khoqand. Khudayar Khan defeated Shah Murad Khan's forces, captured him, and then forgave him at least partly, it seems, as a reward for the service he played in removing Malla Khan from the throne.[15] So began Khudayar Khan's second reign as the Khan of Khoqand (1862–63).

No sooner had Khudayar Khan retaken the throne than he was confronted by yet another rebellion, this one led by his own Qipchaq military commander, 'Alimqul, the chief protagonist in Mulla Yunus's *Ta'rikh-i 'Alimquli Amir-i lashkar*.[16] The

10. TS, fols. 164a–66a.
11. LA, 42–43/f. 34a
12. TS, fols. 178b–80a; LA, 85–86; AIKC, 17–18, 461.
13. TS, fols. 180b–84b; MK, f. 139b.
14. LA, 48/f. 42b. Ya'qub Bek served in this post from circa 1853–58, and again from 1862 until his departure for Kashgar, LA, 85.
15. TS, f. 187b; MK, f. 139b.
16. LA, 51/f. 46a–b.

FIG. 7.1 Muhammad Khudayar Khan.
Turkestanskii Al'bom, 1865–72, Library of Congress, Prints & Photographs Division, LC-DIG-ppmsca-14268.

FIG. 7.2 Military Assembly in Courtyard of Khudayar Khan's Ark.
Turkestanskii Al'bom, 1865–72, Library of Congress, Prints & Photographs Division, LC-DIG-ppmsca-12229.

fallout appears to have begun immediately upon Malla Khan's death, suggesting that the Qipchaqs, who had enjoyed Malla Khan's support, were unwilling to submit to Khudayar Khan and his Sart allies. With the loss of their Shahrukhid patron, 'Alimqul brought all of his loyal commanders to his home in Tashlaq, a village near Andijan, and he proceeded to distribute "forty or fifty thousand *tangas* [silver coins]" as well as weapons among his subordinate commanders and their troops.[17]

The valley was torn apart as the two factions fought for control over Khoqand, an ethnic rivalry that is apparent in the partisan nature of the sources themselves. Niyazi presents a Tajik, or Sart, perspective of the eight-month conflict that favors Khudayar Khan and highlights the bravery of the Sarts in fighting against 'Alimqul and the traitorous Qipchaqs. This contrasts with the pro-Qipchaq narrative of Mulla Yunus that praises 'Alimqul, "The blessed Amir-i Lashkar," who elevated the young son of Malla Khan, Sultan Sayyid Khan (b. 1847; r. 1863–65), as his own Shahrukhid (puppet) in his effort to restore strength and stability to Khoqand.[18] In the end, the Qipchaqs emerged victorious, and Khudayar Khan was left with few options other than to withdraw and seek refuge in Bukhara a second time. 'Alimqul had Shah Murad Khan killed, an event that Niyazi condemns, and which Mulla Yunus fails to mention.[19] The latter chronicler summarizes:

> The order was given to bring Sultan Sayyid Khan, the son of Malla Khan the Martyr, out of Namangan and he was unanimously elevated to the khan's throne. But the management of State affairs such as revenues and expenditures, dismissals and appointments, executions and the minting of coins and all the important affairs [connected with] property and possession were delivered and entrusted to the late Amir-i lashkar. In conformity with this an agreement containing severe and frightful oaths and vows was composed by my own pen. All 'ulama, and great and worthy people, headed by His Majesty the Khan, with sincere hearts put their hands on the agreement and stamped it with their seals. Finishing these affairs [they] set out and entered Kokand.[20]

The following year, in 1864, Russian troops pressed southward from their forts at Perovsk and Vernoe. While Russian plans for further expansion had long been under discussion, Niyazi lays the blame for these losses squarely on 'Alimqul, arguing that

---

17. LA, 50/f. 45a–b.
18. TS, fols. 188a–207a; LA, 50–59/fols. 45a–61a; AIKC, 240.
19. TS, f. 208a–b.
20. LA, 59–60/fols. 61b–62a.

the Qipchaq coup was unjust and that it had enabled the Russians to exploit the discord in Khoqand and advance against little resistance.[21] Before Khoqand could respond, the Russians had taken all of the fortresses of the southern steppe and Khoqand's Kazakh subjects had fallen under Russian control. The puppet Sultan Sayyid himself fled for Bukhara as, Mulla Yunus relates, 'Alimqul "cheerfully set out for Chimkent with the whole army of Kokand and Ferghana and with artillery."[22] 'Alimqul fought hard, but after repelling Cherniaev's forces from Chimkent once, he was forced to withdraw to Khoqand to defend the city, yet again, from a Bukharan invasion. Despite Khoqand's larger military and determined effort, in September 1864, Cherniaev took Chimkent using a stereotypical steppe strategy. Mulla Yunus describes:

> The Russian army of General Cherniaev surrounded Chimkent. A day or two later [Cherniaev], employing a [clever] stratagem, pretended to be put to flight and retreated a little. The stupid Mirza Ahmad Qushbegi became conceited and said: "The Russians have fled and been defeated." He went out of Chimkent with all his forces and pursued the Russians. General Cherniaev turned around, launched an attack, put them to flight and occupied Chimkent . . . Mirza Ahmad Qushbegi and all his subordinates lost their ammunition, arms and outer garments and escaped to Tashkent on horseback with only their whips.[23]

It was just one month after his victory over Chimkent, in October 1864, that Cherniaev led his first expedition against Tashkent. The siege lasted ten days and failed even before 'Alimqul, who was in Khoqand, received word that Ya'qub Beg's forces had successfully defended the well-fortified city against the relatively small Russian force.[24] But for reasons discussed above, Cherniaev was able to return the following year with a more carefully planned strategy to extend the Russian frontier beyond the steppe and establish a Russian colonial foothold in Tashkent. A letter that the newly appointed governor of Orenburg, N. A. Kryzhanovskii, dispatched to Cherniaev on February 25, 1865, includes the following instructions from the Foreign Ministry:

> As for Tashkent, I beg your Excellency vigilantly and closely to observe everything that occurs in this town, and to assist the moral party that wishes to separate from

---

21. TS, f. 209a.
22. LA, 63/f. 67a. See also TS, f. 213a.
23. LA, 68/f. 75a–b.
24. LA, 69/f. 76b and note 257.

hostile Khoqand and through your actions to direct the formation from Tashkent of a polity, independent from Khoqand and Bukhara, but a vassal of Russia.[25]

The ignorant and ambiguous nature of Kryzhanovskii's instructions equipped Cherniaev with considerable autonomy to act as he saw fit within the vague parameters that the Ministry had set for him, parameters that clearly did not forbid him from launching an attack against Tashkent. Morrison concludes, "it is certainly hard to see how he could have been expected to bring the city within the Russian sphere of influence, or create an independent khanate out of it without first attacking the city and expelling the Khoqandi garrison."[26] In any event, with the winter behind him and spring set in, on April 23, 1865, Cherniaev dispatched his response to Orenburg in which he declared that the establishment of a permanent boundary with Khoqand remained unsettled and that, to bring Khoqandi raids to an end, "it is essential that peace and order be introduced into the khanate, and this in turn will be possible only with the establishment of our solid influence in the khanate itself."[27] Less than one week later, Major-General Cherniaev was leading another, considerably larger campaign against Tashkent.

The Russian troops soon reached the Khoqandi fortress of Niyazbek, on the outskirts of Tashkent. Following the same strategy that 'Umar Khan had applied when he took the city on behalf of his brother, the Russians took over the fortress and diverted the Chirchik River, the city's primary source of water. In the hot and dry climate of Central Asia, this ensured that the city's residents would suffer even more acutely while under siege.

In a matter of days, word reached 'Alimqul in Khoqand that the Russians had begun to march against Tashkent. Acting quickly, he dispatched riders to his hakims across the valley and ordered them to dispatch their armies to come to the city's aid.[28] Tashkent remained Khoqand's most important possession, and so, without even waiting for the reinforcements to arrive, 'Alimqul took off to defend the city. Mulla Yunus himself accompanied the Khoqandi army, and, in his very personal account of the events that followed, he describes how 'Alimqul grew distraught when he received word that the people within the city were beginning to come to terms with the fact that they would soon be subjects of the Russian emperor.[29] There had

---

25. For the full reference, see Morrison, "Russia, Khoqand," 187–88 and note. The translation is Morrison's.
26. Morrison, "Russia, Khoqand," 188.
27. Morrison, "Russia, Khoqand," 188. The translation is Morrison's.
28. LA, 74/f. 86b.
29. TS, f. 214b; LA, 75/f. 87b.

for some time been a group of merchants who saw wisdom in handing the city over to the Russians.[30] But with the Russian army camped outside the city walls and the city suffering from growing hunger and thirst, ʻAlimqul feared that pro-Russian sentiments would take root and grow.[31]

ʻAlimqul camped at Keravchi, a short distance from Tashkent, and he sent Mulla Yunus into the city to let the people know that he and his forces had arrived. Mulla Yunus did as ordered, but apparently suffered heat stroke and fell unconscious in the process. His account of subsequent events as they unfolded on May 20, 1865 is as follows:

> On the following day I came to myself due to the sound of cannons. Being utterly feeble as though dead I learnt that on my departure from Keravchi, according to the will of Him who predetermines fate and fixes [the time] of death, the Amir-i lashkar came to Tashkent also and joined battle against the Russian army. When the Russian forces were confused from the cannonade and gunfire of the Muslims, by the predestination of Allah, one bullet [fired] from the Russian army struck the late Amir-i lashkar and he fell from his horse. The Muslim army stopped fighting. He was laid on horseback, and transported into the city. Had it happened an hour or a half-hour later—God knowing better!—the Russian forces would have been defeated and would have fled. But the will of the glorious and most high God was that the vilayat of Turkistan and Ferghana would be passed into the possession of the emperor.[32]

ʻAlimqul had been shot in the stomach. He was lifted from the ground and taken into the city, where soon thereafter he died. On June 27, 1865, the Russian troops breached the city walls and stormed Tashkent. Two days later, the few remaining defenders surrendered to Major-General Cherniaev. For a year, the Russian government considered how it should proceed and, setting aside the original intention of creating a vassal khanate, in August 1866, Tsar Alexander II (r. 1855–81) officially annexed it into the Russian Empire.

As Tashkent remained under siege, many of ʻAlimqul's Qipchaq commanders fled the battle and returned to Khoqand, where they took the opportunity to elevate to the throne a new khan. The candidate they chose was Khudayqul Bek, an unknown figure from a minor Shahrukhid lineage who had apparently previously worked as a

---

30. Morrison, "Russia, Khoqand," 188.
31. TS, f. 214b.
32. LA, 76/fols. 90a–91a.

tailor specializing in the making of waistbands.³³ On learning of the Russian conquest of Tashkent and the elevation of Khudayqul, the Bukharan Amir Muzaffar and Khudayar Khan launched yet another collaborative invasion of the Ferghana Valley, garnering support from local Uzbeks and Tajik troops.³⁴ The campaign met with immediate success, and some forty days after Khudayqul had ostensibly assumed leadership in Khoqand, he was forced to flee the valley, making his way eastward to Kashgar, where the Qipchaqs were deeply engaged in a struggle to wrench Kashgar from Qing hands.³⁵ On July 12, 1865, Khudayar Khan sat on the throne to begin his third and final term as the khan of Khoqand (1865–76).³⁶

YA'QUB BEG BADAULAT, AMIR OF KASHGAR

In the year preceding his death in 1865, 'Alimqul spent a substantial amount of time within the walls of Tashkent anticipating the inevitable Russian return. This was a time of reflection, and a time of planning. Ya'qub Beg is said to have grown nervous as 'Alimqul isolated himself from everyone but Mulla Yunus, who was relaying 'Alimqul's orders and delivering news to his private residence, news that included reports that the political environment in Altishahr had deteriorated considerably and the Kyrgyz had taken, and looted, Kashgar.³⁷ Mulla Yunus reassured Ya'qub Beg that all was as it should be and he informed him that "His Worship, the Amir-i lashkar is thinking and dreaming about making you a padishah."³⁸ Three days later, 'Alimqul assembled the leadership of Khoqand ("the pillars of the state"), including Ya'qub Beg, and, directing his gaze to Buzurg (also Buzruk) Khan, the son of Jahangir Khoja, he announced:

> "You are a töra and the khan of Kashghar. But the rule over the country, taking and giving, punishment and execution, dismissal and appointment, and affairs like these will be entirely in the hands of Badavlat, and you are never to [counteract] him. Content yourself with the titles of Khan and töra and abandon yourself to delights

---

33. MK, f. 142a; TS, f.219b; LA, 77/fols. 91b–92a and note 288. Khudayqul's lineage is traced through his great-grandfather, the unfortunate Sulayman Biy, who ruled for several months before Narbuta Biy took the throne in 1770. Because of the short (May–July 1865) and dubious nature of his elevation, Khudayqul is generally considered to have been illegitimate and so he is not counted among the khans of Khoqand.
34. TS, f. 221a.
35. MK, f. 142a.
36. LA, 77 and note 288; AIKC, 181.
37. Millward, *Eurasian Crossroads*, 118.
38. LA, 69/f. 78a.

and pleasures." He ordered [Buzruk Khan Töra] to swear [to observe this] on the Qur'an. His Worship [Badavlat] asked me for one of my horses for himself. I sent the requested horse [to him] with a golden harness, golden adornment and gilt fringe, and he, happy and content with whatever lot fell [to him], made his way to Kashghar.[39]

And so it was that in 1864, Ya'qub Beg "Badaulat" and Buzurg Khan left Khoqand for Kashgar. While 'Alimqul met his end trying to defend Tashkent from the Russian onslaught, a quite different fate awaited his protégé within the Qing realm.

Ya'qub Beg's successful, though short-lived (1864–77) state in Xinjiang has been interpreted in a variety of ways, most often either as a religiously motivated jihad or as a catalyst for an Uyghur national uprising. Neither accurately characterizes the combination of factors that enabled the Khoqandi commander, former hakim of Khojand, to usurp power and establish himself as the ruler over Xinjiang. The actual factors include: the weakened Qing economy and the inability of the Qing to retain loyalty or maintain military forces by dispatching silver shipments into the region; poor oversight from Beijing during a period of crisis and poorer rule at the local level; and fortunate timing, as 'Alimqul had sent Ya'qub Beg "Badaulat" and Buzurg Khan into Xinjiang in 1864, just as a series of rebellions launched by the Tungan (also known as Dungan or Hui) Muslims—not Turkic Muslims, and not the ancestors of the modern Uyghurs, but Chinese-speaking Muslims from China proper—spread into Xinjiang.

The Tungan rebellions began several years earlier to the east of Xinjiang. But by 1864, they had spread westward feeding on the widespread frustration and despair felt by the Turkic Muslims. There was no uniformity to the rebellions as they spread, no effective leadership, and, other than widespread discontent with Qing rule, no common set of grievances. Rather than a religiously motivated or national uprising, Hodong Kim argues that the 1864 rebellion in Kashgar was a product of the weakening Qing state structures, and it manifested in ways quite similar to the earlier Taiping Rebellion. Some of the confusion regarding the causal factors behind it stem from the fact that, while it did not begin as a religious rebellion, it did take on an Islamic character as religion came to serve as a uniting force against the "infidel" Qing regime.[40]

In 1864, Ya'qub Beg arrived in Kashgar and displaced the poorly organized Kyrgyz rebels. In these early stages of his rise to power, he used Buzurg Khan to rally support

---

39. LA, 70/fols. 78b–79a. For Buzruk Khan, see also AIKC, 113.
40. Kim, *Holy War in China*, 66–71.

among the local populace. But in 1866/7, he dismissed the khoja, who returned to Khoqand where he died in 1869, and turned his attention to the military conquest of Yangi Hisar, and then Kucha, Urumchi, Turfan, and beyond. Ya'qub Beg made alliances with the Tungan and Hui, and with non-Muslim Chinese when it was advantageous to do so. He took the Qing citadel and made Gulbagh his capital. From there, he appointed hakims over his districts, supervised an army of some 40,000 soldiers, dispensed justice, and welcomed British ambassadors who traveled from India to offer military aid and economic relief.[41] From the perspective of the British Raj, there were both economic and political benefits to be gained by replacing the region's former dependency on Chinese markets with improved access to their own in India.

The regime of the Ataliq Ghazi, the honorific by which Ya'qub Beg became commonly known in Kashgar, was not without its flaws, and some of these would prove fatal. Taxes were heavy, economic recovery was slow, and, as had been the case under Wali Khan in the 1850s, local Turkic Muslims found his religious policies and the customs that he enforced to be those of a foreign power. He portrayed himself as a Muslim ruler who had undertaken a mission to bring the people of Altishahr back into the Dar al-Islam—a discourse that explains why chroniclers would retroactively frame his state-building efforts in religious terms. In reality, Ya'qub Beg was primarily a Khoqandi. He was a talented military commander, but with economic crisis continuing and recovery out of reach, it became easy for even his most pious Muslim subjects to reflect longingly on the days of the Qing when silver was plentiful and the people had peace and the privilege of supervising their own spiritual lives.[42] The Ataliq Ghazi and Badaulet Amir of Kashgar's good fortune eventually ran out, and he became acutely ill and died suddenly in late May 1877.[43] Some have argued that he died of natural causes, others that the Qing conspired to have him poisoned. Soon thereafter, Xinjiang was again in Qing hands.

THE SETTING SUN

In July 1867, General Konstantin Petrovich von Kaufman (1818–82) was dispatched to Tashkent to serve as the first Governor-General of Russian Turkestan. Bregel

---
41. Millward, *Eurasian Crossroads*, 120–23.
42. Millward, *Eurasian Crossroads*, 122.
43. AIKC, 512. On the speculations that circulated regarding his sudden death, see Demetrius C. Boulger, *The Life of Yakoob Beg: Athalik Ghazi and Badaulet Ameer of Kashgar* (London: W. H. Allen & Co., 1878), 250–57.

notes that, unlike Cherniaev, Kaufman "was given almost unlimited authority, including the right to wage wars, conduct diplomatic negotiations, and conclude conventions and treaties with the neighboring states at his own discretion."[44] In January 1868, Kaufman forced Khudayar Khan to accept a commercial agreement that granted Russian merchants expanded privileges to live in and travel through Khoqandi territory. In essence, if not by treaty, Khoqand had been reduced to a Russian protectorate: Khudayar Khan was now a Russian vassal.

Several months later war broke out between Russia and Bukhara, and in June 1868 Kaufman forced Amir Muzaffar to accept an official position as a Russian protectorate and permanently sign over all of the territories that he had lost thus far to the Russians, which included Khojand, Urateppe, Jizzakh, and Samarqand.[45] The general contours of Central Asian political history in these years are well known, and, rather than rehearse them here, I focus instead on those developments that unfolded within the Ferghana Valley during Khudayar Khan's third and final reign.

The lack of stability over the two decades that followed Madali Khan's execution had been extraordinarily difficult for Tashkent and Khoqand's territories in the steppe, which had suffered under a revolving door of some twenty-one hakims appointed to govern that realm between 1841 and 1865.[46] With that entire realm stripped from Khoqandi control, the khanate's territory was now once again restricted to the Ferghana Valley, roughly the size it had been at the end of Narbuta Biy's reign at the turn of the century. In 1868, recalling Irdana Biy's success at leveraging Khoqand's relationship with the Qing a century before, Khudayar Khan aimed to establish a similar relationship with his new Russian neighbors.

Quite literally singing Khudayar Khan's praises, Umidi presents Khudayar Khan's third reign as a complete break with that past. Those Qipchaqs who had remained disaffected with his rule after ʿAlimqul's death in 1865 had departed Khoqand to follow Yaʿqub Beg to Kashgar, leaving Khudayar Khan with few enemies to derail his efforts to restore ethnic harmony and the strength of his state. Taking stock of

---

44. EIr, s.v. "Central Asia vii, in the 12th–13th/18th–19th Centuries," 5:201.
45. AIKC, 18. For an analysis of the Russian victory over Khojand that both challenges the imperial narrative and illustrates the importance of approaching the conflict from a local perspective, even those of the invaders, see Inomjon Mamadaliev, "The Defence of Khujand in 1866 through the Eyes of Russian Officers," *Central Asian Survey*, 33, no. 2 (2014): 170–79.
46. AIKC, 18; N. A. Khalfin, *Prisoedinenie Srednei Azii k Rossii (60–90-e gody XIX v.)* (Moscow: Nauka, 1965), 232–33.

this period, Umidi casts him as "a new Timur" and credits him with granting land to people for farming; building bazaars to promote trade; financing imperial architecture, including his new great ark which was completed in 1873 and much of which is restored and remains standing today; and further expanding irrigation to encourage the production of food for local consumption, as well as cash crops and other commodities for export, principally to Russia.[47] Umidi's praise is hyperbolic, but it does not completely miss the mark. It does, however, contrast sharply with much of the received wisdom.

Later histories often characterize Khudayar Khan as having imposed a highly exploitative and even tyrannical rule on his people. Dubrovitskii and Bababekov, for example, conclude that his reign "was even harsher than those of his predecessors," and they reference one contemporary who charged Khudayar Khan with suppressing an attempted coup by secretly executing 3,000 of his subjects, and a second who accused him of having "unleashed a ten-year robbery of his own people, replete with all kinds of plunder and murder."[48] Their account also quotes the Russian imperial-era historian, M. A. Terentev, who listed an array of new taxes that Khudayar Khan is said to have imposed and which, he asserts with no less hyperbole than Umidi, provided "an inexhaustible source of wealth for the greedy khan."[49]

There may be reason to highlight brutal aspects of his reign, as there had been, for example, with 'Alim Khan's reign at the beginning of the century. But these explanations are generally presented uncritically and as part of the systematic portrayal of Khudayar Khan as a despot who would meet his end as a result of "popular rebellion" against his "oppressive rule."[50] Some of the evidence used to support such notions is grounded in historical evidence and does merit consideration. But focusing on just that body of evidence at the expense of all else does more to bolster Russian imperial justifications for having extinguished the khanate and colonized

---

47. MK, fols. 143a–45a. See also the discussion of the commercial environment of Khoqand under Khudayar Khan in Timur K. Beisembiev, *Ta'rikh-i Shakhrukhi: kak istoricheskii istochnik* (Alma-Ata: Nauka, 1987), 66.
48. Dubovitski and Bababekov, "The Rise and Fall," 38. For the references, see Iu. Rossel, "Sredneaziatskaia kul'tura i nasha politika na Vostoke," *Turkestanskii sbornik* (1873), 22:28–29; A. Fedchenko, *Puteshestvie v Turkestan*, vol. 1, pt. 2, St. Petersburg and Moscow, 1875, 95–96.
49. Dubovitski and Bababekov, "The Rise and Fall," 38. See M. A. Terentev, *Istoriia zavoevaniia Srednei Azii* (St. Petersburg, 1906), 2:327. Also relying on Russian sources, Hélène Carrère d'Encausse's provides a strikingly similar depiction of "intense unrest" among the populace in response to Khudayar Khan's "cruel repression" in her chapter, "Systematic Conquest, 1865–1884," in *Central Asia: 130 Years of Russian Dominance, A Historical Overview*, ed. Edward Allworth, 3d ed. (Durham: Duke University Press, 2004), 145–47.
50. EIr, s.v. "Central Asia vii, in the 12th–13th/18th–19th Centuries," 5:202.

the Ferghana Valley than it does to shed light on the actual nature of Khudayar Khan's reign in the context of his times.[51]

Sergei Abashin begins a recent essay on the Russian conquest of Khoqand with the observation that "for some time now the theme of the conquest of Central Asia by the Russian Empire has been a subject of historical generalization."[52] Abashin finds that historians have tended to focus on tropes of conquest, reducing "complex interactions to one supposedly decisive circumstance—economic inevitability, the Great Game, or the individual qualities of military officers."[53] Overlooked are the objectives, motivations, and strategies that informed the decisions and actions of the vast majority of participants in these events. Abashin then goes on to provide an exceptionally detailed microhistory of the 1875 Russian campaign against Oshoba, a small village near Namangan. His essay immerses the reader in three contrasting perspectives to demonstrate that, while the conquest unfolded in a particular way, it meant very different things to different participants. Adjusting the lens away from the sweeping imperial narrative to focus on fine details, he argues, "permits us to understand the conquest not as something planned and proceeding according to that plan, but as a series of successes and failures, discussions and contestations, and decisions which changed as the affair proceeded."[54]

Much like gazing at a skillfully produced impressionist painting, viewing an event or process at a distance gives one a sense of how the various historical strands come together to create the whole. But the closer the reader gets to the event, the easier it becomes to appreciate the multiplicity of agencies, contingencies, and subtle nuances that led history to unfold the way it did. Abashin's case study puts a Khoqandi veneer on Francesca Trivellato's point, discussed in the preface: deeply researched local microhistories have much to offer global history, and there is great value to be found in striking a delicate balance between the two.[55] I would add to Abashin's insightful critique only that it is no less important to move beyond the stereotypes codified in imperial narratives in order to appreciate the complex motivations that led the central actors themselves to make their decisions as well. Khudayar Khan's use of excessive brutality is well documented, but he cannot accurately be defined as an

---

51. As noted in the preface, some archival records regarding this period in Khoqand's history have been published and are available in Troitskaia, comp., *Katalog arkhiva Khokandskikh Khanov*; Troitskaia, *Materialy po istorii Kokandskogo Khanstva*; Nabiev, *Iz istorii Kokandskogo Khanstva*.
52. Sergei Abashin, "The 'Fierce Fight' at Oshoba: A Microhistory of the Conquest of the Khoqand Khanate," *Central Asian Survey* 33, no. 2 (2014): 215.
53. Abashin, "The 'Fierce Fight' at Oshoba," 216.
54. Abashin, "The 'Fierce Fight' at Oshoba," 227.
55. Trivellato, "Is There a Future for Italian Microhistory."

Oriental despot any more than he was "a new Timur" bringing renewed glory to his people. His efforts to bring recovery to Khoqand merit analysis, as do the reasons why those efforts ultimately failed.

Khoqand had long used irrigation projects to expand agricultural production, settle nomads and other migrant populations, and achieve a degree of leverage over those peoples. This began nearly a century earlier, when Narbuta Biy ordered the construction of the Andijan Say, the Ferghana Valley's first large-scale irrigation network. The technique was successful and subsequent rulers embraced it and developed it further. 'Alim Khan's Yangi Ariq transformed Namangan from a small town into a large city at the center of a much more densely populated and productive agricultural zone. 'Umar Khan expanded the Yangi Ariq and ordered the construction of both the Khan Ariq and highly ambitious Shahrikhan Say. The latter canal system alone diverted snowmelt over some 150 square miles in the southeastern part of the valley. Madali Khan continued these efforts and, in the 1840s and early 1850s, even Musulmanqul directed considerable energy toward expanding irrigation, albeit for the benefit of his Qipchaq constituency and not for the population at large.[56] With this legacy in mind, Khudayar Khan set his sights on restoring his khanate's stability and prosperity through the construction of yet another project, the Ulugh Nahr (the "Great Canal," 1868–71), designed to draw water from the Syr Darya west of Andijan.[57] Each of these projects brought water to thousands of farms, and the irrigation networks that the Khoqand government constructed, expanded, and maintained transformed altogether some 593,246 hectares, or roughly 2,300 square miles, of wilderness, pasture, and brush into arable farmland.[58]

The American diplomat Eugene Schuyler was an astute observer, and in the report of his travel through the region in 1873, he was impressed by what he saw. Schuyler found the city of Khoqand to be populated by an estimated 75,000 people and home to a vibrant paper manufacturing industry.[59] He reported that the agricultural economy of the khanate at that time was "in a most flourishing condition," though he did conclude that, especially in the southern part of the valley, "it will be possible to give a greater development to its resources by extending the irrigation system and

---

56. Thurman, "Modes of Organization," 35.
57. Thurman, "Modes of Organization," 35; MTF, f. 81a; AIKC, 532.
58. Thurman, "Modes of Organization," 36 and note. The statistic dates to 1885 which, Thurman notes, "is the earliest measurement available." He concludes, however, that the figure "can be assumed to roughly represent irrigated area at the time of Russian conquest" as Russian efforts to expand irrigation in the valley did not begin until years later.
59. Schuyler, *Turkistan*, 2:11–12.

bringing additional land under cultivation."⁶⁰ As previously observed, the slope of the valley in that particular zone had long hindered the expansion of irrigation. That would change only toward the end of the century, with the introduction of hydraulic pump stations.⁶¹

Over the course of his third reign, Khudayar Khan worked to overcome the ethnic tensions among his Sart, Qipchaq, and Kyrgyz populations. In an effort to achieve this goal, he included among his most trusted inner circle a Qipchaq officer named 'Abd al-Rahman Aftabachi, the son of none other than Musulmanqul, who had previously fought alongside 'Alimqul and whom Beisembiev identifies as a "favorite of Khudayar Khan."⁶² The two were childhood friends, and for the first ten years of Khudayar Khan's third reign, 1865–75, they worked together to rebuild a harmonious environment in the Ferghana Valley. Recovery in Khoqand would no doubt have benefitted from the Khoqand-Kashgar trade, which, despite economic difficulties in Altishahr and political conflict in the region, remained surprisingly strong. According to Forsyth's report of his 1873 mission to Yarkand, caravans still transported between 5,000 and 6,000 loads of merchandise between Ferghana and Altishahr every year, and he personally observed a single caravan transporting 871 loads of cargo valued at 413,890 tanga.⁶³

The ameliatory techniques that Khudayar Khan applied had worked well in the past, but political dynamics in the 1870s were substantially different than they had been during Irdana Biy's reign. Having removed the Jungar threat on their western frontier, the Qing had been happy to govern magnanimously through local Muslim begs that the Qing themselves generously equipped with sufficient resources to maintain a stable economy and manage their own constituencies through incentive or force. During Khudayar Khan's reign, the Russian presence in the region was more akin to a European colonial enterprise with a mission that focused on achieving security for Russian subjects, enforcing governance, and encouraging profit through trade. Local traditions were generally respected in Kaufman's Turkestan Krai, as they had been in Qianlong's Kashgar. But there was no corresponding flow of silver from either the north or the east, and the steady pace of Russian expansion during the 1840s, 1850s, and 1860s had been the cause of considerable hand-wringing. Thus, while the Muslim begs of Kashgar were willing to submit to the "heathen" rule of

---

60. Schuyler, *Turkistan*, 2:55–56.
61. See Maya Peterson, "Engineering Empire: Russian and Foreign Hydraulic Experts in Central Asia, 1887–1917," *Cahiers du Monde Russe* 57, no. 1 (2016): 125–46; Thurman, "Modes of Organization," 112, 227.
62. AIKC, 296.
63. Forsyth, *Report of a Mission*, 481–82, cited in Kim, *Borderland Capitalism*, 180.

FIG. 7.3 Gate to Khudayar Khan's Ark.
Turkestanskii Al'bom, 1865–72, Library of Congress, Prints & Photographs Division, LC-DIG-ppmsca-14908.

the Qing emperor in the 1750s, the Muslim biys of Khoqand were much less enthusiastic about doing the same a century later. Despite his close relationship with Khudayar Khan, 'Abd al-Rahman Aftabachi himself was highly skeptical of Russian intentions and a staunch opponent of maintaining peaceful relations with them.

Matters became even more fraught in the wake of the Russian victory over, and subjugation of, the Khivan Khanate in August 1873. With Khiva reduced to a protectorate, people across the region questioned whether there were any limits to Russian ambitions for expansion. Khoqand's subjects—especially the Kyrgyz and Qipchaqs—grew even more uncomfortable with Khudayar Khan's efforts to maintain a peaceful relationship with Russia.[64] Matters came to a head soon thereafter as a result of Khudayar Khan's introduction of a new tax on his Kyrgyz subjects. This prompted a rebellion, which Khoqand was able to suppress, but Khudayar's decision to punish the Kyrgyz by executing a number of their nobles provoked a sharp response.[65] Kyrgyz rebellions began anew in 1874, and they snowballed into

---

64. MK, f. 145b.
65. AIKC, 18.

something much grander as the Qipchaq troops that Khudayar Khan had dispatched to suppress the Kyrgyz elected to join them instead.

Babadjanov is no doubt correct that the rebels were motivated by their own particular opportunist agendas rather than genuinely leading a religiously motivated resistance to the Russian infidels.[66] But regardless of their true motives, the rebels rapidly united around an anti-Russian platform, and, with ʿAbd al-Rahman Aftabachi at the head of the army, they elevated as their new ruler Khudayar Khan's eldest son, Nasr al-Din, in Andijan.[67] As the rebels moved west toward Khoqand in the summer of 1875, Khudayar Khan fled to Tashkent.[68] What had begun as a small Kyrgyz uprising now drew much broader appeal across the valley, and the rebels hoped that their anti-Russian platform would soon elicit support from Yaʿqub Beg, the Bukharan Amir, Durrani Afghanistan, and other powers within and beyond the region. Their objective was nothing less than the eviction of Russian forces from Central Asia.

ʿAbd al-Rahman Aftabachi aimed to draw support first by demonstrating his already substantial strength against the Russian garrison at Khojand. But word reached Kaufman that the Khoqandi forces were advancing out of the valley, and he quickly dispatched reinforcements from Tashkent. When the Russian troops reached the field, their training and effective use of superior artillery enabled them to outmaneuver ʿAbd al-Rahman's roughly 30,000 Qipchaq soldiers, who rapidly disbanded. ʿAbd al-Rahman fled into Ferghana to seek out Nasr al-Din's younger brother, Murad Bek, so that the Shahrukhid leadership over the khanate could continue. His efforts would fail.

In the wake of the campaign against Khojand, General Kaufman and Colonel Mikhail Skobelev (1843–82) led some 5,000 Russian troops in pursuit of ʿAbd al-Rahman's fleeing soldiers. Umidi suggests that Kaufman had intended to suppress the rebellion and restore Khudayar Khan to the throne.[69] But on August 22, the Russians, including Skobelev, defeated a large Khoqandi force in a fierce battle near Makhram. They then moved on to Khoqand and captured Nasr al-Din, but instead of recalling Khudayar Khan for a fourth reign, Kaufman instead kept Nasr al-Din on the throne and forced him to accept new, even harsher terms. Following this defeat, Russia annexed all Khoqandi territory in the Ferghana Valley to the north of the Syr Darya (which Umidi refers to as "the property of Turan"), including Namangan.[70] Nasr

---

66. Babadjanov, *Kokandskoe Khanstvo*, 557–63.
67. MK, f. 145b; AIKC, 18, 495.
68. MK, f. 146a.
69. MK, f. 146a.
70. MK, f. 147b.

al-Din also agreed to remit some 3,000,000 rubles over the next six years as an indemnity. Khudayar Khan's other children were gathered together and brought to Tashkent, and he himself was sent to Orenburg, where he was instructed to rest and wait for further instructions.[71]

Widespread discontent with the Russian acquisitions in the valley set the final stage of the rebellion in motion and led to the ultimate demise of Khoqand. At the head of the rebellion was 'Abd al-Rahman Aftabachi, who had convinced a mysterious Kyrgyz religious figure named Mulla Ishaq to join his cause and be elevated in Andijan as a pretender under the false name of Pulad Khan (also Pulat, though more correctly, Fulad). The actual Palud Kahn who was a grandson of 'Alim Khan through Murad Khan, 'Alim Khan's son who had killed Sher 'Ali Khan and ruled for one week in 1844.[72] Beisembiev suggests that 'Abd al-Rahman quite deliberately chose Pulad Khan as the figure to build his rebellion around because it enabled him to exploit a dynastic connection with 'Alim Khan, the Shahrukhid ruler who had conquered Tashkent from the Kazakhs. 'Abd al-Rahman aimed to call on 'Alim Khan's legacy "as an ideological reaction to the colonial conquest."[73]

The Pulad Khan rebellion quickly grew to become quite large—the number of rebels reached between 60,000 and 70,000 troops—but it lacked any cohesion and lasted only a few months. Nasr al-Din was forced to seek refuge with the Russians, and, rather than build support through charismatic leadership, Pulad Khan focused on purging any remaining members of Khudayar Khan's family and anyone else he thought may pose a threat to his newfound power. With the rebels divided, Pulad Khan's campaigns were poorly planned, they met with limited success, and they resulted in many thousands of deaths.[74]

Kaufman then placed the exceptionally brutal and now Major-General Skobelev in charge of the effort to bring that rebellion to an end. Skobelev pursued 'Abd al-Rahman Aftabachi and several times defeated him before the Qipchaq commander finally surrendered on January 20, 1876. Andijan had fallen to the Russians less than two weeks earlier and now, with the loss of their commander, all meaningful support

---

71. MK, f. 146b–47b.
72. MK, fols. 147b–149b; AIKC, 343.
73. AIKC, 19; T. K. Beisembiev, "Obraz Alim-khana v Kokandskikh khronikakh i politicheskaiia zhizn' Fergany v XIX v.," in *Kul'tura kochevnikov na rubezhe vekov (XIX–XX, XX–XXI vv.)* . . . (Almaty, 1995), 28–32.
74. MK, f. 148b. Umidi suggests that some 8,300 people were killed in Pulad Khan's purges. See also the dated but detailed account in Richard A. Pierce, *Russian Central Asia, 1867–1917: A Study in Colonial Rule* (Berkeley: University of California Press, 1960), 34–37.

for Pulad Khan came to an end.[75] Skobelev then captured him as well, took him to Marghilan, and executed him there by hanging.[76] On February 2, 1876, Tsar Alexander II announced that the Khanate of Khoqand had been extinguished and the territory of the Ferghana Valley had been formally annexed to the Russian Empire as the Ferghana Oblast, with Mikhail Skobelev appointed its first military governor.[77]

Denied his dream to return to Khoqand for a fourth reign, Khudayar Khan escaped Orenburg with a substantial amount of wealth and horses. He made his way southward and eventually passed into Afghanistan, where he was robbed of everything but his watch.[78] It was there that he met 'Abd al-Rahim Effendi, an Ottoman Turkish merchant who became his close friend and who sponsored Muhammad 'Umar "Umidi" to author the *Maktūbcha-i khan* (MK), a historical poem that provides unique insights into Khudayar Khan's life as the khan of Khoqand, as well as his travels to India, Mecca, Iran, Anatolia, and Baghdad.[79]

According to Umidi, while the two friends were together in Baghdad the Effendi wrote four letters on behalf of Khudayar Khan to the Russian ambassador in Istanbul, who ultimately convinced Tsar Alexander II to permit Khudayar Khan to return to the Russian Empire. Umidi reports that the tsar ordered Kaufman to welcome him to Tashkent and restore his wealth and property.[80] On receiving this welcome news in Baghdad, Khudayar Khan began the long journey home, eager to see his remaining family who were assembled in Tashkent awaiting his arrival. Shortly after passing through Herat, Khudayar Khan stopped to rest for a few days in the small town of Karokh, and it was there that he died in 1881.

FROM KHANATE TO COLONY

The political environment of Khudayar Khan's first two reigns was dominated by wrenching power away from his father-in-law Musulmanqul and his Qipchaq supporters, and then by the residual interethnic conflict among the Qipchaqs, Kyrgyz, and Sarts that remained in the wake of that struggle. His third reign (1865–75)

---

75. Pierce, *Russian Central Asia*, 34–37.
76. MK, f. 149a–b.
77. EIr, s.v. "Central Asia vii, in the 12th–13th/18th–19th Centuries," 5:202. The date corresponds with February 19 in the old Russian calendar.
78. MK, f. 149b. Umidi says he had with him 50,000 som in cash.
79. MK, fols. 150a–54a. See also AIKC, 178–79.
80. MK, f. 153b.

represents a decade-long effort to overcome these obstacles and restore balance to Khoqand in the wake of Russia's annexation of the steppe fortress towns and Tashkent. Setting aside hostilities between the Qipchaqs and his own Sart supporters, Khudayar Khan looked to Musulmanqul's son ʿAbd al-Rahman Aftabachi as a Qipchaq ally, and in 1868 he established a subordinate, but peaceful relationship with Russia.

Yaʿqub Beg's successes in Altishahr offered little in terms of tangible reward for Khoqand, but it drew disaffected Qipchaqs from the valley and for several years helped cool ethnic tensions. Khudayar Khan tried to reinvigorate Khoqand's infrastructure through construction projects and economic recovery by promoting trade and, as had long been the practice in Khoqand, through the expansion and development of new irrigation projects. The Ulugh Nahr canal network was a monumental effort, and Khoqandi Sarts began to increase their production of cash crops, primarily for export to Khoqand's new Russian neighbors.

In this context, Khudayar Khan drew his power not from the unequal distribution of patronage to one or another ethnic group in the valley, but from his alliance with the Russians. A century worth of precedent suggested that this would have been an effective way to transcend ethnic conflict. But Khudayar Khan was unable to chart a stable course forward. The core problem he faced was that the Russian colonial enterprise was very different from that of the Qing. Whereas the Qing had governed from afar through local Muslim mediators who were financially beholden to Beijing, the Russians were present, aggressive, and rapidly expanding their colonial territories in the region. Khoqand had in essence been reduced in stature to a protectorate, and Khudayar Khan's willingness to partner with the Russians presented his opportunistic enemies, and then even his allies, a focal point around which to unite.

Raising taxes on the Kyrgyz set the rebellion in motion, and before long it had transformed into a large and complex popular movement directed against Russia. Khudayar Khan's son Nasr al-Din took the throne as he himself fled for Tashkent in 1875. Soon thereafter, rebels protesting the Russian acquisition of the northern part of the valley put the Russian garrison in Khojand under siege. It remains uncertain whether the Russian Governor-General Konstantin von Kaufman was sensitive to the fact that the more than two decades of Russian expansion had precipitated this crisis. But in 1876 Kaufman saw no other option than to forcibly put down the uprisings, extinguish the Khanate of Khoqand, and establish the newest Russian colonial possession, the Ferghana Oblast, in its place.

CONCLUSION

SCHOLARLY INQUIRY INTO early modern Central Asian history has generally languished behind work on other periods in the region's long history. Citing longstanding theories of regional isolation and decline, the relatively small amount of work that has been produced on Central Asian history in the eighteenth and nineteenth centuries has tended to focus on themes that reify those perceptions. The result has been the perpetuation of the myth that early modern Central Asia remained disconnected and static, unaffected by the currents of world history. Central Asia's presumed isolation from global trade is uncritically adduced to explain the Bukharan crisis of the eighteenth century, and Central Asians' backwardness in culture and technology is cited to explain the subsequent loss of autonomy to the Qing and Russian imperial powers.

This book contends that it was integration, and not isolation, that shaped early modern Central Asian history. I have combined a close analysis of narrative and other sources produced within the region with a connected histories methodology to determine how, during the eighteenth and nineteenth centuries, integrative structures linked Central Asian peoples with globalizing processes, influenced events at the local level, and converged to shape the trajectory of Central Asian history as it moved into the Russian colonial era. In an attempt to provide a fresh perspective on the region's history, this study shifts the analytical focus from the more well-known Bukharan Khanate to the neighboring Khanate of Khoqand.

CONCLUSION — 211

The rise of Khoqand can be traced to the beginning of the eighteenth century, when the Uzbek Ming tribal aristocracy overcame efforts to redefine political legitimacy in the Ferghana Valley in religious terms, as the Makhdumzada khojas had previously achieved in nearby Kashgar. The Ming tribal leader Shah Rukh Biy (d. 1722) is credited with having engineered the rise to prominence of his dynasty in the west-central stretches of the valley. In the context of his time, his achievement mattered only at the local level: the early Shahrukhids were one of several regional powers in the valley, and they were no greater than the Keneges of Shahrisabz, or the Yuz in nearby Urateppe. The population of the valley did grow during this period, as waves of people fleeing the Kazakh and Persian invasions sought refuge there. But it was only in 1740 that the capital of Khoqand was established, and even then, this embryo of a state was truly remarkable only insofar as it had managed to take shape and survive in a difficult regional context.

From the middle of the eighteenth century, the sources present a clearer image of prosperity that was built largely on the lucrative commercial relationship that Irdana Biy put in place with the Qing. The Qing westward campaigns of 1755–59 had brought an end to Jungar state-building ambitions, and they culminated with the end of khoja rule and the Qing annexation of Altishahr as well. This brought the border of China farther to the west than had been achieved since the Tang era, more than 1,000 years earlier. Khoqand established an official relationship with the Qing, and neighboring Kazakh and Kyrgyz leaders followed suit. While Qing records present Khoqand as a subordinate "tributary" power, in fact the relationship was more complex and purposefully vague. For his part, the Qianlong emperor enhanced his prestige in Beijing by claiming to receive tribute missions from such a distant power as Khoqand. For their part, Irdana Biy and his successors reaped other benefits.

The Qing campaign was a resounding success, but it had also been extremely costly. In the wake of that victory, the Qing court recognized that forcibly securing control over Xinjiang by establishing garrisons across such an enormous territory would represent a heavy, sustained drain on the empire's resources. Drawing on an impressive toolbox of diplomatic techniques and strategies, the Qianlong emperor elected to secure the loyalty of local Turkic Muslim nobles with the proverbial carrot rather than the stick. The Qing implemented a series of policies that ensured respect for local traditions, government through the mediation of Turkic Muslim begs, and the appeasement of those begs through land grants and other incentives, including the injection of large amounts of silver into the regional economy. This was an expensive arrangement for Beijing, but it was much less expensive than maintaining large garrisons or launching recurrent campaigns into the region. In the wake of the campaigns against the Jungars, it was the price the Qing were willing to pay for peace on their western frontier.

In that context, Khoqand's official relationship with Beijing equipped Irdana Biy with both political and financial benefits. Politically, he used the size and power of the Qing to enhance his legitimacy in the valley. Financially, he used ambassadorial exchanges to access resources that made his fledgling state grow stronger. Qing sources highlight three different types of exchange that brought profit and opportunity to Khoqand. The official embassies involved a modest but carefully recorded official gift exchange that was always tilted in Khoqand's favor. These exchanges are the best documented, but the least important. More significant was the trade that Khoqand's official ambassadors conducted. The Khoqandi ambassadors that were permitted to travel on to Beijing were granted free travel and the right to tax-free trade in Qing territory. These embassies returned to the valley with enormous amounts of merchandise, which put a substantial amount of wealth at the ruler's disposal. By far the most important profit opportunity, however, was Khoqand's ability to secure the rights of Andijani merchants to expand their commercial network in Xinjiang. Andijanis had been active in Altishahr prior to the Qing conquest, but their activities expanded dramatically in the decades that followed. The Andijani network was perhaps the most direct mechanism that linked Khoqand with the global economy through the Qing, and their activities in the eighteenth and nineteenth centuries helped to transform the Ferghana Valley into an important center for Eurasian trade.

Khoqand's general trajectory of growth in this period did not come without challenges. Early in his reign, Narbuta Biy was confronted by the need to manage the demands of multiple constituencies, including Qipchaqs, Kyrgyz, and other nomadic groups, settled Sarts, Kohistanis, a large migrant population from Altishahr, and various religious groups. Rather than governing through the exercise of Ming political or military superiority, Narbuta Biy engineered a more inclusive solution that appealed to virtually all of these groups. He established strategic marriage alliances with the khojas, incorporated them into the state, and further encouraged their support by financing the expansion of the religious infrastructure. Turning to conflict among the nomadic and settled populations, he ordered the creation of the Andijan Say and Uch Qurghan Ariq, the first large-scale irrigation programs in the valley, which equipped him with a mechanism to exercise leverage over the Kyrgyz, Sarts, and others. This also expanded his agricultural tax base, which enabled him to strengthen his military. By the end of his reign in 1799, Khoqand was the dominant power in the (albeit limited) arena of the Ferghana Valley.

Narbuta Biy's achievements paved the way for his son's revolutionary efforts at political centralization. Pivoting to the north, 'Alim Khan exploited his strategic position on the frontier of both Qing China and Tsarist Russia to transform his father's decentralized collection of city-states confined to the Ferghana Valley into a more centralized and expansive khanate. 'Alim began his reign by purging elements of his father's administration and anyone else he suspected might obstruct his centralization efforts. A cornerstone of this effort involved military reforms, including the development of a more modern and effective standing army that placed a new emphasis on gunpowder weaponry. 'Alim Khan also established an infantry corps of fervently loyal Tajik mountaineers, the Ghalcha, who were under his direct command and whose protection was critical to his centralization efforts.

Within a few years, 'Alim Khan's new military had extended his control beyond the valley to Khojand and Urateppe, and he then launched a successful campaign against Tashkent. With that victory, 'Alim took the title of 'Alim Khan, and he elevated Khoqand as a khanate. Diplomatic ties with the Qing suffered during his reign, but the most critical economic links orchestrated by the Andijanis remained in place. Pressing northward, 'Alim Khan aimed to strengthen his position further by applying the skill and loyalty of his Ghalcha corps to extend Khoqand's territory into the steppe. Khoqandi campaigns northward eventually led to the annexation of what would later become the vilayat of Turkestan, a Khoqandi province that stretched from the border with the Qing westward to Aq Masjid—a steppe fortress that Khoqand established in 1820 on the lower Syr Darya to protect its quickly growing trade with Russia. Indeed, largely because of 'Alim Khan's military reforms, he became the first Central Asian ruler since Tamerlane (d. 1405) to extend a sedentary state's control into the steppe. But 'Alim Khan's ambition exceeded his abilities, and in late 1810, with his loyal Ghalcha freezing as they lay siege to Chimkent, his brother 'Umar and a small group of nobles raced back to Khoqand and staged a coup. 'Alim Khan's tyrannical manner was his undoing, and, as he made his way across the frozen mountain passes on his way back into the valley, his support evaporated. 'Alim Khan was killed as he approached Khoqand, ostensibly preparing to beg for his brother's mercy.

By the time of his death in 1811, 'Alim Khan had repaired his relationship with Beijing, dramatically improved Khoqand's access to Russian markets, and transformed his inherited realm—decentralized and confined to the Ferghana Valley—into a considerably larger, more populous, and much more powerful Khanate. But in the end, 'Alim Khan's legacy benefited his brother, not himself. Narbuta Biy's other son, 'Umar Khan, shared his brother's vision for a strong and expansive state, and he proved to be politically more astute in his efforts to achieve that goal. Where 'Alim had depended on the application of force, his brother had different ideas. 'Umar Khan leveraged the valley's expanding agrarian tax base, revenue from commercial traffic through Tashkent, and proceeds from Khoqand's trade with the Qing to build a broad coalition of supporters.

In the wake of 'Alim Khan's tyrannical regime, 'Umar portrayed himself as the genteel and enlightened calm after the storm, and he exploited the widespread popularity of Timur and his legacy to advance his claim to legitimacy in two ways. First, he had the Altun Beshik legend crafted to link his Shahrukhid ancestry to Timur through Babur, a native of the valley and the last Timurid prince to rule in Central Asia. Second, he and his principal wife Mahlar Oyim, a celebrated poet who wrote under the name Nadira, used patronage to create a Khoqandi court culture that deliberately mimicked the Timurid court of Sultan Husayn Baiqara in late fifteenth-century Herat, at the pinnacle of the Timurid Renaissance. Challenging Bukharan religious supremacy and political dominance in the region, 'Umar encouraged religious figures who had fled persecution and possible death under his brother to return home. He patronized the religious elite, offered them official posts, and financed the construction of grand mosques and madrasas, which earned him a reputation as much for his piety as for his poetry. 'Umar used this support to bolster the religious foundations of his claim to rule as *amīr al-muslimīn* (commander of the Muslims), placing him on equal footing with the Bukharan amir. An analysis of the historical record indicates that 'Umar Khan strategically used both patronage and history writing to support his political agenda and enhance his claim to legitimacy. As later chroniclers grafted his carefully crafted image into their own work, it also secured his legacy as the pious and enlightened 'Umar Khan, "Janat Makān," responsible for creating Khoqand's celebrated cultural renaissance.

In reality, when it served his purpose, 'Umar Khan was capable of unleashing the same level of brutality as his brother. He waged several highly destructive campaigns against the population of Urateppe, and, following in 'Alim Khan's footsteps, he dispatched his army from Tashkent northward into the steppe in a bid to take control of the trade routes crossing the territory of the Kazakh Senior Zhüz. Although he had the good sense to shield his indiscretions from the public eye, 'Umar Khan also appears to have followed the Timurid legacy in terms of his alcohol consumption. According to some reports, excessive drinking contributed to his premature death in 1822, at only thirty-six years old.

The two decades that followed were in some ways a continuation of the trajectory of growth and prosperity that Khoqand had enjoyed since the days of Irdana Biy. 'Umar Khan's son Madali Khan, reviled for his debauchery and his ultimate defeat and death at the hands of the Bukharan Amir Nasrallah, also oversaw Khoqand's farthest territorial expansion northward into the steppe and southward into the Pamirs.

This equipped Khoqand with control over critical trade routes leading to markets in both Russia and China. The expansion of irrigation agriculture continued apace, which enabled Madali to absorb into his state the many thousands of people who migrated from Altishahr and the Pamirs. Faced with a revocation of the favorable Qing trade policies that threatened to limit Khoqand's access to Chinese markets, Madali Khan also launched a military campaign into Altishahr that failed to achieve a single victory, but still managed to realize its ultimate goal. The expense associated with defeating the Khoqandi forces effectively convinced the Qing to restore their earlier policies and even grant Khoqand additional privileges, including the right to have his own *aqsaqals* (elders) collect taxes from Andijani merchants in Altishahr.

The manner of Madali Khan's death provides valuable insight into the nature of legitimacy and the Khoqandi state. Despite such great successes, Madali Khan's reign was plagued by conflict, rivalries, and scandals of his own creation. Many of his offenses were no worse than those committed by other rulers in the region, including his own father. But he made a series of foolish decisions, and his unwillingness to hide his debaucherous behavior from the public eye undermined popular faith in his ability to rule and led to his ultimate downfall. His decision to ignore Islamic law and marry his father's young widow was the last straw.

The Bukharan Amir Nasrallah had good reason to fear Khoqand's rapid expansion, and reports of widespread discontent with Madali Khan's leadership provided the opportunity for Bukharan intervention. When Nasrallah's army approached the valley from Khojand, Madali's own soldiers chose to flee rather than fight to defend his dishonorable reign. Madali was captured and executed, as was his mother. At first glance, the Bukharan invasion appeared to have been a military success, but Nasrallah failed to grasp that the Khoqandis had used him and his Bukharan forces to get rid of Madali. Just ten weeks after the invading army withdrew, the Khoqandis forced the Bukharan hakim from Khoqand and replaced him with another, more suitable Shahrukhid.

To this time, the integrative structures linking Khoqand with the outside world had principally brought new opportunities for growth and prosperity. Khoqand had emerged in the context of the Bukharan crisis, a crisis that was a product of multiple historical processes that had converged in the first half of the eighteenth century to the great detriment of the Bukharan state. In subsequent decades, the rulers of Khoqand had leveraged the Ferghana Valley's access to Qing markets to emerge as a center for transregional trade, they persistently expanded irrigation agriculture to settle waves of migrants in the valley, and they used these new resources to reform the state's military, develop a complex state infrastructure, and expand its territory in virtually all directions. However, at the moment the khanate had achieved its largest size and greatest power, the people of the valley had effectively engineered a regime change. To an extent, Madali Khan's loss in 1842 illustrates the limits of centralized executive authority in the Khanate of Khoqand.

Khoqand would never recover following Amir Nasrallah's execution of Madali Khan, but the reasons had less to do with Madali Khan than with changing historical realities in the region, and across Eurasia. To the east, the Qing preoccupation with the Taiping Rebellion that began in 1850 sent shock waves through the Chinese economy and, by 1853, brought an end to the *xiexiang*, the silver stipend that diverted Qing silver into the hands of Turkic nobles in Altishahr. This severely undermined the stability of the Qing hold over Xinjiang. At precisely the same time, Russian forces to the north began implementing plans to annex Khoqandi outposts in the steppe, beginning, also in 1853, with Aq Masjid. Russian expansion in the steppe was put on hold during the Crimean War (1853–56), but it resumed soon thereafter and culminated with the Russian conquest of Tashkent in 1865.

The Russian military expansion into Central Asia was conducted with several motivations in mind, arguably the most pressing of which was to locate a stable and "natural frontier" where the Russians could garrison their troops and safely defend their soldiers and their subjects. From the vantage point of the steppe outposts, Tashkent seemed to represent just such a frontier. But once it was taken, the destabilization brought about by the Russian presence itself ensured that it would never suffice. As the Russians encroached on the territory of Khoqand, ethnic conflict within the khanate grew fierce. Where earlier administrations had settled populations in strategic locations and used access to irrigation canals and other resources to manage interethnic tensions, the Qipchaq commander Musulmanqul took advantage of the murder of Sher 'Ali Khan to advance his own interests and those of his people, placing the young Khudayar on the throne as his Shahrukhid protégé and son-in-law. High posts and privileges were awarded to Qipchaqs at the expense of other ethnic groups, and the Sarts in particular suffered as their access to land and water resources diminished. Several years later, as Khudayar Khan struggled to wrench regal authority from the Qipchaqs, he turned to the Sarts for support. He emerged victorious, the Sarts unleashed widespread purges against the Qipchaqs, and Khudayar Khan's first two reigns were embroiled in communal conflict.

In his third reign, in the wake of the Russian conquest of Tashkent, Khudayar Khan was determined to return to the more inclusive policies that had benefitted his predecessors. He established a collaborative government administration that included Qipchaqs, Sarts, and others; he ordered the excavation of yet another major irrigation project, the Ulugh Nahr; and he hoped to bring prosperity to the valley by increasing trade with Russians in Tashkent. Khudayar Khan aimed to replicate what Irdana Biy had achieved a century earlier by leveraging his relations with the (also non-Muslim) Qing to return Khoqand to a trajectory of growth, prosperity, and stability.

With the Russians in control of Tashkent and the northern trade routes, emphasizing these commercial linkages would have seemed a desirable goal from the Khoqandi perspective. But following the conquest of Aq Masjid, the Russian colonial presence in Central Asia took on a character that contrasted sharply with that of the Qing. Into the 1850s, the Qing had generally been content to rule from afar and govern through the mediation of local nobility, Turkic Muslim begs, who were compensated generously for their loyalty. Despite Soviet-era claims to the contrary, the Russian presence in Central Asia was more akin to a typical European colonial enterprise. The Russian conquest was an expensive venture, but rather than govern from afar, the Russian colonizers looked to use their superior military technology to impose peace through conquest and submission. Until 1853, the Qing presence in Xinjiang brought wealth into the region. From 1853, the Russian presence provoked fear, anxiety, and destabilization. This was the principal cause of the rising internal political tensions that grew to a crescendo in the 1860s and 1870s, fatally undermined indigenous political authority in Khoqand, and led the Russians to completely extinguish the Khanate in 1876.

Globalization played an important role in the history of Khoqand, both in terms of the opportunities that it provided and the challenges that it presented. But it is no less important to stress the role of historical contingencies. Irdana Biy established an official relationship with the Qing, which the Qing presented as subordinate and which he and Narbuta Biy deliberately exploited to achieve a dominant position over other localized powers in the valley. In analyzing Khoqand's relations with the Qing, historians have tended to focus either on Qing motivations, or on the value of the official gift exchanges that were a key part of these embassies. But the Khoqand khans did not just squander their proceeds on fleeting pleasures: they used the income from their tax-free trade in Qing territory to develop patronage networks.

And Khoqand's greatest objective in dispatching these embassies was to secure the rights for thousands of Andijani merchants to establish themselves across Qing Xinjiang. Exploiting the liberal Qing fiscal policies in the region, the Andijanis effectively linked the Ferghana Valley with the Qing economy and, though that, to the early modern globalizing world.

This revenue stream was a key factor in driving Khoqand's prosperity, and it drew wave upon wave of migrants into the valley from multiple regions. As more groups migrated into the valley—whether their motivation was to flee hardship or pursue opportunity—arable land grew scarce. From Narbuta Biy's reign forward, the Shahrukhid leadership responded by expanding irrigation networks in the valley. For roughly a century, Khoqand oversaw the excavation and maintenance of hundreds of miles of irrigation canals. This required marshalling a massive amount of labor, generally from the communities that would receive the benefit. Ultimately, it converted much of the valley's wilderness, pasture, and brush into arable land that could be turned over to migrant farming communities or used to settle nomadic or semi-nomadic subjects. It is the Khoqandi efforts, and not later Russian policies, that effectively laid the foundations for the cotton economy that would emerge in the late nineteenth and twentieth centuries.

These initiatives brought multiple political and economic benefits. Khoqand used its ability to provide or deny access to irrigation canals as a way to exercise leverage over its subjects while also increasing agricultural revenues. Indian merchant-moneylenders, long active as traders and financiers of agricultural production in the Bukharan Khanate, were welcomed into the valley so that they too might contribute to the expansion of Khoqand's agrarian economy. The revenue retrieved enabled the khanate to strengthen and modernize the state's military, develop the state's built environment, and maintain patronage systems among the tribal nobility, settled farmers, and religious elite. In the process, Khoqand became a more powerful expansionist state—by 1840, the khanate was home to more than 3,000,000 subjects, and its territory extended over some 250,000 square miles, an area thirty times greater than that which Narbuta Biy had claimed just four decades earlier.

The story of Khoqand also illustrates how the early modern process of globalization reshaped the ecology of the Ferghana Valley itself. Recall again the Timurid prince Babur's description of his wilderness homeland punctuated by a few modest cities and farming settlements capable of supporting an army of between 3,000 and 4,000 soldiers. Madali Khan had at his disposal some 100,000 troops and, by the reign of Khudayar Khan, the Ferghana Valley had transformed into a much more densely populated and heavily irrigated agricultural zone. In less than a century, from

FIG. C.1 Great Ark of Khudayar Khan Today.
Author photo.

Narbuta Biy's early efforts to use irrigation canals as a means to leverage control over his subjects to Khudayar Khan's much larger Ulugh Nahr project, Khoqand had transformed nearly 600,000 hectares of brush and wilderness, or 2,300 square miles, into irrigated farmland. This represents roughly 27 percent of the valley—newly claimed arable land above and beyond the preexisting canal networks that drew water from the snowmelt in the alluvial fans around the rim of the valley, for example. Cities that did exist during Babur's time—Andijan, Osh, Marghilan, and such—had grown considerably larger. Namangan, Chust, and other major cities of the late nineteenth century transformed from small towns or villages or, like Khoqand itself, came into existence under the khanate.

At first glance, one might assume that Khoqand's use of water to leverage control over its population in some way supports Karl Wittfogel's model of hydraulic despotism.[1] Wittfogel's political theory posits a powerful centralized authority, an Oriental despot, who used military force to control access to water. In his model, the

---

1. Karl Wittfogel, *Oriental Despotism: A Comparative Study of Total Power* (New York: Random House, 1957).

state used water to control the agricultural producers who were dependent on that water, as well as their production. But looking more closely at Khoqand, one finds that any similarities that may exist on the veneer collapse under closer scrutiny. Such a notion could possibly be sustained if one were to read as fact the chroniclers' portrayal of centralized control that one finds in the fictive propaganda of 'Umar Khan's reign, for example. But to do so would be an error. One need only recall that Madali Khan ruled Khoqand at the peak of its power, and any assumed control over irrigation that he exercised did nothing to enhance his ability to force his people, including his military, to rally to his support in the face of Bukharan invasion.

Rather than providing insight into a despotic state structure, the history of water in Khoqand more effectively identifies the limits of the state. While Khoqand was generally on a centralizing trajectory from the time of Shah Rukh Biy to the reign of Madali Khan, one must resist the temptation to cast it in any way as a "centralized state." To be sure, the chronicles point to the development of a complex and hierarchical structure of bureaucratic offices, as well as efforts to enhance military technology, tax revenue, and control over trade routes. But these same sources also demonstrate that power and legitimacy in Khoqand were perpetually negotiated among multiple constituencies and at the local level. The rise of Khoqand as a major power in the region was a remarkable achievement. But as a state formation it remained relatively decentralized (vis-à-vis states in China and Russia, for example). Its success rested on its ability to mediate and negotiate between competing local interests. Water served not as a mechanism to assert dictatorial power, but as a mechanism to lubricate societal friction and exert leverage. This study therefore joins the chorus of critiques against Wittfogel's suppositions.[2]

Water was at the heart of the transformation of the Ferghana Valley from a sparsely populated "peripheral zone of a peripheral zone" into the most densely populated and heavily irrigated agricultural region in Central Asia. Irrigation projects and access to water in general shaped population movements and settlement patterns throughout much of the khanate's history, and this sheds light on many of the most pressing problems that continue to face the region today. This is notable in the recurrent conflict that has emerged surrounding the ethno-national "exclaves" of Uzbekistan and Tajikistan within Kyrgyzstan, as well as those of Kyrgyzstan and Tajikistan within Uzbekistan, and the large population of modern Uzbeks in and

---

2. For another critique highlighting recent achievements in environmental history, see Ling Zhang, *The River, the Plain, the State: An Environmental Drama in Northern Song China, 1048–1128* (Cambridge: Cambridge University Press, 2016).

around Osh, for example.[3] Although farmers in the valley initially focused their production efforts on fruits, rice, and grains, already from the mid-nineteenth century, cotton became an important agricultural product of the valley as a cash crop, as it remains today. Viewed in this way, even the contemporary Central Asian cotton epic—the underlying cause of the Aral Sea disaster—can be traced back beyond the command economy of the Soviet era to the globalizing pressures of the early modern world.

Khoqand rose and fell in the Ferghana Valley, deep in the heart of the Eurasian landmass, but both the state and its people were anything but insular. It is this point that I would like to touch on one last time before concluding this book. As an integrated part of the globalizing world, I argue that the history of Khoqand merits consideration alongside other small states in Southeast Asia, Africa, India, and perhaps elsewhere that emerged, flourished, and declined on the frontier of expanding imperial powers during the eighteenth and nineteenth centuries.

Roughly twenty years ago, Anthony Reid published the proceedings of three separate conferences that analyzed multiple ways in which small autonomous states in Southeast Asia and Korea had responded to globalizing forces.[4] From the middle of the eighteenth century, these states took a variety of forms, and they confronted the changing pressures of their time in different ways, exhibiting remarkable flexibility and innovation in the process. Reid himself examined the role that the increasingly active commercial economy in Southeast Asia between the mid-eighteenth and mid-nineteenth centuries played in giving rise to these states.[5] Victor Lieberman observed that the most successful of the states in mainland Southeast Asia—Burma, Siam, Vietnam, and Korea—all experienced increasing centralization and militarization, at least partly because they were in constant competition with each other.[6] Other essays engaged the ways that globalization shaped agricultural change, issues of rural monetization, shifting commercial economies, efforts to devise new political strategies in the face of expanding imperial powers, and more.

In both mainland and archipelagic Southeast Asia, global integration in the century preceding the age of high imperialism (post-1850) gave rise to remarkable

---

3. For a study of the ethnic conflicts among these communities today, see Morgan Y. Liu, *Under Solomon's Throne: Uzbek Visions of Renewal in Osh* (Pittsburgh: University of Pittsburgh Press, 2012).
4. Anthony Reid, ed., *The Last Stand of Asian Autonomies: Responses to Modernity in the Diverse States of Southeast Asia and Korea, 1750–1900* (New York: St. Martin's Press, 1997).
5. Anthony Reid, "A New Phase of Commercial Expansion in Southeast Asia, 1760–1850," in *The Last Stand*, 57–81.
6. Victor Lieberman, "Mainland-Archipelagic Parallels and Contrasts, c. 1750–1850," in *The Last Stand*, 27–53.

innovation in cultural and artistic expression, literary production, religious reforms, and new ways to use history in shaping political identities. As a whole, Reid found that these more current understandings of Southeast Asian societies contrast sharply with earlier colonial-era depictions of them as "tyrannical, chaotic, backward-looking and incapable of delivering welfare to their people."[7] One cannot escape the conclusion that the Southeast Asian experience—both in historical context and in its scholarly representation—bears a striking resemblance to that of Central Asia. One finds the same argument relevant for a number of the post-Mughal successor states as well, although he Sikh state (1799–1849) that Ranjit Singh gave rise to in the Punjab is nearly coterminous with the "khanate" period of Khoqand and provides the most obvious South Asian comparison.[8]

Moving westward to Africa, scholars have likewise directed attention to multiple states there that formed nearly conterminously with Khoqand, and also on the frontier of expanding imperial powers. In contemporary northern Nigeria, the Sokoto Caliphate emerged in the early nineteenth century to link dozens of Fulani and Hausa amirs under the leadership of the Muslim reformer and sufi, Caliph Usuman dan Fadio.[9] The Sokoto economy was based in part on its control over trans-Saharan trade routes and the use of slave labor to produce cash crops for export. Sokoto remained an independent, expansionist power for nearly a century, until it fell under the weight of British colonization in 1903. In the mid-nineteenth century, similar forces contributed to the rise of the rival West African power created by "El Hajj" Umar Tal in his native Senegal, Guinea, and Mali (historically known as Western Sudan).[10]

At nearly the same time as Shah Rukh Biy rose to power in the Ferghana Valley, the Asante (Ashanti) Kingdom in modern Ghana combined economic opportu-

---

7. Reid, *The Last Stand*, 5.
8. J. S. Grewell, *The Sikhs in the Punjab* (Cambridge: Cambridge University Press, 1990). For the rehabilitation of the Mughal successor states as important agents in the development of Indian history between the precolonial and colonial eras, cf. Richard Barnett, *North India between Empires* (Berkeley: University of California Press, 1980); C. A. Bayly, *Rulers, Townsmen and Bazaars: North Indian Society in the Age of British Expansion, 1770–1870* (Cambridge: Cambridge University Press, 1983); Muzaffar Alam, *The Crisis of Empire in Mughal North India, 1707–1748* (Oxford: Oxford University Press, 1986); André Wink, *Land and Sovereignty in India: Agrarian Society and Politics under the Eighteenth-Century Maratha Swarajya* (Cambridge: Cambridge University Press, 1986).
9. Murray Last, *The Sokoto Caliphate* (Harlow: Longman, 1967); Mervyn Hiskett, *The Sword of Truth: The Life and Times of the Shehu Usuman Dan Fodio* (New York: Oxford University Press, 1973).
10. David Robinson, *The Holy War of Umar Tal: The Western Sudan in the Mid-Nineteenth Century* (Oxford: Clarendon Press, 1985).

nities made available through trade with Europeans together with the increased availability of modern firearms to begin building a powerful, expansive state that rose over the course of the eighteenth century, parallel with the rise of Khoqand. Distinctions between these two powers include the important role that the slave trade played in the Asante economy and the Europeans' willingness to provide the Asante with large amounts of weapons in exchange for slaves, as well as gold, ivory, and other merchandise. Khoqandi trade appears to have been more multifaceted, and while the Central Asian states purchased weapons from abroad, necessity dictated that they also develop their own arsenal. In 1897, just two decades after Khoqand was extinguished, the Asante was reduced to a British protectorate. It was incorporated into the British Empire's Gold Coast colony in 1902.[11] Meanwhile, in southern Africa, the Zulu Kingdom (1816–97) emerged later than the Asante, but, also like Khoqand, it rose in response to globalizing processes, fell under the weight of those same processes, and left behind a strong legacy that also continues to inform people's lives today.

Many other small non-imperial states rose and fell in the Age of Empire, and they also merit consideration alongside Khoqand. A comparative study of states that emerged, flourished, and collapsed on the frontier of expanding empires in the eighteenth- and nineteenth-century "global age" stands to offer a multitude of theoretical insights into the dialectics of colonial expansion. Other worthy avenues for further investigation include a thorough environmental history of early modern Central Asia, a study of regional politics and the diplomatic relations that Khoqand maintained with Bukhara and Khiva, closer attention to the role that women played at court and in society, intellectual and cultural trends that developed during the lifetime of the khanate, and the legacy of the khanate in such later events as the Andijan Uprising of 1898, the brief Kokand Autonomous Government in 1917–18, and the Basmachi Revolt of 1918–22.[12]

Throughout this book I have demonstrated a number of ways that integrative processes shaped Central Asian history in the eighteenth and nineteenth centuries.

---

11. Ivor Wilks, *Asante in the Nineteenth Century: The Structure and Evolution of a Political Order* (London: Cambridge University Press, 1975).
12. For an introduction to this final point, see Beatrice Forbes Manz, "Central Asian Uprisings in the Nineteenth Century: Ferghana under the Russians," *Russian Review* 46, no. 3 (1987): 267–81. See also Erkinov's work on the subject and Bakhtiyar Babadjanov's foreword in Aftandil S. Erkinov, *The Andijan Uprising of 1898 and Its Leader Dukchi-Ishan Described by Contemporary Poets* (Tokyo: Department of Islamic Area Studies, 2009).

In doing so, I have advocated for the merits of a connected histories methodology that balances a world historical perspective with a deep engagement with historical sources. I hope that readers have found the insights that this approach provides to be valuable. Perhaps more important, I hope that this book will inspire other researchers to direct critical attention to early modern Central Asian history.

GENERAL GLOSSARY

ALTISHAHR: "Six Cities" region of Chinese Turkestan, southern part of modern Xinjiang; often referred to in Khoqandi literature as Yetishahr, the "Seven Cities" region

AQ KIGĪZ: "White Felt," a traditional Mongolian ceremony for elevating a new khan

ARIQ: irrigation canal

ARK: citadel, fortress

BĒGLIK: a fief, or parcel of land under the supervision of a Turkic noble

BID'AH: an "innovation," something, such as a tax, not approved by Islamic law

BĪY/BĪ/BEG/BEK/BEY: Turkic noble

FARSAKH/FARSANG: unit of measure for distance, in Khoqand equaling approximately 5.5 miles

FULŪS: small copper coin, introduced in Khoqand during the reign of Narbuta Biy

GAZ: unit of measure, a length commonly varying between two and three feet, in Khoqand roughly equal to two feet

GHALCHA: Tajik mountaineer population, served as musketeers and artillery corps in 'Alim Khan's Gala Bahādur

ĪSHĀN: honorific title for a venerated sufi saint, common among Khōjas

JĀMA' MASJID/MASJID-I JĀMI': large congregational mosque

JIN: Chinese unit of measurement, equal to 1.3 pounds

KARUN: Qing (Manchurian) term for a frontier outpost

KHĀNAQĀH: a sufi hostel

KHŌJA/KHWĀJAH, PL. KHWĀJAGĀN: title commonly used to refer to sufis, especially among the Naqshbandiyya; in Khoqand, also used in reference to descendants of the earliest Arab conquerors of Central Asia, the earliest Caliphs; also used as a synonym for Sayyid (see below)

LAK/LĀKH: Indian term indicating the numerical figure of 100,000; in Central Asia more commonly used to indicate the figure of 10,000

LIANG: Chinese unit of measurement, equal to 1.3 ounces (same as tael)

MAZĀR: shrine, tomb

MULLĀ: member of the Muslim clergy

MURĪD: student, or a follower of a sufi sheikh

NAHR: river, or an irrigation channel

ŌRDĀ: palace

SART: Central Asian term used to identify a settled agriculturalist, whether Tajik or Turk

SAY: a large irrigation channel that diverts water into many small canals

SAYYID: descendant of the Prophet Muhammad

SHARĪ'A: Islamic law

SUFI/ṢŪFĪ: a Muslim mystic, adherent of a Muslim mystical order, a Ṭarīqa

TAEL: English term for the *liang*, a Chinese unit of measurement equal to 1.3 ounces

TANĀP: Khoqandi unit of measure equal to 3,600 square Gaz (see above), between ¼ and ½ hectares

TANGA: silver coin, same as a dirham

TILĀ: gold coin, same as a dīnār

TÖRE/TŌRA: descendant of Chinggis Khan

'ULAMĀ': plural of 'Ālim, scholarly class of people educated in the study of the Qur'ān and related religious sciences

VILĀYAT: an administrative district, a province

WAQF/AWQĀF: charitable endowment(s)

XIEXIANG: annual Qing silver stipend to Altishahr

YĀSĀ: Chinggisid legal code

KHOQANDI MILITARY TERMINOLOGY

AMĪR: military commander
CHAQMĀQDĀR: flintlock musket
FARANG MILTĪQ: European rifle
GALA BAHĀDUR: also the Sipāh-i Jadīd ("New Army," see below) of Ghalcha (see above) musketeers instituted by 'Alim Khan and dismissed by 'Umar Khan
GHĀZĪ: title for a soldier who leads a fight "for the faith" against non-Muslim forces
JAVĀN/YIGIT/JIGIT: "brave youth," a cavalryman
MILTĪQSĀZ: gunsmith, one who makes muskets or rifles
MĪRGĀN: Khoqandi sharpshooters, or snipers, presumably armed with rifles rather than standard muskets
PHŪR: gunpowder; chemical compound of saltpeter, sulfur, and charcoal
QARĀQAZĀN: "Black Scorpion," the Khoqandi army of irregular troops prior to 'Alim Khan's reign, also known as the Qarāchapān or "Black Robed" troops
QŪRCHĪ: Khoqandi military officer in charge of maintaining the arsenal
SARBĀZ: artillery specialist, infantry
SIPĀH-I JADĪD: the "New Army" of Ghalcha (see above) musketeers instituted by 'Alim Khan and dismissed by 'Umar Khan, same as Gala Bahādur (see above)
SIPĀH-I KUHNA: the "Old Army" under 'Alim Khan, which was larger but equipped with traditional weaponry
TŌPCHĪ: artillery soldier
TUFANG: musket
TUFANGCHĪ: musketeer, one type of infantry soldier
ZAMBŪRAK/ZANBURAK: light field artillery, a small cannon mounted on the back of a camel

KHOQANDI GOVERNMENTAL POSTS

ĀFTĀBACHĪ: "he who holds the pitcher for washing hands," a low official in Khoqand's court administration
AMĪR-I LASHKAR: "Commander of the Army," in Khoqand at times the highest rank in the military administration alongside the Mingbāshi
AMLĀKDĀR: tax collector
ĀQSAQĀL: literally, "white beard," a local elder in a city neighborhood or village, in Khoqand also civil administration post

ATĀBEG: court title for the guardian or tutor of a prince

ATĀLĪQ: high civil administration post for a senior official, oftentimes assigned as an honor

BĀTŪRBĀSHI: military post, head of a vilāyat's army or supervisor of relations with nomads

DĀDKHWĀH: title of middle rank in the civil administration, subordinate to the Atālīq

DĪWĀNBĒGĪ: high rank in government administration, chief fiscal administrator in Khoqand

ḤĀKIM: governor of a vilāyat

HUDĀYCHĪ: mid-rank official subordinate to the Shighāvul, distributed diplomatic gifts at court

MINGBĀSHI: "Commander of One Thousand," in Khoqand the highest rank in the military administration, though second to the Amīr-i Lashkar when that rank was in use

MĪRĀB: official in the civil administration who supervised distribution of water from irrigation canals to farmers working agricultural land

NAQĪB: official responsible for supervising military organization

QŪSHBĒGĪ/KHŪSHBĒGĪ: highest post in the Khoqandi government administration, equal in rank to a governor (hākim) of a province (vilāyat)

SHEIKH AL-ISLĀM: highest post in the legal administration, chief religious and legal authority

SHIGHĀVUL: high official in the court administration; master of ceremonies, responsible for supervising diplomatic exchanges

YASĀVUL: servant to the ruler, appointed at the ruler's discretion to oversee various duties

YŪZBĀSHI: "Commander of One Hundred," mid-level rank in the military administration

BIBLIOGRAPHY

PRIMARY SOURCES

Abdurrakhman-i Tali'. *Istoriia Abulfaiz-khana*. Trans. A. A. Semenov. Tashkent: Akademiia nauk Uzbekskoi SSR, 1959.

Antonova, K. A., and N. M. Gol'dberg, eds. *Russko-indiiskie otnosheniia v XVIII v., sbornik dokumentov*. Moscow: Nauka, 1965.

Antonova, K. A., N. M. Gol'dberg, and T. D. Lavrentsova, eds. *Russko-indiiskie otnosheniia v XVII v., sbornik dokumentov*. Moscow: Nauka, 1958.

Beisembiev, Timur K., ed. and trans. *The Life of 'Alimqul: A Native Chronicle of Nineteenth Century Central Asia*, by Mulla Muhammad Yunus Djan Shighavul Dadkhah Tashkandi. London: RoutledgeCurzon, 2003.

Burnes, Alexander. *Cabool: A Personal Narrative of a Journey to, and Residence in That City, in the Years 1836, 7, and 8 . . .* 2nd ed. London: John Murray, 1843.

Burnes, Alexander. *Travels into Bokhara . . .* 3 vols. London: John Murray, 1834.

Davies, R. H. *Report on the Trade and Resources of the Countries on the North-western Boundary of British India*. Comp. Sir Robert Montgomery. Lahore: The Government Press, 1862.

Fayż Muḥammad Kātib Hazārah. *The History of Afghanistan: Fayż Muḥammad Kātib Hazārah's Sirāj al-tavārīkh*. Trans. R. D. McChesney and M. M. Khorrami. 6 vols. Leiden: E. J. Brill, 2013.

Forsyth, T. D. *Report of a Mission to Yarkund in 1873, under Command of Sir T. D. Forsyth* . . . Calcutta: Foreign Department Press, 1875.

Harlan, Josiah. *Central Asia: Personal Narrative of General Josiah Harlan, 1823–1841.* Ed. Frank E. Ross. London: Luzac & Co., 1939.

Kadyrova, Makhuba. *Nadira, ocherk zhizni i tvorchestva.* Tashkent: Fan, 1967.

Meyendorf, Baron von, ed. *A Journey from Orenburg to Bokhara in the Year 1820.* Trans. Captain E. F. Chapman. Calcutta: Foreign Department Press, 1870.

Minorsky, V., trans. *Hudud al-'Alam: the Regions of the World.* London: Luzac & Co., 1937.

Mir Izzet Ullah. "Travels beyond the Himalaya, by Mir Izzet Ullah. Republished from the Calcutta Oriental Quarterly Magazine, 1825." *Journal of the Royal Asiatic Society* 7 (1843): 283–342.

Mīr Muḥammad Amīn Bukhārī. *'Ubaidullānāma.* IVANU, Ms. No. 1532. Trans. A. A. Semenov. *Ubaidulla-name.* Tashkent: Nauka, 1957.

Mirakshah Munshi, Mullah Zahid Munshi, and Muhammad Tahir Wahid, comps. *Maktubat munsha'at manshurat.* IVANU, Ms. No. 289.

Muḥammad Fazil Bek b. Qadi Muhammad Atabek. *Mukammal-i tā'rīkh-i Farghāna.* IVANU, Ms. No. 5971.

Muḥammad Ḥakīm Khān. *Muntakhab al-tavārīkh: Selected History.* Vol. 2. Ed. by Yayoi Kawahara and Koichi Haneda. Tokyo: Research Institute for Languages and Cultures of Asia and Africa, 2006.

Muhammad Hakimkhon. *Muntakhab at-tavarikh.* Ed. by A. Mukhtorov. 2 vols. Dushanbe: Donish, 1983–85. Facsimile edition of Hajji Muḥammad Ḥakīm Khān b. Sa'id Ma'sum Khān, *Muntakhab al-tavārīkh.* Institute of Oriental Studies and Written Legacy, Academy of Sciences, Republic of Tajikistan, Ms. No. 63.

Muḥammad Sālih Khwāja Tāshkandī. *Tā'rīkh-i jadīdah-i Tāshkand.* IVANU, Ms. No. 5732.

Muḥammad 'Umar Marghīnānī ("Umīdī"). *Maktūbcha-i khān.* IVANU, Ms. No. 1902/V, ff. 130b–156b.

Mulla 'Avaz Muhammad b. Mulla Ruzi Muhammad Sufi ('Attar-i Khoqandi). *Tā'rīkh-i jahān-nūma-ī.* IVANU, Ms. No. 9455/I.

Munis, Shir Muhammad Mirab, and Muhammad Riza Mirab Agahi. *Firdaws al-Iqbāl: History of Khorezm.* Trans. and ann. by Yuri Bregel. Leiden: E. J. Brill, 1988.

Mushrif, Mirzoolim. *Ansob us-salotin va tavorikh ul-khavorqin (Qüqon xonligi tarikhi).* Tashkent: Fan, 1995. In Uzbek.

Nabiev, R. N. *Iz istorii Kokandskogo Khanstva (feodal'noe khoziaistvo Khudoiar-Khana).* Tashkent: Fan, 1973.

Nalivkin, Vladimir, and Maria Nalivkina. *Muslim Women of the Fergana Valley: A 19th-Century Ethnography from Central Asia*. Ed. Marianne Kamp; trans. Mariana Markova and Marianne Kamp. Bloomington: Indiana University Press, 2016.

Niyaz Muḥammad b. ʿAshur Muḥammad Khoqandī. *Tāʾrīkh-i Shahrukhī*. IVANU, Ms. No. 1787.

Noda, Jin, and Onuma Takahiro. *A Collection of Documents from the Kazakh Sultans to the Qing Dynasty*. Tokyo: University of Tokyo Research Center for Islamic Area Studies, 2010.

Pantusov, N. N., ed. *Taarikh Shakhrokhi: istoriia vladetelei Fergany*. Kazan: Tip. Imperatorskago Univ., 1885.

Qayumov, Aziz. *Nodira (Ghazallar)*. Tashkent, 1958.

Qobilova, Zebo. *Amiriy sherʾiiati*. Toshkent: Fan, 2010.

Qodirova, Mahbuba. *Uvaisii, Nodira*. Toshkent: Fan, 1993.

Schuyler, Eugene. *Turkistan: Notes of a Journey in Russian Turkistan, Khokand, Bukhara, and Kuldja*. 2 vols. New York: Scribner, Armstrong & Co., 1877.

Tasmagambetov, I. N., ed. *Istoriia Kazakhstana v Russkikh Istochnikakh XVI–XX vv*. Vol. 2. Almaty: Dayk-Press, 2005.

Thackston, Wheeler M., trans. *The Baburnama: Memoirs of Babur, Prince and Emperor*. New York: Modern Library, 2002.

Troitskaia, A. L., comp. *Katalog Arkhiva Khokandskikh Khanov XIX veka*. Moscow: Nauka, 1968.

Troitskaia, A. L. *Materialy po istorii Kokandskogo Khanstva XIX v. po dokumentam arkhiva Kokandskikh Khanov*. Moscow: Nauka, 1969.

ʿUmarkhon (Amiriy). *Devon: Üzbek tilidagi sheʾrlar*. Tashkent: Fan, 1972.

Valikhanof, Capt., and M. Veniukof. *The Russians in Central Asia . . .* Trans. John and Robert Michell. London: Edward Stanford, 1865.

Valikhanov, Chokan Ch. "O sostoianii Altyshara ili shesti vostochnykh gorodov Kitaiskoi provinstii Nan-lu (Maloi Bukharai) v 1858–9 godakh." In Chokan Valikhanov, *Sobranie sochinenii*, vol. 2, 265–412. Alma-Ata: An Kaz SSR, 1961–72.

Wathen, W. H. "Memoir on the Uʾsbeck State of Kokan, properly called Khokend, (the Ancient Ferghana) in Central Asia." *Journal of the Asiatic Society of Bengal* 3, no. 32 (1834): 369–78.

Zahir al-Din Muhammad Babur. *Babur-nama: Memoirs of Babur*. Ed. and trans. Annette Beveridge. London: Luzac & Co., 1922.

SECONDARY SOURCES

Abashin, Sergei. "The 'Fierce Fight' at Oshoba: A Microhistory of the Conquest of the Khoqand Khanate." *Central Asian Survey* 33, no. 2 (2014): 215–31.

Abazov, Rafis. *The Palgrave Concise Historical Atlas of Central Asia*. New York: Palgrave Macmillan, 2008.

Adle, Chahryar, and Irfan Habib, eds. *History of Civilizations of Central Asia*. Vol. 5: *Development in Contrast: from the Sixteenth to the Mid-Nineteenth Century*. Paris: UNESCO, 2003.

Adshead, S. A. M. *Central Asia in World History*. London: Macmillan, 1993.

Ágoston, Gábor. *Guns for the Sultan: Military Power and the Weapons Industry in the Ottoman Empire*. Cambridge: Cambridge University Press, 2005.

Alam, Muzaffar. *The Crisis of Empire in Mughal North India, 1707–1748*. Oxford: Oxford University Press, 1986.

Alimova, D. A., ed. *Istoriia Uzbekistana (XVI–pervaia polovina XIX v.)*. Tashkent: Fan, 2012.

Askarov, A. A. et al., eds. *Istoriia Uzbekistana*. Vol. 3: *XVI–pervaia polovina XIX veka*. Tashkent: Fan, 1993.

Aslanian, Sebouh David. *From the Indian Ocean to the Mediterranean: The Global Trade Networks of Armenian Merchants from New Julfa*. Berkeley: University of California Press, 2011.

Azadaev, F. *Tashkent vo vtoroi polovinie XIX veka*. Tashkent: Nauka, 1959.

Bababekov, Haidarbek Nazirbekovich. *Qŏqon Tarikhi*. Toshkent: Fan, 1996.

Babadjanov, Bakhtiyar. M. "'How Will We Appear in the Eyes of *Inovertsy* and *Inorodsty*?' Nikolai Ostroumov on the Image and Function of Russian Power." *Central Asian Survey* 33, no. 2 (2014): 270–88.

Babadjanov, Bakhtiyar. M. *Kokandskoe khanstvo: vlast', politika, religiia*. Tokyo and Tashkent: Yangi Nashr, 2010.

Babadjanov, Bakhtiyar. M. "La naqshbandiyya sous les premiers Sheybanides." *Cahiers d'Asie centrale* 3–4 (1997): 69–90.

Bacqué-Grammont, Jean-Louis. "Tûrân, une description du khanat de Khokand vers 1832, d'après un Document Ottoman." *Cahiers du Monde Russe et Soviétique* 13, no. 2 (1972): 192–231.

Balabanlilar, Lisa. *Imperial Identity in the Mughal Empire: Memory and Dynastic Politics in Early Modern South and Central Asia*. London: I.B. Tauris, 2012.

Balabanlilar, Lisa. "Lords of the Auspicious Conjunction: Turco-Mongol Imperial Identity on the Subcontinent." *Journal of World History* 18, no. 1 (2007): 1–39.

Barnett, Richard. *North India between Empires*. Berkeley: University of California Press, 1980.

Bartold, V. V. "K istorii orosheniia Turkestana." In V. V. Bartold, *Sochineniia*, 3: 97–233. Moscow: Nauka, 1965.

Bayly, C. A. "'Archaic' and 'Modern' Globalization in the Eurasian-African Arena." In *Globalization in World History*, ed. A. G. Hopkins, 47–93. London: Plimco Press, 2009.

Bayly, C. A. *Rulers, Townsmen and Bazaars: North Indian Society in the Age of British Expansion, 1770–1870*. Cambridge: Cambridge University Press, 1983.

Beben, Daniel. "The Legendary Biographies of Nāṣir-i Khusraw: Memory and Textualization in Early Modern Persian Ismāʿīlism." Ph.D. diss, Indiana University, 2015.

Becker, Seymour. *Russia's Protectorates in Central Asia: Bukhara and Khiva, 1865–1924*. Cambridge, MA: Harvard University Press, 1968.

Beckert, Sven. *Empire of Cotton: A Global History*. New York: Alfred A. Knopf, 2014.

Beisembiev, Timur K. *Annotated Indices to the Kokand Chronicles*. Tokyo: Research Institute for Languages and Cultures of Asia and Africa, 2008.

Beisembiev, Timur K. "Farghana's Contacts with India in the 18th and 19th Centuries (According to the Khokhand Chronicles)." *Journal of Asian History* 28, no. 2 (1994): 124–35.

Beisembiev, Timur K. *Kokandskaiia istoriografiia: issledovanie po istochnikovedeniiu Srednei Azii XVIII–XIX vekov*. Almaty: TOO Print-S, 2009.

Beisembiev, Timur K. "Legenda o proiskhozhdenii kokandskikh khanov kak istochnik po istorii ideologii v Srednei Azii: po materialam sochinenii kokandskoi istoriografii." In *Kazakhstan, Sredniaia i Tsentralnaia Aziia v XVI–XVIII vv.*, 94–105. Alma-Ata, 1983.

Beisembiev, Timur K. "Migration in the Qöqand Khanate in Eighteenth and Nineteenth Centuries." In *Migration in Central Asia: Its History and Current Problems*, ed. Hisao Komatsu, Chika Obiya and John S. Schoeberlein, 35–40. Osaka: The Japan Center for Asian Studies, 2000.

Beisembiev, Timur K. *Ta'rikh-i Shakhrukhi kak istoricheskii istochnik*. Alma-Ata: Nauka, 1987.

Beisembiev, Timur K. "Unknown Dynasty: The Rulers of Shahrisabz in the 18th and 19th Centuries." *Journal of Central Asian Studies* 15, no. 1 (1992): 20–22.

Beisembiev, Timur K. "Vysshaya administratsiya Tashkenta i yuga Kazakhstana v period Kokandskogo Khanstva: 1809–1865gg." In *Istoriko-kul'turnye vzaimosvyazi Irana i Dasht-i Kipchaka v XIII–XVIIIvv*, ed. M. Kh. Abuseitova and Safar Abdullo, 291–313. Almaty: Dayk-Press, 2004.

Bello, David. *Opium and the Limits of Empire: The Opium Problem in the Chinese Interior, 1729–1850.* Cambridge, MA: Harvard University Asia Center, 2005.

Bello, David. "Opium in Xinjiang and Beyond." In *Opium Regimes: China, Britain, and Japan, 1839–1952*, ed. Timothy Brook and Bob Tadashi Wakabayashi, 127–51. Berkeley: University of California Press, 2000.

Bergholz, Fred W. *The Partition of the Steppe: The Struggle of the Russians, Manchus, and the Zunghar Mongols for Empire in Central Asia, 1619–1758.* New York: Peter Lang, 1993.

Binbaş, İlker Evrim, and Nurten Kılıç-Schubel, eds. *Horizons of the World: Festschrift for İsenbike Togan.* Istanbul: İthaki Publishing, 2011.

Blanchard, Ian. *Russia's "Age of Silver": Precious-Metal Production and Economic Growth in the Eighteenth Century.* London: Routledge, 1989.

Bobobekov, Haidarbek. *Qoqon Tarikhi.* Tashkent: Fan, 1996.

Bosworth, Clifford Edmund. *The New Islamic Dynasties: A Chronological and Genealogical Manual.* New York: Columbia University Press, 1996.

Boulger, Demetrius C. *Central Asian Portraits.* London: W. H. Allen and Co., 1880.

Boulger, Demetrius C. *The Life of Yakoob Beg: Athalik Ghazi and Badaulet Ameer of Kashghar.* London: W. H. Allen and Co., 1878.

Bregel, Yuri. "Barthold and Modern Oriental Studies." *International Journal of Middle East Studies* 12, no. 3 (1980): 385–403.

Bregel, Yuri. *An Historical Atlas of Central Asia.* Leiden: E. J. Brill, 2003.

Bregel, Yuri. "Central Asia in the 12th–13th/18th–19th Centuries." In *Encyclopaedia Iranica*, ed. E. Yarshater, 5: 193–205. Costa Mesa: Mazda, 1992.

Bregel, Yuri. *An Historical Atlas of Central Asia.* Leiden: E. J. Brill, 2003.

Bregel, Yuri. "The New Uzbek States: Bukhara Khiva and Khoqand: c.1750–1886." In *The Cambridge History of Inner Asia: The Chinggisid Age*, ed. Nicola di Cosmo, Allen J. Frank and Peter B. Golden, 392–411. Cambridge: Cambridge University Press, 2009.

Bregel, Yuri. "Tribal Tradition and Dynastic History: The Early Rulers of the Qongrats According to Munis." *Asian and African Studies* 16, no. 3 (1982): 357–98.

Bregel, Yuri. "Turko-Mongol Influences in Central Asia." In *Turko-Persia in Historical Perspective*, ed. Robert L. Canfield, 53–77. Cambridge: Cambridge University Press, 1991.

Brophy, David. *Uyghur Nation: Reform and Revolution on the Russia-China Frontier*, Cambridge, MA: Harvard University Press, 2016.

Brower, Daniel. *Turkestan and the Fate of the Russian Empire.* London: Routledge-Curzon, 2003.

Bukhari, 'Abd al-Karim. *Histoire d l'Asie Centrale par Mir Abdoul Kerim Boukhary* . . . Trans. Charles Schefer. Paris: Ernest Leroux, 1876.

Campbell, Ian W. *Knowledge and the Ends of Empire: Kazakh Intermediaries and Russian Rule on the Steppe, 1731–1917*. Ithaca: Cornell University Press, 2017.

Campbell, Ian W. "'Our Friendly Rivals': Rethinking the Great Game in Ya'qub Beg's Kashgaria, 1867–77." *Central Asian Survey* 33, no. 2 (2014): 199–214.

Canfield, Robert L., ed. *Turko-Persia in Historical Perspective*. Cambridge: Cambridge University Press, 1991.

Cassel, Pär Kristoffer. *Grounds of Judgement: Extraterritoriality and Imperial Power in Nineteenth-Century China and Japan*. Oxford: Oxford University Press, 2012.

Chekhovich, Ol'ga. "O nekotorykh voprosakh istorii Srednei Azii XVIII–XIX vekov." *Voprosy istorii* 3 (1956): 84–95.

Crews, Robert D. *Afghan Modern: The History of a Global Nation*. Cambridge, MA: Harvard University Press, 2015.

Dale, Stephen. "The Legacy of the Timurids." *Journal of the Royal Asiatic Society* 3d ser., 8, no. 1 (1998): 43–58.

de la Vaissière, Étienne. *Histoire des marchands Sogdiens*. Paris: Collège France, Institute des Hautes Études Chinois, 2004. (English translation, *Sogdian Traders: A History*, trans. James Ward. Leiden: E. J. Brill, 2005.)

De Vries, Jan. "The Limits of Globalization in the Early Modern World." *Economic History Review* 63, no. 3 (2010): 710–33.

Di Cosmo, Nicola. "Qing Colonial Administration in Inner Asia." *International History Review* 20, no. 2 (1998): 287–309.

Di Cosmo, Nicola, Allen J. Frank, and Peter B. Golden, eds. *The Cambridge History of Inner Asia: The Chinggisid Age*. Cambridge: Cambridge University Press, 2009.

Dubovitskii, Victor, and Khaydarbek Bababekov. "The Rise and Fall of the Kokand Khanate." In *Ferghana Valley: The Heart of Central Asia*, Frederick S. Starr, 29–68. Armonk, NY: M.E. Sharpe, 2011.

Eaton, Richard M., and Philip B. Wagoner. "Warfare on the Deccan Plateau, 1450–1600: A Military Revolution in Early Modern India?" *Journal of World History* 25, no. 1 (2014): 5–50.

Eden, Jeff. "A Sufi Saint in Sixteenth-Century East Turkistan: New Evidence Concerning the Life of Khwāja Isḥāq." *Journal of the Royal Asiatic Society* 25, no. 2 (2015): 229–45.

Elliott, Mark. "Frontier Stories: Periphery as Center in Qing History." *Frontiers of History in China* 9, no. 3 (2014): 336–60.

Erkinov, Aftandil S. *The Andijan Uprising of 1898 and Its Leader Dukchi-Ishan Described by Contemporary Poets.* Tokyo: Department of Islamic Area Studies, 2009.

Erkinov, Aftandil S. "Fabrication of Legitimation in the Khoqand Khānate under the Reign of 'Umar-Khan (1225–1237/1810–1822): Palace Manuscript of 'Bakhtiyār-nāma' Daqāyiqī Samarqandi as a Source for the Legend of Altun Bīshīk." *Manuscripta Orientalia* 19, no. 2 (2013): 3–18.

Erkinov, Aftandil S. "Imitation of Timurids and Pseudo-Legitimation: On the Origins of a Manuscript Anthology of Poems Dedicated to the Kokand Ruler Muhammad Ali Khan (1822–1842)." Working Paper No. 5, Graduate School Asia and Africa in World Reference Systems, Martin Luther University, Halle-Wittenberg.

Erkinov, Aftandil S. "Noiob Qu'liozma Izidan," *Moziydan Sado* 44, no. 4 (2009): 20–21.

Erkinov, Aftandil S. "Les Timourides, Modèles de Légitimité et les Recueils Poétiques de Kokand." In *Ecrit et Culture en Asie Centrale et dans le Monde Turko-Iranian, X–XIX Siecles*, ed. Francis Richard and Maria Szuppe, 285–330. Paris: Association pour l'avancement des études iraniennes, 2009.

Erkinov, Aftandil S. "Umarkhon tuzdirgan 'Muhabbatnoma' she'riy majmuasi tarikhiy man'a sifatida." In *Markaziy Osiio tarikhi: man'ashunoslik va tarikhnavislik izlannishlari, ilmiy to'plam*, ed. F. Iskhakov, 217–23. Toshkent, 2009.

Erkinov, Aftandil S. "Un Témoin Important du Mécénat de Muḥammad-'Ali Khān, le Manuscrit Supplément Persan 1446 de la BNF." *Studia Iranica* 37 (2008): 129–38.

Fletcher, Joseph. "China and Central Asia 1368–1884." In *The Chinese World Order*, ed. John King Fairbank, 206–24, 337–68. Cambridge, MA: Harvard University Press, 1968.

Fletcher, Joseph. "Integrative History: Parallels and Interconnections in the Early Modern Period, 1500–1800." *Journal of Turkish Studies* 9 (1985): 37–57.

Fletcher, Joseph. "The Mongols: Ecological and Social Perspectives." *Harvard Journal of Asiatic Studies* 46, no. 1 (1986): 11–50.

Fletcher, Joseph. "The Naqshbandiyya in Northwest China." In *Joseph Fletcher: Studies on Chinese and Islamic Central Asia*, ed. Jonathan Lipman and Beatrice Forbes Manz, 1–46. Aldershot: Variorum, 1995.

Flynn, Denis O., and Arturo Giráldez. "Born Again: Globalization's Sixteenth-Century Origins (Asian/Global versus European Dynamics." *Pacific Economic Review* 13, no. 3 (2008): 359–87.

Frank, Allen J. "The Qazaqs and Russia." In *The Cambridge History of Inner Asia: The Chinggisid Age*, ed. Nicola di Cosmo, Allen J. Frank, and Peter B. Golden, 363–79. Cambridge: Cambridge University Press, 2009.

Gaborieau, Marc, Alexandre Popovic, and Thierry Zarcone, eds. *Naqshbandis: cheminements et situation actuelle d'un ordre mystique musulman*. Istanbul and Paris: IFEA et Editions ISIS, 1990.

Geiss, Paul Georg. *Pre-Tsarist and Tsarist Central Asia: Communal Commitment and Political Order in Change*. London: RoutledgeCurzon, 2003.

Geiss, Paul Georg. "The Problem of Political Order in the Khanate of Khoqand: Between Tribalism and Patrimonialism." In *Central Asia on Display: Proceedings of the VII. Conference of the European Society for Central Asian Studies*, ed. Gabriele Rasuly-Paleczek and Julia Katschnig, 53–65. Vienna: LIT, 2004.

Giersch, C. Patterson. "Commerce and Empire in the Borderlands: How do Merchants and Trade Fit into Qing Frontier History?" *Frontiers of History in China* 9, no. 3 (2014): 361–83.

Gommans, Jos. *The Rise of the Indo-Afghan Empire, c. 1710–1780*. Leiden: E. J. Brill, 1995.

Gross, Jo-Ann, and Asom Urunbaev. *The Letters of Khwajah 'Ubayd Allah Ahrar and His Associates*. Leiden: E. J. Brill, 2002.

Gubaeva, S. S. *Etnisheskie protsessy v Ferganskoy doline*. Tashkent, 1991.

Gurevich, B. P. *Mezhdunarodnye otnosheniia v Tsentral'noi Azii v XVII–pervoi polovine XIX v.* Moscow: Nauka, 1979.

Hancock-Parmer, Michael. "Running until Our Feet Turn White: The Barefooted Flight and Kazakh National Identity." PhD diss., Indiana University, Bloomington, 2017.

Hancock-Parmer, Michael. "The Soviet Study of the Barefooted Flight of the Kazakhs." *Central Asian Survey* 34, no. 3 (2015): 281–95.

Hisao, Komatsu. "Khoqand and Istanbul: An Ottoman Document Relating to the Earliest Contacts between the Khan and Sultan." *Asiatische Studien* 40, no. 4 (2006): 963–86.

Hofmeister, Ulrich. "Civilization and Russification in Tsarist Central Asia, 1860–1917." *Journal of World History* 27, no. 3 (2016): 411–42.

Holdsworth, Mary. *Turkestan in the Nineteenth Century*. Oxford: Central Asian Research Centre, 1959.

Holzworth, Wolfgang. "Bukharan Armies and Uzbek Military Power, 1670–1870: Coping with the Legacy of a Nomadic Conquest." In *Nomad Military Power in*

Iran and Adjacent Areas in the Islamic Period, ed. Kurt Franz and Wolfgang Holzwarth, 273–354. Wiesbaden: Dr. Ludwig Reichert, 2015.

Holzworth, Wolfgang. "Relations between Uzbek Central Asia, the Great Steppe and Iran, 1700–1750." In *Shifts and Drifts in Nomad—Sedentary Relations*, ed. Stefan Leder and Bernhard Streck, 179–216. Wiesbaden: Dr. Ludwig Reichert, 2015.

Honchell, Stephanie. "The Story of a Drunken Mughal: Alcohol Culture in Timurid Central Asia." PhD diss., The Ohio State University, 2014.

Howorth, Henry H. *History of the Mongols: From the 9th to the 19th Century*, pt. 2, div. 2. London: Longmans Green and Co., 1880.

Ismailova, J. Kh., and L. G. Levteieva. *U'zbekiston Harbii San'ati Tarikhi*. Toshkent: U'zbekiston, 2012.

Iudin, M. L. *Vziatie Ak-Mecheti v 1853 godu kak nachalo zavoevaniia Kokandskogo Khanstva*. Moscow: Izdatel'stvo Vladimira Bolasheva, 1917.

Juvonmardiev, A. "XVI va XVII asr boshlarida Farghonada dehqonlarning erga biriktirilishi masalasiga doir." ONU 2 (1963): 61–64.

Kamoliddin, Shamsiddin, ed. *Problemy istorii Kokandskogo khanstva: nauchnye diskussii po nekotorym voprosam istorii, istochnikovedeniia i istoriografii Kokandskogo khanstva*. Saarbücken: Lap Lambert, 2013.

Kelly, P. *The Universal Cambist and Commercial Instructor: Being a Full and Accurate Treatise on the Exchanges, Monies, Weights, and Measures, of all Trading Nations and their Colonies . . .* Vol. 1. 2nd ed. London: Lackington and Co., 1821.

Kenensariev, T. *The Kyrgyz and Kokand Khanate*. Trans. Ruby Roy. Osh: Osh State University, 2000.

Khanikoff, Nikolai. *Bokhara: Its Amir and Its People*. Tr. by Clement A. de Bode. London: James Madden, 1845.

Kilian, Janet Marie. "Allies and Adversaries: The Russian Conquest of the Kazakh Steppe." PhD. diss., George Washington University, 2013.

Kılıç-Schubel, Nurten. "Writing Women: Women's Poetry and Literary Networks." In *Horizons of the World: Festschrift for İsenbike Togan*, ed. Ilker Evrim Binbaş and Nurten Kılıç-Schubel, 405–40. Istanbul: İthaki Publishing, 2011.

Kim, Hodong. *Holy War in China: The Muslim Rebellion and State in Chinese Central Asia, 1864–1877*. Stanford: Stanford University Press, 2004.

Kim, Kwangmin. *Borderland Capitalism: Turkestan Produce, Qing Silver, and the Birth of an Eastern Market*. Stanford: Stanford University Press, 2016.

Kim, Kwangmin. "Profit and Protection: Emin Khwaja and the Qing Conquest of Central Asia, 1759–1777." *Journal of Asian Studies* 71, no. 3 (2012): 603–26.

Kočnev, Boris D. "The Last Period of Muslim Coin Minting in Central Asia (18th–Early 20th Century)." In *Muslim Culture in Russia and Central Asia from the 18th to the Early 20th Centuries*, Ed. Michael Kemper, Anke von Kügelgen and Dmitriy Yermakov, 1:431–44. Berlin: Klaus Schwarz, 1996.

Kuropatkin, A. N. *Kashgaria*. Trans. Walter Gowan. Calcutta: Thacker, Spink and Co., 1882.

Lee, J. L. *The 'Ancient Supremacy': Bukhara, Afghanistan and the Battle for Balkh, 1731–1901*. Leiden: E. J. Brill, 1996.

Lee, Wayne E. *Waging War: Conflict, Culture, and Innovation in World History*. Oxford: Oxford University Press, 2016.

Levey, Benjamin Samuel. "Jungar Refugees and the Making of Empire on Qing China's Kazakh Frontier, 1759–1773." PhD diss., Harvard University, 2014.

Levi, Scott C. *Caravans: Indian Merchants on the Silk Road*. Gurgaon: Penguin, 2015.

Levi, Scott C. "Commercial Structures." In *The New Cambridge History of Islam*, Vol. 3: *The Eastern Islamic World, 11th–18th Centuries*, ed. D. Morgan and A. Reid, 561–81. Cambridge: Cambridge University Press, 2010.

Levi, Scott C. "Early Modern Central Asia in World History." *History Compass* 10, no. 11 (2012): 866–78.

Levi, Scott C. "The Ferghana Valley at the Crossroads of World History: The Rise of Khoqand, 1709–1822." *Journal of Global History* 2, no. 2 (2007): 213–32.

Levi, Scott C. "India, Russia and the Eighteenth-Century Transformation of the Central Asian Caravan Trade." *Journal of the Economic and Social History of the Orient* 42, no. 4 (1999): 519–48.

Levi, Scott C., ed. *India and Central Asia: Commerce and Culture, 1500–1800*. Delhi: Oxford University Press, 2005.

Levi, Scott C. *The Indian Diaspora in Central Asia and its Trade, 1550–1900*. Leiden: E. J. Brill, 2002.

Levi, Scott C. "The Legend of the Golden Cradle: Babur's Legacy and Political Legitimacy in the Khanate of Khoqand." In *History of Central Asia in Modern Medieval Studies: In Memoriam of Professor Roziya Mukminova*, ed. D. A. Alimova, 102–18. Tashkent: Yangi Nashr, 2013.

Levi, Scott C. "Objects in Motion." In *A Companion to World History*, ed. Douglas Northrop, 322–26. Chichester, West Sussex: Wiley-Blackwell, 2012.

Levi, Scott C., and Ron Sela, eds. *Islamic Central Asia: An Anthology of Historical Sources*. Bloomington: Indiana University Press, 2010.

Lipman, Jonathon, and Beatrice Forbes Manz, eds. *Joseph Fletcher: studies on Chinese and Islamic Central Asia*. Aldershot: Variorum, 1995.

Liu, Morgan Y. *Under Solomon's Throne: Uzbek Visions of Renewal in Osh*. Pittsburgh: University of Pittsburgh Press, 2012.

Ma, Ning. *The Age of Silver: The Rise of the Novel East and West*. New York: Oxford University Press, 2017.

Macit, Abdulkadir. "Başbakanlık Osmanlı Arşiv Belgerleri Işığında XIX. Yüzıl Osmanlı-Hokand Hanlığı Munasebetleri." MA thesis, Marmara Üniversitesi, İstanbul, 2008.

Mahmudov, Sherzodhon. "The Interrelation of the Kokand Khanate with the Ottoman Empire in the First Half of the Nineteenth Century." In *Proceedings of the XVIth Turkish History Congress*, 287–90. Ankara: Korzayayincilik, 2015.

Mahmudov, Sherzodhon. "Muhammad Khalil Sakhibzade, The Leader of the Naqshbandia-Mujaddidia in Khoqand Khanate and his Embassy Activity." *Arashan gumanitardyk institutunun ilimiy jurnaly* (Kyrgyz Respublikasy Osh Mamlekettik Universiteti) 17–18 (2015): 175–78.

Mahmudov, Sherzodhon. "The Role of Sufis in Deiplomatic Relations between the Khoqand Khanate and India." In *Sufism in India and Central Asia*, ed. Nasir Raza Khan, 39–52. New Delhi: Manakin Press, 2017.

Mahmudov, Sherzodhon. "Sistema administrativnogo upravleniia v Kokandskom khanstve (1709–1876 gg)." PhD diss., Akademiia Nauk Respubliki Uzbekistan Institut Istorii, 2007.

Makhkamov, A. A. "Rol' Kokanda v chainoi torgovle Rossii so Srednei Aziei v kontse XIX–nachale XX veka." ÖIF 7 (1990): 43–46.

Makeev, D. A. *Rossiisko-vostochnye torgovye sviazi na rubezhe Srednevekov'ia i novogo vremeni (XVI–pervaia chetvert' XVIII veka)*. Vladimir: VIT-print, 2013.

Mamadaliev, Inomjon. "The Defence of Khujand in 1866 through the Eyes of Russian Officers." *Central Asian Survey* 33, no. 2 (2014): 170–79.

Mansurov, Shomuhiddin et al. *U'zbekiston harbiy san'ati tarikhi*. Tashkent, 2013.

Manz, Beatrice Forbes. "Central Asian Uprisings in the Nineteenth Century: Ferghana under the Russians." *Russian Review* 46, no. 3 (1987): 267–81.

Martin, Virginia. *Law and Custom in the Steppe: The Kazakhs of the Middle Horde and Russian Colonialism in the Nineteenth Century*. Richmond, Surrey: RoutledgeCurzon, 2001.

McChesney, R. D. *Central Asia: Foundations of Change*. Princeton: Darwin Press, 1996.

McChesney, R. D. "Central Asia in the 10th–12th/16th–18th Centuries." In *Encyclopaedia Iranica*, ed. E. Yarshater, 5:176–93. Costa Mesa: Mazda, 1992.

Mikhaleva, G. A. "O role Orenburga v razvitii torgovykh sviazei Rossii so sredneaziatskimi Khanstvami (vtoraia polovina XVII–nachalo XIX veka." ÖIF 8 (1977): 43–45.

Millward, James A. *Beyond the Pass: Economy, Ethnicity, and Empire in Qing Central Asia, 1759–1864*. Stanford: Stanford University Press, 1998.

Millward, James A. *Eurasian Crossroads: a History of Xinjiang*. New York: Columbia University Press, 2007.

Millward, James A. "Qing Silk-Horse Trade with the Qazaqs in Yili and Tarbaghatai, 1758–1853." *Central and Inner Asian Studies* 7 (1992): 1–42.

Millward, James A. *The Silk Road: A Very Short Introduction*. Oxford: Oxford University Press, 2013.

Mirza Shams Bukhārī. *Tā'rikh-e Bukhāra, Khoqand va Kāshghar*. Tehran: Ayineh-ye Miras, 1998.

Monahan, Erika. "Locating Rhubarb: Early Modernity's Relevant Obscurity." In *Early Modern Things: Objects and Their Histories, 1500–1800*, ed. Paula Findlen, 227–51. London: Routledge, 2012.

Monahan, Erika. *The Merchants of Siberia: Trade in Early Modern Eurasia*. Ithaca: Cornell University Press, 2016.

Montgomery, Sir Robert, comp. *Report on the Trade and Resources of the Countries on the North-Western Boundary of British India*. Lahore: Government Press, 1862.

Morrison, Alexander S. "'Applied Orientalism' in British India and Tsarist Turkestan." *Comparative Studies in History and Society* 51, no. 3 (2009): 619–47.

Morrison, Alexander S. "Camels and Colonial Armies: The Logistics of Warfare in Central Asia in the Early 19th Century." *Journal of the Economic and Social History of the Orient* 57 (2014): 443–85.

Morrison, Alexander S. "Introduction: Killing the Cotton Canard and Getting Rid of the Great Game: Rewriting the Russian Conquest of Central Asia, 1814–1895." *Central Asian Survey* 33, no. 2 (2014): 131–42.

Morrison, Alexander S. "'Nechto eroticheskoe,' 'courir après l'ombre'?—Logistical Imperatives and the Fall of Tashkent, 1859–1865." *Central Asian Survey* 33, no. 2 (2014): 153–69.

Morrison, Alexander S. "Russia, Khoqand, and the Search for a 'Natural' Frontier, 1863–1865." *Ab Imperio* 2 (2014): 166–92.

Morrison, Alexander S. *The Russian Conquest of Central Asia, 1884–1907: A Study in Imperial Expansion*. Forthcoming.

Morrison, Alexander S. *Russian Rule in Samarkand, 1868–1910*. Oxford: Oxford University Press, 2008.

Mukhtorov, Akhror. *Istoriia Ura-Tiube (konets XV–nachalo XX vv.)*. Moscow: Institut istorii, arkheologii i etnografii imeni Akhmada Donisha, AN Respubliki Tadzhikistan, 1998.

Nabiev, R. N. "Iz istorii feodal'nogo zemlevladeniia v Fergane v XVI–XVII vekakh." IAN 3 (1960): 25–34.

Nabiev, R. N. "Novye dokumental'nye materialy k izucheniiu feodal'nogo instituta 'suiurgal' v Fergane XVI–XVII vv." IAN 3 (1959): 23–32.

Nalivkin, Vladimir Petrovich. *Histoire du Khanat de Khokand*. Trans. Auguste Dozon. Paris: E. Ledoux, 1889.

Nalivkin, Vladimir Petrovich. *Kratkaia istoriia Kokandskago khanstva*. Kazan: Tip. Imp. Universiteta, 1886.

Nettleton, Susanna S. "Ruler, Patron, Poet: 'Umar Khan in the Blossoming of the Khanate of Qoqan, 1800–1820." *International Journal of Turkish Studies* 2, no. 2 (1981): 127–40.

Newby, Laura J. *The Empire and the Khanate: A Political History of Qing Relations with Khoqand c. 1760–1860*. Leiden: E. J. Brill, 2005.

Newby, Laura J. "'Us and Them' in Eighteenth and Nineteenth Century Xinjiang." In *Situating the Uyghurs between China and Central Asia*, ed. Ildikó Bellér-Hann et al., 15–31. Aldershot: Ashgate, 2007.

Noda, Jin. *The Kazakh Khanates between the Russian and Qing Empires*. Leiden: E. J. Brill, 2016.

Onuma, Takahiro, Yasushi Shinmen, and Yayoi Kawahara. "Reconsidering the 1848 Khoqand Documents Stored at the National Palace Museum." *Tohoku Gakuin University Review, History and Culture* 49 (2013): 1–24.

Onuma, Takahiro, Yayoi Kawahara, and Akifumi Shioya. "An Encounter between the Qing Dynasty and Khoqand in 1759–1760: Central Asia in the Mid-Eighteenth Century." *Frontiers of History in China* 9, no. 3 (2014): 384–408.

Papas, Alexandre. *Soufisme et politique entre Chine, Tibet et Turkestan: Étude sur les Khwajas Naqshbandis du Turkestan orientale*. Paris: Jean Maisonneuve, 2005.

Parker, Geoffrey. *The Military Revolution: Military Innovation and the Rise of the West, 1500–1800*. 2nd ed. Cambridge: Cambridge University Press, 1996.

Parker, Geoffrey, and Sanjay Subrahmanyam. "Arms and the Asian: Revisiting

European Firearms and Their Place in Early Modern Asia." *Revista de Cultura* (Macau), 26 (2008): 12–42.

Perdue, Peter. "Boundaries and Trade in the Early Modern World: Negotiations at Nerchinsk and Beijing." *Eighteenth-Century Studies* 43, no. 3 (2010): 341–56.

Perdue, Peter. *China Marches West: The Qing Conquest of Central Eurasia*. Cambridge, MA: Belknap Press, 2005.

Peterson, Maya. "Engineering Empire: Russian and Foreign Hydraulic Experts in Central Asia, 1887–1917." *Cahiers du Monde Russe* 57, no. 1 (2016): 125–46.

Pickett, James Robert. "The Persianate Sphere during the Age of Empires: Islamic Scholars and Networks of Exchange in Central Asia, 1747–1917." PhD diss., Princeton University, 2015.

Pierce, Richard A. *Russian Central Asia, 1867–1817*. Berkeley: University of California Press, 1960.

Ploskikh, V. M. *Kirgizy i Kokandskoe Khanstvo*. Frunze (Bishkek): Ilim, 1977.

Potanin, N. I. "Zapiski o Kokanskom khanstve khorunzhago Potanina." *Viestnik Imperatorskogo Russkogo geograficheskogo obshchestva* 18, no. 2 (1856).

Prior, Daniel. "High Rank and Power among the Northern Kirghiz: Terms and Their Problems, 1845–1864." In *Explorations in the Social History*, ed. Paolo Sartori, 137–79. Leiden: E. J. Brill, 2013.

Prior, Daniel. *The Šabdan Baatır Codex: Epic and the Writing of Northern Kirghiz History*. Leiden: E. J. Brill, 2013.

Reid, Anthony, ed. *The Last Stand of Asian Autonomies: Responses to Modernity in the Diverse States of Southeast Asia and Korea, 1750–1900*. New York: St. Martin's Press, 1997.

Rogers, Clifford J., ed. *The Military Revolution Debate: Readings on the Military Transformation of Early Modern Europe*. Boulder: Westview, 1995.

Romaniello, Matthew P. "True Rhubarb? Trading Eurasian Botanical and Medical Knowledge in the Eighteenth Century." *Journal of Global History* 11, no. 1 (2016), 3–23.

Romodin, V. A. "Some Sources on the History of Farghana and the Khoqand Khanate (16th to 19th cc.) in the Leningrad MSS Collections." *Papers Presented by the USSR Delegation at the XXV International Congress of Orientalists*. Moscow, 1960.

Rossabi, Morris. "The 'Decline' of the Central Asian Caravan Trade." In *The Rise of Merchant Empires*, ed. J. Tracy, 351–70. Cambridge: Cambridge University Press, 1990.

Saguchi, Tôru. "The Eastern Trade of the Khoqand Khanate." *Memoirs of the Research Department of the Toyo Bunko (The Oriental Library)* 24 (1965), 47–114.

Saguchi, Tôru. "Kashgaria under the Ch'ing Rule." *Acta Asiatica* 34 (1978), 61–78.

Sahadeo, Jeff. *Russian Colonial Society in Tashkent, 1865–1923*. Bloomington: Indiana University Press, 2010.

Sartori, Paolo, ed. *Explorations in the Social History of Modern Central Asia (19th–Early 20th Century)*. Leiden: E. J. Brill, 2013.

Sartori, Paolo. "Introduction: On Khvārazmian Connectivity: Two or Three Things that I Know about It." *Journal of Persianate Studies* 9 (2016): 133–57.

Schiewek, Eckart. "À propos des exilés de Boukhara et de Kokand à Shahr-i Sabz." In *Boukhara La Noble*. Cahiers d'Asie centrale, ed. Pierre Chuvin, no. 5, 181–97. Tachkent: IFEAC, 1998.

Schorkowitz, Dittman, and Chia Ning, eds. *Managing Frontiers in Qing China: The Lifanyuan and Libu Revisited*. Leiden: E. J. Brill, 2016.

Schwarz, Henry. "The Khwājas of Eastern Turkestan." *Central Asiatic Journal* 20, no. 4 (1976): 266–96.

Sela, Ron. "The 'Heavenly Stone' (Kök Tash) of Samarqand: A Rebels' Narrative Transformed." *Journal of the Royal Asiatic Society* 17, no. 1 (2007): 21–32.

Sela, Ron. *The Legendary Biographies of Tamerlane: Islam and Heroic Apocrypha in Central Asia*. Cambridge: Cambridge University Press, 2011.

Sela, Ron. "Ritual and Authority in Central Asia: The Khan's Inauguration Ceremony." Papers on Inner Asia, no. 37, Indiana University Research Institute for Inner Asian Studies, Bloomington, 2003.

Shamsiev, K. F. "Voprosy istorii Kokandskogo Khanstva v trudakh V. V. Bartol'd." ÖIF 3 (1986): 51–55.

Singh, Sodhi Hukm. *A History of Khokand: From the Commencement of Russian Intercourse Until the Final Subjugation of the Country by that Power*. Ed. Major Charles Ellison Bates. Lahore: Government Civil Secretariat Press, 1876.

Sobolev, Leonid Nikolaevich. *Latest History of the Khanates of Bokhara and Kokand*. Trans. P. Mosa. Calcutta: Foreign Department Press, 1876.

Starr, S. Frederick, ed. *Ferghana Valley: The Heart of Central Asia*. Armonk, NY: M.E. Sharpe, 2011.

Subrahmanyam, Sanjay. "Connected Histories: Notes towards a Reconfiguration of Early Modern Eurasia." *Modern Asian Studies* 31, no. 3 (1997): 735–62.

Subrahmanyam, Sanjay. *From the Tagus to the Ganges: Explorations in Connected History*, Delhi: Oxford University Press, 2012.

Subrahmanyam, Sanjay. *Mughals and Franks: Explorations in Connected History*, Delhi: Oxford University Press, 2012.

Subtelny, Maria. *Timurids in Transition: Turko-Persian Politics and Acculturation in Medieval Iran*. Leiden: E. J. Brill, 2007.

Sultonova, Gulchekhra. "Torgovye otnosheniia mezhdu Bukharskim i Yarkendskim khanstvami v XVI–nachale XVII veka." *Bulletin of IICAS* 11 (2010): 40–48.

Sultonova, Gulchekhra, and Scott C. Levi. "Indo-Bukharan Diplomatic Relations, 1572–1598: the Role of the Actors." In *Insights and Commentaries: South and Central Asia*, ed. Anita Sengupta and Mirzohid Rakhimov, 95–107. Kolkata: Maulana Abul Kalam Azad Institute of Asian Studies; Tashkent: Institute of History, Academy of Sciences, 2015.

Thum, Rian. *The Sacred Routes of Uyghur History*. Cambridge, MA: Harvard University Press, 2014.

Thurman, Jonathan Michael. "Modes of Organization in Central Asian Irrigation: The Ferghana Valley, 1876 to Present." PhD diss., Indiana University, 1999.

Thurman, Michael. "Irrigated Agriculture and Economic Development in the Ferghana Valley under the Qoqand Khanate." MA thesis, Indiana University, Bloomington, 1995.

Togan, Isenbike. "Inner Asian Muslim Merchants at the Closure of the Silk Routes in the Seventeenth Century." In *The Silk Roads: Highways of Culture and Commerce*, Elisseeff, Vadime, 247–63. New York: Bergahn Books, 2000.

Togan, Isenbike. "The Khojas of Eastern Turkestan." In *Muslims in Central Asia: Expressions of Identity and Change*, ed. Jo-Ann Gross, 134–48. Durham: Duke University Press, 1992.

Togan, Isenbike. "A Silent Revolution in 19th Century Central Asia." In *Change and Constancy: Historical Perspectives on the Way to Social Transformation*, 148–55. Conference Proceedings. Beijing: Beijing Forum, 2011.

Topildiev, Nosirjon. *Qo'qon Khonligining Rossiia bilan diplomatic aloqalari tarikhidan (XIX asr–1876 yilgacha)*. Tashkent: Fan, 2007.

Torrey, Charles C. *Gold Coins of Khokand and Bukhārā*. Numismatic Notes and Monographs, No. 117. New York: American Numismatic Society, 1950.

Trivellato, Francesca. "Is There a Future for Italian Microhistory in the Age of Global History?" *California Italian Studies* 2, no. 1 (2011), ismrg_cisj_9025. https://escholarship.org/uc/item/0z94n9hq.

Vohidov, Shadman. *Qo'qon khonligida tarikhnavislik (genezisi, funktsiyasi, namoyandalari, asarlari)*. Tashkent: Akademnashr, 2010.

Von Glahn, Richard. *The Economic History of China: From Antiquity to the Nineteenth Century*. Cambridge: Cambridge University Press, 2016.

Von Kügelgen, Anke. *Die Legitimierung der mittelasiatischen Mangitendynastie in den Werken ihrer Historiker*. Istanbul: Orient-Institut; Würzburg: Ergon-Verlag, 2002.

Waley-Cohen, Joanna. *The Culture of War in China: Empire and the Military under the Qing Dynasty*. London: I.B. Tauris, 2006.

Welsford, Thomas. "The Disappearing Khanate." In *Turko-Persian Cultural Contacts in the Eurasian Steppe: Festschrift in Honour of Professor István Vásáry*, ed. B. Péri and F. Csirkes. Leiden: E. J. Brill, forthcoming.

Welsford, Thomas. *Four Types of Loyalty in Early Modern Central Asia: The Tūqāy-Tīmūrid Takeover of Greater Mā warā al-Nahr, 1598–1605*. Leiden: E. J. Brill, 2013.

Wilde, Andreas. *What is Beyond the River? Power, Authority and Social Order in Eighteenth and Nineteenth-Century Transoxania*. Vienna: Verlag der Österreichischen Akademie der Wissenshchaften, 2016.

Wink, André. *Land and Sovereignty in India: Agrarian Society and Politics under the Eighteenth-Century Maratha Svarājya*. Cambridge: Cambridge University Press, 1986.

Wittfogel, Karl. *Oriental Despotism: A Comparative Study of Total Power*. New York: Random House, 1957.

Zhang, Ling. *The River, the Plain, the State: An Environmental Drama in Northern Song China, 1048–1128*. Cambridge: Cambridge University Press, 2016.

Zhao, Gang. *The Qing Opening to the Ocean: Chinese Maritime Policies, 1684–1757*. Honolulu: University of Hawai'i Press, 2013.

Ziiaeva, D. Kh. *U'zbekistonda harbii ish tarikhidan (Qadimgi davrdan hozirgacha)*. Tashkent: Sharq, 2012.

INDEX

'Abd al-Hamid. *See* Narbuta Biy
'Abd al-Karim Biy Fazli Namangani. *See* chroniclers: 'Abd al-Karim Fazli Namangani
'Abd al-Rahim, 22–24, 29, 30–31, 31n48, 109; sons of, 33, 33n59, 34
'Abd al-Rahman Aftabachi, 204, 205, 206, 207, 209
'Abd al-Rahman Bahadur, 52, 52n2, 53, 54, 72
'Abd al-Wali, 169, 171
Ablay Khan, 35, 48, 54n10, 176
Abu'l Fayz (Abu al-Fayz) Khan, 3, 19, 21–22, 29, 39
Afaqi Khojas, 37, 38, 127
Afaq Khoja, 15, 16
Ahmad Kasani, 15, 128
Akhsi, 11, 12
Ak Mechet. *See* Aq Masjid fortress

Alay Mountains (Pamir-Alay), 9, 69, 82, 139, 142, 164
'Alim Khan, 55, 71–99, 105, 110, 213–14; called 'Alim Ẓālim ('Alim "the Tyrant"), 78, 93; and coinage, 70n51, 76; death of, 152, 213; and irrigation, 112, 203; military of, 83, 83n40, 153, 154, 225, 227; purges, 74, 123, 156; sons of, 21n14, 124, 133, 150, 164, 186, 207; and title of khan, 6, 20, 87–88, 88n65, 99, 124
'Alimqul, 167, 179–80, 191, 193–98, 200, 204
Almaty. *See* Vernoe (Almaty)
Altishahr, 5, 10, 182, 197, 199, 209, 225; conquered, 16, 16n3, 147; Jahangir Khoja and, 137n38, 139–40, 142; Khoqandis in, 60, 62; Madali Khan and, 150, 156, 215; migrants from, 2, 212, 215; Qing and, 32, 36–41, 47–50,

57, 135–37, 144, 189, 211; and silver, 57, 182–84, 186, 216, 226; taxation in, 147, 147n85; trade with, 62–66, 78, 143–44, 157, 204, 212

Altun Beshik ("Golden Cradle") legend, 6, 19, 101–7, 124

Amir Haidar of Bukhara, 83, 84, 109, 122

Amir Muzaffar al-Din, 191, 197, 200

Amir Timur (Tamerlane), 2n4, 21, 89, 99, 100, 100n20, 101, 124

Amu Darya, 32, 43; in maps, 134, 180

Andijan, 46, 66, 71, 119–20, 137, 168, 206–7; in Babur's time, 11, 12, 219; hakims of, 41, 71, 79n21, 87, 160, 190; in maps, 12, 19, 77, 134; Say Canal, 68, 203, 212; Uprising of 1898, 223. *See also* Andijani merchants; Andijanis

Andijani merchants, 44, 64–66; funds levied from, 147, 150, 215; and the Qing, 51, 62–65, 143, 145, 181; and Xinjiang, 51, 73, 77–78, 93, 212, 218

Andijanis, 44, 45n99, 51, 60, 62–66, 212–13

Anglo-Russian Great Game, 173, 174, 202. *See also* Russian Empire, the

Aq Buta Biy, 22, 23, 31

āq kigīz ceremony, 18n6, 100, 225; Khudayar, 165; Madali, 128; Shah Rukh, 18, 95; Sher 'Ali Khan, 161; 'Umar Khan, 95, 95n2

Aq Masjid fortress, 8, 89, 89n71, 121, 132, 134, 157, 160; Khoqand and, 178, 186, 213; known as Kyzyl Orda, 89n71, 134; renamed Perovsk, 134, 177, 179, 180; Russian conquest of, 169–70, 172, 173, 175, 189, 216, 217. *See also* Perovsk Fort

Aqsu, 36, 45, 63, 140; in maps, 26, 37, 134

Aral Sea, the, 7, 25, 28, 121, 150, 168, 175, 221; in maps, 26, 134, 180

Aravan, 68, 77 (map)

Auliya Ata (Djambul/Dzhambul/Jambul; Taraz), 131; in maps, 134, 180

Baba Bek, 33–34, 48

Bababekov, Haidarbek, 16

Babur. *See* Zahir al-Din Muhammad Babur

Baburid Empire. *See* Mughal Empire, the

Badakhshan, 29, 38, 79, 82n38, 133, 134 (map), 136, 147

Baliqchi, 77 (map), 166, 167

Barefooted Flight, 3, 28–30, 176. *See also* Kazakhs

Beijing, 36 (map), 88, 93, 136, 138, 142, 185, 198, 209, 211, 213; Jahangir Khoja executed in, 145, 156; Khoqand and missions to, 41–42, 50, 58–62, 73, 76, 212

Besh Ariq, 34, 71, 77 (map), 153

Bishkek. *See* Pishpek (Bishkek)

Bukhara, 10, 22, 24–25, 44, 133, 154, 161n2; amirate of, 2n3, 98; amirs, 3n8, 39, 56, 84; and Kazakh allies, 25, 27, 28; khanate of, 3, 12–14, 16; and Khoqand, 31, 43, 124, 177; Manghit in, 84, 100; military, 29, 32, 151, 152, 153, 162; rulers of, 21, 123; and Shahrukhids, 73, 96, 120, 122, 122n95, 127, 150

Bukharan Amirate, 2n3, 98, 109, 134 (map), 157, 206

Burnes, Alexander, 150–51, 153
Buzurg Khan (Buzruk Khan Töra), 183, 184, 197, 198–99

Caspian Sea, 131; in maps, 26, 180
Chadak, 14, 16, 17–19, 48, 105; in maps, 19, 77
Chaghataids, 16, 106, 109, 115, 119
Cherniaev, Mikhail, 179, 180–81, 188, 194–96, 200
Chimkent, 89–90, 93, 131, 180, 194, 213; in maps, 134, 180
Chinggisids (Tore, Töra), 6, 29, 34, 99, 100, 108, 124–25; lineage, 20, 88
Chinggis Khan, 25, 89, 125; descendants of, 3, 16, 124; lineage of, 6, 101, 106
chroniclers: ʿAbd al-Karim Fazli Namangani, 52, 106, 110n60; and ʿAlim Khan, 87; Babadjanov, 97; Babur's the *Baburnama*, 11; and Dilshad, 117–18; and Khudayar Khan, 200–201; Mir Muhammad Amin Bukhari, 25; Mirza Qalandar Mushrif Isfarag, 106; Muhammad Fazl Bek, 18, 18n6, 21, 23n23, 102, 105, 110n60, 161, 162, 162n6; Muhammad Salih, 23n23, 87, 88, 89n70, 101, 102, 105; Mulla ʿAlim Makhdum Hajji, 96; Mulla Avaz Muhammad, 22, 32, 40, 102–4, 105; Mulla Mirza Yunus Jan Tashkandi, 168, 168n31, 171n40, 189, 191, 193, 194, 195, 196, 197; and Narbuta, 54n10, 40n80; and Oychuchuk Oyim, 24; and ʿUmar, 95–96, 97, 99, 108, 113, 117, 125, 127, 156, 214, 220; Umidi (Muhammad ʿUmar), 206, 207n74, 208; and Yaʿqub Beg, 199. *See also* literati; Muhammad Hakim Khan Tore (chronicler); Niyaz Muhammad (Niyazi; chronicler)
chronicles, 10, 11, 20, 122, 220. *See also* Newby, Laura
Chu River, 157n126, 173; in maps, 134, 180
Chust, 11, 17, 77 (map), 78, 79, 120, 219
Chusti. *See* Lutfallah, Naqshbandi sufi Sheikh
coinage, 3, 60n24, 182–83, 193, 225, 226; ʿAlim and, 76, 87, 87n64; Narbuta and, 70, 70n51, 70n52, 73; ʿUmar and, 109. *See also* silver
contraband, 64–66
cotton, 57, 61, 134, 160, 160n1, 174, 175, 218, 221
Crimean War, 8, 173, 175, 177, 216

Dilshad (Uzbek poet), 97, 117–19
Durrani administration, 43, 59, 60n23, 206

Fazl Biy, 39, 40, 42, 53, 56
Fort Raim, 168, 173
fortresses: ʿAlim Khan and, 110; at Aulie Ata, 179; at Chahar Kuh, 52; at Deqan Tudah, 20; at Karakol, 132; at Khoqand, 32, 145, 165; in Khoqandi steppe, 8, 122, 160, 186; at Khotan, 140; called Koktonliq Ata, 18, 32; at Merke, 132, 179; of Niyazbek, 87, 195; at Peshaghar, 150, 151, 158; at Pishpek, 132, 179; Russian, 27, 29, 71, 120–21, 132, 133, 157, 173; at Tashkent, 209; at Toqmaq, 132, 179; at

Turkestan, 120, 179; Vernoe (Almaty), 132, 160, 173; at Yangi Hisar, 140; at Yangi Qurghan, 179, 191; at Yarkand, 140; at Yom, 152; at Zamin, 151, 152, 154. *See also* Aq Masjid fortress; Gulbagh

Gala Bahadur, 82, 83, 93, 98, 98n14, 225, 227
Galdan Khan, 16, 26–27, 34
Galdan Tseren, 34
Ghalcha, 82–86, 89–90, 93, 95, 98, 153–54, 213; described, 225, 227
gift exchanges, 41, 44, 46, 50, 59–62, 73, 212, 217; horses and other livestock, 57, 58, 66, 135
gifting, 17, 89, 109, 110, 120, 123, 128
globalization, 8–9, 39, 44, 51, 212, 217–18; processes of, 4, 210, 221, 223
Great Ferghana Canal, 69, 77 (map)
Great Game. *See* Anglo-Russian Great Game
Gulbagh, 137–44, 156, 199

Hajji Bek, 56, 70–71, 74, 78, 161
Hajji Biy Adigini, 45, 47
Hakim Khan. *See* Muhammad Hakim Khan Tore (chronicler)
Hakim Khan (chronicler's grandfather), 53, 56
Hami, 36 (map), 61, 185
Haqq Quli, 137, 138, 144, 148
Hazrat-i Miyan Fazl Khalil (Miyan Khalil/Muhammad Khalil Sahibzadeh/Hazrat Sahibzadeh), 166, 166n22

Herat, 26 (map), 108, 112, 208, 214
horde. *See* Zhüz

Ibraham Biy Keneges, 21, 24, 29, 100
Ibrahim Parvanachi Manghit, 155, 160, 161n2
Idris Quli Biy (also Iris), 52, 53, 54–55, 56, 72, 96
Ili (Qulja), 63, 64, 65, 177; in maps, 26, 37, 134, 180
Ili River, 121, 132, 173
Indian traders, 44, 112–13, 218
Indus River, 43
Irdana Biy, 34, 39–43, 45, 47–50, 54n10, 66; death of, 48, 54, 54n10, 72; and family, 52–53; and motivations, 41n84; prosperous reign of, 48–49, 211, 212; and the Qing, 58–59, 67, 88, 200, 217
irrigation, 9–10, 160, 201, 220; agriculture, 6, 51, 61, 67, 76, 93, 125, 215–16; networks, 68, 69, 73, 111, 112, 203, 218, 219
Irtysh River, 27, 29, 64, 131, 133, 157, 175; in maps, 26, 36, 180
Isfara, 11, 52n2, 78; in maps, 12, 19, 77
Isfayram River, 68, 77
Ishon Buzurg Khoja, 78, 79
Islamic culture, 5, 7, 11, 86, 15, 119, 125–26
Islamic law (sharī'ah), 16, 82, 108, 109, 199, 226; Madali and, 148, 149, 156, 159, 215

Jahangir Khoja, 137–42, 183; the Jihad of the Seven Khojas, 147, 148, 183
Jizzakh, 22, 56, 85, 122, 128, 150–51, 200; in maps, 19, 134

Jungar, 5, 26 (map), 50, 175, 176; Mongols, 3, 3n7, 16, 25, 27–29, 32–39, 47–48, 56; Qing and, 16n3, 27, 135, 204, 211–12

Kabul, 26 (map), 101, 103
Kanibadam, 75, 77
Kasan, 11; in maps, 12, 77
Kashgar, 5, 10, 15, 16, 32, 45, 63, 140; in a map, 19, 26, 36, 37
Kaufman, General Konstantin Petrovich von, 112, 199–200, 204, 206, 208, 209
Kazakhs, 21, 22, 25, 71, 71n53, 79, 89, 131; army, 74, 79–80, 123; documentary records, 54n10; chronicler Choqan Valikhanov, 42, 171, 178, 185; Jungar wars with the, 26, 27, 34, 35, 176; language, 3, 3n7, 35n63; occupations, 48, 50, 96, 120, 211; Russians and, 160, 170, 173, 175–80, 189; Shahrukhids and, 150, 157, 207, 214; steppe, 7, 121; and the Qing, 47n107, 211
Keneges, 21, 22, 28, 53, 120; in Shahrisabz, 21n16, 24, 31, 48, 154, 211. See also Ibrahim Biy Keneges
Keneges Oyim. See Oychuchuk Oyim
Khan Ariq, 111, 203
Khan Padshah, 128–29, 148–49, 152, 155, 156, 159
khan title. See title, of khan
Khiva, 32, 75, 99, 121, 177, 205, 223; in maps, 26, 134, 180
Khivan Khanate, 2, 2n3, 134, 205
Khoja Ahrar lineage, 112, 128
Khoja Bahadur Khan, 133, 153
Khojand, 10, 11, 28–29, 31, 31n47, 42, 163, 213; 'Alim and, 79, 85, 88, 91; hakims of, 22–23, 54, 56, 70, 79, 190, 191, 198; Madali and, 150, 152, 154, 158, 215; in maps, 12, 19, 26, 134, 180; Russians and, 200, 200n45, 206, 209; 'Umar and, 118–20; Yuz tribe of, 39, 48
Khotan, 36, 45, 57, 140; in maps, 26, 37
Khudayar Khan. See Sayyid Muhammad Khudayar Khan
Khudayqul Bek, 196–97, 196n33
Khurasan, 11, 43, 102, 103
Kilian, Janet, 121, 177, 180
Kish. See Shahrisabz (Kish)
Kopal, 173, 134, 180
Kryzhanovskii, N. A., 194–95
Kucha, 63, 199
Kyrgyz, 2, 29, 34, 67–69, 104, 190–91, 197, 204, 212; Adigene tribe of, 41, 42–43, 45; and Altun Beshik legend (Qirghiz), 102n27, 104; Khoqand and, 47–48, 76, 79, 205–6; Khudayar Khan and, 166–67, 205–6; leadership, 160–61; Sher 'Ali Khan and, 163–64, 167; and taxation, 209; troops of, 22, 137
Kyzylorda. See Aq Masjid fortress

Lake Balkhash, 132; in maps, 26, 36, 37, 134, 180
Lake Issiq Kul, 132, 157; in maps, 37, 134, 180
Lashkar Qushbegi, 133, 144
literati, 106, 108, 109, 113, 115. See also chroniclers
Lutfallah, Naqshbandi sufi Sheikh (Chusti), 19, 78, 104–5, 125

Madali Khan. *See* Muhammad 'Ali Khan (Madali)
madrasas, 70, 85, 110, 115
Mahlar Oyim. *See* Nadira
Mahmud Khan Tura, 123, 128
Makhdūm-i A'zam, the "Greatest Master." *See* Ahmad Kasani
Malla Bek/Malla Khan. *See* Muhammad Yar Khan (Malla Bek)
Manchu, 3, 11, 38
Manghit, the, 3n8, 39, 40n80, 56, 84, 98–99, 100, 123, 151
Marghilan, 11, 12 (map), 33, 63, 208, 219; hakims of, 54, 70, 87, 160, 162, 164, 190, 191; Qing and, 41, 137, 138; Shahrukhids and, 66, 119, 155
Ma'sum Khan, 78, 81–82, 91, 84, 89, 108, 128, 129, 130
Mawarannahr region, 10, 25, 28
Mecca, 131, 133
merchants, 44, 49, 63, 64, 140–41, 142, 147, 185, 208; Bukharan, 25, 63n32; Chinese, 43, 57, 66, 143; foreign, 131, 147n85, 181; Indian, 112, 218; Khoqandi, 6, 44–45, 60–65, 77, 133–35, 156; Russians and, 178, 200; Sogdian, 10, 66; and Tashkent, 134–35, 195. *See also* Andijani merchants
migrants, 6, 29, 32, 145n80, 203, 212, 216, 218; from Altishahr, 157, 212; Dilshad and, 117; Jahangir Khoja and, 138; Narbuta and, 51, 61, 69; from Samarqand, 48
military technology, 82, 85, 93, 154. *See also* weaponry
Ming Oyim, 55, 72, 75

Ming, the. *See* Uzbek Ming, the
mining, 26, 57, 174, 183
Miyan Khalil. *See* Hazrat-i Miyan Fazl Khalil
Morrison, Alexander, 174, 174n43, 175, 177, 178, 181, 195
Mughal Empire, the, 6, 9, 100, 108–9, 125
Muhammad 'Ali Khan (Madali), 87, 97–98, 120, 127–30, 132–35, 162–63, 215–16, 218, 220; and the Bukharan invasion, 148–61, 186, 200; and irrigation, 203; and Jahangir Khoja, 138, 141; and Kashgar, 181; and the Qing, 143–45, 147
Muhammad Fazl Bek. *See* chroniclers: Muhammad Fazl Bek
Muhammad Hakim Khan Tore (chronicler), 22, 24n25, 33n57, 131–32; and 'Alim, 81–82, 84, 85, 91–93, 97–98; in exile, 130–31; and Irdana, 40, 52–54, 54n10; and Jahangir Khoja, 137, 137n38, 139, 140–42, 142n65; and Khoqand army, 153, 153n110; and Madali, 128–30, 143–44, 148, 148n94, 149n95, 151n101, 153n110; and Shah Rukh, 21n14; and 'Umar, 110, 117, 118n79, 120n89
Muhammad Rahim Biy, 39, 40n80, 119, 123, 124
Muhammad Sharif Ataliq Mingbashi, 144, 163
Muhammad Yar Khan (Malla Bek), 162, 162n8, 163, 165, 167–68, 172, 185, 189–91, 193
Muimubarak. *See* Qarateppe (Muimubarak)

Musulmanqul Mingbashi, 164–67, 183–84, 186, 203, 216

Nadir Shah, 3, 32, 43, 48, 85
Nadira (Mahlar Oyim), 87, 115–17, 119, 151, 155, 214, 215
Namangan, 17, 34, 41, 56, 193, 206; hakims of, 124, 130, 164–65, 191; later development of, 11, 69, 119, 219; in maps, 19, 77; Shahrukhids and, 66, 75, 203
Naqshbandiya-Mujaddidia sufis, 6, 14, 15, 16, 19–20, 166
Narbuta Biy ('Abd al-Hamid), 49–51, 53–56, 59–61, 66–75, 212–13; chroniclers and, 54n10, 40n80; claimed title of khan, 88n68; and coinage, 70, 70n51, 70n52, 73; death of, 157; grandmother and, 24, 53; and irrigation, 203, 219; and patronage, 93; prosperous reign of, 6, 150, 213; and the Qing, 42n87, 136, 217; and Sarimsaq, 136–37; wife of, 115
Naryn River, 9, 68, 165; in maps, 12, 19, 26, 37, 77, 180
Nasr al-Din Khan, 190, 206–7, 209
Nasrallah, Amir, 149, 151–55, 157–62, 190, 191, 215, 216
Newby, Laura, 2n4, 41, 47n107, 136, 137, 147n85; and 'Alim, 20, 76n10, 88, 92n82; and khojas, 142n62, 144, 183; and the Qing, 43, 46, 58, 76, 138, 139n49, 147; and "tribute" missions, 46n103, 60–62
Niyaz Muhammad (Niyazi; chronicler), 17, 21, 23n23, 32, 143n69, 162, 190–91, 193–94; and 'Alim, 81, 87n63, 90, 92n82; and Ghalcha, 82n38, 83, 85, 98n14; and father, Mulla 'Ashur Muhammad, 78n15; and Khudayar Khan, 167, 167n27, 172, 193; and Madali, 130n8, 148; and Narbuta, 54n10, 70–71; and 'Umar, 96, 111

oases, 10, 36, 37n68, 58, 157n127
Oftab Oyim, 72, 78
Omsk, 131, 134, 175
opium, 65, 98, 135, 142, 147n85, 182
Orenburg, 44, 131, 134, 207, 208; in maps, 26, 180; Russians and, 169–70, 175, 179–80, 194, 195, 207
Osh, 45, 46, 47, 63, 67, 144, 164, 183, 221; in Babur's realm, 11, 219; in maps, 12, 19, 26, 36, 77; Narbuta and, 67, 68
Ottoman Empire, 30, 110n57, 132, 208; Sultan Mahmud I, 30, 109n55; Sultan Mahmud II, 109
Oychuchuk Oyim, 24, 53, 72

Padsha Ata River, 69, 77
Pamirs, the, 7, 132, 136, 139, 215; and the Alay Mountains, 9, 69, 82, 139, 142, 164; Madali and, 127, 133, 150, 152, 157
paper, 65, 203
Perovsk Fort, 172, 177, 179, 193. *See also* Aq Masjid fortress
Perovskii, V. A., 168–69, 169–70, 189
Persian, 32, 50, 119, 135, 211; language, 3, 115; army, 3, 43, 82–83
Peshaghar, 19 (map), 150, 151, 154, 158
Pilakhan, 16, 102
Pishpek (Bishkek), 132, 179; in maps, 26, 37, 134, 180

Qalmaqs, 25, 26 (map), 28, 32–34, 50, 72, 78. *See also* Jungars
Qara Darya River, 9, 68; in maps, 12, 19, 26, 77
Qaraqazan, 82, 227
Qarashahr, 37, 63
Qarategin (Tajikistan), 10, 29, 52n2, 82, 124, 132, 134 (map), 220
Qarateppe (Muimubarak), 33, 33n57, 53, 72
Qarshi, 21, 151
Qianlong emperor, the, 33n55, 60–61; and Irdana, 40–43, 45, 46, 58, 67, 211; and Jungars, 27, 33, 34–38, 50; and Xinjiang, 56, 72, 76
Qing Empire, the, 5–7, 19–20, 36–43, 45–51, 135–44; and Altishahr, 16n3, 32, 57, 189, 211; Andijani merchants and, 62–65, 145, 181; archival records, 54n10, 60, 62–64, 66, 185n91, 211; conquests, 2, 5, 35–36, 39, 211; fiscal affairs, 147, 182, 186, 198, 218; Irdana and, 58–59, 67, 88, 200, 217; and the Jungars, 16n3, 27, 33, 204, 211–12; Madali and, 143–45, 147; military, 29, 35–36, 38, 66, 184–85; Narbuta and, 42n87, 217; Newby and, 2n4, 58, 76, 147; and policies in Xinjiang, 56–58, 72–73, 160, 198–99, 211, 217; and silver, 182, 184, 186, 189, 199, 216, 226; and Tashkent, 125; and trade, 33n55, 44, 145, 215
Qipchaq, 2, 29, 189–91, 193–94, 200, 203–9, 216–17; and Altun Beshik legend, 102, 102n27, 104; massacre of, 168, 168n33; military, 91, 164–68, 183, 186, 196–97; Steppe, 1, 89, 92, 100; and other tribes, 33, 34, 67–68, 160–61, 163, 102n27, 212. *See also* 'Alimqul; Kazakhs
Qulja. *See* Ili (Qulja)
Qunduz, 134, 136
Qurama region, 22, 79, 86, 120
Qurama tribe, 71, 71n53, 152

Rajab, 79, 80; as Diwanbegi, 96; as Qushbegi, 120n88, 123–24
Reid, Anthony, 221, 222
Russian Empire, the, 3, 5, 119n83, 120n86, 173–74, 188–89, 196; colonizing, 2, 7–8, 112, 160, 175, 186, 217; military, 27, 71, 131, 135, 168–69; and the Qing, 29, 35, 64, 177; and trade, 45, 66, 134, 200
Russian tsars: Alexander I, 131; Alexander II, 8, 179, 196, 208; Nicholas I, 166, 173
Rustam Bek, 74, 75, 78

Samarqand, 10, 11, 21, 24, 24n24, 136, 190, 200; ancestral capital, 6, 100; hakims of, 29; migrants from 48, 22, 32
Sarimsaq Biy, 163, 165, 166
Sarimsaq Tura, 89, 89n70, 90, 136, 165
Sariqol (Tashqurghan), 133, 135, 139
Sarts, 23, 47, 68, 75, 190, 226; and ethnic tensions, 160–61, 168, 168n33, 204, 212; and genocide, 216–17; Khudayar Khan and, 166–67, 186, 190, 193, 208–9
Sayyid Muhammad Khudayar Khan, 56, 145, 163–69, 172–74, 185–87,

189–209, 216–19; Ark of, 132, 146; as khan, 165, 165n20
Sayyids, 16, 106n41, 129
Schuyler, Eugene, 76, 203
Shadi Biy, 22, 54
Shah Murad, 56
Shah Murad Khan, 191, 193
Shahrikhan, 111–12, 119, 155
Shahrisabz (Kish), 11, 21, 96, 100, 130, 136; and Bukhara, 22, 120, 131, 158; Hakim Khan and, 131, 148, 148n94
Shah Rukh ('Alim's son), 91, 92, 96, 107
Shah Rukh (Timur's son), 21, 22, 107, 105
Shah Rukh Biy (1709–22), 16–23, 48; leader of the Uzbek Ming, 5, 6, 39, 95, 99, 101, 211; lineage of, 39, 54, 55–56, 70, 105
Shah Rukh Biy (Narbuta's half-brother), 55, 91, 92, 96
Shahrukhid family, 21, 31, 67, 76, 112, 150, 155, 211; Dakhm-i Shahan mausoleum of, 31n48, 92, 164; leadership, 7, 70, 73, 99; lineage, 5, 20, 48, 87, 100, 105, 159, 161; military, 29–30; as rulers, 30, 44, 52, 88, 97–98, 106–7, 160; Uzbek Ming, 124. *See also* Altun Beshik ("Golden Cradle") legend; individual rulers
sharī'ah. *See* Islamic law (sharī'ah)
Sher 'Ali Khan, 161–65, 186, 207, 216
Shughnan, 82n38, 132
silver, 57, 76, 87, 147, 182–84, 204; Altishahr and, 186, 211, 226; stipend, 182, 184, 186, 189, 216, 226; in Xinjiang, 39, 39n75, 66
Skobelev, Mikhail, 206, 207, 208

steppe, 89, 121, 213, 214, 215, 216; southern, annexed, 127, 133, 150, 157, 175, 178; Russians and the, 180, 188, 194
Sulayman Biy, 54, 72, 197n33
Sultan Husayn Baiqara, 108, 112, 113
Sultan Khoja, 86, 113
Sultan Mahmud Khan, 148, 149, 152, 155
Sultan Sayyid Khan, 193, 194
Syr Darya River, 7, 9, 25, 86, 124, 152, 172n41, 178, 179; and irrigation, 69, 203; Kazakhs and, 28, 79–80; in maps, 12, 19, 26, 77, 134, 180; Russians and, 172, 206. *See also* Aq Masjid fortress; Naryn River; Qara Darya River

Taiping Rebellion, 182, 198, 216
Tajikistan. *See* Qarategin (Tajikistan)
Tajiks, 2, 29, 82–84, 85, 90, 93, 163
Tamerlane. *See* Amir Timur (Tamerlane)
Tang Empire, the, 10–11, 41, 62, 211
tanistry, 51–56
Tashkent, 10–11, 20, 22, 86–88, 166, 169, 197–98; 'Alim and, 20, 74, 86–93, 95, 175, 213; hakims of, 87, 89, 162, 163, 165, 168, 189, 200; Kazakhs and, 25, 71, 79n22; Khudayar Khan and, 190–91, 197, 206–7; Madali and, 152, 157, 186, 200; in maps, 19, 26, 134, 180; Qing and, 43, 46, 125; Qipchaqs and, 34, 167; Russians and, 8, 125, 133–34, 175, 180–81, 188, 194–96, 199–200, 206–9, 216–17; Shahrukh-ids and, 48, 49, 71–72, 74, 79, 99, 162, 186; 'Umar and, 96, 120, 150, 214. *See*

also Yunus Khoja; Muhammad Yar Khan (Malla Bek)
Tashqurghan. *See* Sariqol (Tashqurghan)
Tawakkul Tore, 182, 183, 184
tax base, agrarian, 212, 214
taxation, 57–58, 62–63, 82, 138, 145, 151, 179, 199, 201, 209
tax-free trade, 50, 61, 156, 217–18
tea, 60, 129, 135, 143; trade, 45, 61, 65–66, 73, 147
Tian Shan (Heavenly Mountains), the, 9–11, 29, 41, 42, 69, 137; the Kyrgyz and, 47, 67, 76
Timurid Renaissance, the, 95, 101, 107–8, 126, 214
Timurids, 6–7, 15, 98, 100, 101, 119, 125; at Herat, 26 (map), 108, 112, 208, 214; and *Tīmūr-nāma* literature, 100, 125. *See also* Timurid Renaissance
title: of amir, 109, 109n53; of atābeg, 227; of dādkhwāh, 228; of ghazi, 141, 227; of īshān, 225; of khan, 6, 42, 20, 74, 87, 88, 88n65, 99, 124, 197, 213; of khōja, 226
Toqay-Timurid rulers: Subhan Quli Khan, 21; 'Ubaydullah Khan, 21, 25, 91; Wali Muhammad Khan, 103
Toqay-Timurids, 3, 4, 21, 29
trade, 60, 125, 133, 157, 160, 177; with Altishahr, 62–66, 78, 143–44, 157, 204, 212; ambassadorial, 44; by caravan, 4, 10, 64, 111, 178, 179; Eurasian, 212; Khudayar and, 201, 209; sanctions, 143–45, 181; smuggling, 64–66; transit, 42, 45, 51, 62, 135, 143, 179. *See also* silver

trade goods: ceramics, 61; chemicals, 65; Chinese, 42; fruits (fresh and dried), 135; Indian, 65, 135; jade, 57; manufactured goods, 66, 73, 135; medicinal, 45; porcelain dishes, 135; rhubarb, 64, 135, 143, 147; Siberian furs, 66, 134, 135; silk, 61, 65, 134, 135; tobacco, 135. *See also* tea
trade routes, 133, 135, 157, 214, 215, 217, 220, 222; Aq Masjid and, 121, 179
tribute missions, 41, 43, 50, 58, 60, 62, 211
Tsewang Rabdan, 27
Tura Qurghan hakims, 56, 70, 71, 124
Turfan, 36, 63, 199; in maps 26, 36, 37, 134
Turkestan region, 16, 57, 133, 157n127, 225
Turkestan (Yas), 25, 42, 179, 199–200, 204; in maps, 26, 180; Shahrukhids and, 89, 120, 121, 123, 131, 213
Turkic Muslims, 16n3, 37n68, 38, 39, 145, 183, 184, 186, 198–99, 211
Turkic peoples, 1, 14, 47, 82

Uch Qurghan, 68, 164; Ariq, 212
Ulugh Nahr canal network, 209, 217, 219
'Umar Khan, 90–99, 106–13, 117–20, 122–29, 133, 137–38, 147, 213–15; and 'Alim Khan, 79, 86, 150, 154, 227; court of, 115, 117; death of, 131; influential, 55, 158; and irrigation, 111, 203; in the military, 86, 87; reign of, 73; writing under the penname Amīrī, 106, 106n42, 108, 113
Urateppe, 31, 39–40, 53, 88, 97, 122–24,

136, 190, 200; ʿAbd al-Rahim and, 23, 29; ʿAlim Khan and, 83–85, 213; Dilshad resident of, 97, 117, 119; hakims of, 39, 56, 123, 128, 155; Madali and, 143, 150–52; in maps, 19, 134, 180; ʿUmar and, 117–18, 122–24, 214; Yuz in, 22, 33, 48, 56, 211
Uyghur Turks, 2, 16n3, 47
Uzbek amirs, 3, 14, 25, 48, 83, 85, 93, 99
Uzbek Ming, the, 1, 1n1, 14, 22, 31, 53, 211; and Altun Beshik legend, 102, 102n27, 104, 106; Jungars and, 33, 47; Narbuta, 61, 212; Shah Rukh, 5, 16, 19, 20, 48, 95, 99, 101, 211; Shahrukhid lineage and, 1, 124, 160–61; ʿUmar, 99, 109; Yuz and, 33, 40
Uzbek tribes, 22, 23, 47–48, 83, 98, 127, 160; aristocracy, 54, 61, 70, 80

Valikhanov, Choqan, 42, 171, 178, 185
Vernoe (Almaty), 132, 160, 177, 178, 179, 193; in maps, 134, 180

Wakhan, 133, 150, 157
Wali Khan, 182, 183, 184, 185, 199
warfare: Bukharan, 153; Gala Bahadur and, 83; Ghalcha and, 85, 93; infantry, 122; Jungar, 27; Khoqand, 6, 86; Persian, 3; Russian, 131; siege structures (*sarkūb*), 86; snipers, 22, 79, 79n25, 86, 87, 122, 227
water resources, 6, 51, 57, 61, 68, 73, 75–76, 87, 220. *See also* irrigation
Wathen, W. H., 133, 153
weaponry: artillery, 86, 122, 143; bows and arrows, swords and spears, 29–30, 153; cannons and mortars, 82, 153, 154; flintlock muskets, 30, 30n45, 154, 226; gun barrels and locks, 134; gunpowder, 7, 26, 66, 74, 82, 89, 93, 122, 212; heavy artillery, guns, and bombs, 167; matchlocks, 30, 153, 179; muskets, 29–30, 82, 90; rifles reserved for snipers, 79n25; saltpeter, 66, 135
Wittfogel, Karl, 219–20
women poets, 97, 115, 117–19. *See also* Mahlar Oyim (Nadira), Dilshad

Xinjiang, 36, 43–47, 133, 145, 147; Andijani merchants and, 51, 62–63, 65, 93, 181, 182, 212, 218; "New Frontier," 16, 38, 38n70, 50; Qing policies in, 5, 39, 56–58, 72–73, 139, 160, 198–99, 211, 217; Shahrukhids and, 50, 76–77, 88, 150, 156; silver in, 39, 39n75, 57, 66, 182–83, 216

Yaʿqub Bek Badaulat ("The Fortunate One," Ataliq Ghazi), 147, 169, 186, 190–91, 191n14, 197–99, 200, 206, 209
Yangi Ariq ("New Canal"), 75, 111, 203
Yangi Gulbagh. *See* Gulbagh
Yangi Hisar (Yangishahr), 36, 140, 182, 199; in maps, 19, 134
Yarkand, 5, 36, 57, 63, 133, 182, 204; in maps, 26, 36, 37, 134, 180; Qing troops in, 45, 140–41, 185
Yas. *See* Turkestan (Yas)
Yasavi shrine, 120, 120n89
Yunus Khoja, 71, 75, 79–80, 86, 93, 99, 123, 143, 145, 150, 156, 183
Yusuf Mingbashi, 162, 164

Yuz, 22–23, 33, 39–40, 48, 50, 211; and
  Altun Beshik legend, 104;
  Shahrukhids and, 40, 48, 55–56, 123

Zahir al-Din Muhammad Babur, 6, 11,
  12, 88, 106n43; lineage of, 19, 20n10,
  100, 101, 105, 124. *See also* Altun
  Beshik ("Golden Cradle") legend
Zhang Qian, 10
Zerafshan Valley, 28, 29, 151
Zhüz, 35n63, 177, 180, 214; Kishi
  (Junior), 175, 177; Orta (Middle)
  Zhüz, 35, 175, 176, 177; Uly (Senior)
  Zhüz, 26 (map), 175, 176, 180